Sin and Society in Fourteenth-Century England

A Study of the
Memoriale Presbiterorum

MICHAEL HAREN

CLARENDON PRESS · OXFORD

OXFORD
UNIVERSITY PRESS

Great Clarendon Street, Oxford OX2 6DP

Oxford University Press is a department of the University of Oxford.
It furthers the University's objective of excellence in research, scholarship,
and education by publishing worldwide in

Oxford New York

Athens Auckland Bangkok Bogota Buenos Aires Calcutta
Cape Town Chennai Dar es Salaam Delhi Florence Hong Kong Istanbul
Karachi Kuala Lumpur Madrid Melbourne Mexico City Mumbai
Nairobi Paris São Paulo Singapore Taipei Tokyo Toronto Warsaw

and associated companies in Berlin Ibadan

Oxford is a registered trade mark of Oxford University Press
in the UK and certain other countries

Published in the United States
by Oxford University Press Inc., New York

British Library Cataloguing in Publication Data

Data available

Library of Congress Cataloging in Publication Data

Data available

ISBN 0-19-820851-0

1 3 5 7 9 10 8 6 4 2

Typeset by Graphicraft Limited, Hong Kong
Printed in Great Britain
on acid-free paper by
Biddles Ltd, Guildford and King's Lynn

Parentibus Optimis et In Memoriam
W. A. PANTIN

PREFACE

As originating in a D.Phil. thesis, this book owes most to the scholar and great man who suggested the topic to me and supervised my early research on it. The late Dr W. A. Pantin was the first to recognize in the *Memoriale Presbiterorum* a treatise of unusual interest. He communicated to me his conviction that it would repay study and, in the method that was characteristic of his historiographical approach, directed me towards presenting it within a legislative and literary tradition. The pleasure that attends publication would have been much enhanced could he have read the final version. Since his humour had a racy vein, by the discreet standards of a bygone age, I can imagine his delight in the story of the parishioner of Crediton and her troubled pastor who are so central a part of the argument for authorship.

After Pantin's death, his successor at Oriel, Dr Jeremy Catto, became my supervisor and saw the thesis through its final stages. I profited much then from his wide-ranging erudition and judicious criticism. I have profited as much again over the years in which I have never ceased to avail myself of an opportunity during visits to Oxford to test ideas in this and other areas through discussion with him. Latterly he has acted as sub-editor for the series. I am most grateful for the generosity with which he has unfailingly bestowed time and attention.

Among other scholars to whom I am indebted, the following come to mind especially: the late Miss Beryl Smalley, for having led me to the twelfth-century hinterland of my subject and for much kindness besides; Dr Paul Hyams, for stimulating insights into the socio-legal context, conveyed with what I remember as enthusiastic urgency; Fr Leonard Boyle, my association with whom in other work gave me occasions that I did not miss for consultation with the doyen of the study of pastoral manuals; Dr Peter Biller, who had caught from the same source as I a zeal for the treatise and periodically reinvigorated me by reflections on it; and Dr Maurice Keen likewise for encouragement.

Professor Sir Richard Southern in vetting my research proposal on behalf of the Faculty of Modern History gave me shrewdly judged advice on strategy. I had the good fortune to find in my examiners, Dr Roger Highfield and Professor Hugh Lawrence, a courtesy matching their expertise.

My initial research was supported by a Ministry of Education for Northern Ireland Major State Studentship and I remain grateful to the officials who administered the grant for a consideration that went, on more than one occasion, beyond mere efficiency in facilitating my needs.

In calculating the sum of my debts, I am prompted to recall and to acknowledge with pleasure how much my research trips to the British Library over the years have owed to the hospitality of my friend, Mr Peter Cullinane.

A fundamental debt is to my parents, for material and unflagging moral support during the whole of my studies.

J. E. Neale remarked that he had come to understand the mention of a wife in the preface to a book as no mere convention. Over the years in which this study has been in preparation I have had good reason to appreciate the truth of the perception.

MJH
Easter, 1998

ACKNOWLEDGEMENTS

The author is grateful to the following bodies and institutions for kindly granting permission or waiving the requirement to obtain formal permission to quote from unpublished manuscripts in their ownership or custody: the Bodleian Library, University of Oxford; the British Library; the Syndics of Cambridge University Library; the Master and Fellows of Corpus Christi College, Cambridge; Devon Record Office; Exeter Diocesan Registry; the Master and Fellows of Gonville and Caius College, Cambridge; Lincolnshire County Council Archives; the Diocese of Lincoln; the Diocese of Worcester. Use of Westminster Diocesan Archives, Ms. H. 38 is with gracious permission of the Archbishop of Westminster. The author acknowledges with thanks the kind permission of the Revd Leonard E. Boyle, OP, for a quotation from the latter's doctoral thesis. He thanks Boydell and Brewer Ltd. for their ready agreement to his reuse of passages that appeared in a conference paper delivered by him, published under the title 'Confession, Social Ethics and Social Discipline in the *Memoriale Presbiterorum*', in. P. Biller and A. J. Minnis (eds.), *Handling Sin: Confession in the Middle Ages*, York Studies in Medieval Theology, 2 (1998). In the preparation for publication of the present work, he pays tribute to the highly professional contribution to presentation of Mr Jeff New, the copy-editor.

CONTENTS

ABBREVIATIONS

Acton, *Commentary*	John Acton, *Commentary on the Legatine Constitutions*, (printed after Lyndwood, *Provinciale*)
Acton, 'Septuplum'	Cambridge, Gonville, and Caius College, MS. 282/675 ('Septuplum')
ASV, *RA*	Archivio Segreto Vaticano, *Registra Avenioniensia*
—— *RS*	Archivio Segreto Vaticano, *Registra Supplicationum*
Baldwin, *Masters*	J. W. Baldwin, *Masters, Princes and Merchants: The Social Views of Peter the Chanter and his Circle*, 2 vols. (Princeton, 1970)
Boyle, 'A Study'	L. E. Boyle, 'A Study of the Works Attributed to William of Pagula, with Special Reference to the *Oculus Sacerdotis* and *Summa Summarum*', Oxford University, D.Phil. thesis, 1956
Boyle, 'Curriculum'	L. E. Boyle, 'The Curriculum of the Faculty of Canon Law at Oxford', in *Oxford Studies Presented to Daniel Callus*, Oxford Historical Society, NS, 16 (Oxford, 1964)
Boyle, 'John of Freiburg'	L. E. Boyle, 'The *Summa Confessorum* of John of Freiburg and the Popularization of the Moral Teaching of St Thomas and Some of his Contemporaries', in *St Thomas Aquinas, 1274–1974. Commemorative Studies*, ed. A. A. Maurer *et al.* (Toronto, 1974), 245–68 (reprinted in Boyle, *Pastoral Care*)
Boyle, *Pastoral Care*	L. E. Boyle, *Pastoral Care, Clerical Education and Canon Law 1200–1400* (London, 1981)
Boyle, 'The Oculus'	L. E. Boyle, 'The Oculus Sacerdotis and Some Other Works of William of Pagula', *Transactions of the Royal Historical Society*, 5th ser., 5 (1955), 81–110

Brian's Register	Hereford and Worcester Record Office, b 716.093–BA.2648/3 (iii) (Register of Reginald Brian)
Brinton, *Sermons*	*The Sermons of Thomas Brinton, Bishop of Rochester, 1373–1389*, ed. M. A. Devlin, Camden Soc. 3rd ser., 75–86 (1954)
BRUC	A. B. Emden, *A Biographical Register of the University of Cambridge to AD 1500* (Cambridge, 1963)
BRUO	A. B. Emden, *A Biographical Register of the University of Oxford to AD 1500* (Oxford, 1957)
C	Cambridge, Corpus Christi College, MS. 148 ('Memoriale Presbiterorum'); for complete edition, see Haren, 'A Study', ii. For selected interrogatories, see Haren, 'The Interrogatories'
CCR	*Calendar of Close Rolls*
Cheney, 'Legislation'	C. R. Cheney, 'Legislation of the Medieval English Church', *EHR* 1 (1935), 193–224, 385–417
Cheney, *Medieval Texts*	C. R. Cheney, *Medieval Texts and Studies* (Oxford, 1973)
Cheney, 'Textual Problems'	C. R. Cheney 'Textual Problems of the English Provincial Canons', in Cheney, *Medieval Texts*, 111–37
CPL	*Calendar of Entries in the Papal Registers Relating to Great Britain and Ireland: Papal Letters*, ii, iii, ed. W. H. Bliss (London, 1895–7)
CPP	*Calendar of Entries in the Papal Registers Relating to Great Britain and Ireland: Petitions to the Pope*, ed. W. H. Bliss, i (London, 1896)
CPR	*Calendar of Patent Rolls*
CS	*Councils and Synods of the English Church in the Thirteenth Century*, ed. F. M. Powicke and C. R. Cheney (Oxford, 1964)
Concilia	*Concilia Magnae Britanniae et Hiberniae*, ed. D. Wilkins (London, 1737)
Decretum	*Decretum Gratiani*, in *Corpus Juris Canonici*, ed. A. Friedberg, i (Leipzig, 1879)

Digest	The Digest of Justinian, Latin text ed. T. Mommsen and P. Krueger and English translation ed. A. Watson, 4 vols. (Philadelphia, 1985)
DNB	Dictionary of National Biography, ed. L. Stephen and S. Lee, 21 vols. (London 1908–9)
DRO, Chanter 3, 4, 5	Devon Record Office, Exeter diocesan records, Chanter catalogue 3, 4, 5 (Register of John Grandisson, vols. i–iii)
EcHR	Economic History Review
EHR	English Historical Review
EETS	Early English Texts Society
Extravag. Commun.	Extravagantium Communium Liber, in Corpus Juris Canonici, ii, ed. A. Friedberg (Leipzig, 1881)
Extravag. Johannis XXII	Decretales Extravagantes Johannis XXII, in Corpus Juris Canonici, ed. A. Friedberg, ii (Leipzig, 1881)
Feudal Aids	Inquisitions and Assessments Relating to Feudal Aids With Other Analogous Documents Preserved in the Public Record Office AD 1284–1431, i (London, 1899)
Fowler, *King's Lieutenant*	K. Fowler, The King's Lieutenant: Henry of Grosmont, First Duke of Lancaster 1310–1361 (London, 1969)
Haines, *Worcester*	R. M. Haines, The Administration of the Diocese of Worcester in the First Half of the Fourteenth Century (London, 1965)
Haren, 'A Study'	M. J. Haren, 'A Study of the Memoriale Presbiterorum a Fourteenth-Century Confessional Manual for Parish Priests', Oxford University, D.Phil. thesis, 1975
Haren, 'The Interrogatories'	M. J. Haren, 'The Interrogatories for Officials, Lawyers and Secular Estates of the Memoriale Presbiterorum', in P. Biller and A. Minnis (eds.), Handling Sin: Confession in the Middle Ages, York Studies in Medieval Theology, 2 (1998), 123–63
Haren, 'Will'	M. J. Haren, 'The Will of Master John de Belvoir, Official of Lincoln (†1391)', MS, 58 (1996), 119–47

Harper-Bill, *Religious Belief*	C. Harper-Bill (ed.), *Religious Belief and Ecclesiastical Careers in Late Medieval England* (Woodbridge, 1991)
HBC	E. B. Fryde, D. E. Greenway, S. Porter, and I. Roy, *Handbook of British Chronology*, 3rd edn. (London, 1986)
Highfield, 'The Hierarchy'	J. R. L. Highfield, 'The English Hierarchy in the Reign of Edward III', *TRHS*, 5th ser., 6 (1956), 115–38.
Hostiensis, *SA*	Henricus de Segusia (Hostiensis), *Summa Aurea* (Basle, 1573)
Hughes, *Pastors and Visionaries*	J. Hughes, *Pastors and Visionaries: Religion and Secular Life in Late Medieval Yorkshire* (Woodbridge, 1988)
Institut.	*Imperatoris Iustiniani Institutiones*, ed. J. B. Moyle, 5th edn. (Oxford, 1912)
JBAA	*Journal of the British Archaeological Association*
JEH	*Journal of Ecclesiastical History*
JEcH	*Journal of Economic History*
Kowalewski, *Local Markets*	M. Kowalewski, *Local Markets and Regional Trade in Medieval Exeter* (Cambridge, 1995)
LAO, Reg. VIII, IX, XII	Lincolnshire Archives Office, Episcopal Registers VIII–IX (Register of John Gynwell, i–ii), XII (Register of John Buckingham, iii)
LAW	Worcester Cathedral Muniments, *Liber Albus* (A. 5), vol. I
Le Neve, *Fasti*	J. Le Neve, *Fasti Ecclesiae Anglicanae 1300–1541*, revised edn. (London, 1962–7)
LRS	Lincoln Record Society
Lunt, *Accounts*	W. E. Lunt (ed. E. B. Graves), *Accounts Rendered by Papal Collectors in England 1317–1378* (Philadelphia, 1968)
Lyndwood, *Provinciale*	William Lyndwood, *Provinciale* (Oxford, 1679)
MP	*Memoriale Presbiterorum*, cited by folio and column or by chapter as in Cambridge, Corpus Christi College, MS. 148. For edited text see Haren, 'A Study', ii; see also Haren, 'The Interrogatories'
MS	*Mediaeval Studies*
OHS	Oxford Historical Society

Ormrod, *England*	W. M. Ormrod (ed.), *England in the Fourteenth Century*, Proceedings of the 1985 Harlaxton Symposium (Woodbridge, 1986)
Owst, *Literature and Pulpit*	G. R. Owst, *Literature and Pulpit in Medieval England*, 2nd edn. (Oxford, 1961)
Pantin, *Church*	W. A. Pantin, *The English Church in the Fourteenth Century* (Cambridge, 1955)
PL	*Patrologia Latina*, ed. J. P. Migne, 221 vols. (Paris, 1844–1904)
Place-Names Devon	J. E. B. Gover, A. Mawer, and F. M. Stenton (eds.), *The Place-Names of Devon*, 2 vols. (Cambridge, 1931–2)
PMLA	*Publications of the Modern Language Association of America*
Political Songs, ed. Wright	*The Political Songs of England from the Reign of John to that of Edward II*, ed. T. Wright, Camden Soc., 1st. ser., 6 (1839)
PRO	Public Record Office, London
'Reg. Brian 2'	Hereford and Worcester Record Office, b 716.093–BA.2648/3 (iv)
Reg. Hethe	*Registrum Hamonis Hethe, diocesis Roffensis, A.D. 1319–1352*, ed. C. Johnson, i–ii, Canterbury and York Society (1948)
Reg. John of Gaunt	*The Register of John of Gaunt*, ed. S. A. Smyth, Camden Soc., 3rd ser., 21 (1911)
Reg. Mortival	*The Register of Roger Mortival, Bishop of Salisbury, 1315–1330*, ed. K. Edwards, C. R. Elrington, D. M. Owen, and S. Reynolds, i–iv, Canterbury and York Society (1959–75)
Reg. Stapeldon	*The Register of Walter de Stapeldon Bishop of Exeter (1307–1326)*, ed. F. C. Hingeston-Randolph (London, 1892)
Reg. Winchelsey	*Registrum Roberti Winchelsey Cantuariensis Archiepiscopi*, ed. R. Graham, Canterbury and York Society, 51, 52 (1952–6)
RG	*The Register of John de Grandisson, Bishop of Exeter (AD 1327–1369)*, ed. F. C. Hingeston-Randolph, 3 vols. (Exeter, 1894–9)
Rot. Parl.	*Rotuli Parliamentorum*, ii (London, 1767)
SAUO	*Statuta Antiqua Universitatis Oxoniensis*, ed. Strickland Gibson (Oxford, 1931)

SCH	*Studies in Church History*
Sext	*Liber Sextus Decretalium*, in *Corpus Juris Canonici* ed. A. Friedberg, ii (Leipzig, 1881)
SS	Surtees Society
Thompson, *English Clergy*	A. H. Thompson, *The English Clergy and their Organization in the Later Middle Ages* (Oxford, 1947)
Thompson, 'Will'	A. H. Thompson, 'The Will of Master William Doune, Archdeacon of Leicester', *Archaeological Journal*, 72 (1915), 233–84
TLS	*The Times Literary Supplement*
TRHS	*Transactions of the Royal Historical Society*
VCH	*The Victoria History of the Counties of England*
Walsh, *Scholar and Primate*	K. Walsh, *A Fourteenth-Century Scholar and Primate Richard FitzRalph in Oxford, Avignon and Armagh* (Oxford, 1981)
X	*Libri Decretalium Gregorii IX*, in *Corpus Juris Canonici*, ed. A. Friedberg, ii (Leipzig, 1881)

I

The Memoriale Presbiterorum*:*
A Confessional Manual With a Social Focus

The *Memoriale Presbiterorum* is a part of that great body of writing for the instruction of parish clergy which is so prominent a feature of the intellectual life of the English church in the thirteenth and fourteenth centuries. In contrast to some of the other manuals, which range widely over the pastoral cure, the treatise is exclusively devoted to confessional technique. Transmitted anonymously, it purports to have been written for a friend in the first instance. The address 'amice karissime' occurs internally at various junctures. That it is more than a convention has powerful support in the manuscript tradition. The final chapter is an addendum, an edited letter on the law governing the burial of a pregnant woman, in response to a scruple raised by the original, unnamed recipient. Tacked on after the concluding formula of the treatise proper, it is an evident and unique departure from the main subject.

As a manual for confessors, the treatise proper is a thoughtful application of the continental canonical tradition to the mid-fourteenth-century English scene by a puritanical though sensitive observer. Its historical interest is on a number of levels. First, it is noteworthy precisely as the work of a reformer of wholly orthodox bent, whose denunciation is as severe of abuse in ecclesiastical structures as in secular. If the primary import of this point needs less emphasis now than formerly, this is partly an effect of the uncovering of similar sources and of the consequent perception that the pre-Wyclifite church contained, at its middle levels certainly, a ferment of self-criticism.[1] Then, as regards wider history, especially as its study is conducted under the pervasive influence of the *Annales* school, the *Memoriale Presbiterorum* is a fertile source. It is sharply focused on the social dimension of confession. From being a didactic manual it thus becomes, for the historian, in large part both a vehicle of social doctrine and a reflection of the milieu to which it is directed. The author is a fierce critic of contemporary society

---

[1] Cf. Pantin, *Church*, 211, 238.

which, in its middle and lower strata, he subjects to systematic review
from the unusual perspective of penitential discipline. His strictures,
when controlled by the documentary evidence and the views of other
commentators, are valuable as the concerns of someone who feels deeply
about social abuses—most notably those which proceed from the malpractices of officialdom—and who has considerable experience of this
latter aspect of his subject.

Little acumen is required to discern that the author can hardly have
known so well, or have been so preoccupied with, the class of officialdom
which he excoriates, unless he lived shoulder to shoulder with it. Even
in the abstract, therefore, his comments assume a further importance.
They are not simply an additional source of social and administrative
history, supplying the defects of a documentation which is weakest, especially as regards administrative history, on the very points on which
the author is so acute.[2] Though its content may be applied in that way,
the significance of the *Memoriale Presbiterorum* is larger than its specific utility. With its strong opinions on a range of issues, the treatise
is one of the most idiosyncratic products of a profession, that of the
ecclesiastical lawyer and administrator, whose contemporary influence
was unparalleled but which, apart from bare details of training and
career, is largely without face.[3] Its author need not be taken to be a
typical representative of his profession for him to serve as a caution-
ary example. Moreover, his associates in the episcopal circles to which
he belonged, on the identification proposed below, can be traced in
sufficient number to reinforce the caution. His is a class towards which
both contemporaries and historians have been at kindest reserved, and
more often outrightly hostile. Commenting on the novelty of the perspective opened up by a study of episcopally inspired reform in York,
Professor R. B. Dobson mused on how startled the late Hamilton
Thompson would have been by the 'implicit rejection of his own—the
orthodox—view that late medieval English prelates and canons were
the personification of "the conservative mind of the ecclesiastical
lawyer" '.[4] Episcopal government in the diocese of Exeter, the setting,
as is argued, of the treatise, and in the two dioceses—Worcester and
Lincoln—in which its author as identified was official, will be a

---

[2] Cf. J. Scammell, 'The Rural Chapter in England from the Eleventh to the Fourteenth
Century', *EHR*, 86 (1971), 19–20.
[3] Cf. D. M. Owen, *John Lydford's Book* (London, 1974), 15–16.
[4] R. B. Dobson, reviewing Hughes, *Pastors and Visionaries*, in *TLS*, 15–21 Sept. 1989,
p. 1008.

related theme of this study. The principal theme will be how urgently the conservative legal mind could generate and propagate reforming views. On the argument for identification, the author of the *Memoriale Presbiterorum* becomes the ecclesiastical lawyer-administrator from fourteenth-century England of whose personal convictions and preoccupations we know most. The impression is as surprising, perhaps, as it is edifying.

Another, large, area of the subject's historical interest is the correspondence of views between the *Memoriale Presbiterorum*'s author and Richard FitzRalph, archbishop of Armagh (1347–1360) and champion of the secular clergy against the friars. This was an aspect noted by the late Dr Pantin,[5] whose shrewd suggestion of influence is supported by the argument for identifying the circle in which the author moved. The insinuation is strong that his powerful and puritanical personality, or the viewpoint at least which he so passionately advocates, contributed to FitzRalph's outlook on the pastoral cure and was responsible in particular for a fusion of ideas that became hugely significant for FitzRalph the controversialist—the primacy of restitution in the confessional regime and the friars' alleged shortcomings in respect of it. The elaboration of this hypothesis requires a more direct address to the development of FitzRalph's pastoral concerns and to his polemical stance than can be attempted here. Apart from such specific inquiry, however, the effect of the present study is to offer a contextual framework within which to view FitzRalph's involvement in controversy and new material for explaining the 'apparently sudden change of heart' as regards the mendicant friars that has always been a puzzle for his biographers.[6]

Paradoxically, the interest of the treatise would seem, at first sight, to be least in terms of its original purpose—of serving as a manual. Though an argument from surviving manuscripts is hazardous, its circulation would not appear to have been large. There are no known medieval literary references to it and, aside from the extant copies, only one piece of direct evidence for its currency. This is a bequest made of it by the late-fifteenth-century theologian Robert Tehy to the senior fellow of Magdalen College[7]—hardly the readership that the author might have envisaged. Various explanations may be adduced. It is likely

[5] Pantin, *Church*, 206.
[6] Walsh, *Scholar and Primate*, 349. See further, M. J. Haren, 'Richard FitzRalph and the Friars: The Intellectual Itinerary of a Curial Controversialist', in J. Hamesse (ed.), *Roma Magistra Mundi. Itineraria Culturae Medievalis* (Louvain-la-Neuve, 1998), i. 349–67.
[7] See *BRUO* 1854. I am grateful to Dr R. M. Ball for bringing this reference to my attention.

that those very qualities which have been isolated as making the work so valuable to the historian militated against its success as a pastoral manual. As Dr Pantin remarked: 'One of the most disastrous and blighting effects of Wycliffism was that, for the first time in the history of this country, it associated criticism with heterodoxy.'[8] How far this may have affected a work as explicit as the *Memoriale Presbiterorum* is imponderable, but the background can hardly have been ideal. Other factors may have been at least as significant and, if these are correctly diagnosed, an important part of the interest of the work is its very failure to establish itself. The competition from several quarters was formidable. As already observed, didactic literature aimed at raising the competence of parish clergy was a thriving genre. The most successful example of the type, judged both by the criterion of surviving manuscripts and by the authority of its instruction, was the *Oculus Sacerdotis* of William of Pagula, from whose work several other treatises derived their inspiration or even formally took their point of departure.[9] This is the case with, for instance, the *Regimen Animarum* and Mirk's 'Instructions for Parish Priests', which borrow from the *Oculus* and are otherwise evidently influenced by it, and with the *Cilium Oculi Sacerdotis* and John de Burgo's *Pupilla Oculi*, which expressly set out to supplement or improve on the work from which they take their titles.[10] The *Memoriale Presbiterorum* is remarkable in that it appears to be wholly independent not only of the *Oculus Sacerdotis* itself but of William of Pagula's other writings also, though it is possible that its author was indirectly influenced by Pagula's lead, of which there might well have been discussion in Oxford legal circles.[11] The medieval reader conferred no premium on originality in these matters. It must be acknowledged too that the *Memoriale Presbiterorum* was, from a canonistic viewpoint, both less thorough and less informed than its direct rival, the *Prima Pars* of the *Oculus Sacerdotis*, a manual for confessors written by Pagula *c.*1326–8, after he had completed the two other parts of the *Oculus*.[12] The tone and bias of the *Memoriale Presbiterorum* are, moreover, quite different from those of the *Prima Pars Oculi*. Pagula's approach is deeply influenced by the thirteenth-century developments in moral theology, which he merges subtly with the canonistic rulings in a measured, dispassionate, 'academic' style, where his own opinions do not intrude. The *Memoriale Presbiterorum*, apart from its other idiosyncrasies, is

---

[8] Pantin, *Church*, 238.   [9] See Boyle, 'The *Oculus*'.
[10] See Pantin, *Church*, pp. 202–5, 213–17.   [11] Cf. below, p. 43.
[12] See Boyle, 'The Oculus', 106.

marked by a strong legalism in its approach to confessional technique and by a punctilious, remorseless concern for abstract justice, as is particularly evident in its burning preoccupation with restitution. Part of its criticism of the friars as confessors is their alleged readiness to sacrifice the requirements of justice to the penitent's peace of mind. At issue is the divergence between a legalistic and a psychological approach to confessional practice. Those great developments in moral theology on which Pagula drew, mediated to him by the *Summa Confessorum* of John of Freiburg,[13] were the achievement above all of the friars' schools. The *Memoriale Presbiterorum* reads as though the author himself knew that he was engaged in an action to retrieve ground and that the opposition which he faced was an accomplished one.[14] On this point, he is not so much a conservative as a reactionary. Though the evidence of circulation indicates some demand for the most austere section of the treatise, his suffered the handicap, perhaps, of being an unpalatable prescription. The programme purveyed was not designed for a consumer-led market. Indeed, in the ecclesiology of the episcopal regime which is the context argued for the treatise, a consumer-led market represented the subversion of a disciplinary framework founded firmly on the monopoly of the parish and diocesan structure. Within that framework, the concern was for the right ordering of society on a model of inflexible moral principle. Social discipline so conceived is one of the treatise's central preoccupations.

[13] See ibid. 103, and Boyle, 'John of Freiburg'.
[14] Even in the course of a passage critical of the friars he can acknowledge that they are 'good clerks'. MP, fo. 16ra.

2

Text, Authorship, and Dating

The five known extant manuscripts of the *Memoriale Presbiterorum* are: Cambridge, Corpus Christi College, MS. 148 (referred to as C); London, Westminster Diocesan Archives, MS. H. 38 (referred to as W); Oxford, Bodleian Library, MS. Selden Supra 39 (referred to as S); London, British Library, MS. Harley 3120 (referred to as H); and Cambridge University Library, MS. Mm. v. 33 (referred to as U).[1] C, the earliest, a copy made at least one remove from the archetype, is dated palaeographically to the first half of the fourteenth century. H, an early-fifteenth-century manuscript containing frequent corruptions, is of particular interest for its unique colophon which describes the treatise as having been 'composed' by 'a certain doctor of decrees' (sc. canon law) at Avignon in 1344.[2]

Internal Evidence For Authorship and Dating

The information of H's colophon is open to doubt. An immediate point of criticism is its title for the treatise, 'Memoriale Sacerdotum'. Although the element 'Memoriale' probably derived from the work of William Durand ('Speculator') printed under the title *Aureum Confessorium et Memoriale Sacerdotum*,[3] from which the *Memoriale Presbiterorum* takes certain of its dogmatic material,[4] it is unlikely that the title of the latter work was originally *Memoriale Sacerdotum*. It is more likely that at some point in transmission to H the title *Memoriale Presbiterorum* was changed in order to broaden the address and that this change was incorporated in the colophon. In favour of this judgement is the fact that 'presbiter' occurs in the proem and at other junctures internally where 'sacerdos' would have served as well, and that in so far as there is inconsistency in usage the inconsistency occurs in H. Thus H, despite its title, has the incipit 'Cum animadverterem quam

---

[1] For an outline description and stemma, see Appendix.   [2] Cf. below, p. 220.
[3] Printed as an appendix to Gulielmus Durandus, *Repertorium Aureum*, in id., *Speculum Juris* (Frankfurt, 1592).
[4] MP, a. x–xii, fos. 5ʳ–6ʳ.

plures presbiteros parochiales . . .' (on this point confirming C's 'Cum animadverterem quam plurimos presbiteros parochiales . . .'). The heading of the first chapter in the text of H (fo. 3ᵛ) reads 'Qualiter *sacerdos* parochialis in audiendo confessionem alicuius se debet habere erga confitentem' against C's reading *presbiter*, but, revealingly, the title of the same chapter in the table of contents to H agrees with that of C in reading *presbiter*. Not only, therefore, is the reading *presbiter* intrinsically stronger but it also has the more convincing manuscript support, to the limited extent that discrimination on this point is possible. The consideration cautions against an over-literal acceptance of the colophon.

Of direct concern to the argument for authorship is the colophon's reference to a doctor of decrees and to place of composition. The form 'a quodam doctore decretorum' seems in the abstract unlikely to be authorial. Whether it replaced an illegible name or was wholly an interpolation based on what might have seemed a likely construction, especially from the final section of the treatise,⁵ is speculative. More firmly, the degree—if attributed to the author at time of writing— is almost certainly wrong. On internal evidence the treatise would not be judged the product of a doctor of canon law. The display of canonical erudition is lacking.⁶ In this regard, the contrast with the works of William of Pagula—including most aptly the *Prima Pars Oculi Sacerdotis*—is marked. Moreover, the author has a pronounced tendency to turn for his authority rather to civil law.⁷ Even as regards civil law, the content of the treatise is not technical. The subject did not require that it should be. What might be deduced from the treatise as regards the author's academic status is that he was in disciplinary orientation a lawyer rather than a theologian, that he had evidently studied civil law, that as an English civilian his civil law was propaedeutic to canon law, but that it is unlikely that he was at time of writing a doctor of decrees.

Strictly on legal content, the treatise would be dated 1312 × 1317, the earlier parameter being established by a reference to the Council of Vienne,⁸ the later by John XXII's promulgation of the *Clementines*,

---

⁵ See the description of contents, below, p. 76.

⁶ This is true of his lack of citations as of his specific unfamiliarity with the *Clementines*.

⁷ See e.g. MP, fos. 31ᵛ, 37ʳᵃ, 41ʳᵇ, 47ᵛᵃ, 60ᵛᵇ, 61ʳᵃ, 61ᵛᵇ, 62ʳᵃ, 62ʳᵇ, 66ᵛᵇ, 68ᵛᵃ, 69ʳᵇ, 95ᵛᵇ, 96ʳᵃ. The majority of these civilian references are to the law (or, twice, 'laws') or in the form 'legitur' without specification.

⁸ MP, fo. 15ʳᵃ.

to which there are no references. Although even as late as 1333 there was complaint at Oxford that the *Clementines* were being neglected,[9] William of Pagula, writing in the 1320s was familiar with them.[10] In so far as the silence might be deemed to confirm the conclusion already reached that the author possessed a lower level of legal expertise, its implication in the abstract for close dating is imponderable. Discussion of a *terminus ante quem* derived from silence on the legislation of the Council of London (1342) may be postponed, as the consideration is affected by the supposed place or context of composition.

H's connection of the treatise with Avignon cannot be confirmed or excluded from internal content. The author was evidently an Englishman[11] of Canterbury province.[12] Once—just over two-thirds of the way through the treatise—he uses 'here' ('hic'), where the context must be England.[13] While this should mean that that part of the treatise at least was written in England, it is perhaps compatible with a supposition that the author, if writing at Avignon, was not long out of his native country. He refers in passing late in the treatise to the fact that papal (and episcopal) penitentiaries daily grant testimonials to confitents.[14] The remark might reflect experience, but can hardly be pleaded with urgency to that effect.

Supplementing these meagre gleanings, the firmest information about the author is that he had a friend for whom the treatise was written and who consulted him subsequently about a problem relating to the burial of a pregnant woman, thus occasioning an addendum to the treatise.[15] Otherwise, internal evidence bearing on the author is confined to the documentation throughout the treatise of his strong views on a range of issues. Some of the most pronounced—his strictures on officialdom, his preoccupation with restitution, and his criticisms of the mendicant friars—have been signalled in Chapter 1. His strictures on officialdom include a particular concern with forensic abuse. That he was himself a secular is a priori likely from the treatise's concern with the expertise of secular clergy. The conclusion is in keeping with the author's knowledge of or anxiety about general administrative practice.

---

[9] *SAUO* 132. Cf. Boyle, 'Curriculum', 135–6, 137–8, 150–1.

[10] See Boyle, 'A Study', i. 159–60.

[11] He refers to 'foundlings': C, fo. 26vb ('fundlinges'); W, fo. 22^r ('foundlynges'); H, fo. 33^r ('fundelyng'); also to impleading by writ in the king's court and 'per vadium et plegium' in the courts of magnates: C, fo. 75^v.

[12] An inference from his references to provincial legislation. Cf. below, p. 76.

[13] MP, fo. 67vb.   [14] MP, fo. 84vb.   [15] Cf. above p. 1, and below, pp. 20, 77.

It is confirmed by the combination of his criticism of friars with, on one idiosyncratic point, criticism of monks.[16] There will be occasion to refer to these traits later in this chapter and, in the main, they will be the subject of detailed examination in Chapters 5 to 12.

Silence of the Bibliographical Tradition

The early bibliographers throw no light on the question of authorship. The treatise, in C, is noticed only by Tanner,[17] in passing, under the name of Robert Grosseteste, as having the same incipit as a Commentary on the *Disticha Catonis* wrongly associated with him.[18] M. R. James is incorrect in stating that Tanner elsewhere attributes it to a Thomas de Hanneya.[19] Thomas de Hanneya is, rather, credited by Bale[20] and Tanner[21] with authorship of the *Memoriale Iuniorum*, written in 1313, the first four words of whose incipit ('Cum animadverterem quam plurimos doctores')[22] are the same as those of the *Memoriale Presbiterorum*. The *Memoriale Iuniorum* is a textbook of grammar.[23] Thomas de Hanneya is known to have been at the Roman curia before writing his treatise,[24] but he has no connection with the *Memoriale Presbiterorum*. The incipit, 'Cum animadverterem quam plurimos', derives from the *Disticha Catonis*[25] and hence lent itself to a didactic work. As noted already,[26] the title *Memoriale* in the case of the *Memoriale Presbiterorum* is probably borrowed from a work of William Durand. Dr Pantin tentatively suggested Thomas Fastolf as a possible author, on the basis of his legal eminence and contemporary residence at Avignon,[27] where

---

[16] Dr Pantin allowed for the possibility that he was a monk (Pantin, *Church*, 206) but chapter b. lxi of the treatise—discussed below, pp. 12–13, 152—weighs against this.

[17] T. Tanner, *Bibliotheca Britannico-Hibernica* (London, 1748), 350, col. a.

[18] See S. H. Thomson, *The Writings of Robert Grosseteste* (Cambridge, 1940), 245.

[19] James, *Catalogue*, i. 337.

[20] J. Bale, *Scriptorum Illustrium Maioris Britanniae Catalogus*, 2nd edn. (Basle, 1557–9), part ii, p. 156.

[21] Tanner, *Bibliotheca*, 376.

[22] 'Memoriale Iuniorum', Oxford, Bodleian Library, MS. Bodl. 643, fo. 134ᵛ. For further details of the work, see R. W. Hunt, 'Oxford Grammar Masters in the Middle Ages', in *Oxford Studies Presented to Daniel Callus*, Oxford Historical Society, NS, 16 (1964), 175 and n. 3, 182 and n. 2. For the author, see also *DNB*, viii. 1190; there was a Thomas de Hanneye, canon of Poughley priory, Berks., in 1314; see *Registrum Simonis de Gandavo*, ed. C. T. Flower and M. C. B. Dawes, Canterbury and York Society (1934), ii. 818–21.

[23] See Hunt, 'Oxford Grammar Masters', 175, n. 3.   [24] Ibid. 182, n. 2.

[25] Cato, *Collectio Distichorum Vulgaris*, Prologus, in *Minor Latin Poets*, ed. J. W. and A. M. Duff (London, 1934).

[26] Cf. above, p. 6.   [27] See Pantin, *Church*, 21, n. 3, 205 n.

he compiled the first collection of decisions of the Rota.[28] There is no more specific reason, however, for connecting him with the *Memoriale Presbiterorum*.

A Clue to Authorship? The Will of William Doune

The initial clue in a series of inferences towards identification of the author came from research on the careers of fourteenth-century ecclesiastical lawyer-administrators, a class to which the author might plausibly be deemed to belong. In context of a search for the author, as on notable counts in its own right, the extant fragment of the will of Master William Doune attracts interest.[29]

William Doune held the archdeaconry of Leicester from 1354 until his death, which had occurred by 21 June 1361.[30] His will as it survives is undated. It was made after he had become rector of Swalcliffe, Oxon., to which he was instituted on 15 February 1360, and when he had already been rector for a sufficient period to have spent considerable sums on the fabric of the rectory.[31] He was in no immediate expectation of death[32] and a likely occasion for settling his affairs would have been his departing in autumn 1360 for the papal curia, on a journey from which he was not in fact to return.[33] A reference to the unborn child of Alice de la Lee favours the will's being made in England. Part of the collection known as Snappe's Formulary,[34] it comprises Northamptonshire Record Office, Box X643 no. 1, fos. 56–61 (formerly fos. clvii–clxii). Doune's will is distinct from the items that precede and follow.[35] The medieval foliation suggests the loss of three folios preceding and one following the extant fragment. The will, defective at

---

[28] His career is outlined in *BRUO* 2174–5. For the collection, comprising thirty-six cases, between December 1336 and March 1337, see *Dominorum de Rota Decisiones Novae, Antiquae et Antiquiores* (Cologne, 1581), 631 ff.

[29] See Thompson, 'Will'; cf. D. M. Owen, *The Medieval Canon Law: Teaching, Literature and Transmission* (Cambridge, 1990), 14, 19–21, 32, for some of the other points of interest.

[30] *CPP*, i. 320, when the canonry and prebend of Empingham in Lincoln cathedral was described as consequently vacant. Cf. ibid. 370, 381.

[31] LAO, Reg. IX, fo. 225ᵛ. Cf. Thompson, 'Will', 268.

[32] This is clear from a bequest to his chaplain at Epwell in Swalcliffe parish, conditional on his continuing to serve him; it is also suggested by the qualification 'si me supervixerit' in bequests to the vicar of Melton Mowbray and the chaplain of Wothorpe and by the provision, 'si . . . me premoriatur', referring to the former. See Thompson, 'Will', 277 and n. 2, 268.

[33] See below, p. 200.   [34] Cf. Owen, *Medieval Canon Law*, 35–6.

[35] Fo. clix has a 'monts' watermark: cf. C. M. Briquet, *Les Filigranes* (Paris, 1923), no. 11675, but without hatching.

beginning and end, would therefore be thought most plausibly a quire of eight folios. Unnoticed by the editor, there is one variation of hand within it. The passage continuing from 'Item lego partui qui est in ventre Alicie uxoris Ricardi', with the words[36] 'de la Lee de parochia de Swalclif, si nascatur masculus et vocetur post me Willelmus, xls.' and concluding[37] 'domino meo Lincolniensi et tercio meliorem domino meo Wigorniensi episcopis, et executoribus meis tres alios anulos', is in weaker, more spidery writing than the rest. The text of the will is elsewhere at least in part a copy. Comparison of the second hand with that of matter putatively written by William Doune, decades before, in Grandisson's register is inconclusive, but the particular variation cannot readily be explained otherwise than by assuming that what survives is part of the original quire of the will in its final draft and that the testator himself intervened in the copying to write rather than dictate bequests additional to pre-existing dispositions. The formulary contains at fos. 42ʳ–43ᵛ[38] a sentence by William Doune in a case involving Osney abbey.[39] One may speculate accordingly that the quire containing the will came from Osney, which was a beneficiary in it[40] and which, as will be seen, held some of Doune's possessions.

There are three principal correspondences between the outlook of William Doune, as revealed by his will, and the views of the author of the *Memoriale Presbiterorum*. The most idiosyncratic is the testator's evident anxiety over the integrity of property left in safe-keeping at the monasteries of Ford and Osney. To the abbot and convent of Ford he bequeathed five marks and quittance of debts,

provided that they shall have faithfully guarded and delivered to my executors my goods there deposited, concerning which I have an indenture under the abbot's seal; then and not otherwise shall they have these legacies and enjoy them and otherwise not but my executors shall [sc. in case of irregularity] convene them in the secular court for two marks of annual pension and one robe, being in arrears and unpaid annually for eleven years, the obligation in respect of which under their common seal is in my great coffer standing in the dorter of Osney.[41]

The abbot and convent were to be excused from rendering the goods on deposit and from forfeiting the legacy if their failure resulted from

---

[36] Thompson, 'Will', 273.   [37] Ibid. 274.

[38] Of this section, fo. 43 was formerly foliated cxxix.   [39] Cf. below, p. 198, n. 52.

[40] That the will took effect is shown by the abbot of Eynsham's acknowledgement of his legacy. See *Documents Illustrating the Activities of the General and Provincial Chapters of the English Black Monks, 1215–1540*, ed. W. A. Pantin, iii, Camden Society, 3rd Ser., 54 (1937), 37.

[41] Thompson, 'Will', 270.

loss, as through fire or theft, 'if such transpired without[42] fraud or fault of the abbot and convent or any single person of them'.[43] However, if they did not respect the indenture and were of bad faith, they were to be forced to honour the obligation in full and the pension and robe were to be exacted. To Abbot Thomas Cudelyngton and the convent of Osney Doune left twenty marks, for common uses at the disposition of the abbot, with an additional mark for each canon and further bequests to individual canons and to the abbot's household. The legacies were on condition that the abbot and convent

shall have faithfully guarded and shall have fully and faithfully delivered the money, books, silver vessels and other goods of mine deposited with them, such as are manifest at least in general in an indenture sealed with their common seal and in accordance with what I faithfully specify in a memorial or inventory drawn up by me in the matter and affixed to and enclosed in the present testament and in accordance with the exigency of the said indenture, in which the goods in question are not specified, but the chests and coffers (*ciste et coffre*) are sealed with my seal and are locked with keys which I have.

They were similarly left quittance of a debt of twenty pounds and of an annual pension of forty shillings which was in arrears for three or four years.[44]

The ingenuity of these provisions documents well a stricture of the *Memoriale Presbiterorum*, when under the title (b. lxi), 'De religiosis thesaurum et bona alia penes se deposita occupantibus et illicite consumentibus', the author considers a particular instance of how monks incur the obligation of restitution:

Almost all rich people of the present day, as well clerics as lay, deposit their monies and treasures in religious houses for safe-keeping and it often happens that such depositors, before they have recovered and have had what was deposited, pay the debt of nature, and the religious with whom the goods in question were deposited hide and misappropriate the same, sometimes opening the chests (*cistas*) with a substitute key and sometimes hiding the chests in secret places, asserting even with an oath that they have in their possession nothing whatever from the goods thus deposited and so they convert the goods surreptitiously to their own uses. But such religious believe that they do not sin thereby, in that they celebrate and represent themselves as celebrating for the soul of the depositor; but certainly in this they are very badly mistaken. Accordingly, as thieves and encroachers on and unlawful detainers of the property of another, they are bound to making restitution in the last particular of all the goods in question to the heirs or executors of the true lord of the goods, in as much as it was never the pleasure of the true lord of the

---

[42] The edition has 'sive', which I interpret however for 'sine'.
[43] Ibid. 271.   [44] Ibid.

things thus deposited that they should in any respect remain in the possession of those with whom they were deposited.[45]

The second principal correspondence between the *Memoriale Presbiterorum* and William Doune's will is their common sensitivity to forensic abuse. In particular, the author criticizes the professional witnesses or jurors whom he dubs 'choir leaders':

It often happens that witnesses receive, against the laws, from the party producing them, a great salary for giving testimony, to the restitution of which they are variously obliged by law. [Take the case,] if a witness shall have received a salary for maintaining falsehood in any court, ecclesiastical or secular, in accordance with the regular practice of those choir leaders on assizes and inquisitions, who in no way wish to tell the truth unless they shall have received money from one side or the other or perhaps from both. And frequently, the party which has justice on its side gives to such inquisitors, let us say ten, for telling the truth: if the opposing party shall have given twenty, they will give their corrupt opinion for that side which has made the larger gift to them, unjustly depriving the other party of its right. And many other liars depose falsehood in the ecclesiastical courts.[46]

William Doune bequeathed to his uterine half-brother, Aymer Fitzwarin—who had appointment as sheriff and escheator of Devon[47] —twenty marks and twelve silver spoons, 'on condition that never so long as he lives he stand on any jury nor take oath before the king's

---

[45] 'Fere omnes divites moderni tam clerici quam laici, pecunias suas et thesauros in domibus religiosis causa salvo custodiendi deponunt et frequenter contingit quod taliter deponentes, antequam suum huiusmodi depositum repecierint et habuerint, debitum nature persolvunt, et religiosi penes quos bona huiusmodi fuerint deposita ipsa bona occultant et occupant, quandoque cistas clave adulterina aperiendo et quandoque ipsas cistas in secretis locis occultando, asserentes eciam cum iuramento quod nichil penitus de bonis sic depositis penes se habent, et sic bona illa furtive in usus proprios convertunt. Set tales religiosi credunt se non peccare in hoc, pro eo quod ipsi celebrant et se fingunt celebrare pro anima deponentis; set certe in hoc errant pessime. Unde, tamquam fures et rei aliene invasores et illiciti detentores, tenentur ad restitucionem omnium bonorum huiusmodi heredibus vel executoribus veri domini bonorum in solidum faciendam, pro eo quod nunquam placuit vero domino rerum huiusmodi depositarum quod res ipse penes ipsos depositarios aliquo modo remanerent.' MP, fos. 71ᵛ–72.

[46] 'Multociens contingit quod testes recipiunt contra iura a parte producente magnum salarium pro testimonio perhibendo, ad cuius restitutionem varie de iure sunt astricti. Si igitur testis receperit salarium pro falso in quacunque curia, ecclesiastica vel seculari, perhibendo, secundum quod regulariter faciunt isti ductores chorearum in assisis et inquisicionibus, qui nullo modo veritatem dicere volunt nisi ab altera parcium vel forsan ab utraque pecuniam receperint. Et frequenter pars que iusticiam fovet dat talibus inquisitoribus pro veritate dicenda pone decem: si pars adversa dederit viginti, pro illa parte dicent sensum suum corruptum, que plus sibi donavit, partem aliam iniuste privando suo iure. Et multi alii falsi in causis ecclesiasticis falsitatem deponunt.' MP, fos. 69ᵛ–70ʳ.

[47] As sheriff 1348–50 (again in December 1361); as escheator in 1348. See *List of Sheriffs for England and Wales*, PRO List and Indexes, 9 (London, 1898), 35; *List of Escheators for England and Wales*, PRO List and Indexes, 72 (London, 1932), 33.

justices or other secular persons nor serve as one of the twelve jurymen nor ever induce anyone to do so, but laying aside and abandoning all such barratries [*talibus baratriis*], of which he is much suspected—let me say no more—he serve God as a faithful Christian and do worthy penance for the past'.[48]

Regarding the third principal correspondence, there is a difficulty which would seem to forbid Doune's authorship of the treatise. The difficulty is superficial, but it might easily obscure an essential similarity of outlook between treatise and will. The author of the *Memoriale Presbiterorum* is a fierce critic of the very class of officialdom to which Doune belonged, and indeed of abuse of the particular office which Doune held. Both in the section of the treatise devoted to interrogation of the penitent according to his social and vocational status,[49] and in that devoted to the obligation of restitution as it affects the various categories of penitent,[50] the author berates the misconduct of ecclesiastical administrators. Most relevant in the present context is his castigation of archdeacons:

If one may say so, the archdeacons of our time and their servants and others also who have charge of ecclesiastical jurisdiction as regards making correction of sins, like the hounds of hell, not only barking but also savaging, on many occasions unduly oppress their subjects from exquisite and feigned causes and extort money variously from them . . . They care about and have as their object making themselves a great pouch from the correction of souls precisely in the measure that correction of souls has become wholly alien to them. All who do such things against the statutes of the sacred canons, as being useless and unprofitable servants and even outright brigands, offend God gravely in these respects, on which account it is laid down in the law that if an archdeacon or anyone else, visiting his subjects by ordinary law, shall have oppressed in procurations the churches subject to him, in accordance with what they do who bring with them, when they visit, a burdensome household and hunting dogs and more horses than is permitted them by law—which infirmity is common to almost all the archdeacons of our time—he is bound to restitution of the damage inflicted by him beyond what is permitted him by law, in the following manner, namely, that he is obliged to render to the church which he thus oppressed whatever he received, personally or through his agents, beyond what was due and, notwithstanding, he is obliged to render as much again

---

[48] Thompson, 'Will', 272.

[49] 'Circa officiales et decanos rurales iurisdiccionem ecclesiasticam exercentes': MP, fos. 19ᵛ–20ᵛ.

[50] The most notable passages are in the chapters entitled 'De archidiaconis et eorum ministris'—quoted in part below—and 'De officialibus et correctoribus recipientibus pecuniam pro penitencia pro peccato notorio per eosdem iniuncta': MP, fos. 65ʳ–66ʳ.

from what is his; and so he is obliged to restitution in double, for example: some-one has oppressed a church in ten; he is obliged to restitution of twenty . . . Moreover, the members of archdeacons' households are not content unless they receive gifts from the persons visited and, if they shall not have received gifts, they oppress such persons . . . And if he shall have done this, the recipient is bound to restitution in double the amount, to be made within the month to him from whom he received it. Otherwise, such a recipient incurs penalty of suspension, *ipso iure*, until he shall have made satisfaction of the double amount, as has been said; and, notwithstanding, he who inflicted the damage, for the reason touched on, or even oppressed anyone, is obliged to restitution of the damage and to making compet-ent satisfaction for the damage to those who suffered it, in respect of the oppres-sion thus caused by him. And let not the lord archdeacon believe, nor any of his people, that he can be relieved by law from the penalty of restitution in this way of what has been received wickedly and contrary to the prohibition of the law, if he who gave remitted to them afterwards, spontaneously, of his grace, whatever he gave them in time of visitation, because an ecclesiastical person who gives in this way is only the proctor, not the lord, of the ecclesiastical goods and so could not remit to anyone, against the prohibition of the law, what by law could not be so remitted. Wherefore, in consideration of these matters, very many archdeacons and their servants are subject to grave perils in these days.[51]

[51] 'Si phas esset dicere, archidiaconi nostri temporis et eorum ministri et eciam ceteri qui ecclesiastice presunt iurisdiccioni, quoad correccionem peccatorum faciendam, tamquam canes infernales non solum latrando set eciam devorando, suos subditos multociens ex causis exque-sitis et fictis gravant plus debito, et pecunias varie extorquent ab eisdem . . . Tantum enim curant et ad hoc agunt ut sibi faciant marsupium magnum correccione animarum quantum in ipsis est penitus exulata. Omnes talia contra statuta sacrorum canonum facientes, tamquam ministri inutiles et pigri et eciam vere predones, Deum in hiis graviter offendunt, propter quod cavetur eciam in iure quod si archidiaconus vel quivis alius suos subditos iure ordinario visitans ecclesias sibi subditas in procuracionibus gravaverit, secundum quod faci-unt illi qui ducunt secum quando visitant onerosam familiam et canes venaticos et plures equos quam a iure sibi permittitur, que infirmitas est communis quasi omnibus archidiaco-nis nostri temporis, tenetur ad restitucionem dampni per ipsum dati ultra id quod sibi a iure permittitur, isto modo videlicet quod tenetur ecclesie quam sic gravavit reddere quicquid per se vel per suos plus debito recepit, et nichilominus tenetur reddere tantumdem de suo; et sic tenetur ad restitucionem dupli, verbi gracia: gravavit quis ecclesiam in decem, iste tene-tur ad restitucionem viginti . . . Preterea familiares archidiaconorum non sunt contenti nisi dona recipiant a personis visitatis, et, si dona non receperint, gravant personas tales . . . Quod si fecerit, recipiens tenetur ad restitucionem dupli eius quod recepit faciendam illi a quo illud recepit, infra mensem. Alioquin sic recipiens penam suspensionis incurrit ipso iure donec de duplo illo satisfecerit ut dictum est; et nichilominus ille qui dampnum dedit ex causa pre-tacta vel eciam quemquam gravavit tenetur ad restitucionem dampni ac ad satisfaciendum dampnum passis competenter, pro gravamine per ipsum sic illato. Nec credat dominus archidi-aconus vel aliquis de suis quod possit liberari de iure a pena restitucionis huiusmodi male et contra iuris prohibicionem perceptorum si ille qui dedit postea de sua gracia eis sponte remisit quicquid tempore visitacionis dedit, quia persona ecclesiastica taliter donans rei eccle-siastice procurator est tantum et non dominus, et sic contra iuris prohibicionem non posset cuiquam remittere quod de iure non poterit sic remitti. Unde, istis consideratis, gravibus subiciuntur periculis quamplures archidiaconi et eorum ministri hiis diebus.' MP, fo. 65ʳ⁻ᵛ.

William Doune went to considerable lengths to have restitution made of extortions for which he was responsible:

And for the love of God, within a month after my death let there be made, principally in my archdeaconry of Leicester and then in the whole diocese of Lincoln, a general proclamation that whoever at any time has felt himself to have been unduly oppressed or harassed by me, or has been able to say and show, at least with probability, that I extorted or received something from him against justice and good conscience—excepting only archidiaconal procurations, which I sometimes received in the said archdeaconry without having discharged the office of visitation, on account of which I have above[52] ordained to be done in the said archdeaconry other services of piety and alms in recompense, such as I can at present make—if [he] show[s] probable evidences of the injurious and illicit extortion and receipt and swears the truth of the assertion (as to the value or otherwise or sufficiency or insufficiency of which evidences and oath, having regard to the qualities of persons and the amounts in question, I wish it to be at the judgement and conscience of my executors, in as much as nothing specific of the kind occurs to me at present, with the exception of certain receipts by my servants from the vicar, as they have said, of Melton Mowbray, in respect of which I have above bequeathed him to a markedly greater value, and because I perhaps extorted from the same vicar against right conscience a certain obligation of ten pounds, I have above remitted and remit it to him, and I ask that he may remit [sc. the fault] to me, because I do bitterly reflect (*iam amare recogito*)[53] that many superiors deal very badly with their subjects, rather they plunder them, of which number I was and am one, may God of his ineffable mercy pardon me), then my executors shall restore and make good, in as far as shall be right and proper, all and single that has thus been illicitly extorted and received, in so far as my goods not bequeathed in the present testament to other uses or to persons known or unknown may suffice in this respect.[54]

Quite apart from his interpretation of *iam amare recogito*, it seems that Professor Hamilton Thompson read Doune's sentiment here as evidence of that abuse of archidiaconal power for which there is otherwise a good deal of literary and some documentary evidence. This is not so much apparent from his introduction to the will—where he merely cites the evil reputation of archdeacons from the twelfth century onwards and remarks that 'William Doune was acutely conscious

---

[52] This may refer to various substantial bequests for the repair of churches in the archdeaconry. Thompson, 'Will', 269.

[53] 'iam amare recogito': ibid. 280. Thompson, ibid. 251, rendered, 'for that I now bitterly consider in myself': whether 'iam' is taken to be purely intensificatory or as suggesting a change of mind is, in the abstract, a matter of stylistic judgement. My rendering here is conditioned by my general argument.

[54] Ibid. 243–4.

of the temptations of his office and its unpopularity'—as from a reference afterwards, in his Ford Lectures, to Doune's praying 'God's forgiveness for exactions and extortions in which, however, he was careful to point out that he merely followed the example of his brethren'.[55] Even when every allowance is made for the accommodation of idealism to pragmatism over a period of some twenty years, it is evident that such a perspective would make Doune an unlikely candidate for authorship of the *Memoriale Presbiterorum*. Doune's provisions can, however, be read quite differently, as an indication not so much of abuse —of which, as regards extortions, he was firmly conscious of only one lapse and that by his servants—as of extreme sensitivity to abuse. From that perspective, Doune's candidacy is strengthened rather than otherwise by his confessions of guilt. The benign reading of Doune's scruple is in fact reinforced by the display of similar scrupulosity on the part of his own official and successor, John de Belvoir.[56] The sensitivity thus evinced by Doune to his servants' conduct—it seems as though they may have been questioned on the legality of receipts—might itself be held a further point of correspondence between will and treatise. There is here implicit acceptance of the moral precept, strongly emphasized by the author of the *Memoriale Presbiterorum*, that principals are responsible for the acts of their deputies.[57]

Verbal or stylistic comparison between a treatise and a will is probably bound to be an unproductive exercise. Some dissimilarity may be noted at once from one of the passages cited above, in the will's use of 'barratries', which occurs nowhere in the *Memoriale Presbiterorum*, for the alleged malpractices of Aymer Fitzwarin. The only features observed to be common to the two writers are: occurrences of 'insolidum' ('completely' or 'to the enth'), which is so frequent in the *Memoriale Presbiterorum* as to be a trait and of which there are a few instances in the will;[58] a single instance in the will of the phrase 'et non sicut in iure cavetur', of which there are several near examples in the treatise;[59] an uncompelling near-resemblance of phrase;[60] and a use of

[55] Ibid. 244. Cf. Thompson, *English Clergy*, 60–1.
[56] See below, p. 210.   [57] MP, fo. 65ᵛ. Cf. MP, fo. 67ʳ.
[58] See e.g. MP, fos. 57ʳᵇ, 63ᵛᵇ, 64ᵛ, 65ʳᵇ, 66ʳᵇ, 67ᵛᵇ, 68ᵛ (x 2), 69ᵛ, 71ʳ, 72ʳ, 76ʳ, 77ᵛ (x 2), 78ᵛᵇ, 79ʳ, 79ᵛ; cf. Thompson, 'Will', 267(x 2), 268, 270, 284.
[59] Thompson, 'Will', 268. Cf. 'de iure novo sic cavetur'; 'per canonem quo cavetur'; 'in iure cavetur'; 'cavetur in iure sic'; 'cavetur eciam in iure'; 'in diversis legibus cavetur': MP, fos. 16ʳ, 17ᵛ, 30ᵛ, 61ᵛᵇ, 65ʳᵇ, 95ʳᵇ.
[60] MP, fo. 68ᵛᵇ: quandoque nichil quandoque modicum; cf. Thompson, 'Will', 271: 'nichil vel modicum'.

the term 'corrupta' in the sense of sexually experienced.[61] In isolation, none of the correspondences of outlook is, perhaps, all that remarkable. Even the anxiety over the deposits with the two monasteries seems to be part of a more general circumspection on Doune's part: he left a bequest too to his bailiff at Swalcliffe, Robert Saundres, conditional on his faithfulness in answering to the executors for goods in his keeping and administration, and another to Richard Medmenham, one of his executors, on a similar condition.[62] Nor can it be supposed that Doune, though his testamentary arrangements reveal an unusually forceful and punctilious character, was the only depositor of his time to fear for his valuables. The coincidence of the several areas of sensitivity is however sufficiently arresting to prompt further investigation of Doune's career as a test of his suitability for authorship.

An ostensible consideration against is academic standing. Within one possible range for dating the treatise[63] and on the best reconstruction of Doune's academic career,[64] he would have been in the early stages of legal study at time of writing. Even at time of redacting, if that is to be distinguished, he would have been at just about halfway in his progress to the doctorate in civil law. (In 1343 he is described as 'in utroque iure scolari',[65] and in 1349 as 'licentiato in legibus',[66] shortly after which he must have proceeded doctor of civil law.[67]) Though the colophon might, on the case for his authorship, be taken as slight evidence for his having proceeded doctor of canon law at some stage, there is no documentary evidence to this effect and the documentary evidence is formally against.[68] Manifestly, he does not meet an understanding of the colophon as representing the *Memoriale Presbiterorum* to have been 'composed' by someone who was a doctor of decrees in 1344. Any postponement of a *terminus ante quem* which is already disturbingly late, is excluded.[69] As already noted, however, the treatise on internal evidence would not be judged the product of a doctor of canon law. Doune's lacking that status at the supposed time of composition is

---

[61] MP, fo. 26ʳ (a. xli); cf. Thompson, 'Will', 278.   [62] Ibid. 278, 283.
[63] See below, pp. 28–30.   [64] See below, p. 43.
[65] ASV, *RS* 4, fo. 89ᵛ. Cf. *CPP*, i. 63.   [66] ASV, *RS* 21, fo. 52ʳ.
[67] See below, p. 43.
[68] Even to the end of his career, references to his degree in both episcopal and papal sources have him as 'legum doctor', which is best understood as 'doctor of civil law'. In his will, however, he bequeathed his own 'repetitiones' and 'lectura' which would most naturally be understood to be in canon law: they follow references to Innocent III and Guido de Baysio and precede a bequest of the *Sext*. Thompson, 'Will', 282.
[69] See above, pp. 7–8, below, pp. 27–8.

not, therefore, cogent. Indeed, his relative juniority as a lawyer may be thought another circumstance—additional to what is known of his outlook—compatible with his candidature.

A more serious consideration is the fact that Doune was not at the attributed date a priest, and could accordingly have had no direct experience as a confessor in the formal sense.[70] He did not receive a benefice with cure until he was instituted, as a simple clerk, to Georgeham, Devon, on 4 November 1344.[71] He had already had papal dispensation to hold three benefices, including one with cure, without being obliged to reside or to be ordained priest,[72] and in April 1345 he was still only a deacon.[73] That Doune was not a priest at the date assigned by the colophon is probably not, however, a sufficient reason to exclude him from authorship. It would be entirely compatible with the gulf between knowing and doing, so marked in medieval culture, that someone having no practical experience of his subject (at least as regards sacramental confession) should write authoritatively from a level of abstract learning and be received as an authority accordingly. There are many observations in the *Memoriale Presbiterorum* on the behaviour of penitents and on the peculiar difficulties which they pose that read most naturally as the observations of a confessor—and one of standing too—but that can accommodate themselves also, if the prompting is sufficiently strong, to the other supposition. There is nothing in the treatise which definitively establishes that the author was a priest. From 1335 Doune appears in the household of John Grandisson, bishop of Exeter.[74] That fiercely idealistic prelate, with whom he seems to have had a family connection,[75] must have spotted his fitness for episcopal service and have patronized him. By 1336 he was acting as Grandisson's

---

[70] For the consideration affecting a civil lawyer's promotion to priesthood, see below, p. 35, n. 155.

[71] *RG*, iii. 1345.

[72] ASV, *RS* 4, fo. 89ᵛ; cf. *CPP*, i. 63. ASV, *RA* 76, fo. 111ʳ⁻ᵛ; cf. *CPL*, iii. 112. The terms of both supplication and letter are slightly ambiguous. Doune, who was illegitimate, was dispensed to hold the benefices without being promoted to sacred orders or being obliged to reside otherwise than if he were legitimate. The qualification is best understood as preparing the way for his being licensed, as he subsequently was, under *Cum ex eo*.

[73] *RG*, ii. 992, in a licence, dated 20 April 1345, under *Cum ex eo*, for him to study (sc. civil law). He was still a deacon, still evidently studying civil law, in the year commencing 20 September 1348, when his licence was renewed. Ibid. 1068.

[74] See below, p. 39.

[75] Grandisson's mother, Sybil, was a granddaughter of Sir Fulk Fitzwarin. See G. E. Cokayne, *The Complete Peerage*, vi (London, 1926), 61–2. Doune's mother had evidently married a Fitzwarin.

registrar, or perhaps rather as one of his registrars.[76] In a petition to the pope preferred on Doune's behalf in 1343, he was described as the bishop's 'dilecto et familiari', who had faithfully served him for many years.[77] The views of a man of whom the bishop thought so highly and who must have been perceived as a rising star might well be accepted as worth having, particularly by an incumbent within the diocese.

Authorship: The Recipient of the Treatise

An inference to identification of the original recipient of the *Memoriale Presbiterorum* provides crucial support for the argument so far. On the hypothesis that motivated the search, the document from which the inference derives comes from precisely the right source, the Exeter register, even if its date is earlier than might have been expected. On 25 November 1332[78] Bishop Grandisson wrote to John de Leghe, vicar in the collegiate church of Crediton, advising him over the burial of a parishioner who had died while pregnant:

Nostro supplicasti edoceri responso si parochiane tue, que pregnans, fetu ab utero non soluto, diem clausit extremum, ecclesiastica dari debeat vel denegari sepultura. Ad quod respondemus—sequendo sentenciam Hostiensis in Summa—*Extravagantes*—de Consecracione Ecclesie vel Altaris; *Vers. quid si mulier pregnans*—Quod si certus esse valeas fetum esse mortuum, per judicium cyrurgici periti[79] in illa pericia, et obstetricum veritatem experiencium per imposicionem baculi in ore mulieris mortue, ipsam sepeliri minime prohibemus; nec, eciam, consilium tibi damus, set te tue consciencie in premissis duximus relinquendum.

With this compare the case in the chapter appended to the *Memoriale Presbiterorum*, 'De muliere gravida mortua sepelienda cum partu vel non':

Tuis amice karissime apicibus michi postquam tractatum suprascriptum per me tibi missum perlegeras rescripsisti quod quedam mulier pregnans in tua decessit parochia cuius corpus una cum fetu suo Christiane tradidisti sepulture, et ob hoc tibi insidiantes invidie flamma te tamquam homicidam in hoc asserunt deliquisse. Unde ut quid tenere debeas de cetero in hoc casu periculo tue anime precavendo tibi rescriberem supplicasti.[80]

---

[76] See below, pp. 40–2.   [77] ASV, *RS* 4 (formerly 5), fo. 89ᵛ.
[78] *RG*, ii. 673–4. The year is derived contextually, the entry itself being dated, apart from the date of day and month, merely 'ut supra'. DRO, Chanter 4, fo. 158ʳ.
[79] The edition reads 'perito' mistakenly.
[80] MP, fo. 95ʳ. In Haren, 'A Study', ii. 326, I take *periculum*, the reading of H, into the text. I see this now to be an error and *periculo* to be the stronger reading.

(The author supplies accordingly an exhaustive analysis, based on the *Summa Aurea* of Henry of Susa (Hostiensis).)[81]

There were two issues in such an eventuality—determining the condition of the foetus and the propriety of burying in consecrated ground. Though theoretically distinct, they were in practice intricate. In the addendum the circumstances are recapitulated elliptically: the friend had given Christian burial to mother and foetus; therefore he had incurred the charge of homicide. There was genuine doubt whether Christian burial was permitted. The answer depended on whether the foetus was considered as part of the mother or as an entity in its own right. An older line of thought, as the author explained, had held that the woman should not be opened but be buried intact. At the other extreme was the view that the foetus should be delivered by section, baptized if live and buried if it subsequently died. In between was the view that there should be no section if the foetus were evidently dead. This had been the implication of the instruction given by Bishop William Briwere's statutes (1225 × 1237) for Exeter diocese, who ordered section 'if the infant is believed to be alive'.[82] One may deduce from Grandisson's reply that he too tended to this view, though he was markedly coy—no doubt in deference to the dissension among the authorities. Evidently, the author's friend had not ordered section. Indeed, the conscientious pastor, if moderately informed, must have been in a quandary between legal scrupulosity and the sensitivities of his parishioners, for the consensus of authority dictated that were the foetus removed dead it could not be buried in the cemetery. Whether Leghe had observed some lesser procedure to ascertain the foetus's condition is unclear. Perhaps Grandisson was endorsing what had been done on this point. More likely not: what he recommends comes straight from Hostiensis. The dispute—to conflate the sources now—may rather have been occasioned by Grandisson's answer. But even if the lesser procedure had been followed, some would undoubtedly have felt that only section could give certainty. At Crediton there would have been more advice than usual—and than was profitable.

Little clear external light can be shed on an association of William Doune and John de Leghe. Inference is possible from an entry in the Exeter register, dated 3 March 1329, recording a dispute between Robert de Doune, rector of the church of Ringmore, in south Devon, plaintiff,

---

[81] Cf. Hostiensis, *SA*, iii. tit. 'De consecratione ecclesiae vel altaris', art. 8, col. 394.

[82] See *CS*, ii. 234.

and John Stibba—vicar of the neighbouring parish of Ermington —and William Strode, executors or administrators of the late John de Leghe, of the diocese, over a breviary.[83] From coincidence of dates, the John de Leghe here may perhaps be taken as the clerk presented to the north Devon rectory of West Putford on 21 June 1328.[84] West Putford was vacant on 1 March 1329 and Robert de Leghe was instituted on 8 April.[85] That the vicar of Ermington had been nominated to act in the estate of a benefice-holder on the other side of the county might indicate that John de Leghe had goods in south Devon and was connected with the Ermington area. (At the very least the details as interpreted would suppose intercourse across a diocese whose terrain might suggest caution on this point.) Why Robert de Doune felt moved rather promptly to claim a breviary from the goods of John de Leghe is a matter of surmise. There was at least a social relationship.

There is no firm evidence of kinship between Robert de Doune and William, but there is a certain argument from location. Of the several possible origins of William's toponymic, Down Thomas, in the parish of Wembury, south Devon, has the strongest claim. In his will he makes such solicitous provision for Isabella Pipard, who resided with his sister, as to have led Hamilton Thompson to suggest that she may have been his daughter.[86] The Pipard family had land in Down Thomas.[87] (Isabella might have been a kinswoman on the side of William's mother, to whose identity there is at present no clue, other than that she married into a cadet branch of the Fitzwarins.) A further, slight, consideration in favour of the location is the 'Thomas' element in the designation of the manor. This dates from the early fourteenth century[88] and is probably from 'Thomas le Squier', referred to in 1346 as a previous holder.[89] Thomas was a well-established name in the family

---

[83] *RG*, i. 470–1. Robert de Doune's character as rector emerges from a visitation inquiry of 1342, where it is recorded 'multa bona ibi tempore suo fecit in construendo domus novas et antiquas reparando': G. G. Coulton 'A Visitation of the Archdeaconry of Totnes in 1342', *EHR* 26 (1911), 117.

[84] *RG*, iii. 1264.   [85] Ibid. 1270.

[86] Thompson, 'Will', 272–3, 277–8. For the suggestion that she may have been his daughter, see ibid. 245, n. 2. The care shown in these provisions is in keeping with the striking tenderness of remarks in the *Memoriale Presbiterorum* on women's psychology, for example, on the confessor's attitude to adultery and fornication; even where the woman is a willing partner, the confessor is to consider the possibility that she was 'seducta falsis promissionibus causa extorquendi ab ea carnalem copulam sibi factis, quo casu micius debet secum agi quia mulieres fragiles sunt valde et mollia habent corda'. MP, fo. 47ʳ.

[87] *Feudal Aids*, i. 380 (AD 1316).

[88] The 1316 reference is the first known occurrence of it.

[89] *Feudal Aids*, i. 401; cf. *Place-Names Devon*, 260.

of William Doune.[90] Wembury, Ermington, and Ringmore are three
points of a small territorial triangle. Finally, if William Doune were a
native of the area it would be peculiarly appropriate that he should have
been a witness to the probation on 16 November 1338 of the will of
Sir Richard de Champernon, lord of Modbury, a fact which was originally omitted from the register and was somewhat awkwardly inter-
polated.[91] But that circumstance may, of course, be entirely accidental, a
reflection simply of Doune's official activity.

The element 'Legh' occurs in the place-names Challonsleigh and
Elfordleigh (both corresponding to the medieval Legh), in the parish
of Plympton St Mary, somewhat north of Wembury and in the same
hundred of Plympton.[92] However, other derivations of the toponymic
are, in the abstract, equally possible. In fact, Johns de Leghe of putatively quite different provenance appear in the surviving ordination
lists for the episcopate of Walter de Stapledon (1308–26). One figure
—who may conveniently be designated John de Leghe (1), was to be
ordained[93] subdeacon at a ceremony in the conventual church of Totnes,
to the presentation of Sir Robert de Stockay, knight, on 22 December
1319.[94] There were three other general ordination ceremonies in that
month—at Lawhitton, in Cornwall, on 2 December; at Stokenham (in
Coleridge hundred), on 16 December; and at Paignton, on 27 December.[95] While Totnes, Stokenham, and Paignton are in vicinity, the choice
of Totnes as against Lawhitton must be thought indicative in general
terms of the ordinand's provenance. Moreover, although Robert de
Stockay had lands in scattered locations,[96] it is noteworthy that he appears

---

[90] It was the name of his legitimate half-brother (see Thompson, 'Will', 276), of an illegitimate half-brother—his father's son (see ibid. 275)—of his late sister, Thomasine (see ibid.
279), and of his father's niece, Thomasine, daughter of John Lynham (see ibid. 275). Hamilton
Thompson suggested that William's father might have been Thomas Doune or Estdoune,
who presented to the rectory of East Down, between Barnstaple and Combe Martin, in 1339,
but observed against this that whereas William's father's heir was Thomas, the patron who
presented to East Down in 1363 was Philip Doune: ibid. 236. The Pipard evidence in favour
of Down Thomas also makes the Thomas le Squier referred to a more likely figure. In favour
of a connection with East Down, however, is the fact that Georgeham, the rectory which
William later held, though of different patronage, is nearby.

[91] See below, p. 41.   [92] Cf. *Place-Names Devon*, 252–3.

[93] Strictly, the lists are evidence of intention to be ordained rather than of actual ordination. See W. J. Dohar, 'Medieval Ordination Lists: The Origins of a Record', *Archives*, 20:
87 (1992), 17–35. In references below I use 'ordained' as shorthand, except where a substantive point arises.

[94] *Reg. Stapeldon*, 527.

[95] This is to omit the small ceremony held in the chapel of the prior's chamber at Plympton
on 9 December.

[96] See e.g. *Feudal Aids*, i. 358–9, 371, 381, 400.

in 1303 as holding a fee in Torridge, in the parish of Plympton St Mary.[97] He would seem an eminently suitable supporter of a Leghe of Challonsleigh/Elfordleigh. His candidate, John de Leghe, appears subsequently as deacon, ordained on 20 September 1320, this time in the parish church of Axminster, and priest, ordained in Exeter cathedral on 19 September 1321.[98] From him must perhaps be distinguished John de Leghe (2), who was ordained acolyte at the same ceremony as his namesake, in Totnes, on 22 December 1319,[99] since canon law forbade the reception of subdiaconate and a minor order on the same day.[100] The same consideration as already adduced concerning the ordinand's provenance applies, and it is reasonable to think that Johns de Leghe (1) and (2), if distinct at all, were related. Whether John de Leghe (1) is identical with the candidate who was to be ordained acolyte in Exeter cathedral on 22 September 1319[101] cannot be established, though the interval would be convenient if he intended to proceed to major orders at a proximate ceremony. His missing the September ceremony would conveniently explain double reception in December. But there is some slight risk of confusion with a John de Leghe who appears among a list of those tonsured in the hall at Cuttingbeak, close to St German's priory in Cornwall, on 18 June 1318,[102] from whom must in turn be distinguished the recipient of tonsure—putatively therefore John de Leghe (4)—listed for the Cornwall archdeaconry under the date 21 December 1308.[103] John de Leghe (4) could a fortiori be the acolyte of 22 December 1319.

Of these figures, the best candidate/s for a 'Doune connection' must be John de Leghe (1)/(2). Since (2), if distinct, is the less advanced he is the more readily identified with the candidate for tonsure, unfortunately without any note of provenance, in the chapel of Paignton on 21 December 1314. That list also includes, again without provenance, the names William de Doune (tonsure) and Robert de Doune (acolyte).[104] The coincidence of the names William de Doune and John de Leghe here is intriguing but of uncertain significance. There is a William de Doune to be tonsured in Stapledon's first and vast ordination list of

---

[97] Ibid. 353.   [98] *Reg. Stapeldon*, 530, 533.   [99] Ibid. 527.

[100] Lyndwood, *Provinciale*, 310 (b); v. tit. 11, *ad vocem* 'canonicas sanctiones', citing Hostiensis, Joannes Andreae and John of Freiburg. For laxity on the point, see Haines, *Worcester*, 166–7.

[101] *Reg. Stapeldon*, 523.   [102] Ibid. 518.

[103] Ibid. 453. There is other evidence in the ordination lists of 'de Leghes' from Cornwall.

[104] Ibid. 500: a Robert de Doune was tonsured at Totnes on 22 December 1313.

21 December 1308.[105] Here, presumably because the archdeacons were commissioned to examine the ordinands, the candidates were listed by archdeaconry and William is included in the (southern) archdeaconry of Totnes. He may or may not be the same as the William de la Doune ordained acolyte in the more northerly parish church of South Molton on 18 December 1311.[106] The 'la' variation in the second case does not exclude assimilation, since the form 'La Doune' is attested for Down Thomas itself in 1303.[107] There are no means of distinguishing further the Williams of 1308 and 1314. Since there is no confusion of the name during Grandisson's pontificate, one of the two somehow passed out of the record. On the argument for the local provenance of the future archdeacon testator, it is likely that one of them is to be identified with him, despite the fact that neither is noted in the ordination lists as having been dispensed for illegitimacy.[108] Such notes do occur in Stapledon's register—as, for instance, the qualification 'legitimatus', presumably meaning dispensed, against several acolytes among those ordained on 22 December 1313[109]—but not often enough to carry conviction as to the consistency of his registrars' practice on the point, especially in regard to minor orders. A clue to practice may be offered by the case of Thomas Cros, tonsured on 6 August 1314, against whose name is the detail, 'de soluto genitus et soluta, cum quo Dominus dispensavit, tunc, ibidem'.[110] The implication is that normally there was a separate procedure. In the ordination list of 21 December 1308, the qualification 'legitimatus' appears for a subdeacon of the Totnes archdeaconry[111] but there is no note against any in the great list of minor ordinands and the same is true of the list of 21 December 1314, which, while much shorter, included approximately one hundred persons tonsured and fifty ordained acolytes. William Lyndwood, indeed, held that in the case of minor orders the bishop's conscious act of conferring on a candidate of illegitimate birth conveyed implicit dispensation.[112]

No more than the Williams de Doune can the Johns de Leghe be clarified finally. The first reference to John de Leghe of Crediton is his association with three others as executor of the testament of Mr Walter de Esse, late canon of that church, on 9 July 1329.[113] While family or

---

[105] Ibid. 452.   [106] Ibid. 484.

[107] *Calendar of Inquisitions post Mortem*, iv (Edward I), p. 88, no. 139. Cf. *Place-Names Devon*, 260.

[108] Cf. above, n. 72.   [109] *Reg. Stapeldon*, 490.   [110] Ibid. 499.   [111] Ibid.

[112] Lyndwood, *Provinciale*, 27 (a); i. tit. 4, *ad vocem* 'dispensatione sufficienti'.

[113] *RG*, i. 513. He is titled 'vicar'.

territorial connection offers on the evidence a probable basis of the relationship between William Doune, taken as author of the *Memoriale Presbiterorum*, and John de Leghe, taken as its recipient, the connection cannot be established precisely from the documentation. That, however, is tangential to the main argument, which may conveniently be summarized as read from the local context outwards. In this perspective, the foundation is the bishop's letter to John de Leghe of Crediton. It is not supposed that the case at Crediton was unique in fourteenth-century England. The point of interest is less the burial than the neurosis surrounding it, reflected variously—on the supposition that the case is indeed the same—in the episcopal register and in the addendum to the treatise. If the treatise is on this basis assigned to the Exeter context, the next question is whether one figure in or from that context is, in the state of the evidence, more eligible than another as a candidate for authorship. Study of Grandisson's regime[114] shows that certain salient preoccupations of the author were topics of sensitivity within it. To that extent any member of the episcopal circle might voice them, and the possibility remains that if we could know their individual views in sufficient detail any one might on that score compete with William Doune as a figure to whom the treatise might be referred.[115] Notably, William of Nassington, a more senior member by far than Doune of Grandisson's administration, is credited with having written an instructional work which shows interesting parallels with the *Memoriale Presbiterorum*.[116] For that matter, anyone in Exeter might have had cause to observe sailors, on whom the *Memoriale*, uniquely within the genre, carries a chapter. At this stage William Doune's will can be appealed to as revealing several idiosyncrasies in common with the treatise: suspicion of monks as 'bankers', sensitivity to forensic abuse, and hypersensitivity to the obligations of restitution. Beyond the will, a further shared idiosyncrasy is afforded by a strong inference towards Doune's hostility to the mendicant orders,[117] of which there is no trace in William of Nassington's outlook as known. Finally, on the tangential point, one may return to topography and to the social bonds within small communities. The treatise—still more its addendum—was written a little *de*

---

[114] See below, Chap. 3.

[115] The *fasti* of Grandisson's administration have been constructed by D. J. Cawthron, 'The Episcopal Administration of the Diocese of Exeter in the Fourteenth Century, With Special Reference to the Registers of Stapeldon, Grandisson and Brantingham', London University, MA thesis, 1951.

[116] See below, pp. 57–60. [117] See below, p. 209.

haut en bas, by a member of the 'sublime and literate' class: for whom better, perhaps, than a school chum?

On these several grounds, William Doune of known figures makes the strongest bid. In the absence of confirmatory attribution to him, his authorship is a hypothesis based on circumstance. But it is a hypothesis against which there is no ultimately telling consideration and for which there is an accumulation—rather, a convergence—of detail. While there can be no guarantee that Doune's primacy as a candidate is not a trick of the evidence in its survival for him, the fact is of some moment that the strength of his personality has left separate imprint—in his own will and in the will of his client John de Belvoir.[118] On this count too he is eminently suitable as author of a treatise whose sustained forcefulness is a remarkable feature. Finally, however, Doune's authorship must remain a construction on evidence that is partial. In deference to that reservation, the remainder of this study, in so far as it surveys the doctrine of the *Memoriale Presbiterorum*, will as a general method preserve the reference to 'author' rather than to Doune. By the same token, the account of Doune's career, reviewed in Chapters 3 and 13 as the career of the strongest candidate within the surviving evidence for authorship of the treatise, will distinguish between those elements in the composition of his outlook that are derivable from his context as reconstructed from the other documentation, and those that would follow were he by conclusive demonstration established as the author.

Dating

The case made for the treatise's provenance has implications for dating. Within the context as identified, an obvious *terminus ante quem* is provided by the legislation of the Council of London of 1342, justly described as 'the most significant body of provincial legislation in the later Middle Ages'.[119] Several of the rulings from the series published in May 1343 bear on matters of concern to the author, particularly as regards lay intrusion on ecclesiastical rights and jurisdiction and as regards tithing and pecuniary penances. Grandisson attended the council.[120] Detailed comparison between the legislative programme and

---

[118] See Haren, 'Will', 135–7.

[119] B. Bolton, 'The Council of London of 1342', *SCH* 7 (1971), 147. On the three series of constitutions elaborated by the council, see also Cheney, 'Legislation', 415–17, and id., 'Textual Problems', 122.

[120] See *RG*, ii. 968.

the *Memoriale Presbiterorum* must be deferred.[121] It may be noted simply that the areas of correspondence between the treatise and the matters discussed in London (especially the great series of clerical measures)[122] are substantial. Though the council's achievement was considerably less than its ambitions, the complete absence of reference to it by Doune—considered as author—cannot escape notice. The silence would in those terms be prima facie evidence that the treatise was written—if not before the council met—at least before the text of the legislation, published in May 1343, came to hand.[123] In that case, the areas of correspondence referred to would be taken to suggest that Grandisson was one of the assembly's most active members, not only voicing his own views but channelling to his fellow prelates the elaborated preoccupations of his circle. We know by his letter excusing himself from personal attendance at the largely abortive meeting summoned for October 1341 that he submitted a dossier on heads of reform.[124]

The inferred identification of the recipient of the *Memoriale Presbiterorum* provides a framework that might explain this silence. Though what can be known of John de Leghe's career is meagre and is complicated by the fact that there was putatively more than one cleric of the name, there are grounds from it for speculating that the *terminus ante quem* for the substance of the addendum to the treatise might be the end of 1338. The letter to the friend, that constitutes the addendum, refers to the pregnant woman as having died 'in your parish' and to the criticisms as promoted by 'the flame of envy'. While it is not impossible that the reference is to a former parish, it would be peculiarly appropriate if the context were still that in which the problem had arisen. On 31 December 1338 a John de Leghe had collation of the 'officium ministeriatus'—the office which replaced the original vicarage—in the new collegiate church of Ottery St Mary.[125] The fact that on 17 September following an appointment was made, unfortunately without detail of the manner of vacancy, to the 'vicaria parochialis alias curata' in Crediton,[126] creates a presumption that the John de Leghe

---

[121] Points of correspondence will be noticed in the course of examining the treatise's social doctrine, in Chaps. 5–11.

[122] The series printed in *Concilia*, ii. 696–702.

[123] See *The Register of Ralph of Shrewsbury, Bishop of Bath and Wells 1329–1363*, ed. T. S. Holmes, ii, Somerset Record Society, 10 (1896), no. 1712, for the archbishop's letter of publication, dated 19 May 1343.

[124] *RG*, ii. 971.

[125] Ibid., iii. 1323. For the relationship between the *ministeriatus* and the vicarage, see the ordinance as recapitulated in the papal confirmation; ibid., i. 123.

[126] Ibid., iii. 1325.

of Ottery St Mary is the John de Leghe of Crediton. If he is, it is hardly too much to think that his change of benefice was related to the local controversy and scandal to which, despite his circumspection, he had given rise. The appointment in Ottery St Mary was within the bishop's gift. Probably Grandisson felt some responsibility towards an incumbent who had acted scrupulously and whose claims to consideration in the aftermath would have been urged by one of the bishop's confidantes.

External evidence suggests too a plausible genesis of the writing of the treatise. Grandisson had conducted what appears to have been a rather thorough visitation of the church at Crediton, following which, on 1 July 1334, he issued a new statute. He referred to the extreme breadth of the cure attaching to the vicarage, noted the burdens on it, and made new arrangements for the upkeep of the vicar. He also removed from him the duty of attending choir except on solemn festivals or when he was not otherwise engaged.[127] The new concentration on the cure might have inspired a request to the author or have moved him spontaneously to think of a manual. The specialization might also have sparked the flame of envy to feed on the tinder of an alleged pastoral incompetence.

Internal and external evidence combine to offer a *terminus post quem* for about the last third of the treatise. A puzzling chapter, unique in the genre, on the fraudulent conduct of 'collectors of the procurations of a legate or other nuncio of the apostolic see'[128] may be construed as having its origins in a sharp quarrel between Grandisson and Master Durantus, the *locum tenens* of the papal collector Bernard de Sistre, in May–June 1337.[129] The point of criticism in the chapter differs from that underlying the quarrel, and the complaint voiced in the treatise may have been prompted by more general discussion within the bishop's circle, even preceding the attack on Master Durantus. However, if a connection were supposed between the quarrel as it is documented and the comments of the *Memoriale Presbiterorum*, there might be established a period of some eighteen months, maximally, within which the original treatise was completed from the advanced stage which the chapter in question represents, was transmitted and received its addendum. The fact that the friend had to correspond with the author rather than

---

[127] *RG*, ii. 752–4.   [128] MP, fo. 66ʳ⁻ᵛ. See below, pp. 177–80.

[129] *RG*, i. 217–18, 298–300. More information on the nature of the dispute emerges from the bishop's subsequent letter of complaint, apparently to a member of the curia, ibid. 302–4. For comment on the dispute, see Lunt, *Accounts*, pp. xxx–xxxi. Lunt was misled by a heading in the episcopal register into identifying the addressee of the subsequent letter of complaint as Bertrand de Monte Faventio, cardinal deacon of Santa Maria in Aquiro. Cf. below, p. 180.

consulting him orally may be significant, indicating perhaps that he applied to him in the course of an academic year. The addendum might thus have been written from Oxford in the year 1337–8.[130]

Evidently, the dating contemplated here has a bearing on the reconstruction of Doune's academic career if his authorship is accepted: Doune as author would, by this calculation, have to have been a master of arts by the time that he first begins to be active in Grandisson's service for his study of civil law to have been reasonably in course within the limit proposed. This, however, as will be seen later, is not quite certain,[131] and the considerations adduced for dating the treatise 1337 × 1338 are insufficiently strong to constitute a parameter. John de Leghe both might have been pursued by a sense of unease into his new charge and, as an object of the bishop's favour, might have continued to attract envy. As regards the hypothetical pretext of the writing of the treatise, even if the idea had been generated by the needs of Crediton the execution might have been deferred. Provision for conduct of the ministry at Ottery would no doubt have been a project especially close to the bishop's heart.

If the treatise with addendum were to be dated 1337 × 1338, or at all events before the legislation of the Council of London could be taken into account, what is to be made of the colophon to the Harleian manuscript? It remains evidence linking the *Memoriale Presbiterorum* with Avignon in 1344. Of the two elements, the place-date is somewhat stronger than the year-date, since the latter if written in figures at any point would be more vulnerable to error, though in the Harleian manuscript the final part is written in full, 'quadragesimo quarto'. In fact, William Doune is known to have been accompanying Bishop Grandisson on his trip to the curia in the summer of 1343. The supplication presented in the bishop's name on Doune's behalf and granted on 6 July of that year refers to him as 'dilecto et familiari suo magistro Willelmo de Donne, in utroque iure scolari, secum iam ad vestre sanctitatis presentiam veniente'.[132] The episcopal party left Dover on or shortly after 25 May—the date of commission to the vicars general.[133] Grandisson was back in his diocese by 12 September.[134] William Doune is known to have been in the diocese by 12 January 1344.[135] It is not to be excluded that the treatise was left behind for

---

[130] There are no references to Doune in Grandisson's register between 7 September 1337 and 4 April 1338. *RG*, ii. 847, 870. Cf. below, p. 40.
[131] For the details below pp. 39–41.   [132] ASV, *RS* 4 (formerly 5), fo. 89ᵛ.
[133] *RG*, i. 973.   [134] Ibid. 977.   [135] Ibid. iii. 1341.

copying after the party's trip to Avignon and that a scribal note of completion was later elaborated into the colophon as it stands, or that the colophon, less date of completion of the publication copy (and less author's degree), was already drafted or appended to the exemplar. However, another explanation must be entertained. The next reference to Doune in the episcopal register after January is under the date 7 July 1344, when he witnessed the first exercise of a faculty granted to the bishop on 6 July of the preceding year—part of a great batch of graces granted to him as of that date—to create notaries public by apostolic authority.[136] Grandisson had received a similar privilege on a previous visit to the curia. On that occasion he had left Dover on 23 October 1331[137] and had landed again at Sandwich on 9 February 1332.[138] His exercise of the faculty to create notaries public—granted on 17 December 1331—followed shortly after his return to England. Before reaching his diocese he had created Nicholas Aunger notary, in London, on 7 March.[139] There can be no certainty that he would have wished to avail himself of the privilege so promptly on the later occasion, but it can be shown that on 7 July 1344 he had not had it for nearly as long as the date of grant would imply. Although the faculty is dated, as is normal with common papal letters, by the date of grant of the corresponding supplication, the evidence of the papal register is that it was expedited not earlier than 11 March 1344 and probably some little time thereafter. Here the registers of importance are not *Registra Vaticana*, the fair copies on which the *Calendar of Papal Letters* for the period is based,[140] but *R[egistra] A[venioniensia]*, which represent the primary registration. The quire in which Grandisson's faculty to create four notaries public is registered is one of twenty-four leaves (fos. 258–81) of *RA* 224, having the heading 'I Quaternus litterarum de Tabellionatu anni secundi' (sc. Clementis VI). It is quite clear from internal organization that the quire was kept as such during the process of registration rather than being a series of double leaves later assembled, and this confirms that the contemporary serial numbers accorded to the individual entries correctly reflect their original sequence. In this sequence the Grandisson item is number 100 ('c'),[141] which follows immediately an item dated '5 Idus Mart', anno secundo' (sc. 11 March 1344) and follows less proximately items dated in February and March of the same year, interspersed with others of

---

[136] Ibid. ii. 986–7.   [137] Ibid. 637.   [138] Ibid. 638.   [139] Ibid. 639.

[140] The faculty to Grandisson is calendared in *CPL*, iii. 144, from ASV, *RV* 162.

[141] ASV, *RA* 224, fo. 277^r.

earlier date. Since the date of the preceding item represents grant rather than registration, it persuasively sets a minimum *terminus post quem* for the registration of the Grandisson item, which is followed three entries later by an item granted on 16 March.[142] The possibility that for some reason registration of the Grandisson faculty was simply overlooked in the preceding *anno domini* year and, although expedited earlier was registered late, can be excluded by the fact that a similar pattern is noted in relation to a number of other grants made to him at the same time.[143]

With allowance of an interval for expedition to the register of the contextual letters actually granted in the spring of 1344, there is reason accordingly to think that a significant amount, at least, of the Grandisson business dated 6 July 1343 was not processed until the early summer of the following year. In the case of the faculty to create notaries, an apt criterion of delay is afforded by the example of the similar grant to Grandisson on 17 December 1331, of which he probably had possession before he left Avignon and which was certainly in his hands by 7 March. Later, in the pontificate of Boniface IX, recipients of *novae provisiones* (that is, confirmatory provisions) were required to have their letters expedited to the register within eight months or forfeit the grace.[144] This was a regulation of a specific abuse and was designed to ensure that those already holding title to benefices did not obtain and keep indefinitely in reserve precautionary grants of new title which they had no intention of processing until a rival claim or some other pressing occasion arose. There is no evidence for a similar regulation in the pontificate of Clement VI, nor does it have direct implications for the types of grant obtained by Grandisson, but it is a useful indication of what at the maximum might be considered tolerable time for expedition where the recipient was tardy. Why the process was so slow in

---

[142] Ibid. fo. 277ᵛ.

[143] Grandisson business dated 6 July 1343 registered with grants dated February–March/April 1344 has been noted as follows: (1) *RA* 74, fos. 336ʳ–337ʳ; (2) ibid., fos. 337ᵛ–338ʳ; (3), (4), (5), (6) ibid., fo. 250ʳ⁻ᵛ; (7), ibid., fo. 251ʳ; (8), (9), ibid., fos. 252ᵛ–253ʳ; (10) *RA* 76, fo. 111ʳ⁻ᵛ; (11), (12), ibid., fos. 165ʳ–166ᵛ. Of these, only (1)–(2), and (8)–(9) are of a type susceptible to improvement by backdating.

[144] *Regulae Cancellariae Apostolicae: die päpstlichen Kanzleiregeln von Johannes XXII. bis Nikolaus V.*, ed. E. von Ottenthal (Innsbruck, 1888), 59–60. I am grateful to Dr Patrick Zutshi, with whom I discussed the interval necessary to expedite letters in the period, for drawing my attention to this regulation, as also for the suggestion that delays must often have been due to difficulties with proctors.

the case of the grants made to Grandisson on 6 July 1343 is unknown. It is unfortunate that of the letters issued to him under that date no original, from which the name of the proctor responsible for it could be recovered, appears to survive.[145]

Doune's re-appearance in the Exeter register in July 1344 after an interval of months and the first use of a faculty which was expedited so late is only one aspect of a suggestive coincidence. There is a hint of a strong association, quite obscured by Hingeston-Randolph's re-arrangement of entries in the printed edition, between this part of the register[146] and Doune personally. In the sequence of the register, the creation of the notaries occurs first[147] in a quire of twelve folios, which begins with folio 122[148] and which follows the quire (fos. 110–21) that accompanied the bishop in 1343 at least as far as Dover.[149] At the beginning of the quire, on fo. 122^{r-v}, are registered two items, dated 13 January and 9 February (sc. 1344),[150] concerning Launceston priory, a house for which, incidentally, Doune had a marked affection.[151] Next is entered the text of Clement VI's faculty, of date 6 July 1343, to create the notaries, followed at once (on fo. 123^r) by the record of three uses of it, on 7 and 15 July and on 20 October; the witnesses to the act of 7 July are named: William Doune, Nicholas Aunger, and Thomas David. Immediately after the third use of the faculty is a heading for

---

[145] P. N. R. Zutshi, *Original Papal Letters in England 1305–1415* (Vatican City, 1990), p. 94, no. 187, prints an unrelated letter obtained during the bishop's visit to the curia.

[146] DRO, Chanter 3.

[147] The content of this quire of ten extant folios, beginning at fo. 122 and ending with an unnumbered, blank folio (= 130A), is partially duplicated in the next quire, but the argument from association of material is unaffected.

[148] The quire ends with the unnumbered blank folio intervening between DRO, Chanter 3, fos. 130 and 131. The fourth and eleventh folios of the quire have been cut out (leaving only an inner rim in both cases) without loss of text as between the third and fifth folios (fos. 124 and 125 respectively). Since the entry on fo. 130^v is complete there and since the final folio of the quire is blank, there is no contextual guidance as to whether the removal of the eleventh folio resulted in loss of text.

[149] The commission to the vicars-general is registered at ibid., fo. 119^r. In the abstract this could be a later entry from an interim registration—of which there is evidence elsewhere in Grandisson's register—but a jotted item, evidently *pro memoria*, at the foot of fo. 118^r, being a dimissory letter issued at London on 18 May 1343, is explicable only on the supposition that this quire accompanied the bishop, as perhaps it did even to Avignon.

[150] The year-date is wanting and is derived contextually. A heading on DRO, Chanter 3, fo. 122^r gives the pontifical year as 'xvii'.

[151] He left ten marks in his will to its fabric fund, a half-mark to each canon, with an extra half-mark to a particular canon, and to the prior in perpetuity a silver vessel belonging to his late father and adorned with his father's escutcheon. Thompson, 'Will', 267, 274.

the change of year to AD 1345, with, as the first item of that year's business at this point and the last item on fo. 123ʳ, registration of the licence for absence to study under *Cum ex eo* granted to Doune, as rector of Georgeham, on 20 April 1345. Doune's dispensation is registered in the same hand and ink as the entries recording the notarial creations on 15 July and 20 October and, judged on these similarities as well as on positioning and spacing, the business would seem to have been entered at the same time—probably, in view of the disparity of dates, from an interim record or draft. The business on fo. 123ᵛ begins in a different hand and ink. Although hardly any general register business is recorded for the year 1344–5, and although the register commonly opens the year at 25 March, it is improbable that the positioning of the April entry here is a true reflection of the diocesan scene since October.[152] It is more likely that some special reason caused the issue of the first licence under *Cum ex eo* for William Doune to be noted at this point.

If there was thus an association between the notarial business and Doune, its basis is a matter of guesswork. Perhaps he had, as a notary public himself, witnessed all three uses of the faculty, and not just the first, where witnesses' names are recorded, and that may have been enough to suggest the juxtaposition. Alternatively, if the source were an interim record, that may have been Doune's notes where the business was preserved together. Nothing in the Exeter register establishes that he had been to the curia in 1344 and had personally brought back the notarial faculty together with the other letters, thus engendering an association so close between himself and the notarial business as to make it peculiarly appropriate that his *Cum ex eo* licence should be 'filed' at this point. The absence of reference to him for months at a time has been noted in previous years and taken as suggesting that he may have been away at university.[153] That is a possibility in this instance too, though the institution to Georgeham on 4 November 1344[154] and the issue of the first licence to him under *Cum ex eo* in April of the following year might suggest, rather, that he returned then to the study which the papal dispensation of 1343 was undoubtedly intended to facilitate and which a sequence of licences shows that he maintained

---

[152] This is more likely to be due to the loss of a quire or to the non-transference of business from an interim record to the final register than to inactivity. An item transacted on 16 December 1344, when Doune was also present, was entered in the preceding quire. DRO, Chanter 3, fo. 119ʳ. Hingeston-Randolph speculated on the loss of quires, *RG*, iii., p. lvii.

[153] See below, p. 43.   [154] *RG*, iii. 1345.

continuously thereafter, still as a deacon,[155] until he completed the doctorate in civil law.[156] The most compelling reason, within the hypothesis of authorship, for thinking that Doune was at the curia in 1344 is the colophon to the Harleian manuscript. This could be explained by supposing that the treatise was brought to Avignon in 1343 and copied there, perhaps being returned to England with the batch of papal letters. As already observed,[157] there is a strong implication that the thinking expressed in the treatise regarding restitution and friars exercised an important influence on Grandisson's protégé, Richard FitzRalph, resident at the curia from 1337 until the summer of 1344. If the treatise were thought to have been left with anyone, then FitzRalph must be the prime candidate for its custody. However, it is tempting to explain the colophon by suggesting that the long delay in the processing of the papal letters necessitated the dispatch of an agent from the diocese either to recommission a proctor or to act as proctor himself.[158] There may have been other business. A papal letter of 11 September 1344 ordered the bishop to cease molesting the proctors of Adhémar Robert, cardinal priest of Sant' Anastasia, in levying the fruits of the parish church of Axminster,[159] which he held annexed to the prebend of Warthill in York cathedral. The rights of the prebendaries of Grindale and Warthill in the parish were a long-standing subject of contest.[160] Grandisson's predecessor, Stapledon, had made a determined but unsuccessful effort to recover it,[161] and Grandisson himself had sequestrated the rectory in 1334 on grounds of the neglect of its

---

[155] Honorius III's decretal, *Super specula*, X. 3. 50. 10, forbade study of civil law to priests and dignitaries (holders, *inter alia*, of *personatus*—'parsonages' of precedence) rather than to holders of parish churches as such. Cf. *Sext.*, 3. 24. 1. Since Doune was dispensed by Clement VI from promotion or residence otherwise than if he were legitimate and was then licensed under *Cum ex eo*, which dispensed from promotion to priesthood as well as sanctioning non-residence, he was able by remaining a deacon to avoid the strictures of *Super specula*, while studying civil law. For the general application of *Cum ex eo*, see L. E. Boyle, 'The Constitution "Cum ex eo" of Boniface VIII', *MS* 24 (1962), 263–302 (reprinted in id., *Pastoral Care*).

[156] See below, p. 43.   [157] See above, p. 3; cf. below, Chap. 12.

[158] William of Nassington, later a prominent member of the bishop's administration, had been proctor in the impetration of at least one letter relating to Grandisson's appointment to Exeter in 1327. See Zutshi, *Original Papal Letters*, p. 74, no. 149.

[159] *Clément VI (1342–1352) lettres closes, patentes et curiales se rapportant à la France*, ed. E. Déprez, J. Glenisson, and G. Mollat, 3 vols. (Paris 1910–61), i. 1100; *CPL*, iii. 10.

[160] For the origin of the rights, see C. T. Clay, *York Minster Fasti, Being Notes on the Dignitaries, Archdeacons and Prebendaries in the Church of York Prior to the Year 1307*, ii, Yorkshire Archaeological Society, Record Series, 124 (1959), 153–4.

[161] See *Reg. Stapeldon*, 38–40.

buildings.[162] When Adhémar Robert acquired title to the prebend in
York is unclear. John de Thoresby had a royal grant of it on 10 July
1343,[163] but he appears to have been displaced by the cardinal, who was
in occupation as late as 1349.[164] From the moment when Grandisson
heard of the cardinal's interest he would have recognized a formidable
opponent, and might well have taken steps to enter and maintain his
objections. At all events, if the bishop found need, for whatever reason,
to have his affairs handled anew at the curia, Doune would have been
an eminently suitable envoy, following the experience gained from his
recent visit, which may even have been thought of as preparing him
for such an eventuality. Bishop Stapledon used his first registrar, John
de Launceston, for missions outside the diocese in 1316 and 1321,
appointing him in the latter year one of his proctors at the curia.[165] We
know from his will that at some point in his career Doune had transacted business there, for to Master Thomas Pepir he left

a certain quire covered without in white leather, containing commissions made in
the Roman curia and apostolic letters and the praxis and terms in causes in the
Roman curia and positions and articles and many other useful things, written almost
entirely in my hand and in part containing a membrane of parchment in which
are written letters or copies of letters of commissions and other matters of bishops
and certain other matters which I put together (*que recollegi*) in the time of my
youth when I stood in the services of the lord bishop of Exeter.[166]

If it is not quite certain that the 'Roman' was contemporaneous with
the episcopal matter, the insinuation to that effect is strong. He may
have used the visit of 1343 to the purpose, though the time available
for direct observation would have been curtailed by the fact that the
curial holidays ran from 29 June to 15 September.[167] No time after
1343–4 would appear to be as suitable a point to which to refer the
experience.

---

[162] *RG*, ii. 770. For other references to the rectory, see ibid. 176–7, 241 (where the bishop
complains, AD 1329, that the prebendary's claim is founded not on papal or episcopal grant
but on royal authority only), 372–3 (AD 1328), 380, 493–4 (AD 1329), 658, 684 (AD 1332),
687, 688–9 (AD 1333), 772 (AD 1334), 794 (AD 1335), 1262 (AD 1366).

[163] *CPR (1343–1345)*, 57. Cf. Le Neve, *Fasti*, vi. 86.

[164] *CPR (1348–1350)*, 279. Cf. Le Neve, *Fasti*, iv. 86.

[165] See *Reg. Stapeldon*, p. viii.

[166] Thompson, 'Will', 284. Cf. Owen, *The Medieval Canon Law*, 32. Richard de
Medmenham received a larger collection of the type, not explicitly Doune's own making.
Thompson, 'Will', 282.

[167] See B. Guillemain, *La Cour pontificale d'Avignon (1309–1376), étude d'une société* (Paris,
1962), 52.

If the original treatise was written before Doune's first known trip to Avignon, what was 'composed' at Avignon in 1344 would be taken to have been a redacted version, for the benefit of the wider public—'ad informacionem iura non intelligencium'. The extent of editing is imponderable. As observed, there was not occasion to incorporate reference to the Council of London. The redaction must minimally have consisted of uniting the treatise and addendum, the opening words of which as preserved—'Tuis amice karissime apicibus michi postquam *tractatum suprascriptum* per me tibi missum perlegeras rescripsisti'—are evidently in part editorial. Even so, the union is rough: the treatise ends with a short prayer of benediction; the addendum is presented as such, its sole connection with the treatise being autobiographical. For such a limited redaction, the term 'compositum', literally understood as a placing together, is so precise a description that it may well be authorial. The remainder of the colophon, except for the author's degree and the title of the treatise, carries conviction, both in its length and in its insistence on the legalistic element, though it is possible that somewhere in the transmission a scribe had caught the author's spirit and style. On the case for Doune's authorship, 'a quodam doctore decretorum'—already suspect—is inaccurate, at least as regards time of redaction. On one line of argument, it is likely that no author's name ever attached. The choice of Avignon as the formal place of publication may have proceeded from discretion. The circumstances which provoked the addendum may be construed as a factor against wider publication in the short term. The treatise is insistent on the confessor's responsibility to avoid any betrayal, direct or inadvertent, of what has been confessed to him, a responsibility which extends even to denying the bishop information should he press for it, and which covers all idle talk, of a type which is represented as being frequent, from which inferences could be drawn.[168] Though the bond postulated between John de Leghe and William Doune was not sacramental, and though the basic facts were known within at least part of the diocese and to some, no doubt, within the bishop's circle, the confidence was a serious one and may even have been followed by Leghe's approaching, on Doune's advice, the episcopal penitentiary. The confidence itself and the local sensitivity reflected in it could easily have set up a conflict of concerns, between the desire to inform, even on the issue which having arisen so sharply in one case might well do so elsewhere, and the claims of discretion.

[168] MP, fos. 82rb–82^v.

The anonymity of Avignon may have seemed to offer a solution. By 1343–4 the sensitivity would perhaps have subsided. Leghe may even have been dead,[169] and this may have been the circumstance by which the unpublished treatise with its epistolary addendum returned to the author's hands. But he may equally have borrowed it or used a copy, if he had retained one, and published with his friend's benison. While the exact circumstances are unlikely ever to be illuminated further, there is the ground of suspicion that the mystery that surrounded authorship of the work and that so long defied resolution was present, indeed was deliberately introduced, at the beginning of its public life.

---

[169] No more is heard of Leghe after the collation of 1338. On 22 January 1349 Sir John Payn, priest, had collation of the *ministeriatus* with annexed canonry and prebend in Ottery St Mary, but there is no note of predecessor nor of circumstances of vacancy. *RG*, iii. 1372.

3

The Career of an Ecclesiastical
Administrator I:—Exeter

The strength of the case for William Doune's authorship prompts close
scrutiny of his career. For more than a quarter of a century his activity
can be followed in considerable detail in the surviving registers of Bishops
Grandisson of Exeter, Gynwell of Lincoln, and Brian of Worcester.
The focus of this chapter is on how far his experience at Exeter and
the character of Grandisson's episcopate may have moulded the outlook of the treatise, whose doctrine will be studied in Chapters 4 to
11. The question also arises how far Doune's formation at Exeter and
the views expressed in the treatise—considered as from his pen—were
significant for his later conduct of affairs and legacy as a senior administrator. That will be examined in Chapter 13.

Doune's Career at Exeter

The first firm notice of William Doune in Bishop Grandisson's register is the record of his presence in Exeter cathedral at the election of
Dean Richard Brayleghe, on 9 September 1335 and again on 18 and
22 September, during a continuance of the same business.[1] At this stage
he may already have the style 'Master'. As will appear, the fact is not
quite established, and the point is of sufficient importance for the evidence to be set out.

The list of 9 September records as present 'Magistris(?) W. de
Nassyngtone, Benedicto de Pastone, Galfrido Ectone et W. Doune'.[2]

---

[1] *RG*, ii. 797, 803. A William de Doune, 'domicello, nostre diocesis, literato', who was
appointed, with Master Richard de Todewelle, vicar of Sidmouth, to administer the goods
of the rector of Rockbeare, on 13 November 1332, may plausibly be thought a relation: ibid.
664–5. Cf., however, Thompson, 'Will', 237–8, where the two are identified. On 16 April
1347 there are references to William de Doune 'domicello nostro' in connection with the
custody of Polsloe priory. *RG*, ii. 1015.

[2] DRO, Chanter 4, fo. 193ᵛ. The ending of the introductory title is unclear and may be
for 'Magistro' rather than as taken in *RG*, ii. 797. A composite list, introduced by 'Magistris'
is recorded on the second occasion: ibid. 803 (read below from DRO, Chanter 4, fo. 195ᵛ).

Of these, both Nassington and Paston were certainly 'Master'; Geoffrey Ectone cannot be otherwise shown to have been a master and he occurs elsewhere without the title.[3] On the second occasion the list is: 'presentibus Magistris J. de Northwode, W. de Nass., R. Bonde, David Alyam, R. de Bysshopleghe, W. de Donne, W. de Brauntone et aliis.' Of these, all the figures preceding Doune can be shown to have the style 'Master'; W. de Brauntone's status cannot be confirmed nor is his identity certain.[4]

Doune recurs intermittently in the following years. He is named as witness to an act at St Buryan, during an episcopal progression, on 12 July 1336 ('presentibus personis superius expressis, et Magistris David Alyam, N. Aunger, notariis publicis, et Willelmo Doune, clerico'),[5] and as present at the probation of the will of Sir William de Ferrars on 14 December of the same year.[6] The formula on the latter occasion, 'presentibus Magistro Benedicto de Pastone et Willelmo Doune, clerico', deters an unambiguous conclusion from the documentary usage that he was by now entitled 'Master', though the positioning of the conjunction in the list of 12 July 1336 makes this on balance probable.[7] The fact that the entry of 14 December 1336[8] is in the hand taken, on evidence discussed below, to be Doune's own is of ambivalent import. It may be that he denies himself the title 'Master' as not having attained it: or he may be thought to have the less need to identify himself by full style. The description 'clerico' in the act of 14 December 1336 more persuasively indicates function in the episcopal household than mere personal status, as it seems likely to do too in the instance of 12 July 1336 and as it evidently does in the next listing in which he occurs. This is as a witness to Grandisson's appeal on 7 September 1337 against archiepiscopal visitation of the free chapel of Bosham. On this occasion he is certainly 'Master'.[9] Incepting in the spring of 1337 would have resulted in his being regent during the whole of the next year. Superficially, the evidence is against this. On 4 April 1338 he is named

On the third occasion, the list, comprising names that occur in the previous composite lists and headed by W. de Nassington, is not prefaced by a title: ibid.

  [3] See *RG*, ii. 655 (AD 1332), 1337 (AD 1337); *CPR (1330–1334)*, 178 (AD 1331).
  [4] Cf. *RG*, ii. 803, 878, 1249, 1361, 1366, 1504.   [5] Ibid. 821.   [6] Ibid. 834.
  [7] As it is taken in *BRUO* 587, in the case of the reference under 9 September 1335.
  [8] DRO, Chanter 4, fo. 205ᵛ.
  [9] *RG*, ii. 847: 'presentibus Magistris David Alyam, notario publico, Willelmo de Doune, clerico, Willelmo de Braybroke, domicello, et Thoma Pictore, de Wodestoke, ac me Nicholao Aunger, publico auctoritate apostolica notario'.

in the Exeter register at the probation of a will.[10] He was witness in Exeter cathedral at the appropriation to the chapter of St Merryn in Cornwall on 25 May 1338,[11] and at the benediction of the abbot of Newenham on 31 May.[12] However, these occurrences cannot perhaps be taken firmly to establish that he was in the diocese continuously in the spring to early summer of 1338. His appearance on 4 April might just reflect the fact that term ended on that day, the vigil of Palm Sunday, and that in 1338 it and the day before were non-teaching days.[13] A modest licence in the prelude would have permitted his return. By the same token, 31 May 1338 was Whitsun, and in the interval from 23 May until the Whit recess there was in the formal programme only one teaching day,[14] over which might conceivably have been thrown what Italians call a *ponte*. If he was at Oxford, leaving rather punctually at the first opportunity, he might of course have been in either faculty. The record does not, however, safely exclude the possibility that he was regent. Accordingly, the question when he became a master of arts must remain open.

On 16 November 1338, he acted at the probation of the will of Sir Richard de Champernon, lord of Modbury, where his name as the last witness is in the form 'et me Willelmo Doune'. The entry is an interpolation in the register text, written in a different hand and ink to that of the register at this point and inserted round the title to the next section.[15] However, since the hand of the interpolation differs from that which will shortly be considered as having a definite claim to be Doune's, the attesting formula must be taken to indicate his responsibility for the memorandum which is here registered rather than for the physical insertion of the attesting formula itself. He next occurs on 19 August 1339, as having delivered 'within the outer door of the episcopal manor of Clist' a commission concerning Carswell priory.[16] On the next day, still at Clist, he was present with the official of the diocese, Mr William de Crowthorne, and others 'in the chancery chamber of the said manor' at a resignation and institution in respect of parish benefices.[17] He was present with others in Chudleigh church when Mr Richard Gifford, rector of Ashwater, the bishop's commissary in the matter, proved the will of the vicar of Dawlish on 18 January 1340, and again six days later, with Nicholas Aunger, in the chancery chamber of Chudleigh

[10] Ibid. 870. [11] Ibid. 876. [12] Ibid. 878. [13] Cf. *SAUO* 4.
[14] Ibid. 6. [15] DRO, Chanter 4, fo. 218. Cf. *RG*, ii. 894.
[16] Ibid. 916. [17] Ibid.

when Crowthorne, the official, granted administration to the executors.[18] He reappears just over a year later in a memorandum attested by himself as a notary public and dated 5 February 1341 to record probation of the will of Hugh de Courtenay, earl of Devon. On this occasion he has the title 'scriba eiusdem domini nostri Exoniensis'. The title is accorded to others—David Alyam, Robert Peyke, and Nicholas Aunger—in the witness list,[19] but the form of attestation indicates that 'scriba' in Doune's case implies custody of the register at this point. The clause reads: 'et me, Willelmo de Doune, clerico Exoniensis diocesis et notario publico et scriba eiusdem domini nostri Exoniensis, qui eciam interfui in probacione testamenti domini Willelmi de Botriaux, prout superius est expressum.'[20] Doune is not in fact named in connection with the latter transaction, dated 17 January 1341, at the point of its registration earlier on the same page.[21] The reference of 'prout superius est expressum' is most cogently taken to be simply to the substance of the entry in question. The definite information, necessary precisely because the name does not appear above and supplied here in a hand different to that of the interpolation noted previously as regards probation of the will of Sir Richard de Champernon,[22] would therefore be an autograph contribution of Doune himself. Neatly, the hand identified here as Doune's can be seen also at a subsequent juncture concerning the earl of Devon's will, being a memorandum by Doune of the commission of its administration on 24 March 1341.[23] The implication is that, as one of several registrars at this point, he is particularly associated with the entry of matter for whose original confection he was responsible.

In the interval between the two stages of the processing of the earl of Devon's testament, Doune occurs once, explicitly as a notary public, among the witnesses to the obedience of the abbot of Dunkeswell, received on 22 February, in the chapel at Chudleigh.[24] After the testamentary item there is no further note of him until almost a year later, when on 15 February 1342, in the chamber at Chudleigh, explicitly as the bishop's notary ('notario suo') and in his presence, he applied the episcopal seal to the quittance then granted over the administration of the goods of the earl of Devon and drew up the record of the proceeding.

---

[18] Ibid. 920–1.   [19] Ibid. 940.   [20] Ibid. and DRO, Chanter 4, fo. 235ʳ.
[21] *RG*, ii. 936. Cf. DRO, Chanter 4, fo. 235ʳ.
[22] Sc. the interpolation at ibid., fo. 218ʳ.
[23] Ibid., fo. 237ᵛ (first entry on the page). For text, see *RG*, ii. 946–7.
[24] *RG*, ii. 943.

Here, too, he entered it in the register. The other named witnesses were Masters Benedict de Pastone and Richard Langacre and Master Nicholas Aunger, 'alias connominato Marshal'.[25]

The pattern of activity noticed so far may be misleading in that there is reason to think that Grandisson's surviving *Registrum commune* is in part defective as a record of diocesan business. However, Doune's activity as noticed is compatible with the hypothesis that his working membership of the bishop's staff was heavily punctuated by recurring absences, some at least of which must have been spent at the university. The course of his studies in civil law may be reconstructed only broadly. A bequest in his will suggests that he had been a member of Merton, but no precision is possible.[26] In a provision to him on 18 October 1349, ultimately ineffective, of a canonry of Exeter, notwithstanding his church of Quainton and the portion of St Endellion, he is addressed as licentiate in (sc. civil) laws.[27] By 16 June 1351 he had proceeded to the doctorate.[28] His study need not have been continuous before the commencement of the licences to him under *Cum ex eo* which, from the grant of the first, on 20 April 1345,[29] give a clearer chronology. For instance, he appears to have spent the spring of 1341 in Exeter diocese, and there may have been a significant break from university in the year 1343–4, when he made one and possibly a second trip to Avignon.[30]

From February 1342 until the first *Cum ex eo* licence there are four references to Doune in the episcopal register. The first is his presence in Chudleigh at the institution of Thomas Dyngele as rector of St Creed, Cornwall, on 12 January 1344,[31] which is of importance in establishing that Doune had indeed returned from Avignon after the trip of the previous summer. The fact that an act concerning Bodmin priory, dated at Chudleigh, 30 November 1343, was registered in the hand attributed above to Doune is congruent but, in the abstract, is uncertain evidence to the same effect, since the duplication elsewhere of material in the register suggests that registration was, on occasion at least, done from an interim copy and thus may have been postponed.[32] The second reference to him is his witnessing the creation of Mr Robert

[25] Ibid. 953. Cf. DRO, Chanter 4, fo. 241[r].

[26] Thompson, 'Will', 271. Cf. below, p. 62.

[27] *CPP*, i. 182; *CPL*, iii. 345. ASV, *RS* 21, fo. 52[r].   [28] *CPL*, iii. 432.

[29] *RG*, ii. 920.   [30] See above, pp. 30–8.   [31] *RG*, iii. 1341.

[32] For the Bodmin item, see DRO, Chanter 3, fos. 119[v]–120[r]. Cf. *RG*, ii. 979–81. For duplication of matter in the register, see particularly Chanter 3, fos. 122[r]–127[r], repeated at ibid. 131[r]–136[r], and cf. remarks by Hingeston-Randolph at *RG*, ii. 1002 n. and 1008 n.

Shutlesworth as notary public, on 7 July 1344,[33] the background to which has been discussed in Chapter 2. The third is the record of his own institution as rector of Georgeham, Devon, on 4 November 1344.[34] The last is his presence at Chudleigh as a witness to the grant of administration of the will of Thomasia, wife of Sir John de Cheverstone, on 16 December 1344.[35] Thereafter, the only references to him are in respect of the grant of the licences under *Cum ex eo*.[36] The first of these, as already noted, was granted on 20 April 1345 and accorded leave of absence until the Michaelmas following.[37] The deduction must be that Doune was intending to return to Oxford immediately at this point. The licence was renewed for a year on 19 October,[38] and thereafter annually until 1348 inclusive.[39] He resigned Georgeham by November 1349,[40] having been admitted to Quainton, Bucks., on 1 September preceding.[41] In view not least of his close family connections with the diocese, signalled in detail in his will, it may reasonably be presumed that he did not lose contact with Exeter during the rest of his career. However, there is no further reference to him in the episcopal register for almost six years: on 31 August 1355, as episcopal commissary 'verbotenus deputatus', he presided at Chudleigh over the purgation of a clerk. The confirmation of continuing association with Grandisson is a useful complement to the evidence of the will.[42]

The Character of Grandisson's Episcopate

Grandisson's episcopate began in the shadow of violence. Only the six-month tenure of James Berkeley separated him from a vacancy occasioned by the murder of Bishop Stapledon at the hands of the London mob on 15 October 1326. It would be surprising had the crime not affected him deeply. His response when summoned to a provincial council in the capital in January 1329 was sharp. To the archbishop he expressed astonishment, 'more than can be explained in words . . . how

---

[33] *RG*, ii. 986–7.   [34] Ibid., iii. 1345.

[35] Ibid., ii. 989. In view particularly of the frequency of Thomas and derivatives noted in Doune's family (see above, pp. 22–3), she may have been a relation.

[36] Cf. above, p. 34.

[37] *RG*, ii. 992, where it is interpreted as constituting leave until Michaelmas 1346. The form is, however, until Michaelmas 'tunc proxime sequens'. My interpretation of the next licence, whose date is not given, is determined accordingly.

[38] Ibid. 1002. Hingeston-Randolph has dated this to the year 1346, but it will be rather for the academic year 1345–6.

[39] Ibid. 1009, 1031, 1068.   [40] Ibid., iii. 1401.

[41] LAO, Reg. IX, fo. 240ʳ (roman numeration).   [42] *RG*, ii. 1166. Cf. below, p. 63.

that place . . . should be chosen for the reformation of clergy or realm or for other utility of the church'. Whatever others might do, he himself could not attend, either honourably or safely, where a people burdensome to God and Church had so recently erupted into such cruel savagery, the bruit of which, demanding vengeance, daily increased from earth in the ears of the Lord of hosts. He took his cue from Augustine's Letter to Bishop Nectarius.[43] There was no distinguishing innocent and guilty, only the guilty and the more guilty. Even if the fraudulent plea of the Londoners were credited, that the governors of the city could not restrain the mob, it followed that the venue was unsuitable. Let others do as they would; he could not but think that the common mind for mischief still held among the citizenry. If the whole human race was prone to wickedness, how much more those whom the devil himself led at will, bound as they were under anathema and separated from grace? The price of attendance at such a convention was discretion of speech, and this was impossible for those who should not only reprove the guilty deed in what they said but inflict corporal correction for it. The pope had promised an inquisition into the circumstances of Bishop Stapledon's death and the belief was widespread that it would be committed to Grandisson himself, so that there would be special risk for him to appear in person. Moreover, such damage had been done to his hospice in London that he had nowhere to lodge. He concluded with a plea that, on account of the dangers from those who were ill-disposed, the archbishop should not divulge his views except to their fellow-bishops—if even to them.[44]

Though written for the occasion, this more than routine letter of excuse reveals one of Grandisson's most pervasive traits, an overtly Augustinian pessimism about fallen human nature. 'The vice of elation, seething in the lust of domination, twists down every crooked path and more ardently seeks that which is forbidden than that which is lawful', is his proem to a mandate over a disputed incumbency—though one, admittedly, in which the unlawful claimant's position was so entrenched and supported as to result in real violence.[45] The perception, aggravated by his horror of affront to the person of clerks, is at

[43] Cf. *PL*, xxxiii. 316–17.   [44] See *RG*, i. 449–50.

[45] Ibid., ii. 1052 (5 July 1348). The dispute was over the church of Kilkhampton, between Sir Theobald de Grenville and his client and kinsman, Mr Walter de Merton, on the one hand, and Sir John de Raleghe and his client, Thomas de Cruce, on the other. The circumstances are narrated at length by Hingeston-Randolph in the preface to his edition; *RG*, iii., pp. lx–lxii.

the root of his lively regard for order. 'Apprehendite disciplinam' drops from his pen as the ready complement of 'Nolo mortem peccatoris': this in a letter to no less a personage than Hugh de Courtenay, earl of Devon, with the brusque greeting 'Amendement dalme' and the counsel 'que vous depart Dieu vous amendez'.[46] The order that he regards is a hierarchical one in which the spiritual function is exempt from scrutiny.[47] If the sentiment recalls *Unam sanctam*, the protest in another context that nowadays those glory more who inflict more injury on holy mother church recalls *Clericis laicos*, though in fact it directly echoed a particular tradition in Exeter diocese.[48] Every undergraduate draws the lesson from the fate of Boniface VIII that the high ecclesiastical doctrine was *passé*. This was less evident to contemporaries. The rhetoric, hardly less than the substance, of Grandisson's correspondence confirms as much in his case. 'Coment soioms noundigne, sumes Ministres et lieu tenantz Jhesu Crist en cest pais', he asserts in the letter to the earl of Devon already cited.[49] He had previously been more explicit. At the beginning of his episcopate, deeply in debt to the papal Camera, he had written to Courtenay for financial assistance and had received instead advice on the need to live within his means. The advice was acknowledged, with sardonic thanks,

although the sons of Holy Church neither should nor can teach or judge their masters nor their spiritual fathers . . . And although we are of tender age, we know whether it is fitting to offer explanation of all our deeds. And please to understand, sire, that we have so long at the schools of clerks and prelates learned to render our lesson that we ought not from these sciences to take licentiate in another school. Wherefore, sire, you must pardon us if a prelate does not betake himself to the school of a knight, for St Paul says 'He that is spiritual judges all things but is judged of no one.'[50]

Courtenay was his cousin by marriage and the prophet no doubt felt the need accordingly to establish the independence of his calling against the pretensions of patronizing familiarity. Whatever the prompting that evoked it, however, the tone is revelatory of deeply laid convictions. These come to the surface whenever ecclesiastical liberties are

---

[46] Ibid., i. 294–5. The letter is to be dated 22 December 1335.   [47] Ibid. 203.

[48] Ibid., ii. 946, in a letter of date 1341. The complaint is voiced again in response to an incident in 1348; ibid. 1041. The language is undoubtedly derived from the strongly worded statute on lay incursions of Bishop Quinel of Exeter (1287), whose outlook on several points anticipates and evidently influenced Grandisson's. Cf. *CS*, ii. 1038.

[49] *RG*, i. 294.   [50] Ibid. 203.

in jeopardy. 'Does not the Lord say "Touch not mine anointed."?'[51] 'No power is attributed to laymen of judging the Lord's anointed.'[52] 'To laymen and those exercising an office of secular power no licence or faculty pertains of judging priests and other ministers of the church, whom the word of Truth with prophetic mouth on occasion calls gods, on occasion angels.'[53] Even to read, believe, or speak ill of a bishop occasions peril to the soul in its implied slight on God, whose servant he is.[54] A proceeding against clerks is a 'contempt of the king of kings who judges the universe in equity'.[55] In standing against infringements that were the preoccupation of most medieval bishops, Grandisson unfailingly finds the ground of elevated and unyielding principle. His handsomely illuminated thirteenth-century psalter opens to the touch at a scene of Becket's martyrdom.[56] Among the schools in which he had trained was that presided over by Jacques Fournier, to whom, on his elevation as pope, his sometime pupil wrote warmly and whose own reforming credentials are well established.[57]

Explicit in Grandisson's stance is an anxious awareness that perceived weakness encourages abuse. 'The impiety of persecutors is the more strongly enflamed against churches and ecclesiastical persons the more half-hearted the opponents whom it encounters,' he observes in re-action to a violent attack on his manor of Tawton by Sir Theobald de Grenville and some fifty adherents, including members of other prom-inent north Cornish families, in 1347.[58] Grandisson could hardly be reproved for half-heartedness. In his mind is the exhortation, 'Cry so that you cease not; like a trumpet lift up your voice'.[59] To some, the urgency appeared strident. Its force was palpable. At the beginning of the episcopate, in the correspondence referred to, Hugh de Courtenay accused the bishop of singularity. It was a charge to which he happily owned: 'that please God and the singular Virgin we are well singular and single [sc. single-minded and frank] and not double like those of

---

[51] Ibid., ii. 946 (in a letter dated 16 March 1341). Cf. the sentiment of Bishop Quinel, 'Nolite tangere christos meos et in prophetis meis nolite malignari, quod de prelatis eccle-siarum intelligimus esse dictum': *CS*, ii. 1038.

[52] *RG*, ii. 947 (in a letter dated 18 June 1341).

[53] Ibid. 962 (in a letter dated 10 August 1342).

[54] Ibid., i. 204 (in a letter to Lady Courtenay about her husband's attitude, 1328/9).

[55] Ibid., ii. 964 (in a letter dated 11 November 1342).

[56] London, British Library, MS. Additional 21926, fo. 13ᵛ. Grandisson bequeathed the book to the Lady Isabella, daughter of Edward III: ibid., fo. 6ʳ.

[57] See B. Schimmelpfennig, 'Zisterzienserideal und Kirchenreform. Benedikt XII. (1334–1342) als Reformpapst', *Zisterzienser-Studien*, iii (Berlin, 1976), 11–43.

[58] *RG*, ii. 1026–27.   [59] Ibid. 946 (in a letter dated 1341); cf. above, n. 48.

the world.'[60] An ecclesiastic who may be identified as Walter Meriet, chancellor of Exeter cathedral, told him baldly how his regime was regarded, drawing the implication either that the folk of the parishes actually were wickeder than all others or that the government to which they were subjected was over-severe. Grandisson in reply disclaimed asserting that his parishioners were, taken as a whole, wickeder than others, because that would be undignified—even though perhaps it might be open to him to do so.[61]

Meriet points up, in fact, a dilemma for the reader of the register: how far to interpret the business that it contains as a reflection of the peculiarly acute problems of the diocese and how far to attribute it to the bishop's temperament.[62] Undoubtedly, this was censorious— of clerical shortcomings as much as of lay. A delinquent prior, for instance, is dismissed as a 'useless shadow upon the earth, a tree baneful as it is sterile'.[63] But undoubtedly, too, high-handedness—to the extent that it may be diagnosed in his composition—is mitigated by high-mindedness. There can be no mistaking that his subjects' welfare bulked large in his thinking; nor is there need to suppose that in its direction to their welfare his thinking was as invariably sombre as it was serious. 'Bring to due consideration', he briskly exhorts the personnel of his consistory court, in the regulations promulgated for it in 1336, 'that the common sense of joy is lost if there is concealed mulcting of the people.'[64]

The high concept of ecclesiastical dignity and office revealed by the register is thus paralleled by a high concept of the responsibility attaching. On occasion, in Grandisson's dealing with the incursions of secular authority, the two dimensions intertwine. In February 1341, publishing in French the articles of excommunication against infringers of ecclesiastical liberty to the earl of Devon and the royal commissioners in Devon and Cornwall, 'bound by our office and distrained by our conscience', he includes a careful explanation of the effects of excommunication, 'so that God may never of our hands seek the blood of your souls'.[65] Though he need not, in his evident sincerity, be thought wholly indifferent to the advantage of dramatic presentation, the effect is unhistrionic. It is a part with the general and sustained conscientiousness in the conduct of his government as an enterprise requiring

---

[60] Ibid., i. 203.   [61] Ibid. 284 (in a letter to be dated 1334).

[62] Cawthron, 'Episcopal Administration', 146, notes the increase in excommunications for assaults on clerks under Grandisson but also their relative frequency under his successor, Brantingham.

[63] *RG*, ii. 837.   [64] Ibid. 807.   [65] Ibid. 943.

total commitment. In May 1336, in a mandate directed to the president of the Exeter consistory, he revoked all commissions previously issued by him—except those to his officials and commissaries general and the officials of his peculiar jurisdiction—on the grounds that 'we reside continuously in our diocese'.[66] Apart from occasional absences, such as to attend at provincial council or on his two trips to the papal curia at Avignon, continual residence seems indeed to have been the hallmark of the episcopate.[67] A mandate to the dean of Exeter just before Christmas 1335 requiring him to enact penal statutes against absent vicars choral reveals, in its intensity of language, the high concept entertained of the responsibility of ecclesiastical superiors as much as concern with the substantive issue. The dean is enjoined 'by the sprinkling of the precious blood of Jesus Christ'—an ejaculation that occurs also in Grandisson's will[68]—'. . . that considering carefully what is incumbent on you by the assumption of a part of our solicitude' he take action accordingly.[69]

It is not unreasonable to deduce from the register a corresponding rigour in regard to the residence of benefice-holders, though putative deficiencies in the preservation of business—especially for the later decades of the episcopate—forbid the clear delineation of a policy. Mr Walter Botriaux, rector of St Ruan, Lanyhorne, and prebendary of Exeter and Glasney, was the object of a proceeding on the point in 1339 in the course of which he was firmly adjured to 'remain and persist in that vocation in which he was called'[70]—his parish cure. The later, polemical adoption of the same watchword from Corinthians by FitzRalph[71] suggests the seriousness of vocational constancy in Grandisson's moral code. Among Botriaux's offences was that, 'having abandoned and deserted the cure of souls, hospitality, and residence there, he notoriously wandered . . . to and through various places, here and there, unlawfully and temerariously enmeshing himself then and now in secular business, wholly unbecoming his priestly state and forbidden by law'.[72] He had also abused a licence under *Cum ex eo*,[73] granted him for study in Oxford or elsewhere in England, 'to seek out other

---

[66] Ibid. 814.
[67] Cawthron, 'Episcopal Administration', p. xii, calculates twenty absences in the forty-one years of the pontificate but points out their short duration, with the effect that there are only six recorded constitutions of vicars-general: ibid. 39.
[68] *RG*, iii. 1557.   [69] Ibid., ii. 807.   [70] Ibid. 913.
[71] 'Unusquisque in quo vocatus est frater in hoc permaneat apud Deum' (Cf. 1 Cor. 7: 24): Sermon 90 ('Proposicio' of 5 July 1350), in A. Gwynn, 'The Sermon Diary of Richard FitzRalph', *Proceedings of the Royal Irish Academy*, 44 C (1937), 57.
[72] *RG*, ii. 911.   [73] On this licensing system, see Boyle, 'The Constitution'.

cures of souls and otherwise to engage in various other unwonted activities'.[74] Licences for absence are granted, both—as here—for the highly respectable motive of study[75] and for administrative service, including service with secular lords, though sometimes both types come with reservations: 'with effect that he return to his church during Lent', in a licence for study granted in 1336;[76] 'with effect that he return to his church in Advent and Lent', in a licence of the same year for service with the earl of Warenne;[77] 'so that he teach from his study', in a licence of 1355.[78] There is clear evidence in a mandate from this latter year of special sensitivity on the subject of beneficed clerks in secular service. Whereas those who have cure of souls, and especially those to whom are committed the keys of the church, are obliged, like anxious shepherds, to wake over the flock in their keeping and to keep the watches of the night, the bishop observes with sorrow the reluctance of curates to reside in person and their disposition instead to 'betake themselves under strained excuses to the services of magnates and of other lords, sometimes to such as do not fit their order, and—what is more detestable—on occasion, even when not summoned to these services they insinuate themselves and procure their appointment, in order to lead a dissolute life at their own whim'.[79] The distinction between being summoned and insinuating oneself concedes a certain pragmatism, compatible with the fact that licences for administrative service are registered, though not in great numbers. The problem may have become more acute in the period following the Black Death and the reference to the additional responsibility derived from possession of the keys suggests that in the bishop's mind was his concern with the administration of confession, now becoming a critical issue.[80] Particular factors apart, however, the tone of the mandate is in keeping with what is a general preoccupation of Grandisson on the issue of pastoral accountability. From the evidence of the proceeding against Botriaux, the sentiment may plausibly be credited to the episcopate as a whole, with whose ethic of commitment it accords. In fact, as regards *Cum ex eo* licences,

---

[74] *RG*, ii. 912. Botriaux did not in fact hold plurality of cures, though he had in 1330, during his first period of non-residence for study, had licence to receive feoffment of the manor of Alcester (Warks.), which might explain the reference to 'unwonted activities'. When he was admitted to St Just-in-Penwith (Cornwall) in 1340, he resigned Lanyhorne. Cf. *BRUO*, i. 228.

[75] Despite Grandisson's strictures, Botriaux had a further licence for a year at Oxford or elsewhere in England on 20 November 1340. *RG*, ii. 929–30.

[76] Ibid. 811.   [77] Ibid.   [78] Ibid. 1175.   [79] Ibid. 1174.

[80] Ibid., i. 557; ii. 853, 1128, 1143–7, 1208.

we know that Grandisson kept a strict eye on their aftermath. William Kaignes, who had had one from 1333–5, was challenged, mistakenly, for failure to proceed to priesthood within a year of its termination.[81]

One particular aspect of accountability is articulated explicitly and at several junctures, the personal responsibility of office-holders. In September 1333 a mandate to the president of the Exeter consistory complained that rural deans, elected by the benefice-holders of the deaneries, were on their own authority—or rather temerity—appointing substitutes, 'men less fitted, entirely without substance, of light opinion, commanding little or no credibility in law'; to these suspect persons they were committing also their authentic seals of office, over which special care ought to be exercised. The consequence—'which we relate with sorrow and contemplate with a heavy sigh'—was 'various inextricable falsehoods, both in and out of judgment'. The practice was to be stopped and those elected to the office instructed that, 'since their industry is deemed to be elected in this context', they should not, except where there was a lawful impediment, exercise the office by deputy or commit the seals. In the event of unavoidable substitution, the deputy was to be approved by the president of the consistory. A heavy fine, of 100 shillings to the cathedral fabric, was prescribed for breach of the regulation.[82] The problem was not wholly resolved, for it is referred to again in the bishop's carefully detailed enactments for his consistory court, published on 3 February 1336. These provide that public notice be given how recourse is to be had against those assumed to the offices of the deaneries for the faults of their surrogates—the deans themselves, as principals, to be summoned personally to the next consistory 'for contempts contracted by their surrogates'. Moreover, subjects aggrieved by such deputies, 'under colour of their office or otherwise', were invited to depose to the bishop concerning their plaint, personally or by proxy, orally or in writing, and were assured of remedy.[83] This policy initiative combines themes which are pronounced in the *Memoriale Presbiterorum*: the responsibility of principals for the conduct of their agents and a particular sensitivity to abuses of office and to forensic deficiencies.[84]

Nearly related as a target of Grandisson's reforming zeal or—in so far as it is necessary or possible to make the distinction—of his

---

[81] See Owen, *John Lydford's Book*, 26–7. Cf. L. E. Boyle, 'Aspects of Clerical Education in Fourteenth-Century England', reprinted in id., *Pastoral Care*, 28.

[82] *RG*, ii. 713.   [83] Ibid. 808.   [84] See below, p. 85.

administration's, is the behaviour of archdeacons, particularly in the context of visitations and procurations. The general behaviour of archdeacons is an important theme of the *Memoriale Presbiterorum*. As has been noted above,[85] sensitivity on the subject of archidiaconal procurations is pronounced both in the *Memoriale Presbiterorum* and in William Doune's will. Indeed, as will be shown later, there is a further strong insinuation as to the large dimensions that it assumed in William Doune's outlook from the fact that this same concern was inherited by—at least it is emphatically evidenced in the records of—the administration of Lincoln in the last quarter of the century, when his former official in the archdeaconry, John de Belvoir, was official of the diocese.[86] As the evidence somewhat uncertainly presents itself in the register, Grandisson's initiatives appear to come after the period when Doune was most associated with Exeter and the date of the *Memoriale Presbiterorum*. That reading of the record—and Doune's evidently deep personal concern—might well suggest that seeds of which he was the principal sower had taken root. There can, however, be no certainty on the point. In an abstract construction, it must be thought that a more plausible flow of ideas would be from Grandisson to his administration, but a two-way exchange cannot be discounted. A rather similar question arises over the genesis of the hostility to the mendicant friars, to be examined later.

A mandate to the official principal on abuses in visitations took as its point of departure Bishop Quinel's statute 'Eterni largitor premii' of 1287. This had sought to remove the profit motive from the imposition of pecuniary penances during archidiaconal visitation by requiring that such fines be paid not to the visitors but to the uses of the churches that were visited. The penalty for infringement of the provision was to be payment of twice the amount (*in duplum*) to the fabric of the cathedral church, in addition to restitution itself.[87] The fact that there was thus a native legislative tradition on the subject at Exeter probably resulted in the topic's being live within Grandisson's circle. Discussion of it within the circle might easily be the source of the attention given it in the *Memoriale Presbiterorum* as well, perhaps, as of the author's insistence on the principle of *restitutio in duplum*. Unfortunately, Grandisson's mandate here is without date—beyond the fact that it sets as its terminus the forthcoming feast of St Peter in Chains (1 August). It is dated by the editor from position as relating to the

[85] See above, pp. 14–17.   [86] See below, pp. 211–14.   [87] *CS*, ii. 1034–5.

year 1346 but, as he observes, there is chronological confusion of entries at this point due putatively to the copying of entries from separate memoranda.[88] If that dating is right, the action would coincide rather neatly with the ending of the long tenure of the archdeaconry of Cornwall by Adam de Carleton and his replacement by John of St Paul (1346–9). Under the general application, there is a nuance of particular address: the 'just and reasonable statute' of his predecessor has 'from excessive indulgence on our part been brought into contempt by some'. The vice of corrupt self-seeking (*ambitionis*) has so blinded the eyes of certain of his archdeacons (there were four in Exeter cathedral)—'as well the eye of intellect as of administration, of which the one ought to be pure, the other circumspect'—that they do not in the course of visitation proceed as they ought by zeal for justice, 'including by a moderate unsheathing of the spiritual sword', to secure the repair and supply of defects on the part of those responsible. Instead they impose excessive pecuniary penalties, in levying which they then show the zeal for censures that ought originally to have been employed. The archdeacons are now to be admonished, in set terms, to make complete restitution within a month, to the local churches, of all sums thus illicitly received to date and appropriated to their own profit, under penalty, as provided in Quinel's statute, of double payment to the fabric of the cathedral church. If the admonitions are unheeded the bishop proposes to proceed against them 'by all ways and means legally available to us'.[89] The acknowledgement of remissness need not perhaps be taken too seriously: remissness does not seem to have been Grandisson's besetting fault, and he had a record of vigilance as regards abusive profiting from jurisdiction. The prologue to his regulations for the conduct of his consistory court, issued on 3 February 1336, lamented 'the blindness of proper and private advantage, rather the rapacity, jealous of all equity' reportedly affecting various court personnel and resulting in the 'taking our subjects as objects of prey'. Judges were accordingly directed to inflict corporal correction for crimes of delinquency. Commutation was restricted to pressing cases. It was specified, though without particular comment, that the same be observed by archdeacons' officials. The conclusion to the regulations provided that fines imposed to date throughout the whole of his pontificate should not be levied without special mandate of the bishop, under his seal, and that the rolls containing them should, rather, be transmitted to him.[90]

---

[88] *RG*, ii. 1008 n.   [89] Ibid. 1008–9.   [90] Ibid. 808.

While the consistory regulations demonstrate Grandisson's concern over a particular source of corruption in the earlier period, there is also clear evidence that he was preoccupied specifically with abuses of archidiaconal authority in the second half of the 1340s. His undated mandate, just discussed, would certainly not be out of place at that time. The evidence is an initiative on the more technical subject of archidiaconal procurations. It is likely that he had always maintained a rigorous position in their regard, linking the collection of procurations firmly to personal visitation. So much is implied by a letter issued in 1342 on behalf of the veteran Adam de Carletone. Adam was so impeded by bodily infirmity that he could not , 'as is proper', himself discharge the office of visiting the churches of his archdeaconry of Cornwall, and accordingly could not exact the procuration due under that head. However, he maintained personal residence in Exeter cathedral, 'to the honour of that church', and the bishop appealed to the rectors and vicars of the archdeaconry to subvent him 'by way of courtesy and goodwill on your part'.[91] The obligations falling on him by reason of his office, as well as his loss of the procurations through inability to visit, were pleaded by Adam in the act by which he exchanged his archdeaconry with John of St Paul for the rectory of Brington, Hunts.[92] Whether, as suggested, because of this particular change of personnel, or on some other count, the bishop was subsequently drawn to specific regulation. A mandate of 25 June 1348 to the official principal, the commissary general, and the officials of the peculiar jurisdiction referred to 'frequent clamorous complaints', 'daily growing', that some archdeacons were 'so blinded by the vice of damnable corrupt self-seeking [*ambitionis*]' that they 'unjustly and unduly, rather, sacrilegiously' levied their procurations without personal visitation. The levying of procurations or of other sums by colour of them without personal visitation was to cease forthwith under penalty of excommunication, binding as well the offending archdeacons as their officials or other agents. The obliqueness of the measure may reflect the fact that John of St Paul had powerful connections.[93] The bishop was conscious of other difficulties. He made, as he was bound to do, specific exception where the archdeacon was armed with a papal privilege on the point. Grandisson himself, as archdeacon of Nottingham, had had dispensation to visit by deputy.[94] Moreover, he was conscious that his present regulation did nothing to remedy past exaction, but he promised to address this issue 'in

[91] Ibid. 956–7.   [92] Ibid. 957–8.   [93] Ibid. 958.   [94] *CPL*, ii. 101.

opportune time'.[95] The concessions hint at the intractability of the problems that he faced. As already noted, the issue of archidiaconal procurations is an important one in the *Memoriale Presbiterorum*, and the legal technicalities relating to them will be discussed in that context.[96]

Grandisson's sense of responsibility as a governor combined with singleness of purpose and outlook to defend a classically simple model of ecclesiastical organization founded on the parish unit. An explicit instance of the concern, in circumstances where no claim to privilege was in question and where no formal prejudice could be generated, is his inhibiting the nuns of Canon's Leigh in 1356 from receiving parishioners at services, precisely because of the deleterious effects on parish churches.[97] But the general trait is most palpable in the register's testimony to his jealousy both of private chapels and of chapels of ease. Causing celebration—or, rather, profanation—in his chapels without any known privilege or episcopal licence and in contravention of direct prohibition was one of several abuses by the newly created earl of Devon against which Grandisson complained to the archbishop of Canterbury in 1335. There the offence takes its place with disruption of testaments and impeding ecclesiastical corrections, and follows a list of encroachments on ecclesiastical jurisdiction alleged against the servants of the earl of Cornwall.[98] The encroachments of the great and their detachment from a parochial structure was one dimension of the problem. Grandisson was no less concerned about the consequences of chapels when they were a response to local topography. While acknowledging that problems of travel were a legitimate cause of the foundation of chapels of ease, he was alive to the tendency of 'those who by abuse call themselves parishioners of the chapels' to become 'elated'—that vice again—as 'degenerate sons' against the mother church.[99] In the case of the chapel of Marldon within the parish of Paignton, Devon, in 1348, an aggrieved body of parishioners took sanctions against their vicar's suit to protect his rights by agreeing to withhold certain traditional funeral dues—refusing to light the bier or to make what they considered discretionary offerings more than a mass-penny, 'with a false piety contaminated by the poison of envy' using the money saved to distribute largesse to the poor and on occasion removing the bier-cloth.

---

[95] *RG*, ii. 1050.   [96] See below, pp. 91–3.

[97] *RG*, ii. 1185–6 (24 April 1356).

[98] Ibid. 293–4. For a general mandate, issued in 1336, against celebration in forbidden places, see ibid. 836.

[99] Ibid. 1056.

As a reprisal, the bishop suspended the chapel.[100] More drastically, in 1351 he ordered the demolition of a chapel—'a house of idolatry', as he stigmatized it, those having resort to which were in consequence sacrificing to idols and practising sorcery (the cult was of an image of St Mary the Virgin). The chapel had been built by the Augustinian priory of Frithelstock without his licence or blessing and in contravention of his order.[101] It would be possible to deduce from the heavy incidence of licensing in the early years and the infrequency of licensing in later years that the antipathy to chapels developed during the pontificate.[102] It is perhaps more likely, however, that the number of licences issued in the early years of the pontificate represents the regularizing of a *de facto* situation, in conditions of considerable difficulty, rather than indicating an initial tolerance. On this reading, the Frithelstock solution would show his true feeling, in a context untrammelled by lay interests and where his authority had been directly flouted. A few years later, somewhat apologetically restricting celebration in the chapel of St Salvator, Ottery, he lamented how some folk were 'unstable, sad to say, in faith'—a teetering revealed by their preference for 'chapels and profane oratories'—and recalled how he had had certain chapels of the diocese, which had been 'built without our knowledge', in some cases suspended and in others utterly demolished.[103] The perceived risk evidently was that resort even to a thoroughly respectable foundation might encourage wider defection.

Besides the 'note of conspiracy' overt in the circumstances of Marldon chapel, Grandisson was on his guard against a more insidious restlessness on the part of parishioners, threatening to sound order. This, as he diagnosed it, was a disposition to 'seduce themselves perilously with various and strange doctrines'.[104] Precisely what was referred to in context is unclear. Grandisson was suspicious of vagabond influences. In

---

[100] Ibid. 1057.

[101] Ibid. 1110–11. For comments on the cult and on the limitation of episcopal power in effect over it, see N. Orme, 'Bishop Grandisson and Popular Religion', *Reports and Transactions of the Devonshire Association for the Advancement of Science, Literature and Art*, 134 (1992), 110–13.

[102] Dr Margaret Steele, in a most interesting study of Grandisson's outlook as derived principally from his reading inclines to this view. M. W. Steele, 'A Study of the Books owned or used by John Grandisson, Bishop of Exeter (1327–1369)', Oxford University, D.Phil. thesis, 1994, p. 177, n. 65, where it is calculated that in the period from 1328 to 1332 Grandisson licensed over 100 chapels. Dr Steele relates the concern evinced by Grandisson in marginal comments hostile to chapels on a text of pseudo-Isidore in Eton College MS. 97, formerly an Exeter cathedral book, fos. 16 and 88ᵛᵃ, to his destruction of the Frithelstock chapel.

[103] *RG*, ii. 1157–8 (1 July 1355).   [104] Ibid. 1056.

a mandate of 13 February 1341, addressed to the dean and subdean of Exeter cathedral and to the official of the diocese, Mr William de Crowthorne, over a feigned miracle at Exeter, he recalled St Paul's warning (2 Cor. 11: 14) that the angel of Satan had the capacity to transform himself into an angel of light and—a countryman's image—'to cheat the skill of the hunter with the assumed simplicity of a guileful vixen'. Not every spirit was worthy of belief. The incredulity of Thomas had turned out to be of more profit to us than the readiness of the other disciples. Among the triflers against whom one must guard, special vigilance was needed against 'worthless and unknown strangers'.[105] Perhaps Marldon was admitting extraneous preachers, friars even. Certainly it is not difficult to see here, in Grandisson's tendency to fuse the unauthorized and the unorthodox, the not-too-distant counterpart of hostility against the intrusions of the mendicant orders into parish discipline. In a combination of sensitivities, one instance of his objections to an unauthorized chapel involved the Augustinian friars of Dartmouth. The issue, whose history is related at length in a process dated 4 September 1347,[106] was complicated by the bizarre intrusion of a suffragan— the archbishop of Damascus—and, no doubt, by an underlying tension between Grandisson and the friars. This latter dimension is revealed by the fierce language used of them in 1351 when they had allegedly overrun the church of Townstal, Dartmouth's parish. Then, the bishop identifies them as 'disciples of Antichrist, disguised in the habit of religious'.[107] The implications of this aspect of Grandisson's outlook, the early evidence of criticisms of the mendicant friars within his circle and the correspondences with the full-blown campaign against them by his protégé, Richard FitzRalph, require separate consideration.[108]

The picture that emerges from the episodic business of the register is complemented by other sources. On the argument of the present study, the *Memoriale Presbiterorum*, whose doctrine is reviewed in detail below, itself sheds valuable light on the thinking of Grandisson's circle, as it in turn reflects it. The same may be suggested, with due reservation, of the vernacular poem *Speculum Vitae* which two manuscripts among a large tradition associate with William of Nassington.[109] The

[105] Ibid. 942–3. [106] Ibid. 1027–31. [107] Ibid. 1108–9.
[108] See below, pp. 185–9, 198–200.
[109] See H. E. Allen, 'The *Speculum Vitae*—Addendum', *Publications of the Modern Language Association of America*, 32 (NS, 25) (1917), 133–62; C. Brown and R. H. Robbins, *The Index of Middle English Verse* (New York, 1943), 40; V. Nelson, 'Problems of Transcription in the *Speculum Vitae* MSS', *Scriptorium*, 31 (1977), 254–9.

reservation is twofold. In the first place, there must be more residual doubt over the authorship of the *Speculum Vitae* than over that of the *Memoriale Presbiterorum*. However, Nassington's authorship is wholly probable,[110] and the probability is greatly strengthened by the case for the authorship of the *Memoriale Presbiterorum*, with which it has certain prominent interests in common.[111] The second reservation derives from the northern affiliations of the poem[112] that (in default of a critical edition) may be taken to indicate provenance. Thus, if it is indeed by William of Nassington it must be more plausibly deemed to have been written during the York rather than the Exeter phase of his career, though it is reasonable to suppose that the views expressed in it were forming earlier.

William of Nassington was one of several members of a family of Lincolnshire origin, active at a senior level in York diocese during the period (1312–27) when Grandisson held the archdeaconry of Nottingham, who were recruited to the Exeter administration.[113] Mr Thomas Nassington became Grandisson's official in 1329 and archdeacon of Exeter (1331–*c*.1345),[114] and Mr John de Nassington became canon of Exeter (1328), bishop's chancellor (by January 1329), and archdeacon of Barnstaple (1330).[115] William of Nassington, described by Grandisson in 1328 as 'dear and special clerk, our counsellor',[116] became canon of Exeter cathedral in the following year.[117] By 1332 he was Grandisson's chancellor,[118] and in that year had appointment as auditor of causes at Exeter.[119] For some fifteen years he was one of the most prominent figures in Grandisson's administration, serving both within the diocese and as proctor outside it, including at the Roman curia in 1329.[120] A commission of particular interest as regards the views expressed in the *Speculum Vitae* was his appointment to inquire into the excesses of advocates and proctors of the Exeter consistory court in 1336.[121] On

---

[110] The case for William of Nassington's authorship of the *Speculum Vitae* has been eloquently argued by Dr Jonathan Hughes in an unpublished paper of which he kindly sent me a copy. See also I. J. Petersen, *William of Nassington, Canon, Mystic and Poet of the Speculum Vitae* (New York/Berne/Frankfurt am Main, 1986).

[111] See below pp. 59–60, 109–10.

[112] See V. Gillespie, 'The Literary Form of the Middle English Pastoral Manual with particular reference to the *Speculum Christiani* and Some Related Texts', Oxford University, D.Phil. thesis, 1981, p. 134. Cf. Hughes, *Pastors and Visionaries*, 148.

[113] Cf. D. N. Lepine, 'The Origin and Careers of the Canons of Exeter Cathedral, 1300–1455', in Harper-Bill (ed.), *Religious Belief*, 93, 105.

[114] *RG*, i. 499, 529; iii. 1285, 1349; *CPL*, ii. 321.   [115] *RG*, i. 67; iii. 1267.

[116] Ibid., i. 167.   [117] Ibid., i. 245.   [118] Ibid., ii. 650.

[119] Ibid., ii. 662.   [120] Ibid., i. 476.   [121] Ibid., ii. 809.

25 May 1343, with William Crowthorne, the official of the diocese, and Benedict de Paston, he was appointed vicar-general of the diocese during Grandisson's absence at the Roman curia. About this time, following the appointment of his associate, William de la Zouche, former archdeacon of Exeter, as archbishop of York, William of Nassington evidently began the transfer of his principal activity to York diocese, where he served as archbishop's chancellor, as vicar-general during the vacancy of the see of Durham in 1345, and subsequently as an auditor of causes of the court of York.[122] By 1355 he was official of Salisbury diocese, under Bishop Robert Wyvil, in which position he appears to have continued until his death, *ante* June 1359.[123]

The *Speculum Vitae* is a lengthy treatise of moral and elementary dogmatic instruction organized around various traditional groups of seven—the seven petitions of the Lord's Prayer, the seven gifts of the Spirit, the seven vices, the seven virtues, and so on—but including in the course of the exposition a whole range of what would now be called catechetics. In addition, it incorporates a good deal of social commentary and criticism, particularly under the analysis of the vices. Much of this is evidently prompted by the poem's principal source, the *Somme le Roi*, written in 1279 by the Dominican Friar Lorens, confessor of Philip III of France.[124] While it is tempting to think that Grandisson, who had not only studied in Paris but had enjoyed close relations with the Dominicans,[125] might have introduced William of Nassington to the work, this cannot in itself be used as an argument for the authorship of the poem. Such a specific channel of dissemination need not be postulated. The *Somme* was translated into Kentish prose in 1340 by a monk of St Augustine's, Canterbury, Dan Michael of Northgate.[126]

It is in the correspondence of concerns between the *Speculum Vitae* and the *Memoriale Presbiterorum* that the rapport between the thinking within Grandisson's circle and the poem may most plausibly be detected. These correspondences are most pronounced in the poem's

---

[122] See *BRUO*, ii. 1339, for references to the Register of William la Zouche, fos. 282ᵛ and 268ᵛ—the appointment as vicar-general of Durham and auditor of court of York, respectively. For fuller details of Nassington's York career, see Petersen, *William of Nassington*, 18–20, 33–7.

[123] *BRUO*, ii. 1339.

[124] See *The Book of Vices and Virtues*, ed. W. N. Francis, EETS, os, 217 (1942), pp. xi–xix. Cf. Pantin, *Church*, 225.

[125] He was consecrated in the Dominican church in Avignon. *RG*, i. 322–3 and cf. *RG*, i. 169–170 and A. G. Little and R. C. Easterling, *The Franciscans and Dominicans of Exeter* (Exeter, 1927), 47. For the evidence of his bequests, see below, pp. 209–10.

[126] *Ayenbite of Inwit*, ed. R. Morris, EETS, os, 23 (1866).

exposition of Rapine and Calumny—the third and fourth branches of Avarice. Under Rapine are grouped six classes: common robbers; false executors; false debtors; covetous lords; covetous prelates; and lastly a miscellany of officials, deans, bedells, bailiffs, and sheriffs. Calumny affects eight classes: false plaintiff; false defendant; false witness and juror; false advocate; false procurator and attorney; false notary and clerk; false judge and justice; false maintainer and counsellor. This careful and specialized survey of administrative and legal personages and of forensic abuses in the *Speculum* owes much to the *Somme le Roi*.[127] The interest might, in the abstract, as well be associated with Nassington's experiences at York as at Exeter. However, the fact that it is a pre-occupation shared with the author of the *Memoriale Presbiterorum* suggests that it developed at Exeter, where, as noted above, Nassington was not only engaged in the practice of law but was closely involved with Grandisson's consistorial reforms.

The poem's strictures on legal officers will be noted in the course of reviewing their treatment in the *Memoriale Presbiterorum*. For the moment it will suffice to cite a passage of the *Speculum Vitae* that illustrates a dominant concern both of the *Memoriale Presbiterorum* and of William Doune as testator, and that relates directly to themes considered as characteristic of Grandisson's outlook. The treatment of prelates under the fifth subdivision of Rapine—the breathtakingly forthright comment implicit in the schematic placing is from the *Somme le Roi*—recalls Grandisson's general sense of governmental responsibility and a specific antipathy evinced by him:

> Prelates of holikirke so fre
> þurgh miʒt of þair autorite
> done þair sugettes grete outrage
> and putten þam to grete costage
> qwen þai þam visite þai make maistries
> þai raisin of þam grete procuracies
> and qwat þai aske þai most pay
> for þai dar nouʒt agayn þam say
> þos þat þus done oute of cours
> þai may þurgh riʒt becalde robbours.[128]

The *Myrour to Lewde Men and Wymmen*, a prose version of the *Speculum Vitae*, renders the content of the same passage as follows: 'Coueitous prelates of Holie Chirche beþ þei þat setteþ imposiciouns

[127] Cf. 'Somme le Roi', London, British Library, MS. Royal 19 C ii. fos. 13ʳ–14ʳ.
[128] 'Speculum Vitae', Oxford, Bodleian Library, MS. Bodley 446, fo. 90ʳ.

upon hir sugettes and chargeþ hem wrongfulliche in her visitaciouns, and makeþ hem to paye þat hem lust or what þei wole aske, or elles trauailleþ hem by sompnynge to appere in fer stedes and in oþer maner processe tile þey haue what þei wole. þei may wel be cleped raueynoures.'[129] This is only one of several junctures at which the *Myrour* seems to be informed by a level of understanding that is independent of the poem and that allows its author to handle the common theme with remarkable acuity. There is no clue to his identity, beyond the fact that he appears to have written in a south-western dialect, and for composition no improvement is possible on the date *c.*1400 deduced from the survival of manuscripts.[130] By mere content, however, the *Myrour* has a claim to be regarded as a witness to the continuing vigour of an outlook.

There remains to be noted explicitly another large, and this time firmly established, source for understanding the character of Grandisson's episcopate: the evidence for his intellectual interests—or rather the more explicit evidence, with discount of his determined building programme at Exeter cathedral and at his collegiate foundation of Ottery St Mary, a programme that itself testifies silently but permanently to a grand concept of episcopal office. His patronage of Richard FitzRalph is more readily classified under the head of intellectual interest, as FitzRalph was not recruited to the administration. The particular importance of their association in context of the present study will emerge from Chapter 12. For the moment it may be noticed as offering a fleeting insight into Grandisson's circumspection as a talent-spotter. In a letter apparently dating from 1328, Grandisson, following an investigation conducted by him on the point, dismisses a reservation that he had entertained regarding FitzRalph's suitability as a candidate for orders.[131] The implication here is that FitzRalph received major orders —as he later received episcopal consecration—at Grandisson's hands. It is impossible to establish the title by which he received them—it was probably supplied by Grandisson himself—but the occasion reveals a particular instance of a career progression that is unlikely to have been as unusual as it might appear, considered here in isolation, among Anglo-Irish clerics in the fourteenth century.[132] Its special interest derives from FitzRalph's later prominence, from Grandisson's

---

[129] *A Myrour to Lewde Men and Wymmen: A Prose Version of the Speculum Vitae edited from B. L. MS. Harley 45*, ed. V. Nelson (Heidelberg, 1981), p. 135, ll. 8–13.

[130] See ibid. 25, 51.   [131] *RG*, i. 173.

[132] I am grateful to Dr Virginia Davis for some enlightening preliminary conclusions from a database of Irish clerical careers in England in the later middle ages.

shrewdness in recognizing his qualities early, and from his disposition to attach to himself, evidently with some deliberation, new talent of very diverse provenance. Behind every recruitment to his service or circle must be imagined, no doubt, some 'taking up of references' or inquiry where the promising candidate's background or outlook was less than thoroughly known or where there was any reason for hesitation.

Of later appearance, as far as the evidence goes, was the association with another prominent theologian, Thomas Buckingham, fellow of Merton 1324–40[133]—a college with which, as has been noted, William Doune must also have had a connection, of uncertain date. (Merton's establishment was primarily of arts scholars intended for theology, but there was some provision for canon law and for civil law as a preliminary to it.[134]) Thomas Buckingham was, 1346–c.(?)1349, chancellor of Exeter cathedral and, it seems, disputed there on an aspect of his major theological preoccupation, the compatibility of divine predestination and human free will.[135] There is direct evidence for Grandisson's concern to promote a strong theological tradition at his cathedral.[136] Apart from its contemporary topicality, the subject of the disputation is likely to have been of high interest to him, who was by training a theologian and in outlook so evidently Augustinian.

The cultivation of outstanding theologians and the recruitment of a core of reflective lawyers to his administration fits a model that Grandisson, with engaging self-consciousness, presented of his episcopacy in 1346. Writing to the Black Prince, who was collecting matériel for his French expedition, the bishop protested the scholarly quality of his life: 'I do not greatly love to have horses, or grooms, or dogs, or falcons, but sire, of chaplains, clerks, and books have I sufficient for my estate.'[137] Disingenuousness aside, the picture presented is in keeping with what otherwise emerges. Grandisson's interest in books is particularly well documented. From one of his letters we have a vignette of a provincial collector's method of acquiring books in Oxford that is

---

[133] See *BRUO*, i. 298–9.

[134] See R. Highfield, 'The Early Colleges', in J. I. Catto (ed.), *The Early Oxford Schools* = *History of Oxford University*, i (Oxford, 1984), 245.

[135] For the context, as being probably Exeter, see Pantin, *Church*, 114 n. For Buckingham's thought more generally, see M. D. Chenu, 'Les Quaestiones de Thomas Buckingham', *Studia Medievalia in Honorem R. J. Martin* (Bruges, 1949) and B. R. de la Torre, *Thomas Buckingham and the Contingency of Futures: The Possibility of Human Freedom* (Notre Dame, 1987).

[136] *RG*, i. 307–8. The letter, dated 1349, is translated in Pantin, *Church*, 115–16.

[137] Quoted from the French original, PRO, Ancient Correspondence, LIV, no. 67, in F. Rose-Troup, *Bishop Grandisson Student and Art Lover* (Plymouth, 1929), 21.

fresh still in the days of Thornton's or Waterfield's catalogue. In 1329, near the beginning of their documented relationship, FitzRalph reserved on his behalf with Mr Richard de Ratforde a copy of St Augustine's sermons and the vendor was asked to keep an eye out for other rare theological volumes and classic sermon material.[138] We can glimpse that Grandisson lent to his clients. William Doune made provision in his will for the return of the letters of Peter of Blois, belonging to the bishop—a detail, incidentally, supporting what may be surmised of their continuing relationship.[139] The explicit cult of books and of humanism in the *Philobiblon* has made the circle centred on that other episcopal patron, Richard de Bury of Durham, the most historically palpable intellectual coterie of fourteenth-century England.[140] Grandisson's circle has a substantial claim to notice as another of the type. Though its ethos seems more severe—there is no hint at Exeter of the humanist spirit —the disparity on this measure must be partly specious. FitzRalph is a common link, and William Doune, as putative manualist, has his counterpart among Bury's clients in John Acton. If Thomas Buckingham may properly be counted part of Grandisson's 'circle'—and we do not know when their association commenced nor how deep it was—then he too has his Bury counterpart in Thomas Bradwardine.[141] These are not sealed units. Through Oxford and the two bishops' London residences there may be thought to have been constant contact and exchange.[142] Richard de Bury himself had a link with Exeter: he had formerly held the prebends of Crediton, acquired in 1327,[143] and Penryn, acquired in 1330.[144]

In default of a treatise by Grandisson on the importance of his reading to him, insights must be derived in piecemeal fashion. How productive the approach proves in his case has been shown by Dr Steele's study.[145] His regard for *auctoritas* and for primitive models is

---

[138] *RG*, i. 240.   [139] Thompson, 'Will', 275. Cf. above, p. 44.

[140] See J. de Ghellinck, 'Un bibliophile au XIV siècle: Richard d'Aungerville', *Revue d'Histoire Ecclésiastique*, 18 (1920), 271–312, 482–502; 19 (1923), 157–200. N. Denholm-Young, 'Richard de Bury (1287–1345)', in *The Collected Papers of N. Denholm-Young* (Cardiff, 1969), 1–41. Richard de Bury, *Philobiblon*, ed. M. Maclagan (Oxford, 1960).

[141] Richard de Bury was dead by the time that Buckingham became chancellor of Exeter. As regards the divergence of view between them, Bradwardine must be judged further from a 'humanist' cast of mind than Buckingham, though the criterion is not useful. See principally G. Leff, *Bradwardine and the Pelagians* (Cambridge, 1957).

[142] On the significance of the bishops' London residences, see W. J. Courtenay, *Schools and Scholars in Fourteenth-Century England* (Princeton, 1987), 104–5.

[143] *CPR (1327–1330)*, 191; *CPL*, ii. 275; *RG*, 191.   [144] *CPR (1327–1330)*, 495.

[145] Cf. above, n. 102.

marked.[146] It may be suggested that the latter interest is close to that which becomes the motive force of Richard FitzRalph's defence of classic ecclesiology.[147] There is clear evidence that in rereading Augustine's *De Civitate Dei* in the mid- to late 1350s he had FitzRalph's cause in mind.[148] The concern for judicial reform evident in the register is mirrored by signs in the annotations and marginalia of a marked interest in the beginnings of a legal system, the character of high priests and judges, and the corresponding role of bishops.[149] Other reflections on the responsibility of bishops were prompted by his reading of Gregory the Great's *Regula Pastoralis* and the *Canones Apostolorum*.[150] Similarly, his concern with administration is apparent in his attention to the letters of Gregory the Great.[151] The annotations on the *Canones Apostolorum* suggest a particular rigour as regards non-communication with excommunicates that accords well with the tone of the register.[152] His reading of *De Civitate Dei* gave him ample scope to draw lessons about warfare, why God permits it, the theory of just war, and the moral approximation of victors and vanquished.[153] This line of analysis may plausibly be thought to underlie the pronounced interest of the *Memoriale Presbiterorum* in problems of restitution arising from acts of war.[154] For the most part, the *Memoriale*'s discussion of the problems is unoriginal, being derived largely from the *Summa Aurea* of Hostiensis.[155] There can be no doubt, however, that the work of extracting the doctrine of Hostiensis on the penitential dimensions of war by a member of his circle would have been highly congenial to Grandisson. His reading indicates that the topic of Thomas Buckingham's disputation would have been no less congenial to him, for his adherence to Augustine was without prejudice to his belief in man's free will.[156] Grandisson's outlook both as reader and pastor lends

---

[146] Steele, 'A Study', 139, 141.

[147] Cf. M. J. Haren, 'Friars as Confessors, the Canonist Background to the Fourteenth-Century Controversy', *Peritia*, 3 (1984), 516.

[148] Steele, 'A Study', 166, citing marginal comments in Oxford, Bodleian Library MS. Bodley, 691, fos. 160rb, 211ra.

[149] Steele, 'A Study', 139, 151, 152. Dr Steele has remarked on the peculiar force of his notes concerning law and judgment, ibid. 153.

[150] Ibid. 152, 155–6.   [151] Ibid. 142.

[152] Cf. above, p. 48.   [153] Steele, 'A Study', 157–8.

[154] MP, chap. b. xl: 'De predonibus et raptoribus qui in bellis bona aliorum rapiunt': fo. 62vb; chap. b. xli, 'De bello quando dicitur iustum et quando non': fos. 63^r–64^r; chap. b. xlii, 'De hiis qui recipiunt predam ex dono predonis': fo. 64r; chap. b. xliii, 'De uxore et familia predonis': fo. 64^{r-v}; chap. b. xliv, 'De hiis qui res raptas seu depredatas emunt': fos. 64^v–65^r. Cf. Pantin, *Church*, 210.

[155] See Hostiensis, *SA*, cols. 1469–74.   [156] Steele, 'A Study', 147, 151.

support to the manuscript authority that locates Buckingham's disputation at Exeter.[157] Lastly, as regards the correspondence between Grandisson the scholar and literary patron and Grandisson the working bishop and man of action, may be particularly noted the fact that early in his episcopate he wrote a Life of Thomas Becket,[158] that he had a continuing interest in the relationship of *regnum* and *sacerdotium*,[159] and that he had a particular and related regard for the Letters of St Anselm.[160] The exact nature of his interest in Anselm's Letters is shown by the note in his own hand, dated 9 April 1364, his seventy-third year, and renewed by him three years later, bequeathing a copy of them to successive archbishops of Canterbury: 'hic infra potest videri status tam ecclesie quam regni Anglie[.] Utinam renovetur per Christum dominum nostrum qui vivit et regnat rex regum et summus sacerdos pontifex in eternum[.] Amen Amen[.]'[161] The inscription could be, and may have been thought of as, the epitaph of his own pontificate.

---

[157] Pantin, *Church*, 114, n. 2.   [158] Steele, 'A Study', chap. 6.   [159] Ibid. 251.
[160] Ibid. 145.   [161] London, British Library, MS. Cotton Cleopatra C. XI, fo. 8ʳ.

4

The Memoriale Presbiterorum: *Genre, Sources, and Wider Affinities*

Genre and Sources

The *Memoriale Presbiterorum* is indebted to three principal strands of the tradition of penitential writing. Indirectly, it stands in a line of development from that departure of twelfth-century theology characterized by Grabmann as the 'biblical-moral movement'.[1] The members of the movement were distinctive for their interest in practical morality, an interest that readily converged with and promoted the burgeoning theology of private penance which is so notable a feature of twelfth-century Parisian thought.[2] This theology emphasized the interior quality of sin and of repentance and, as a counterpart, the role of the confessor in diagnosing the extent of the penitent's fault, through prolonged examination, and prescribing a remedy for it. The most important figure of the 'biblical-moral movement', who represents equally the concern with practical morality and with confession, was Master Peter the Chanter, precentor of Notre Dame (d. 1197). Peter's own massive *Summa de Sacramentis et Animae Consiliis*,[3] an investigation of moral topics through the device of casuistry, was a product of his teaching rather than a manual designed for ready use in a pastoral context. However, he must be judged an important influence on the much more practical *Summa Confessorum*[4] of the English theologian Thomas de Chobham (written *c*.1215), which despite its title has been rightly described as a 'manual of the pastoral care in general'.[5] Chobham's *Summa* was a source for

---

[1] M. Grabmann, *Die Geschichte der scholastichen Methode nach den gedruckten und ungedruckten Quellen*, ii (Freiburg im Breisgau, 1911), 476–501.

[2] See P. Anciaux, *La Théologie du sacrement de pénitence au XIIe siècle* (Louvain/Gembloux, 1949).

[3] Peter Cantor, *Summa de Sacramentis et Animae Consiliis*, ed. J.-A. Dugauquier (Louvain/Paris, 1954–67).

[4] *Thomae de Chobham, Summa Confessorum*, ed. F. Broomfield (Louvain/Paris, 1968).

[5] Boyle, 'A Study', i. 224; but cf. Broomfield, (ed.), *Thomae de Chobham: Summa*, p. xxiv. On another aspect of his contribution, see F. Morenzoni, *Des écoles aux paroisses: Thomas de Chobham et la promotion de la prédication au début du XIIIe siècle* (Turnhout/Paris, 1995).

the *Oculus Sacerdotis* of William of Pagula, and therefore constitutes a direct link between the earlier, Parisian phase of pastoral writing and the fourteenth-century English scene. There is no sign of its having been used by the author of the *Memoriale Presbiterorum*.

The elaboration of the internal dimension of morality challenged an older penitential model that was classically concerned with the object-ive character of the sinful act and of satisfaction for it, and that pur-ported to inflict penalties by tariff rather than administer prescriptions judged to take account of the range of circumstantial factors bearing on a particular penitent's guilt. In fact, the transition from the rigour of the early penitentials, in so far as it was ever general, to the individually orientated approach took place over a lengthy period of modification.[6] Indeed, one of the favourite metaphors of the later regime, that of the confessor-physician,[7] was inherited from the early-eleventh-century *Decretum* of Burchard of Worms.[8] Although the analysis of the twelfth-century theologians was sufficiently disturbing in its most radical pre-sentation to provoke controversy,[9] it evoked little substantive debate on its essential premisses. It triumphed with relative ease on ground that had been prepared for it, and its triumph ultimately represented, in the value theoretically placed on conscience, a distinctive contribu-tion to western civilization. The impact of the 'internal' analysis can be estimated not least by its reception beyond theological circles, in canonical jurisprudence.

Already by the time of Peter the Chanter there was a well-developed interest among lawyers in the subject of penance. Burchard of Worms is one example. The outstanding early contribution was that of Gratian, who incorporated into the section *De Poenitentia* of his *Decretum* the pseudo-Augustinian work *De vera et falsa poenitentia*. The authority of this section went far to establish the requirement of oral confession.

---

[6] On penitentials which allowed a measure of discretion on the confessor's part, see T. P. Oakley, *English Penitential Discipline and Anglo-Saxon Law in their Joint Influence* (New York 1923), 65, and id., 'The Penitentials as Sources of Medieval History', *Speculum*, 15 (1940), 211. Cf. the argument of P. J. Payer, 'The Humanism of the Penitentials and the Continuity of the Penitential Tradition', *MS*, 46 (1984), 340–54. For perception of their inflexibility, see R. Blomme, *La Doctrine du péché dans les écoles théologiques de la première moitié du XII siècle* (Louvain, 1958), 109, 202.

[7] See e.g. Broomfield (ed.), *Thomae de Chobham, Summa*, 240–1.

[8] *PL*, cxl. 943–1014, the nineteenth book of which is entitled 'Corrector et medicus'.

[9] As attended Peter Abelard's exposition, on which see *Peter Abelard's Ethics*, ed. D. Luscombe (Oxford, 1971), pp. xxxii–xxxvi, 22–5, 44–7; D. Luscombe, *The School of Peter Abelard: The Influence of Abelard's Thought in the Early Scholastic Period* (Cambridge, 1969), 194, 211, 276–8, 295–6.

Gratian's work was ill-suited, though, as a guide to confessional practice. The results of the twelfth-century developments in canon law
were first summarized for the confessor in the *Liber Poenitentialis* of
the Englishman Robert of Flamborough, composed probably between
1208 and 1213 and not later than 1215.[10] No direct influence of
Flamborough's work has been traced on the *Memoriale Presbiterorum*.
However, the *Liber Poenitentialis* is of considerable interest for an assessment of the *Memoriale Presbiterorum* in that it exhibits a tension, that
was never wholly resolved in the literature and which has particular
importance for the *Memoriale Presbiterorum*, between the doctrine that
penances are arbitrary, at the confessor's discretion, and the authority
of canonical penances. Not only implicitly—by his listing the canonical
penances in Book V of his *Liber*—but also explicitly, Flamborough, while
accepting that penances might be mitigated or increased 'from considered
reasons', displayed a reverence for the canons that did not escape criticism in his own day.[11]

If Flamborough, for all that as a canon of St Victor he must have
been quite familiar with developments on the theological side at Paris,[12]
is an ambivalent witness to the impact of the theologians' analysis on
the canonical tradition, that tradition began, from the second decade
of the thirteenth century, rapidly to absorb the implications of the new
outlook. A particular spur to the canonists' concentration of intellectual effort on penance was the decree *Omnis utriusque sexus* of the Fourth
Lateran Council of 1215, imposing throughout western christendom
an obligation of annual confession to the penitent's 'proper priest'.[13]
Among the lawyers' productions which subsequently issued on the
subject of confession, two may be selected for particular mention in
tracing the pedigree of the *Memoriale Presbiterorum*, the *Summa de
Casibus* of Raymund of Peñafort, written in 1225, and the *Summa Aurea*
of Henry of Susa (Hostiensis), written *c.*1253.

The main importance of Raymund's *Summa* in the present context
is that he took over, as Robert of Flamborough had not, the doctrine
of the circumstances of action as a main thrust of his approach to
the conduct of confession. This device, inherited from the classical

[10] See Robert of Flamborough, *Liber Penitentialis*, ed. J. J. Firth (Toronto 1971), 8–9.

[11] See J. J. Firth, 'The *Penitentiale* of Robert of Flamborough: An Early Handbook for
the Confessor in its Manuscript Tradition', *Traditio*, 16 (1960), 552.

[12] The complex of associations is summarized by L. E. Boyle, 'The Inter-Conciliar Period
1179–1215 and the Beginnings of Pastoral Manuals', in F. Liotta, *Miscellanea Rolando Bandinelli
Papa Alessandro III* (Siena, 1986), 54.

[13] X. 5. 38. 12.

rhetorical tradition,[14] had received much elaboration from the twelfth-century literature on penance, notably from Alan of Lille in his *Penitenciale* (*c*.1175–85)[15] and in diffusely casuistical fashion from Peter the Chanter. Raymund formulated the circumstances in the rhyming couplet:

Quis, quid, ubi, per quos, quoties, cur, quomodo, quando,
Quilibet observet, animae medicamina dando.[16]

It was in this form, generally mediated through the highly influential *Summa Confessorum* (completed *c*.1298) of the Dominican John of Freiburg, who adapted Raymund's work in the light of the century's theological developments,[17] that the doctrine of circumstances reached the manualists of fourteenth-century England. The *Memoriale Presbiterorum* too received the doctrine in this form, though by way of the *Summa Aurea* of Hostiensis.

With Raymund of Peñafort, the circumstance 'Quis' was the point of departure for an examination of the penitent on the basis of his station in life. Raymund offered special instruction on the interrogation appropriate to a limited number of classes: religious, secular clerics, princes, knights, merchants, burgesses and citizens, peasants.[18] The guidance as regards secular persons was extremely brief, however. Raymund's treatment of the matter is notable rather for what it set in train than for what it delivered. What it set in train was accomplished principally within the canonical tradition. It is noteworthy that John of Freiburg, a theologian, added nothing of significance to Raymund's scheme in his own *Summa Confessorum*, though he did return to the subject of interrogation according to dignity, state, and office in a minor work, the *Confessionale*, which he wrote for the less expert confessor.[19] The elaboration within the lawyers' tradition began with the Bolognese

---

[14] The major study is J. Gründel, *Die Lehre von dem Umständen der menschlichen Handlung im Mittelalter* (Münster, 1963). See also D. W. Robertson, Jr, 'A Note on the Classical Origin of the Circumstances in the Medieval Confessional', *Studies in Philology*, 43 (1946), 6–14, and, with specific reference to the line of development discussed here, M. J. Haren, 'Social Ideas in the Pastoral Literature of Fourteenth-Century England' in Harper-Bill (ed.), *Religious Belief*, 46–7.

[15] *PL*, ccvii. cols. 1153–6.

[16] Raymund of Peñafort, *Summa Confessorum* (Rome, 1603), 463–4.

[17] John of Freiburg, *Summa Confessorum* (Paris, 1519). For admirable discussion, see Boyle, 'John of Freiburg'.

[18] Raymund of Peñafort, *Summa Confessorum*, 466–7.

[19] 'Confessionale': Oxford, Bodleian Library, MS. Laud Misc. 278, fos. 354ʳ–363ᵛ. See P. Michaud-Quantin, *Sommes de casuistique et manuels de confession* (Louvain/Lille, 1962), 44.

canonist Johannes de Deo, whose *Liber Penitentiarius* (written in 1247), attempts a comprehensive survey of the vices of the various classes of society.[20] The work, which is divided into seven books, is wholly devoted to confessional technique. The personal status of the penitent is considered in two separate contexts. In Book I, which contains fifteen titles on penance in general, several conditions of penitent are considered. So, instruction is provided on the confession of the infirm (chapters 1, 2),[21] of the healthy (chapter 3), of servile and free,[22] religious, women, widows, and beguines.[23] Books V and VI review ecclesiastical and secular occupations, respectively. The clerical persons comprise the pope, cardinals, papal chaplains, patriarchs, archbishops, bishops, abbots, monks, deans, archdeacons, archpriests, provosts, treasurers, masters of schools, precentors, canons of cathedrals, teachers, advocates, counsel, and priests.[24] The secular persons considered are emperor, king, duke, margrave (*marchio*), count, baron, knights, merchants, and peasants.[25] The sins of rulers are expounded in terms to become familiar in the literature of complaint:

> Counts sin especially in that they believe that it is licit for them to dismiss their wives and take others on their own authority, which was never licit for them nor will be. In the second place, they sin gravely in that they distrain churches and ecclesiastical persons, contrary to ecclesiastical liberty, contemning the keys of the church . . . In the third place, they sin gravely in that they exhaust the faculties of their subjects unjustly . . . They sin too in tithes, first-fruits and offerings, which they do not pay . . . They sin too against justice in oppressing the poor . . .[26]

Although the form of these sections is denunciatory, the confessional purpose is retained: they end for the most part with a formula recommending their use as an interrogatory by the confessor.

Johannes de Deo's detailed programme for the penitent's examination on the basis of his station in life established a separate tradition within the genre. Within a few years it was absorbed and developed by the great *Summa Aurea* (*c.*1253) of another canonist, Henry of Susa (Hostiensis). This is the principal source of the *Memoriale Presbiterorum*, through which the doctrines discussed above, particularly those of Raymund of Peñafort and Johannes de Deo, were transmitted to the author. The *Summa Aurea* includes a detailed review of the classes of

---

[20] Oxford, Bodleian Library, MS. Laud Misc. 112, fos. 325^r–338^v. See Michaud-Quantin, *Sommes*, 26–7.

[21] *PL*, xcix, cols. 1085–6.   [22] Ibid., col. 1086.

[23] (?) 'pyrocarae'. Ibid., col. 1088.   [24] Ibid., cols. 1089–107.

[25] See MS. Laud Misc. 112, fos. 335^v–336^v.   [26] Ibid., fo. 336^r.

penitents, based on the scheme of Johannes de Deo, and it contains a powerful statement in practical form of the obligation of restitution in cases of injury or theft.

The *Summa* is not a confessional work but a survey of canon law, its organization being that of the five books of the *Decretals*, with the inclusion of additional titles. Penance is discussed in Book V, under the canonical title 'De penitentiis et remissionibus'.[27] This section, containing sixty-two subdivisions, was capable of forming a separate tract, and in fact had a circulation independent of the *Summa*.[28]

The *Summa* proceeds by question and answer. The opening chapters of this title deal with the nature of penance and contrition and with sin as the subject of confession (chapters 1–11). The elaboration of circumstances follows that of Raymund.[29] A consideration of the personal status of the penitent ensues by way of answer to the question, 'To whom must confession be made?' In this respect, as in the range of persons dealt with and the order in which they occur, Hostiensis's account is modelled—without acknowledgement—on that of Johannes de Deo.[30] The consideration of the vices of each is, however, fuller than in the latter.

Having established the proper confessor for each class, Hostiensis considers general aspects of confession: when it should be made; how the priest should behave towards the penitent; what factors impede penance and what factors induce to true penitence (chapters 46–7); the effect of true penitence (chapter 51); the factors which prevent relapse after true penitence (chapter 52); the obligations of the priest towards his confitent and vice versa (chapters 53–4); a theological discussion of whether penance should be reiterated (chapter 55), an enumeration of the circumstances (largely stemming from canon law) when it must be reiterated (chapter 56), and a discussion of the question whether sins once remitted ever return (chapter 57); finally may be included under this head two matters indirectly related to penance—whether good works benefit the person in mortal sin, and the effect of indulgences (chapters 58, 59). Chapter 60 is a list of the penitential canons.

The final two chapters of this title (61–2) are devoted to the obligation of restitution in certain cases, and provide the best account of this matter to be found in the whole continental tradition of confessional

---

[27] Hostiensis, *SA*, cols. 1385–483.   [28] See Gründel, *Die Lehre*, 416.   [29] Ibid.
[30] Hostiensis, *SA*, v, tit. 'De penitentiis et remissionibus', sections 15–44. The only variation from Johannes de Deo is that 'comes' is not included in the list of secular persons, presumably as being an unnecessary distinction from 'procer seu baro'.

literature. Chapter 61 ('Quibus et qualiter, a quibus et in quantum facienda est restitutio male acquisitorum') surveys the classes most likely to incur the obligation: prelates, the mother of a child whom her husband wrongly supposes to be his, wreckers, those who receive booty, court officials, usurers, those who give alms illegally, and so on. Chapter 62 explains the form to be used in making restitution.

The *Summa* of Hostiensis is used extensively in the *Summa Confessorum* of John of Freiburg. Among the manualists of fourteenth-century England, its influence can be seen in the *Septuplum* of John Acton and in the encyclopaedia 'Omne Bonum' (*c.*1375),[31] as well as in the *Memoriale Presbiterorum*. Otherwise, however, Hostiensis's influence in this context is less than might have been anticipated. John of Freiburg, the structure of whose *Summa* was based on that of Raymund, did not accommodate the valuable analysis of restitution. In particular, William of Pagula's *Oculus Sacerdotis*, for which the *Summa* of John of Freiburg is a principal source, and the manuals inspired by the *Oculus* escape both the heavy social orientation of Hostiensis's programme and its minute, legalistic concentration on the question of restitution.

While the *Summa* of Hostiensis is by far the most important influence on and source for the *Memoriale Presbiterorum*, another source, to which reference has already been made,[32] may be recapitulated here. That is the short work of the late-thirteenth-century canonist William Durand (d. 1296), printed as *Aureum Confessorium et Memoriale Sacerdotum*, from which the *Memoriale Presbiterorum* may take the first part of its title and from which it takes certain dogmatic material.

The Structure and Content of the *Memoriale Presbiterorum*

Unlike some treatises which range more widely over the pastoral cure—such as the *Summa* of Thomas de Chobham or the *Oculus Sacerdotis*, viewed as an entity—the *Memoriale Presbiterorum* is exclusively devoted to confessional technique, of which it is an exhaustive treatment. It is therefore akin to the *Prima Pars* of the *Oculus Sacerdotis*. To the extent

---

[31] For the latter work, see L. F. Sandler, 'Face to Face With God: A Pictorial Image of the Beatific Vision', in Ormrod, *England*, 228–35, who ascribes it to James le Palmere, an exchequer clerk. *Omne Bonum* repeats the whole of Hostiensis's interrogations on the seven deadly sins; see London, British Library, MS. Royal 6 E vi, fos. 37ᵛ–38ʳ. These interrogations, unacknowledged, are also the basis of a short tract in Oxford, Bodleian Library, MS. Bodl. 490, fos. 118ʳ–132ʳ, an early fourteenth-century manuscript.

[32] Above, p. 6.

that it includes dogmatic material, this is subordinate, being designed
to prepare the confessor for the instruction of the penitent.

The *Memoriale* consists of 218 chapters. In C, the first 119 chapters
are numbered under the letter 'a' and the remainder under 'b'. This
division, reproduced in W but not in H, is in fact nothing more than
a convenience of numbering. The work is formally a unit. It may, however, conveniently be considered as falling into some seven sections.

The first two chapters deal with the reception of the penitent,
the second being an account of the cases in which the priest may
absolve a penitent from another parish. There then follows a dogmatic
section (a. iii–xi) on the articles of faith, the decalogue, the works of
mercy, and sin. This material is based in part on Pecham's 'Ignorantia
Sacerdotum'[33] and in smaller part on William Durand's *Aureum
Confessorium*. A general statement of the importance of the circumstances
(derived from William Durand's account, already mentioned) and
of the manner of confession (a. xii–xiii)—precedes the programme of
interrogation.

The interrogation consists (a. xiv–xlii) of inquiry into the seven deadly
sins and the circumstances, and examination of the penitent on the basis
of his station in life. The questionnaire on the seven sins is a repeti-
tion of the corresponding section of Hostiensis's *Summa Aurea*. The
latter also provides the inspiration of the chapters dealing with the
various classes, though as will appear from more detailed consideration,[34] the author of the *Memoriale* modifies his source to suit his purpose, adding material to the questionnaires on several of the classes
considered by Hostiensis and inserting several classes not found in
the latter's schema. He also omits, presumably as being beyond the
sphere of the parish confessor, a number of persons—such as the higher
ecclesiastical and secular dignitaries—traditionally included in the
programme.[35]

The central portion of the work is devoted to canonical material of
the type found in the *Prima Pars* of the *Oculus Sacerdotis*,[36] though this
is not a source. So, there is the essential information on the cases in
which the penitent must be remitted to higher authority (a. xliiii–xlv)
and on those in which confession must be reiterated (a. xlvi). Then
follows a list (a. xlix–b. xii) of the penitential canons. The method of
presenting these resembles that adopted in the *Confessionale* of

---

[33] For this statute's importance, see Boyle, 'A Study', i. 257–8.
[34] See below, Chapters 5–11.   [35] For further details, see below, pp. 82–3.
[36] See Boyle, 'The Oculus'.

Marchesino di Reggio d'Emilia—a Franciscan who is thought to have been lector at Imola and Bologna and whose work is plausibly dated *ante* 1315—though it does not seem that the *Confessionale* is a source for the *Memoriale*. Marchesino's list of fifty-seven canonical penances derives in the main from the corresponding section of Hostiensis's *Summa Aurea* (with the addition of ten not found in Hostiensis's list), and either this work or the *Summa Confessorum* of John of Freiburg, which reproduces Hostiensis's catalogue, is the probable source for Marchesino. However, while Hostiensis's list was really only an index to the location of the penances in the *Decretum Gratiani* and *Decretals*, Marchesino followed up the references and provided the full text of the canon in each case. Similarly, the *Memoriale Presbiterorum* includes for each penance the full text or a résumé of it. In effect, it is not presumed that the confessor will have an opportunity to consult the material for himself.[37] Conversely, and in contrast to the practice of Marchesino and, in general, of the other lists of penances referred to above, no references are given to the canons; this accords with the author's practice throughout the work.[38]

Because of the unusually prominent place given to the penitential canons in the *Memoriale*, it affords one of the best examples in the genre of that dichotomy between the doctrine of the arbitrary character of penance and continuing reverence for the canonical prescriptions, which was noted above in connection with the *Liber Poenitentialis* of Robert of Flamborough. The rationale of the application of these penances is set out in a. xlviii. The author's bias is certainly in favour of the imposition of the canonical penance.[39] However, this instruction is modified to the extent that if the confessor, having imposed the canonical penance, decides that it is expedient 'to modify or shorten or prolong the time of penance, as the quality of the offence and the condition and dignity of the person of the sinner requires', he may do so,[40] and if he does

---

[37] See MP, fo. 48vb, where the author offers the following apology: 'Istas penitencias a canone statutas in variis capitulis decretorum et decretalium reperire poterit scriptas diligens indagator, set capita capitulorum hic non inserui causa brevitatis et pro eo quod libros canonicales non habes nec plerique confessores habent nec eciam iura canonica audiverunt. Preterea querendo concordancias huiusmodi mens tua forsan obtenebraretur et pocius errares quam vera saperes.' Cf. MP, fo. 80^v, where he explains his omitting various incidental questions, 'relinquendo illa studiosis copiam librorum habentibus'.

[38] Only in the list of excommunications are canonical references supplied.

[39] See MP, fo. 31^v: 'si igitur repereris certam penitenciam statutam a canone pro peccato, illam de iure debes iniungere et non aliam. Alioquin si aliam iniunxeris, ex quo certa penitencia a canone est statuta, falsa dicitur illa penitencia per te iniuncta.'

[40] Ibid., fo. 32^r.

this 'from a true cause', 'he shall not be said to have imposed a false penance, but a true one'.[41]

The catalogue of penances includes eighty-three canons and is a more detailed and comprehensive account than that of any of the treatises considered above, none of which serves as an adequate source. It appears to be—as the author himself implies that it is[42]—the fruit of his own researches in the *Decretum* and *Decretals*. It is interesting, as a comment on the list's excellence within its own terms, and on the continuing influence of the penitential canons, that it circulated—in at least one manuscript[43]—separately from the rest of the text. The section on canonical penances concludes with an account of arbitrary penances—which may be applied in accordance with the penitent's condition—and with other related material of a general nature (b. xii–xxvii).

The author next proceeds to the subject of restitution (b. xxviii–lxxii). First are discussed a number of general legal points of difficulty in this connection.[44] Then are considered the obligations of various classes and persons, notably administrative officials, to make restitution of unjust gains. This section is therefore, in one respect, the obverse of the examination of the classes in the earlier part of the work, and like the interrogatories, owes its inspiration and much of its legal content to the relevant sections of the *Summa Aurea*. Here again, however, the author's contribution is considerable and he reveals a marked zeal for his subject.[45] It is a trait which is shared by other moralists of the middle and later part of the century, notably Richard FitzRalph, Thomas Brinton, and William Langland.[46]

Following the account of restitution is a discussion of several other topics preliminary to absolution, such as contrition (b. lxxiii) and the continuing relationship between penitent and confessor, of which both must be reminded (b. lxxiiii–lxxv). Then follows instruction on the manner of absolution in the case of an excommunicate (b. lxxvii–lxxviii).

---

[41] Ibid.   [42] Ibid., fo. 48[vb].

[43] Oxford, Bodleian Library, MS. Selden Supra 39, fos. 4[r]–68[r].

[44] See further, below p. 83.   [45] See e.g. MP, fos. 63[vb]–64[r], 75[v], 80[rb]–80[v].

[46] For FitzRalph's doctrine on restitution, see e.g 'Sermons', Oxford, Bodleian Library, MS. Bodley 144, fo. 1[v]. Cf. A. Gwynn, 'Richard FitzRalph, Archbishop of Armagh', *Studies*, 25 (1936), 83–4; id., 'Archbishop FitzRalph and the Friars', ibid. 26 (1937), 58; id., 'The Black Death in Ireland', ibid. 24 (1935), 36; Walsh, *Scholar and Primate*, 364–5. For Brinton's doctrine see Brinton, *Sermons*, i. 147–8. For Langland's, see *Piers Plowman*, ed. W. W. Skeat (Oxford, 1968), C. VII, 256–8, 296 ff., 304 ff., 309–10, 342 ff.; C. IX, 235 ff.; and for criticism of the friars on this point, ibid., C. XXIII, 316–17.

In the course of his discussion of contrition (b. lxxiii), the author raises a question concerning the value of indulgences. He deals with them in general terms. Nothing specific connects the subject with Clement VI's statement of the treasury theory of indulgences in the jubilee bull 'Unigenitus Deus',[47] issued in the year preceding the supposed date of the *Memoriale*. The author is clearly sceptical of their value in practice—there is no criticism of the authority issuing them —on the grounds that the requirement of true penitence is rarely fulfilled. His insistence that indulgences do not remove the necessity of performing the enjoined penance is in keeping with his rigorous regard for the canonical sanctions, and is less equivocal than the doctrine of Raymund of Peñafort and Hostiensis, both of whom counselled the performance of the penance without holding that it was essential.[48]

The penultimate section of the treatise is a list of excommunications, papal, legatine, and as relevant to Canterbury province. This is the least impressive part of the *Memoriale* and may be contrasted with the corresponding sections of the *Oculus Sacerdotis*. The excommunications are not well organized; b. lxxxxvi is an addendum, out of place, of papal excommunications. The list does not claim to be comprehensive and may have been compiled in haste or without adequate sources to hand.[49] Some seventeen cases of excommunication in the *Decretals*, three from the *Sext*,[50] and ten from among what later came to be the *Extravagantes Communes*, up to the end of the pontificate of John XXII, are omitted; there are no excommunications from the *Clementines* nor from the collected *Extravagantes* of John XXII, with neither of which the *Memoriale* displays any acquaintance elsewhere, though the author does refer to the Council of Vienne.[51] The latest papal excommunication listed is that of Clement V's 'Quia nonnulli', dated 1306.[52] The latest English excommunication listed is Pecham's sentence against corruptors of nuns from the Council of Lambeth (1281).[53] It is noteworthy in this regard that a compendium of censures that circulated in Canterbury

---

[47] *Extravag. Commun.* 5. 9. 2.

[48] MP, fo. 81ᵛ. Raymund of Peñafort, *Summa*, iii, tit. 'De penitentiis et remissionibus', sect. 63, pp. 494–5; Hostiensis, *SA*, cols. 1483–90.

[49] The author claims to have set down the cases 'quatenus ad presens occurrere michi potuit', MP, fo. 90ʳ.

[50] Excluding *Sext*. 3. 23. 3, 'Clericis Laicos', and 5. 12. 3, 'Exiit qui seminat'; both were obsolete, the latter being suspended in 1322.

[51] MP, fo. 15ᵣᵃ. On the slow reception of John XXII's decrees, see Boyle, 'Curriculum', 159–60.

[52] *Extravag. Comm.*, 5. 10. 4. MP, b. lxxxx.   [53] MP, fo. 94ʳ. *CS*, ii. 911.

province, probably as a result of a statute of the Council of London of 1309, ordering regular publication of the papal and English excommunications included Clement V's 'Quia nonnulli' as its latest papal excommunication.[54]

The final section of the work as originally envisaged consists of general information and exhortation (b. lxxxxvii). There follows the addendum, discussed above, on the procedure to be observed in the burial of a pregnant woman.

The Distinctive Character of the Treatise

The two outstanding characteristics of the *Memoriale* are its puritanical and legalistic approach to penance—as evidenced principally by the author's emphasis on the canonical penances and on the overriding necessity of restitution as a prerequisite of absolution in cases where the obligation has arisen—and its concern with social vices. The social dimension will be explored in detail in Chapters 5 to 11. The general rigourism may be more briefly considered.

A much larger proportion of the work is devoted to the two topics of canonical penance and restitution than in any of either the continental or English treatises within the genre. Evidently the emphasis is an idiosyncrasy of the author, and it is linked on both counts with another idiosyncrasy, his distrust of mendicant confessors.[55] The association is suggestive of deeply rooted convictions whose origins may plausibly be traced to the tradition described above. One feature of that tradition is the extent to which it was indebted for its later evolution to canon lawyers. It may not be altogether fanciful to suppose that the laxity which the author of the *Memoriale* and FitzRalph, among others, alleged to be a feature of the confessional practice of the friars might in part at least have been a reflection of a different approach to penance, an intrusion, informally, of moral theology into the judicial forum. The hypothesis requires caution in view of the unexceptionable doctrine

---

[54] For the statute of the Council of London, see *CS*, ii. 1274–7. For the possible influence of this statute on William of Pagula, see Boyle, 'A Study', i. 329–30. No text of the complete compendium is known at present. Knowledge of it derives from Robert of Finingham (*c.*1320–50). Cf. Boyle, 'A Study' i. 330–3. Cambridge University Library MS. Dd. vii. 14, fos. 7ʳ–9ᵛ, which is probably associated with it (cf. Boyle, 'A Study', i, and *CS*, ii. 1275, n. 1), does not contain the papal excommunications and therefore cannot represent its full content. (I owe my introduction to this matter to Professor Boyle, 'A Study', i, and by communication.)

[55] See below, Chapter 12.

presented by Raymund of Peñafort (a Dominican and canonist)
and John of Freiburg (a Dominican and theologian) in the thirteenth
century, and in view of the strong—indeed rigid—attachment to the
canonical penances evinced by the Franciscan Marchesino di Reggio
d'Emilia.[56] However, if the critics' complaints in this respect are not
to be dismissed as merely partisan, and they are too numerous and
consistent to be disposed of summarily, there may be some merit
in advancing a corrective to the motive commonly ascribed to mendicant confessors,[57] even though the hypothesis can be no more than
tentative.

The strength of the *Memoriale*'s attachment to the canonical penances may be one part of the explanation of its independence of the
Summula prescribed by Bishop Quinel for Exeter diocese in 1287.[58]
Its silence as regards Quinel's important statutes for Exeter diocese,
which influenced Grandisson himself,[59] may readily be explained by
the evident address of the treatise as transmitted in the manuscripts
to a readership within Canterbury province as a whole.[60] The same
consideration would explain its preferring Pecham's syllabus over
Quinel's *Summula* as a source of dogmatic matter.[61] However, its ignor-
ing a treatise which—if the argument for provenance is accepted—the
author must have known or to which, at all events, his circle would
have directed his attention, may be highly significant. The *Summula*
patronized by Quinel presents the penance to be assigned by the confessor as wholly at his discretion, when regard is had to the circumstances.[62] While the alternative claims of canonical authority and
moderating judgement had been a dilemma from early in the tradition

---

[56] For Marchesino's rigidity, see his *Confessionale*, 60. The *Summa* of the Franciscan,
Astesanus de Asti, written in 1317 is another example cautioning against neat categorization
on the point. It contains a list of the penitential canons which, though shorter and less elaborate than that of Marchesino, was influential, eventually achieving a separate status from
the *Summa* and even being printed separately. Cf. Michaud-Quantin, *Sommes*, 59.

[57] See e.g. Chaucer, *Canterbury Tales*, ed. F. N. Robinson (London, 1966), I. (A) 221–2:

> Ful swetely herde he confessioun,
> And plesaunt was his absolucioun,
> He was an esy man to yeve penaunce,
> Ther as he wiste to have a good pitaunce.

[58] See *CS*, ii. 1018. Cf. ibid. 1077. Quinel adopted rather than wrote the treatise. See
J. Goering and D. S. Taylor, 'The *Summulae* of Bishops Walter de Cantilupe (1240) and
Peter Quinel (1287)', *Speculum*, 67 (1992), 576–94.

[59] See above, p. 52.

[60] Its 'local' legislation does not descend below provincial level.

[61] Cf. above, p. 73.   [62] See *CS*, ii. 1075.

of new penitential writing, as the case of Robert of Flamborough illustrates, Quinel's stance could hardly go further in its concession to the capacity of the individual confessor. The *Memoriale*, by contrast, while recognizing that the penance will be discretionary where no canonical penance exists,[63] and while tolerating some flexibility in application,[64] both teaches explicitly that the canonical penance is to be preferred (other penance being stigmatized as false),[65] and by exhaustive listing reinforces that preference solidly. So pronounced is the concern that it is tempting to suggest that the emphasis may even have been a corrective to Quinel's approach of which, in the abstract certainly, the author strongly disapproved.

By contrast, the *Memoriale*'s apparently complete independence of the works of William of Pagula is undoubtedly to be ascribed rather to lack of access to them than to choice. The *Prima Pars Oculi*, the last section of the *Oculus Sacerdotis* to be written, dates from 1326–8.[66] This and the *Summa Summarum* (1319–22) would have provided the author on several points with superior legal reference than that he had available. Though his emphasis as regards penitential discipline clearly differs from Pagula's—principally as regards the social dimension of interrogation, the level of guidance on restitution, and, once more, the primacy of the canonical penance[67]—there can be no doubt that he would have benefited from Pagula's superior scholarship, of whose initiative he may have known, but whose writings he cannot have had to hand.

Literary Affinities of the *Memoriale Presbiterorum*

The concentration on class and occupational behaviour from a pastoral perspective, which is already marked in the thought of Peter the Chanter and his circle[68] and which, in professional terms, was continued particularly within thirteenth-century canonist writing, is closely related to wider literary developments. Unsurprisingly, and with overt pastoral purpose, it is paralleled in certain strands of the literature of vices

---

[63] MP, fo. 31vb.   [64] Ibid., fo. 31va.

[65] Ibid., fos. 31va, 55^r–v.   [66] See Boyle, 'The Oculus', 106.

[67] William of Pagula holds that priests should know the canonical penances (of which he lists fifty-seven) in order to have an idea of what is appropriate, but the actual imposition is at the discretion of the confessor, who should adjust as necessary in individual circumstances. 'Oculus Sacerdotis': Oxford, New College MS. 292, fos. 2^r–3^v, 13^r–16^v. The emphasis is quite different from that of the *Memoriale Presbiterorum*, and the proportion assumed by the topic is of a wholly lesser order.

[68] See esp. Baldwin, *Masters*.

and virtues. Its effect is evident, for instance, in the *Somme le Roi*, and in the treatises that translate and derive from it, of which the *Speculum Vitae* has been specially mentioned. At a more general level of development—putatively the most influential—is comprised the literature of satire and complaint, where the object is as often to provoke reform as to deride or to entertain.[69] The outflow from penitential literature to the literature of complaint can be seen in the *De Planctu Ecclesiae* of the Portuguese Franciscan Alvarus Pelagius, written *c.*1330 at the papal curia, where the author was for a time major penitentiary.[70] Its second book (to which the title really applies) is divided into ninety-three *articuli*, of which thirty-six concern the responsibilities and failings of the various offices and classes, ecclesiastical and secular. The *De Planctu* owed much to the Bolognese tradition in this matter, and to Hostiensis's *Summa Aurea* in particular. In turn, it is a source of the *Septuplum* of the canonist John Acton, which among the pastoral manuals of fourteenth-century England most resembles the *Memoriale Presbiterorum* in its focus on the social context of sin.[71]

Reciprocity between the moral and satirical dimensions[72] is evident on the level of content even when, as usually, it is impatient of demonstration on the level of direct influence. The effect is various. At times, as in the case of *Piers Plowman*, the moral and satirical combine in the same work in such a way as to make them impossible to disentangle. In other cases, as in that of Chaucer[73] or in some of the so-called political songs,[74] the satirical perspective is overt and dominant. For England, the interaction has been explored most extensively in relation to sermon literature.[75] The *Memoriale Presbiterorum* both

---

[69] For a general survey and categorization, see J. Coleman, *English Literature in History 1350–1400: Medieval Readers and Writers* (London, 1981), 60–156.

[70] Alvarus Pelagius, *De Planctu Ecclesiae* (Lyons, 1517).

[71] See Haren, 'Social Ideas', 48–9.

[72] See B. Smalley, *The Study of the Bible in the Middle Ages*, 3rd edn. (Oxford, 1983), 245.

[73] An enlightening investigation of Chaucer's rapport with moral and moralizing literature is found in J. Mann, *Chaucer and Medieval Estates Satire: The Literature of Classes and the General Prologue to the Canterbury Tales* (Cambridge, 1973).

[74] See J. R. Maddicott, 'Poems of Social Protest in Early Fourteenth-Century England', in Ormrod, *England*, 130–44; G. Kane, 'Some Fourteenth-Century "Political" Poems', in G. Kratzmann and J. Simpson (eds.), *Medieval English Religious and Ethical Literature: Essays in Honour of G. H. Russell* (Cambridge, 1986), 82–91; J. Taylor, *English Historical Literature in the Fourteenth Century* (Oxford, 1987), 236–56.

[75] Owst, *Literature and Pulpit*. Cf. H. Leith Spencer, *English Preaching in the Late Middle Ages* (Oxford, 1993), esp. 65–8. For recent evaluation of the social teaching and criticisms of clerical commentators in general, see S. H. Rigby, *English Society in the Later Middle Ages: Class, Status and Gender* (London, 1995), 306–16.

indicates another point of pastoral contact by which the sensibilities of contemporaries to social vice might be roused and poses a recurring conundrum of the interaction between moral and satirical: how far do these perspectives reflect one another and how far the real world?[76] In a sense, of course, the real world is moulded by their perceptions: an exaggerated or distorted idea of the abuses prevalent in society can have an importance only vaguely related to the actual extent of the abuses: witness in near-contemporary context the agitation over papal provisions. However, an answer to the question as posed must be at least an aspiration of historical inquiry. The fact that, as a review of the classes of society from a strictly professional perspective, the *Memoriale* has close affinities with the literature of satire and complaint must be remembered in evaluating its social content. The following account of its views will attempt to set them in context and control them by reference to the documentary record and to the legislative and moralistic tradition, and through comparison with other critics. The treatise's correspondence with contemporary conditions and its assessment of those conditions have each a historical interest.

[76] For remarks on the problem in relation to the 'political' songs, see Maddicott, 'Poems', 140 and in relation to literary works in general, see R. H. Hilton, *The English Peasantry in the Later Middle Ages* (Oxford, 1975), 20–1.

5

Society Under Scrutiny I:
The Examination of Court Personnel
and Ecclesiastical Administrators

Society Under Scrutiny

The interest of the author of the *Memoriale Presbiterorum* in social behaviour is evinced mainly in two sections of the treatise, as they have been distinguished in Chapter 4: under the heads of the interrogation of the penitent according to his or her status, and of the obligation of restitution as it falls on different categories of penitent, whether in terms of status or of sins committed. In the treatise, the *ad status* section opens, 'beginning from the part of greater dignity',[1] with two chapters on regular clergy—one on simple religious and a second on regular office-holders—followed by two on secular clergy, clerics, and priests. There are then surveyed in sequence: officers of ecclesiastical administration (officials and rural deans); lawyers (advocates and proctors); seneschals and bailiffs of secular jurisdiction; knights; merchants and burgesses; servants (the questions asked dictate this translation of *servientes* here, though at its recurrence, under the head of restitution,[2] the term may alternatively or in addition mean 'sergeants'); sailors (apparently a unique occurrence in confessional literature); villeins; married women; and children (with whom the section on interrogation concludes).[3] Several of these types recur in the section on restitution, which also considers types related to them (such as a variety of other court personnel) and types not specifically introduced in the section on interrogation. So, under the head of restitution are discussed, among others: temporal lords who burden their subjects with tallages and exactions (b. xxxviii); peasants who withdraw from their lords services due and customary (b. xxxix);

---

[1] 'a parte digniori incipiendo': MP, fo. 13rb.   [2] Ibid., fo. 68rb.
[3] For the text (with translation) of the main part of this section, see Haren, 'The Interrogatories'.

archdeacons and their servants (b. xlv); officials and correctors who impose pecuniary penances (b. xlvi); the collectors of procurations of a papal legate or nuncio (b. xlvii); lay bailiffs who invade the goods of churches (b. xlviii); judges, ecclesiastical and secular (b. xlix); assessors and counsellors of judges (b. l); apparitors, bedells, and other servants of judges (b. li); bailiffs and sergeants of magnates (b. lii); physicians (b. liii); advocates (b. liiii); false and corrupt witnesses (b. lv); accusers and denouncers of crimes (b. lvi); those who enact unjust statutes (b. lvii); religious who occupy and illicitly consume goods deposited with them (b. lxi); and pardoners (b. lxx). In addition, under this head, are considered various technical moral cases, several of which go back to the days of Peter the Chanter and all of which had received extensive elaboration from the thirteenth-century canonist tradition, particularly in the *Summa Aurea* of Hostiensis, the principal source of the *Memoriale*'s treatment. These problem cases include: prelates alienating the goods of their churches (b. xxix); the salaries of the harlot and actor (b. xxxii); supposititious birth (b. xxxiii); occupation of wreck (b. xxxiiii); looting in time of fire (b. xxxv); the obligations of a maître d'hôtel in respect of his guests' property (b. xxxvi); and the especially detailed analysis of questions arising from seizure of goods in war (b. xl–xliv).[4]

It will be evident that the sequence of the topics dealt with under restitution is less structured than that of the interrogatories. If, as is possible, this is a sign of haste in the writing of this part of the treatise, there is no stinting in the treatment accorded to the topics once introduced: the section on restitution occupies about one-quarter of the whole and represents the most thorough review of the subject in the medieval English didactic tradition. Restitution is of its nature a socially orientated dimension of morality. The review of the treatise's social doctrine here and in the following six chapters, under the general heading in each case of examination, merges the content of the section on restitution with that of the section on interrogation, whose more orderly classification it broadly follows, except that the treatment of clerics is moved from pride of place in favour of giving prominence to the author's more pronounced idiosyncrasies (chief of which is his concern with administrative malpractice and the vices of officialdom), and that, in the interests of economy, a small miscellany of penitents has had to be artificially grouped together.

---

[4] See above, p. 64, n. 154.

The Examination of Court Personnel and
Ecclesiastical Administrators

That men of law were generally slaves to avarice was an axiom of the literature of complaint. An *exemplum* of Jacques de Vitry consigns advocates to the company of Nero in an infernal bath of gold.[5] In Peter Cantor's *Verbum Abbreviatum* they are dealt with immediately after usurers, as being 'in cupidity, a like class of men':[6]

This class of men antiquity reproves, not only for their cupidity but also for the worthlessness of their office. For, as pugilists, runners, heralds, and officials of this type were worthless and abject, so too advocates; for no one became an advocate except as a remedy for his poverty, so that he might secure livelihood by his office. Today, too, this class of men is most to be reprehended for cupidity and negligence.[7]

John Gower saw an analogy between the advocate and the prostitute, 'que nisi sit donum nescit amare virum',[8] and Langland imagined that:

> Men of lawe lest pardoun hadde • that pleteden for mede,
> For the sauter saveth hem nouȝte • suche as taketh ȝiftes,
> And namelich of innocenz • that none yvel ne kunneth.[9]

It was explicitly with an eye to the composition of his audience that Richard FitzRalph, expounding the Lord's Prayer during a general procession in London, developed the petition 'Give us this day our daily bread' into an argument against unjust gain, whether in war, in the market, or in court:

And especially on account of the narrators and advocates present, it was shown that they eat the bread of others when they receive more than another, equally learned, though inferior in opportunity, should wish to receive. Of every such it was proved that they affirm 'Give us our bread' without reason, for the bread is not theirs. So it was said of others who do justice, receiving for it a reward, since what is thus received is not theirs, for nothing ought to be given in return for justice.[10]

The criticisms of outsiders to the legal profession, civil, common, or ecclesiastical, tended to be confined to generalities. Canonists were

---

[5] *The Exempla or Illustrative Stories from the Sermones Vulgares of Jacques de Vitry*, ed. T. F. Crane, Folklore Society, (1890), p. 14, c. xxxvi.

[6] *PL*, ccv. 159.

[7] Ibid., 160. For these and other critics, cf. Baldwin, *Masters*, i. 193; ii. 131.

[8] John Gower, *Vox Clamantis*, vi, cap. 1, 1. 44 (ed. Macauley, p. 231).

[9] William Langland, *Piers Plowman*, ed. Skeat, B. vii, 38–40.

[10] 'Sermons', Oxford, Bodleian Library, MS. Bodley 144, fos. 40ᵛ–41ʳ.

more specific. 'This would be most difficult,' says Joannes de Deo, 'to narrate all the excesses of advocates; yet I . . . an ancient doctor of decrees, will do a little and narrate those things of which posterity should beware.'[11] By the beginning of the fourteenth century, following the *Summa* of Hostiensis and the *Speculum Juris* of William Durandus,[12] the six sins which John enumerated had given way to a thorough examination of the technicalities of injustice.[13] The *De Planctu Ecclesiae* of Alvarus Pelagius, in part an adaptation of Hostiensis's exposition, surveyed minutely the offences of advocates, counsel and assessors, proctors, witnesses, accusers, notaries, and judges (of whom he listed over seventy sins, providing thereby an excellent *via negativa* exposition of the duties and requirements of the office).[14]

The concern of the *Memoriale Presbiterorum* with legal officials is untypical of English confessional manuals, as indeed is its intensive examination of the classes in general. As has been noted in Chapter 4, it is dependent for much of the material of its interrogations on the *Summa Aurea* of Hostiensis. There is ample indication, however, that the author had a personal interest in the shortcomings of the legal profession. While his treatment of advocates,[15] witnesses,[16] and delators of crimes[17] is based on his source, his article on archdeacons and their ministers[18] has no model in Hostiensis and is a consideration of a class much neglected in the *Summae Confessorum*. In addition, while his interrogation of officials and rural deans[19] owes something to Hostiensis, it appears largely to be a contribution of the author, and his treatment of the assessors and counsellors of judges,[20] and of apparitors,[21] though suggested by Hostiensis, contains much apparently original comment. Many of the points with which he deals had been the subject of legislation by popes, by provincial and diocesan synods, and by prelates in framing regulations for their own courts.

One feature of the author's examination of those involved in the exercise of ecclesiastical jurisdiction is his concentration on the 'small fry'—the executives rather than the principals. It will be seen that this

---

[11] Joannes de Deo, *Liber Poenitentiarius* (*PL*, xcix), 1105–6.

[12] See above, pp. 70–2. Guillelmus Durandus, *Speculum Juris* (Frankfurt, 1592).

[13] On the more general literary perceptions of forensic corruption, see J. Aberth, *Criminal Churchmen in the Age of Edward III: The Case of Bishop Thomas de Lisle* (University Park, Pa., 1996), 85–93.

[14] Alvarus Pelagius, *De Planctu Ecclesiae*, art. 35–41 (ed. Lyons, 1517, fos. 141ᵛ–145ʳ).

[15] MP, a. xxxiv ('Circa advocatos et procuratores'), b. liv. ('De advocatis').

[16] Ibid., b. lv.   [17] Ibid., b. lvi.   [18] Ibid., b. xlv.

[19] Ibid., a. xxxiii.   [20] Ibid., b. l.   [21] Ibid., b. li.

is also a characteristic of his treatment of secular administration and
one shared with other contemporary critics. Grandisson's strong sense
of the personal responsibility of office-holders and his vigilance over
their shortcomings has already been noted.[22] If this was the source of
the author's bias, there is wider evidence from late-medieval administration to justify it. The dispute in which Archbishop Arundel acted
as a mediator in 1401 between the archdeacon of Ely and Bishop John
Fordham offers details of 'forms of corruption and maladministration
among the archdeacon's ministers which have significance beyond the
particular circumstances at Ely: it confirms . . . with specific examples
. . . the bad character which is normally ascribed to these administrators.'[23] Grandisson's mandate of 1333 requiring rural deans to
exercise their office personally rather than commit their functions to
inadequate deputies gives an insight both into the delegation of authority at a relatively humble level and into the occasion for malpractice
that it might afford.[24]

    While much of what the *Memoriale* has to say could as well apply
to the officers of higher jurisdictions, its comments do seem to be best
understood with reference to inferior courts in which, as Maitland put
it, 'you will get inferior law'.[25] Its interrogation of 'the officials of
bishops or of archdeacons or their deans'[26] would seem to be most aptly
directed to the latter two categories: 'First you [sc. the confessor] shall
say this: "Have you heard the laws, civil and canon, so that you shall
know to judge justly in each and every ecclesiastical case?", for he who
is ignorant of the laws deals perilously and acts against his conscience,
if he presumes to take up the office of judgment, and thus heads for
hell.'[27] The query finds an echo at a later period in Lyndwood's comments on these very classes: 'for commonly these rural deans are inex-
pert and ignorant of the law'[28] and 'for commonly these officials have
little expertise in the law'.[29] Similarly, the *Memoriale*'s criticism of
judges[30] seems hardly appropriate to the highly professional personnel

----

[22] See above, p. 51.   [23] M. Aston, *Thomas Arundel* (Oxford, 1967), 89.
[24] *RG*, ii. 713.
[25] F. W. Maitland, *Roman Canon Law in the Church of England* (Cambridge, 1898), p. 43.
[26] MP, a. xxxiii.   [27] Ibid., fo. 19ᵛ.
[28] Lyndwood, *Provinciale*, lib. ii, tit.i, p. 79, gloss *ad vocem* 'audire presumant'.
[29] Ibid. 81, gloss *ad vocem* 'committatur'.
[30] 'Nonnulli eciam talium iudicum, iura penitus ignorantes, officiis maxime ecclesiasticis,
circa quod et in quibus maius vertitur periculum anime, se immiscent et sentencias iniquas
et iniustas ferunt, eo quod iura per que debent suas consciencias informare numquam audierunt
vel intellexerunt, et sic plerosque ledunt minus iuste.' MP, fos. 66ᵛ–67ʳ.

of the upper strata of ecclesiastical administration at this period. Even
when applied to the officials of archdeacons, however, there is some
evidence to suggest that such criticism requires qualification, though
little enough is known of the personnel at this level. The official of the
archdeacon of Cornwall in 1328, who drew Grandisson's ire by refusing to render a sum of six marks seized from certain false pardoners
of the Holy Sepulchre, was Master Richard de Chuddele.[31] Of the
officials of the Worcester archdeaconries in the first half of the century, it has been observed that most of them were entitled 'magister'
and their professional character is apparent.[32] Some of them graduated
into episcopal service and others were employed as ad hoc commissaries of the bishop.[33] At Winchester during Adam Orleton's episcopacy the three men styled 'official of the archdeacon of Winchester'
are all given the title 'master',[34] though there is no external evidence
to justify it. Of eight officials of the archdeacons of Ely between 1374
and 1382, all were masters,[35] though their professional character probably owes something to the fact that there was a university in the
diocese, just as the presence of the university of Oxford in Lincoln diocese meant that the officials of the bishop's administration tended to
be national rather than local in their backgrounds.[36] The fact, however,
that at Ely two of the archdeacons' officials acted at the same time as
advocates in the bishop's court is 'significant of the differences in
status and qualifications demanded' of officers in the higher and lower
jurisdictions.[37] At Norwich there appears, too, to be a preponderance
of masters among those archdeacons' officials whose names we know.[38]
The five identifiable archdeacons' officials in Salisbury diocese during
Mortival's pontificate (John de Tarent, Robert de Shirwode, John Legh,
Thomas de Hamme, and Robert de Ayleston) are all entitled 'master'.[39]
Ayleston went on to a distinguished career in royal service, becoming

---

[31] *RG*, i. 426–7.   [32] Haines, *Worcester*, 43.

[33] See ibid. 40–3, for an outline of what is known of these officials in the diocese.

[34] See R. M. Haines, 'Adam Orleton and the Diocese of Winchester', *JEH* 23 (1972), 20;
id., *The Church and Politics in Fourteenth-Century England: The Career of Adam Orleton*
(Cambridge, 1978).

[35] See Aston, *Thomas Arundel*, 108 n.

[36] See C. Morris, 'A Consistory Court in the Middle Ages', *JEH* 14 (1963), 153.

[37] See Aston, *Thomas Arundel*, 108 n., where the question of the experience of lower legal
officials is discussed.

[38] Of ten officials listed for the several archdeaconries, 1315–75, by F. Blomefield, *An Essay
towards a Topographical History of the County of Norfolk* (London, 1806), iii. 659–61, eight
appear to be Masters.

[39] See *Reg. Mortival*, i. 288; ii. 194–6, 434–5; iii. 99, 152 n.

keeper of the privy seal.[40] John de Belvoir, William Doune's official in the archdeaconry of Leicester, would powerfully serve to deter generic condemnation were it not that one might suppose him to have been chosen with particular care.[41]

Archdeacons' officials are named relatively seldom in episcopal registers, and indeed the impression which emerges from the lists that can be compiled, incomplete as they are, may well be distorted, for one might expect the more distinguished of the class to find personal mention more readily. Still, what we know of them from this source suggests that they were often more highly trained than their critics would lead one to suppose. On the other hand, while deputies of such officials are not named, there are occasional indications that they existed.[42]

Again, though a bishop's register may sometimes afford the names of rural deans, little information may be forthcoming about their qualifications. Eleven persons are named as holding rural deaneries in Rochester diocese during the episcopate of Hamo Hethe. None of them is entitled 'master'. But the fact that the dean of Malling, Bartholomew de Crowthorne (1349), is found to take the place of the commissary of the official of Rochester in the consistory court, on two occasions—in May 1347 and October 1348—implies a degree of professional competence.[43] On the debit side, we find that John de Carletone, rural dean of Rochester, in May 1332 is given two days to answer the charge of having pronounced certain persons excommunicate, 'having omitted the order of law, without first giving the canonical warning or having specified the cause and without having reduced it to writing'.[44] We do not know whether the charge was justified. Nor do we know the offence for which John Aylbern, dean of Isleham, was in January 1332 inhibited by the bishop's commissary from the office of advocate in divorce cases, under penalty of 100 shillings, to be distributed in alms by the bishop.[45] Rural deans, as we shall see, did not have power of judgment in marriage cases, and it is interesting to find that they should have appeared as advocates in a higher court, as the officials of the archdeacons did at Ely.[46]

Restrictions imposed by bishops on the judicial powers of inferior courts are a recurring feature of thirteenth-century local legislation. It

---

[40] See *BRUO*, i. 83.   [41] See Haren, 'Will', 123, and below, pp. 209–10.
[42] See *Reg. Mortival*, i. 268, for the *locum tenens* of the official of the archdeacon of Salisbury (1319).
[43] See *Reg. Hethe*, ii. pp. xx, 911.   [44] Ibid., i. 475–6.
[45] Ibid. 467.   [46] Aston, *Thomas Arundel*, 108 n.

is in one respect part of a trend towards increasing centralization, but it also reflects—as is shown by the frequent distinction between the matters to be handled by archdeacons on the one hand and rural deans on the other—a lack of confidence in the capacity of these courts, particularly those of rural deans, to handle certain highly sensitive cases. Bishop Richard Poore's synodal statutes for Salisbury (1217 × 1219) forbade the determination of a doubtful marriage case by an archdeacon, 'dean', or priest without consultation with the bishop.[47] It is not clear whether this is to be interpreted as implying competence when there was no doubt in the case,[48] but much more definite rulings were to follow. Though the Council of Oxford did not mention archdeacons in this context, it inhibited rural deans from hearing any marriage case in future, 'since in matrimonial cases great discretion is necessary, for which reason it is dangerous for them to be handled by the simple'.[49] As Lyndwood explains it, this is to be interpreted to the effect that they may not do so 'by reason of their office or on pretext of any custom'.[50] The anonymous statutes issued shortly afterwards did deal with archdeacons; while following Oxford in forbidding rural deans to examine any kind of marriage case, they allowed archdeacons or their officials to do so except where there was question of a divorce, in which event only the bishop or his deputy could act.[51] As for those who took cognizance of marriage cases 'nomine proprio',[52] the legatine Council of London (1237) stipulated simply that where abbots, archdeacons, or 'deans' had cognizance of these 'by privilege or approved custom', they should not proceed to a definitive sentence before first deliberating with the bishop of the diocese and obtaining his opinion.[53] The 'deans' of this ruling are not rural deans, already debarred by the Oxford legislation, but deans of a major church.[54] Certainly, William Raleigh's statutes for Norwich (1240 × 1243) made no concession in this respect to custom as regards rural deans ('decani vel subdecani'); they were not to handle or terminate matrimonial or criminal cases except by

---

[47] *CS*, ii. 85, c. 78.

[48] See J. Foster, 'The Activities of Rural Deans in England in the Twelfth and Thirteenth Centuries', Manchester University, MA thesis, 1955, p. 69, who thinks that it probably does not imply such competence.

[49] *CS*, ii. 113, c. 25.

[50] Lyndwood, *Provinciale*, ii, tit. i, p. 79(b), gloss *ad vocem* 'audire presumant'.

[51] *CS*, ii. 147, c. 42.

[52] See the explanation of this by Lyndwood, *Provinciale*, ii, tit. 1, p. 81 (a), gloss *ad vocem* 'pronuncietur'.

[53] *CS*, ii. 255–6, c. 23.   [54] See Acton, *Commentary*, 59 (b), *ad vocem* 'decani'.

special grant of the bishop,[55] while his statutes for Winchester (1247), which probably preceded an agreement as to the respective jurisdictions of himself and the archdeacon of Surrey,[56] forbade not only deans ('decani nostre diocesis') but archdeacons and their officials to handle or terminate matrimonial or testamentary cases, or criminal or civil cases involving deposition or deprivation of benefice, 'or other cases particularly pertaining to our cognizance'.[57] However, in the agreement which followed with the archdeacon, limited rights were conceded to the latter in matrimonial cases.[58] His arrangement was repeated by his successor,[59] and externally has a parallel in William Bitton's statutes for Wells (1258).[60]

The reiteration of this legislation may be a comment on its efficacy, and there is a suggestion that in the late thirteenth century at least the rural dean might exercise a *de facto* matrimonial jurisdiction despite the prohibitions, with the consent of the parties.[61] However, such defiance can hardly have been widespread, for restrictive legislation of the type detailed above seems to peter out in the mid-thirteenth-century and is not a feature in the later decades. The author of the *Memoriale* does not make it clear whether he regards rural deans as having matrimonial jurisdiction. A question regarding unjust judgments, particularly in a matrimonial case, is included in his interrogation of officials and rural deans,[62] but it may well be intended for the former, though in view of the fact that he is otherwise sensitive to the mishandling of matrimonial business,[63] he might have been expected to be more specific in the present instance. Nor is it apparent whether the officials whom he has in mind on this count are those of bishops or of archdeacons; they are examined jointly.[64]

The author of the *Memoriale* is in fact concerned with a variety of injustices in the exercise of office rather than with these fundamental questions of jurisdiction. The abuses with which he deals can be documented, occasionally by actual examples and frequently from episcopal and provincial statutes. Varying forms of extortion bulk large among the offences of which he complains, particularly by archdeacons on their visitations,[65] lending substance to Hamilton Thompson's view that their

---

[55] *CS*, ii. 353, c. 51.   [56] See ibid. 413, n. 4.   [57] Ibid. 413, c. 68.
[58] Ibid. 413, n. 4.   [59] Ibid. 718, c. 78.   [60] Ibid. 608, c. 40.
[61] Foster, 'Activities', 70.   [62] MP, fo. 20ʳ.   [63] See below, p. 104.
[64] MP, a. xxxiii.   [65] See the passage cited, above pp. 14–15.

activity in the later middle ages had become little more than 'a money raising exercise'.[66]

In his complaint about the equipage of archdeacons on visitation[67] the author had an eye to legislation. The Third Lateran Council, in an attempt to curtail the 'burdensome household' of visiting prelates, had laid down in detail the maximum number of horses that might accompany them: in the case of archdeacons, five or seven, and in the case of deans, two. Those who customarily used less were not to increase the number. Hunting-dogs and hawks were forbidden.[68] The ruling was referred to by the Council of Oxford.[69] The measure was, of course, aimed at reducing the expenses of the progress and was related to another matter—itself the subject of much legislation—the system of procuration, whereby in theory the costs of the visitation were recovered and which in practice constituted a source of profit to the visitor. Though there were several important supplementary rulings, some of which attempted to fix the maximum procuration which a visitor might receive, according to his dignity—in the same way that an attempt had been made to fix the number of his household—the basic law on the subject was that of the Fourth Lateran Council, which, while confirming that the visitor was entitled to receive sustenance, stipulated that procurations should not be burdensome, that they were due only to a prelate visiting in person, and that one was to suffice per day.[70] This regulation and the restriction on the size of the household were repeated, with reference specifically to archdeacons' visitations, by Bishop Poore in his statutes for Salisbury (1217 × 1219).[71] Chapter 20 of the legatine Council of London (1237), dealing with the duties of archdeacons, decreed that they should exact only moderate procurations and should take with them only a modest household and a modest number of horses. They should not accept bribes nor commit extortion under penalty of double restitution to pious uses, at the bishop's will.[72] This general exhortation to restraint was rehearsed in the statutes for Chichester diocese (1245 × 1252).[73] However, in July 1252, as a result of an appeal

---

[66] Thompson, *English Clergy*, 63; cf. id., 'Diocesan Organization in the Middle Ages, Archdeacons and Rural Deans', *Proceedings of the British Academy*, 29 (1943), 153–5. The continued vigour of the rural chapter at this time has been ascribed to the profits which it generated, see J. Scammell, 'The Rural Chapter in England from the Eleventh to the Fourteenth Century', *EHR* 86 (1971), 2.

[67] See above, p. 14.   [68] X. 3. 39. 6.   [69] *CS*, ii. 114, c. 27.

[70] X. 3. 39. 23.   [71] *CS*, ii. 93, c. 104.   [72] Ibid. 254. Cf. *MP*, fo. 65[rb].

[73] *CS*, ii. 457–8, c. 34, p. 23.

by the suffragans of Archbishop Boniface, Innocent IV issued a decretal which went beyond the ruling of the Lateran Council in that it specified that the procurations of visiting prelates—including archdeacons as well as archbishops and bishops—were in no case to exceed the sum of four marks.[74] It was this 'new constitution' which Bishop William Bitton required archdeacons to observe, in his statutes for Bath and Wells, a few years later,[75] and it was probably what Bishop Giles of Bridport had in mind when he condemned an attempt by archdeacons to augment the procuration allowed them in the canons by requesting lodgings out of charity.[76] There do not appear to be any further references to the measure in English legislation, and indeed it was in conflict with another decretal of the same pope, included in the *Sext*, forbidding visitors to receive their procurations in money.[77] The latter was confirmed by Gregory X, who added that they might not even receive a procuration in victuals from places which they did not actually visit.[78] Boniface VIII, however, did allow the visitor to receive the procuration in money, but forbade him to receive more than one per day, even though he visited several places.[79] For the later period, the maximum amount of procurations was regulated by Benedict XII's detailed constitution on the subject, issued in 1336. This dealt with the procurations of visiting prelates in the four traditional 'national' areas of western christendom, the French, German, Spanish, and Italian, England being included, as usual, in the German 'nation'. In the case of archdeacons who visited in person, the maximum daily procuration was forty silver tournois, or ten in the case of archpriests, a term synonymous here with rural deans. In no case, it was stipulated, was anything further to be demanded, and if custom ordained a lesser payment, this was to remain unaffected by the constitution.[80] Prelates must moderate their expenses in keeping with the size and resources of a particular house, within the maximum limits set down. In the case of archdeacons who had a papal

---

[74] See *Annales Monastici*, ed. H. R. Luard, i (Rolls Series, 1864), 300–1.

[75] *CS*, ii. 613–14, c. 53.   [76] Ibid. 553, c. 4.   [77] *Sext.*, 3. 20. 1.

[78] Ibid. 2.   [79] Ibid. 3.

[80] The Council of London's constitution on the subject (1342), did not refer to Benedict XII's ruling and simply took the 'usual amount' as being the correct procuration. Thus, when visitors were accompanied by a number in excess of that laid down by the canons, those visited should be free to pay a procuration, in cash—at the 'usual' figure—or in victuals, which were more difficult to estimate. Dependent chapels were to be reckoned as included in the procuration for the mother church, which was liable at the rate normal for one church in the diocese. *Concilia*, ii. 698–9. For the authority of Benedict XII's decretal, see Lyndwood, *Provinciale*, iii, tit. 22, p. 221 (a), gloss *ad vocem* 'personaliter'.

privilege to visit by proxy and to receive procurations in ready money, the maximum amount was to be thirty silver tournois.[81] Such privileges are a common feature of the *Calendar of Papal Letters* in the fourteenth century, with the exception of the pontificate of John XXII, who appears to have pursued a policy of curtailing them.[82] They are usually granted for a period of three years, though the indult could be renewed. The privileges are of two kinds: where no mention was made of the procurations, they appear merely to have constituted a licence to the non-resident archdeacon—usually an alien—to discharge the duty of annual visitation by deputy; but the clause allowing the procurations to be collected is frequently included.[83] Limitation of the amount to be collected—that it should not exceed thirty silver tournois—seems to be an innovation of Benedict XII, though it appears shortly before the issue of the constitution, *Vas Electionis*.[84]

Grandisson's rigour on illicit receipt of procurations has been noted,[85] as has William Doune's personal sensitivity on the subject.[86] When abused, procurations constituted simply a form of taxation under cover of an approved system for the recovery of expenses. In the interrogation of officials and rural deans, the *Memoriale* deals with levies which had less specious claim: 'Item, have you ever imposed tallages on poor priests, perhaps for the enrichment of your household, and if they did not deliver to those to whom you wished, in accordance with your desire, did you aggrieve them in their goods or did you weary them with labours or cause them to be wearied?'[87] The subject of tallage is one met with occasionally in local legislation. In the early years of the thirteenth century the bishop of Worcester informed the dean of Gloucester that he had promulgated sentence of excommunication against those who exacted or paid six pence, 'nomine strenarum', in that archdeaconry, and inhibited him from making such exactions. They are described as being annual impositions on each church and chapel.[88] Twelve pence is the sum mentioned in a statute of Bishop Gervais of Winchester (1262 × 1265) condemning a similar exaction, 'which to conceal the depravity of simony . . . some fictitiously refer to as a gift, some indeed as archdeacon's pig'.[89]

---

[81] *Extravag. Commun.*, 3. 10. 'Vas electionis'.   [82] See *CPL*, ii. 440–1.
[83] For examples of the first type, see ibid. 24, 55, 57, 58, 60; and of the second type, see ibid. 33, 47, 68, 72, 81.
[84] See ibid. 531, 533, 536.   [85] See above, pp. 51–2, 54–5.
[86] See above, p. 16.   [87] MP, fo. 20rb.
[88] *CS*, ii. 115, n. 3.   [89] Ibid. 721–2.

Tallage by archdeacons, deans, and their officials was, in fact, forbidden by the Council of Oxford, which in this followed a ruling of
the Fourth Lateran Council.[90] Glossing the Oxford canon, Lyndwood
debates 'whether an archdeacon may exact anything from his subjects
by way of a charitable subsidy, in a case where he has not visited and
therefore could not have procurations?', and concludes that he may not,
'since archdeacons ought to make no exactions and exact no tallage from
their subjects to their own use'.[91]

Archdeacons' tallage was, of necessity, confined to clerics. Other
aspects of the 'money-raising exercise' had wider application. The section of the *Memoriale* devoted to restitution contains a chapter on officials
who inflict a corporal penance and then commute it to a pecuniary one,
thereby in effect tolerating the sin.[92] The abuse was satirized by Chaucer
—though specifically with reference to the lifting of excommunication—
in his portrait of the apparitor[93] (" "Purs is the ercedekenes helle" seyde
he"[94]), and the author of the 'Poem on the Evil Times of Edward II'
observes that:

> . . . thise ersedekenes that ben set to visit holi chirche,
> Everich fondeth hu he may shrewdelichest worche;
> He wole take mede of that on and that other,
> And late the parsoun have a wyf, and the prest another,
> At wille,
> Coveytise shal stoppen here mouth, and maken hem al stille.[95]

Elsewhere he complains of the corruption of officials and deans:

> Mak a present to the den ther thu thenkest to dwelle,
> And have leve longe i-nouh to serve the fend of helle to queme;
> For have he silver, of sinne taketh he nevere ȝeme.[96]

The distinction between simoniacal tolerance of sin and pecuniary
penance was a difficult one to maintain in practice. There is a well-
known story of Thomas Gascoigne that, when the clergy of the diocese of St Davids petitioned Bishop de la Bere (*c.*1452–3) to free them
from their concubines, he refused to do so on the grounds that he would

---

[90] Ibid. 115; cf. X. 3. 39. 6, and X. 5. 37. 3, the latter being a direction of Alexander III
that the archdeacons of Coventry cease unlawful exactions.
[91] Lyndwood, *Provinciale*, iii, tit. 22, p. 221 (a), gloss *ad vocem* 'pro visitatione'.
[92] MP, b. xlvi.   [93] *Canterbury Tales*, I(A), 649–50; 653–8.   [94] Ibid. 658.
[95] *Political Songs*, ed. Wright, 344, ll. 49–54; cf. ibid. ll. 192–210.
[96] Ibid., ll. 195–8.

thereby lose 400 marks, in that he received a noble each from the priests for having them.[97]

Pecuniary penance itself was only grudgingly accorded a place in corrective discipline by canon law, common and local, and by its interpreters. Innocent IV's decretal 'Venerabilibus' acknowledged an archbishop's right to impose fines 'in accordance with the custom of the region', 'in cases where he had power of excommunication'.[98] This was their sole explicit sanction in the decretal collections, and Joannes Andreae, being clearly hostile to the institution, interpreted restrictively.[99] The general canonical principle in regard to them equated the imposition of pecuniary penances with dispensation and confined their use to prelates exercising the latter power. Archdeacons were considered incapable of dispensing from a statutory, that is, a canonical, penalty and, where such existed, were therefore excluded from commuting it to a pecuniary one.[100] In the English context, Ottobuono's statute 'Deus Omnipotens'[101] forbade receipt of money by archdeacons for notorious mortal sin—the type, that is, of which judicial notice would be taken. John Acton interpreted his prohibition as referring to the receipt of money 'directly' (i.e. as a bribe for toleration) and 'indirectly' (to redeem the corporal penance inflicted),[102] but without commenting on the prevalence of either practice. However, while the strict letter of the law denied the power of commutation to archdeacons and, by implication, to inferior prelates, a concession to 'custom' was necessary even on the level of theory.[103] Two constitutions of Archbishop Stratford (1342–3)

---

[97] Thomas Gascoigne, *Loci e Libro Veritatum*, ed. J. E. T. Rogers (Oxford, 1881), 35–6. For systematic toleration at Ely (*c*.1375) see Aston, *Thomas Arundel*, 93, 279.

[98] *Sext.*, 5. 11. 7.

[99] 'Dum allegatur haec decretalis quod prelati ecclesiastici imponere et exigere possunt poenas pecuniarias, respondetur quod haec decretalis probat contrarium, cum de consuetudine dicat haec licere quasi non de iure.' Joannes Andreae, *Novella in Sextum* (ed. Venice, 1571), *ad* 5. 11. 7, fo. 163[vb]. For the general opinion of the canonists on pecuniary penance, see F. D. Logan, *Excommunication and the Secular Arm in Medieval England* (Toronto, 1968), 143–4.

[100] The best statement is by the fifteenth-century glossator, Nicholas de Tudeschis ('Abbas Siculus'), on X. 5. 37. 3: 'archidiaconi, qui in criminibus dispensare nequeunt, poenam pecuniariam imponere non possunt, ubi iure alia statuitur'; see *Corpus Iuris Canonici cum Glossis* (ed. Lyons, 1671), ii. col. 1856, *ad vocem* 'licet'. Where there was no statutory penalty, the penance was arbitrary, ibid. 1857, gloss *ad vocem*, 'penam pecuniariam'.

[101] *CS*, ii. 768–9.

[102] See Acton, *Commentary*, 116 (b), *ad voces* 'pecuniam recipiant', 'ab ipso delinquente'.

[103] Lyndwood, who recognized two preconditions for the imposition of pecuniary penance —that the judge must have power of dispensation over the crime and that even then discretion might be used only in *ex officio* proceedings, since where the interest of a third party

bore on the subject—'Accidit novitate perversa', which belongs to the series of canons actually published by him, in May 1343, and 'Quoniam reus', from the unpublished series.[104] The topic of 'Accidit novitate' was actually lay interference with ecclesiastical jurisdiction, and the matter of pecuniary penances was raised only incidentally, as one of the areas allegedly affected. Perhaps for this reason, its assertion of the legitimacy of their imposition and of the redemption of corporal penance was peculiarly forthright,[105] occasioning Lyndwood, when he came to gloss it, some difficulty in reconciling it with traditional opinion.[106] 'Quoniam reus', by contrast, was a measure of internal ecclesiastical control. It was severely critical of commutations, as being tantamount to the hiring of sin, and attempted to curb their use in the case of recidivists. Money was not to be taken beyond the second occasion for a notorious offence, under penalty of twofold restitution within a month to the fabric of the cathedral church and of suspension from office in case of defiance. Commutations of corporal penances were forbidden, unless for 'great and urgent cause'. On the other hand, local ordinaries were to see that they did not impose excessive corporal penances on delinquents so that the latter were compelled to redeem them 'causative et per obliquum', by a heavy sum. Such commutations, when they were made, were to be moderate.[107] This intended reform constituted only a partial restriction of the discretionary aspect, which otherwise remained, both as to the imposition of a fine and to its amount. Grandisson too was conscious of the difficulty. Although his consistorial reforms purported to insist on corporal rather than pecuniary penalties, he recognized that pressure from below might result in commutation.[108]

Pecuniary penances were, in fact, too useful a device to be abandoned, despite the obvious dangers. It has been shown that penances were not usually imposed on persons of dignity so as to ruin their social standing

was present, this must be satisfied by strict justice—pointed out that the first requirement excluded archdeacons, but made provision for the modifying force of 'consuetudo praescripta'; see *Provinciale*, 52 (a), gloss *ad vocem* 'poena canonica'; cf. ibid. 261 (b), *ad voces* 'juste poterunt', 'licet'.

[104] For these, respectively, see *Concilia*, ii. 707–8, 700; they are included in Lyndwood, *Provinciale*, 261–2 and 323, respectively. On the three series of constitutions elaborated by the Council of London, 1341–2, under Stratford, see Cheney, 'Legislation', 415–17; id., 'Textual Problems', 122; Bolton, 'Council of London of 1342', 147–60.

[105] It stated, without qualification, that ecclesiastics could licitly impose corporal or pecuniary penances on their subjects and justly commute corporal penances; see *Concilia*, ii. 707.

[106] Lyndwood, *Provinciale*, 261 (a), *ad vocem* 'licet'.

[107] *Concilia*, ii. 700.　　　　[108] See above, p. 53.

and hence their authority.[109] Glossing Stratford's requirement of an urgent cause for commutation, Lyndwood recognizes as such 'the fact that it is a noble person or such that his reputation would be greatly injured thereby [namely, by the infliction of a corporal penance], and that it would engender grave scandal, for the avoidance of which the truth of justice is sometimes omitted'.[110] The author of the *Memoriale* too, for all his criticism of the abuses of the system, allows of an exception in the case of a 'grave and noble person'.[111] Indeed, at one point Lyndwood introduces an argument which, if pursued, could have justified the substitution of pecuniary for corporal penances even in the case of persons of no consequence; as he points out, for them the former might be a greater penalty.[112] In practice, 'there seems little doubt that monetary penances were preferred, at least by those who could afford them'.[113] A report of the parishioners of Boston to the vicar-general of Lincoln in the late fifteenth century records 'that many crimes are revealed from time to time before the official but there is no correction in respect of them, except a pecuniary one, for it had not been seen here that anyone did public penance unless he were a very poor man'.[114]

---

[109] See R. Hill, 'Public Penance: Some Problems of a Thirteenth Century Bishop', *History*, 36 (1951), 221. For a legislative example of class distinction in this respect, see William de Blois's statutes for Worcester (1229), which specified that corrupt witnesses and their suborners, if they were of mean estate, should be flogged, but if they were persons of some dignity, should be fined; see *CS*, ii. 131, c. 65. See also the explanation of pecuniary penance —'maxime si convictus sit liber homo'—in the writ, 'Circumspecte Agatis', ibid. 974. Acton recognizes the relevance of the offender's 'idoneitatem alias conditionem', *Commentary*, 54 (a), *ad vocem*, 'crimina puniant'. Nevertheless, prominent men did sometimes undergo public penance in the fourteenth century, as witness that enjoined on Sir Robert de Colville; see *CPL*, iii. 142, and, for its performance, E. L. G. Stones, 'The Folvilles of Ashby-Folville, Leicestershire, and their Associates in Crime, 1326–47', *TRHS*, 7 (1957), 129. For Bishop Bateman's insistence that Robert, Lord Morley, perform public penance through the streets of Norwich for incursion on the episcopal manors, see *DNB*, i. 1316 and A. H. Thompson, 'William Bateman, Bishop of Norwich, 1344–55', *Norfolk Archaeology*, 25 (1935), 122. On public penance in a later period, see M. Bowker, 'Some Archdeacons' Court Books and the Commons' Supplication Against the Ordinaries of 1532', in D. A. Bullough and R. L. Storey, (eds.), *The Study of Medieval Records: Essays in Honour of Kathleen Major* (Oxford, 1971), 308.

[110] Lyndwood, *Provinciale*, p.325 (b), gloss *ad vocem* 'urgente causa'.

[111] 'Si tamen officiales et ministri huiusmodi ceperint pecuniam ab aliqua persona gravi et nobili quam non decet vel forsan non expedit pro suo peccato notorio per ipsos penitencie pupplice subici corporali et pecuniam sic receptam in pios usus duxerint convertendam, satis poterit tollerari, dummodo per eosdem nichil fraudis penitus committatur.' MP, fo. 66ʳᵇ.

[112] Lyndwood, *Provinciale*, v, tit. 15, p. 325 (b), gloss *ad vocem* 'corporalium'.

[113] *An Episcopal Court Book for the Diocese of Lincoln 1514–1520*, ed. M. Bowker, Lincoln Record Society, 61 (1967), p. xvi.

[114] M. Bowker, *The Secular Clergy in the Diocese of Lincoln 1495–1520* (Cambridge, 1968), 36. It appears that at this period, commutation was an effect of officiousness and of the severity of penances imposed: ibid. 35, 21.

Further to what might be called the profits of jurisdiction, the *Memoriale* includes a question concerning charges made for inductions: 'Item, did you ever receive from any rector or vicar, alb, cow or other temporal equivalent for his corporal induction into or investiture in his church or vicarage, to be performed by you?'[115] Such charges were the subject of two chapters of the first series of constitutions of the Council of London of 1342. The canon 'Nova et insatiabilis cupiditas' was directed against the excessive fees which, it was alleged, were charged for letters of institution of clerks to benefices, for letters of their admission to them, and for letters of ordination, on grounds of the cost of writing and sealing the documents. In addition, it was said that letters of archdeacons and their officials concerning inquisitions over vacancies in benefices were not delivered to the presentees until they made an excessive payment. The canon laid down a scale of fees: not more than twelve pence to be charged for the writing of letters over inquisitions, institutions, or collations or for commissions to induct or for certificates of induction, and not more than six pence for letters over any sacred orders. Since ordinaries, it was emphasized, were responsible for the salaries of their servants, no tips were to be exacted for the minor officers—such as those who sealed the letters, or janitors and so on. Anyone extorting a sum in defiance of the above was to be required to make twofold restitution within a month, under penalty of suspension from office and benefice in the case of a beneficed clerk, and of suspension from entry to church in the case of an unbeneficed clerk or layman, until due satisfaction was made.[116] The canon 'Item quia archidiaconi' dealt specifically with charges for induction. Archdeacons and their officials and other ministers of the province, it was alleged, refused to induct to benefices or to give certificates of induction until they received an immoderate sum of money. But, unlike the *Memoriale* which implies that nothing may be received for discharging this function, Stratford's constitution allowed a procuration—to cover expenses —of up to forty pence to an archdeacon, or two shillings to an archdeacon's official, performing the induction. The inductee was to be at liberty to pay in cash or in kind, and the penalty for anyone who

---

[115] MP, fo. 20ᵛ.

[116] *Concilia*, ii. 696–7. This constitution is not included by Lyndwood in his *Provinciale*, and he ignores it in discussing charges for institution or for letters anent. While suspicious of such charges, as bordering on simony, he seems to allow of them on the understanding that the office for which the salary is paid is not 'de substantia rei agendae', and provided that the work done is commensurate, *Provinciale*, iii, tit. 6, p. 138 (a–b).

exacted more than these maxima or who refused to issue a certificate of induction on some pretence, was to be *ipso facto* suspension from office and entry to a church, until due satisfaction was made.[117] It is to be noted, however, that Lyndwood thought that the archdeacon might receive a customary offering in excess of these charges without incurring the penalty of the statute.[118]

The interrogatory in the *Memoriale* to be put to officials and rural deans also deals with several procedural abuses of which they may be guilty. These include harassment in citation and in compurgation, and irregular excommunication. The first is described in these terms: 'Item, have you cited or fixed a term to any subject of yours—for the sake of aggrieving or harassing him—in the ultimate bounds of your jurisdiction, or in a place excessively remote from that where the subject dwelt and thus he was fatigued by labours and superfluous expenses, and perhaps gave you something in redemption of the labour?'[119] Two important rulings in canon law restricted the powers of papal judges-delegate to cite defendants outside their cities and dioceses. Canon 37 of the Fourth Lateran Council enacted that no one should be summoned to judgment by virtue of apostolic letters beyond two days' journey from his diocese,[120] while a decretal of Boniface VIII imposed further limitations. Where plaintiff and defendant were of the same city or diocese, the case was not to be commissioned to judges outside of these boundaries, except in certain specified cases, where one of the parties was particularly influential locally or where the impetrants pleaded fear of their adversary. In no case could the defendant be summoned beyond one day's journey from his city or diocese.[121] These regulations had reference only to the procedure of judges appointed by apostolic letters, though the canon of the Lateran Council was cited in the agreement reached between Pecham and his suffragans over summonses of the latter to the archbishop's court.[122] There seems to be no thirteenth-century local legislation on citation by officials of bishops or of lower authorities, though in the case of the bishop of Norwich, a complaint is recorded that his officials oblige accused persons to travel twenty or thirty miles for purgation.[123] Archbishop Stratford's provincial

---

[117] *Concilia*, 697.

[118] Lyndwood, *Provinciale*, iii, tit. 6, p. 141 (b), gloss *ad vocem* 'indebite'.

[119] MP, fo. 20[r].   [120] X. 1. 3. 28.

[121] *Sext.*, 1. 3. 11.   [122] *CS*, ii. 925, c. 17.

[123] *Registrum Epistolarum Johannis Pecham*, ed. C. T. Martin, i (Rolls Series, 1882), 178; cf. *CS*, ii. 650, n. 2.

constitutions of 1342 did rule upon the point. Officials and servants of bishops, archdeacons, and other ordinaries of the province, it was complained, cited defendants for compurgation to places outside their jurisdiction or to remote parts within it, so that the accused were forced to pay a fine or sometimes to confess to a crime that they had not committed and to undergo a penance rather than inflict labours on themselves and their compurgators. Henceforth, persons defamed who wished to purge themselves were not to be summoned from one deanery to another nor to other than well-known places within it.[124] Lyndwood approved of this, pointing out that, apart from the consideration of expense, it was desirable that the purgation should take place where the defamation had arisen, on the canonical principle 'that the evil should die where it arises'.[125]

There was scope for abuse in the matter of compurgation itself: 'Item, did you ever impose on anyone defamed an excessively heavy purgation and so being compelled by necessity he redeemed his harassment, paying money to you on this account?'[126] Both the *Decretum Gratiani* and the *Decretals* contain directives on the number of compurgators to be produced by persons of various rank. So, seven compurgators of the same 'order' were to be produced by a priest, three by a deacon. Fifteen of the same degree were required for the purgation of a noble.[127] There was, however, room for discretion in fixing the number required; another text of the *Decretum*, regulating the compurgation of a priest, suggested three, five, or seven 'good and neighbouring priests', or more if the bishop saw fit.[128] Certainly, the gravity of the crime involved could lead to an increase in the number of compurgators required, and in fact the canons specifying a fixed number of compurgators were not considered authoritative by Lyndwood, whose view was that 'today . . . the number in this case is arbitrary'.[129] In England, synodal statutes repeatedly warn that purgation shall not be delayed 'from day to day, as an occasion of taking money', and that the canonical number shall not be exceeded.[130] Bishop Fulk Basset's statutes for London diocese (1245 × 1249) forbade malicious insistence on purgation, and practices

---

[124] *Concilia*, ii. 700.
[125] Lyndwood, *Provinciale*, v, tit. 14, p.313 (b), gloss *ad vocem* 'ad alium'. In regard to archidiaconal citations in the sixteenth century, Bowker, 'Some Archdeacons' Court Books', 307, found little to support the Commons' complaints.
[126] MP, fo. 20ʳ.   [127] *Decreti* IIa pars, 2. q. 5. 12; ibid., 13.   [128] Ibid. 19.
[129] Lyndwood, *Provinciale*, v, tit.14, p. 313 (b)–314 (a), gloss *ad vocem* 'sextae manus'.
[130] See *CS*, ii. 73, c. 39; 194, c. 80; 458, c. 35.

such as the requirement of an excessive number of compurgators, the assignment of an inconvenient place, or prorogation of the time set.[131] Bishop William Bitton's statutes for Wells (*c*.1258) required archdeacons to limit the number of compurgators to five in the case of a less serious offence—except where a 'principal person' was involved—and ten or twelve in the case of a major crime.[132] Archbishop Stratford, in 1342, in a constitution probably unpublished,[133] specified that not more than six compurgators should be prescribed in the case of a crime like fornication and not more than twelve in the case of adultery or a more serious crime.[134] While, as has been noted, Lyndwood rejected the authority of the canons in the *Decretum Gratiani* fixing the number of compurgators, he accepted the force of this present constitution.[135]

Practice reflected the uncertainty of the law on the point. The numbers of compurgators recorded as having been assigned by a late-thirteenth-century court in the archdeaconry of Sudbury, Norwich diocese, are modest: three and five compurgators were required in cases of alleged association with an excommunicate, five in the case of adultery, five and seven in cases of incest.[136] In 1314 Archbishop Greenfield of York reduced the number of compurgators in the case of charges brought, during his visitation, against the chaplain of Treeton, from the twelve prescribed by his correctors to six or eight, and changed the place of compurgation for a more convenient one.[137] The purgation imposed upon Reginald de Hadham, prior of Westminster, in 1307 by Abbot Walter de Wenlok, with whom he was in dispute, was certainly burdensome; he was required to purge himself 'cum vicesima quarta manu' of the charges brought against him—a number probably calculated as being in excess of the prior's support in the convent.[138] Examples near to the time of Stratford's attempt to establish maxima indicate the problem with which his constitution was intended to deal. We find that fourteen compurgators are required of a man charged with adultery, in Rochester diocese (1343),[139] while in

---

[131] Ibid. 650, c. 80.   [132] Ibid. 609, c. 42.
[133] See references at above, p. 27, n. 119.   [134] *Concilia*, ii. 700.
[135] Lyndwood, *Provinciale*, v, tit. 14, p. 314 (b), gloss *ad vocem* 'duodecimae manus'.
[136] See A. Gransden, 'Some Late Thirteenth-Century Records of an Ecclesiastical Court in the Archdeaconry of Sudbury', *Bulletin of the Institute of Historical Research*, 32 (1959), 62–9.
[137] *The Register of William Greenfield, 1306–1315*, ed. W. Brown and A. H. Thompson, pt. ii, Surtees Society, 149 (1934), 175, no. 1041.
[138] See E. H. Pearce, *Walter de Wenlok, Abbot of Westminster* (London, 1920), 174.
[139] *Reg. Hethe*, i. 633.

Canterbury in 1348 there is a case of an accused who is convicted of adultery but who clears himself of incest by thirty-six compurgators.[140]

On irregularity in the form of excommunication, the query to be put ('Item, did you ever pass any sentence of excommunication, major or minor, against anyone, without writing, and without committing to writing the cause for which you passed it, or did you otherwise promulgate sentence of excommunication without due maturity?')[141] is a technical one, based on a canon of the Council of Lyon. This required that the judge pronouncing sentence of excommunication should commit to writing the reason for it and, when lawfully requested, should provide a copy of the document to the excommunicate within one month of his passing the sentence.[142] 'Due maturity' is probably to be understood with reference to the canon of the Fourth Lateran Council, decreeing that sentence of excommunication should only be passed after a 'competent admonition'.[143]

The matters of jurisdiction and procedure so far discussed bear upon the office of the judge. As for the other personnel of a court, the *Memoriale Presbiterorum* includes sections on the interrogation of advocates and proctors, and on the duty of restitution as it affects advocates, judges, their assessors and apparitors, and witnesses and delators of crimes.

Although the offices of proctor and advocate were theoretically distinct—the essence of the one being power of attorney and of the other, legal expertise[144]—the interrogatory provided for them in the *Memoriale* does not in fact comprise a separate consideration of their functions. For general purposes they were often assimilated.[145]

For his chapters on the interrogation of advocates and proctors, and on the duty of restitution as it affects the former, the *Memoriale* depends on Hostiensis,[146] supplying on occasion explanatory glosses on the latter's account. So it expounds the law affecting the person of the

---

[140] *The Royal Commission on Historical Manuscripts, Eighth Report, Appendix*, part i, sec. 2 (London, 1881), 337 (a).

[141] MP, fo. 20ʳ.   [142] *Sext.*, 5. 11. 1; cf. *CS*, ii. 631–2, and 1040–1.

[143] X. 5. 39. 48. Bishop Quinel's statute on excommunication required triple admonition in the presence of witnesses, who could testify to its having been given, see *CS*, ii. 1040–1.

[144] See Lyndwood, *Provinciale*, i, tit. 17, p. 74, *ad vocem* 'advocatus'.

[145] See J. Sayers, *Papal Judges Delegate in the Province of Canterbury 1198–1254* (Oxford, 1971), 221; R. Helmholz, 'Ethical Standards for Advocates in Theory and Practice', *Proceedings of the Fourth International Congress of Medieval Canon Law* (Vatican City, 1975), 284–5. Lyndwood, elaborates the distinction: *Provinciale*, i, tit. 17, p. 74 (b), gloss *ad vocem* 'advocatus'.

[146] Cf. above, pp. 70–2.

advocate:[147] neither religious nor secular clerics in sacred orders—and particularly priests—may act as advocates, except in certain cases. Religious were forbidden by a ruling in the *Decretals* from acting in court except for utility of their monastery and at the command of their abbot.[148] Secular priests or beneficed clergy, on the other hand, were originally forbidden—by canon 12 of the Third Lateran Council—from practising in the secular forum only.[149] The legatine Council of London in 1237 implicitly recognized the right of beneficed clergy to plead, when it ordained suspension from office and benefice as the penalty for advocates who were guilty of malpractice,[150] and it was cited to this effect in the synodal statutes for Chichester (1245 × 1252), which repeated the Lateran canon, with a qualification: 'And this in the civil. In the ecclesiastical court, however, they are to be admitted, if they wish to practise, in accordance with the legate's constitution published concerning them.'[151] Gregory IX, however, extended the prohibition to include the ecclesiastical forum, with the exception of certain cases,[152] and the effect of the new ruling is seen shortly afterwards in Walter de Cantilupe's statutes for Worcester diocese (1240).[153] Archbishop Greenfield of York in 1308, following in this a regulation of his predecessor Wickwane, forbade priests and clerics having cure from practising in the consistory court 'except in the cases conceded by law'.[154]

So far as concerns the professional ethics of advocacy,[155] there is a notable point of difference between the modern and medieval conception of the office. The latter required the advocate to assess in advance the justice of a case which he was called upon to undertake and to act or refuse to act accordingly.[156] Archbishop Stratford's important ordinances for the Court of the Arches (1342) contain an explicit statement of the duty.[157] The *Memoriale Presbiterorum* questions the advocate on whether he acted against conscience in defending the wicked.[158]

---

[147] MP, fo. 69[rb].   [148] X. 1. 37. 3.   [149] Ibid. 1. Cf. *CS*, ii. 26–7, 64, c. 11.

[150] Ibid. 259, c. 29.   [151] Ibid. 465, c. 66.   [152] X. 1. 37. 3.

[153] *CS*, ii. 314, c. 75.   [154] Ibid. 314–15 n.

[155] For a judicious overview, see Helmholz, 'Ethical Standards', 283–99.

[156] MP, fo. 21[r]. Cf. Helmholz, 'Ethical Standards', 285–6.

[157] *Concilia*, ii. 689. Among the articles drawn up in January 1377 to be sworn to by advocates and proctors of the bishop of Ely's consistory court, is one to the effect that 'causas improbas vel penitus desperatas et ex mendacibus allegacionibus compositas non fovebunt scientes, seu malam conscientiam habentes quomodolibet de eisdem. Quod cum sciverint, seu malam conscienciam habuerint, ipsas omnino dimmittent.' See Aston, *Thomas Arundel*, 407, art. 5.

[158] MP, fo. 21[r].

If defence of an unjust case was considered unethical, so too was an obstructive insistence on points of law. Advocates were sometimes required to take an oath prior to their admission to practise in a court, specifically eschewing this among other abuses.[159] The *Memoriale* shows a particular concern for unjust delays in matrimonial cases.[160] These were peculiarly delicate;[161] their settlement might depend largely on the veracity of the parties; furthermore, while the partners to a disputed union were in theory required to separate for the duration of the case, they did not always do so in practice.[162] Certainly, the handling of matrimonial cases receives much attention in English diocesan and provincial legislation. A number of versions of Bishop Richard Poore's synodal statutes for Salisbury diocese (1217 × 1219) against false witnesses and perjurors—whose absolution is reserved to the bishop and his penitentiary—make a special ordinance 'concerning advocates or others suborning false witnesses and concerning the false witnesses themselves, suborned, for the dissolution of lawful, contracted marriages or for the impeding of future lawful contracts.'[163] Canon 4 of the Council of Oxford (1222) excommunicated advocates 'who in matrimonial cases maliciously put exceptions in the way or cause them to be put, to prevent true marriages from taking due effect or to prolong the proceedings of the case, contrary to justice',[164] and canon 45 prescribed that the advocate who opposed a marriage after sentence had been given for it should be deprived of his office for one year, unless the judge should hold him excused on account of a justifiable error or probable ignorance.[165]

---

[159] See the statutes of the consistory court of Lincoln (1334), c. 9, in *Concilia*, ii. 573; and Bishop Richard de Kellawe's statutes for Durham, c. 12, in *Registrum Palatinum Dunelmense*, ed. T. D. Hardy, (Rolls Series, 1875) iii. 579. Cf. canon 29 of the Legatine Council of London (1237), which besides requiring a general oath declared that no advocate should be admitted to matrimonial cases—or to cases concerning elections—without swearing in each case to act faithfully. *CS*, ii. 258–9. The Ely articles of 1377 included a specific undertaking to this effect, see Aston, *Thomas Arundel*, 407, art. 4. Stratford's constitutions for the Court of the Arches, on the other hand, prescribe only a general form of oath for the advocates on the point, requiring respect for the rules of the court; see *Concilia*, ii. 695(b).

[160] MP, fo. 21rb. The remarks do not derive from Hostiensis.

[161] For the difficulties facing the courts, especially in establishing contract, see M. M. Sheehan, 'The Formation and Stability of Marriage in Fourteenth Century England: Evidence of an Ely Register', *MS* 33 (1971), 228–63.

[162] See Aston, *Thomas Arundel*, 68, 101, 107. In two matrimonial cases before the official of the archdeacon of Ely in 1374, the defendants contracted marriage while the case was undecided, probably with the collusion of the official, ibid. 103–4.

[163] See *CS*, ii. 77, n. d; cf. ibid. 231.   [164] Ibid. 107.

[165] Ibid. 120. Lyndwood's interpretation is that the advocate is thus debarred from advocacy in all the courts of the province, not simply in that in which he offended. *Provinciale*, i, tit. 17, p. 75, gloss *ad vocem* 'privatus existat'.

The general principle underlying the *Memoriale*'s treatment of judges, witnesses, and assessors, as in that of advocates, is that where damage has been unjustly inflicted, restitution must be made. A similar consideration applies to delators of crimes, for whom a form of apology in the case of defamation—based on Hostiensis[166]—is supplied. Ignorance of the law on the part of judges does not excuse them from responsibility for the effects of their judgments.[167] The legatine Council of 1237 allowed judges who were in doubt over a point of law to seek counsel at the expense of the parties.[168] It was the function of the assessors to advise the judge in this fashion and they gave their opinion in a formal instrument—a 'consilium'—which was not, however, binding on the judge.[169] It was generally agreed that the assessors, unlike the judge, were entitled to receive a salary from the parties,[170] and this is the point of the restrictive practice whereby, according to the *Memoriale*, some judges demanded a share of the salaries of the assessors and other court officials before admitting them to a case.[171] The assessor is morally responsible for deficiencies in his counsel,[172] and if the judge, having exercised due diligence, is deceived in this manner, he is excused from the obligation of restitution in respect of the damages inflicted by his judgment.[173] Otherwise, the duty of restitution in the judge's case is absolute and the law takes no cognizance of a remission by the injured party.[174] As for the witnesses, they may receive expenses, but the author distinguishes between this and the extortion of a salary—effectively a bribe for testimony—as practised allegedly by the 'choir leaders' of whom he complains.[175] The ecclesiastical courts made more extensive use of witnesses in cases between party and party than their secular counterparts at this period.[176] Indeed, the king's courts were hostile to promissory witnesses,[177] and while compurgation was frequently used in manorial and borough courts—as was the case in the ecclesiastical courts—its use in the royal courts was restricted at this period to certain personal actions, such as some cases of debt, and

---

[166] MP, fo. 70ᵛ.   [167] Ibid., fo. 67ʳ.   [168] CS, 259, c. 29.

[169] See P. Fournier, *Les Officialités au moyen âge* (Paris, 1880), 25, 206.

[170] See Baldwin, *Masters*, i. 191; Fournier, *Les Officialités*, 25.   [171] MP, fo. 66ᵛᵇ.

[172] Ibid., fo. 67ᵛ.   [173] Ibid.   [174] Ibid., fo. 67ʳᵃ⁻ᵇ; cf. *Sext.*, 1. 3. 11.

[175] MP, fo. 69ᵛᵇ. See above, p. 13.

[176] For the use of witnesses in the ecclesiastical courts, see B. Woodcock, *Medieval Ecclesiastical Courts in the Diocese of Canterbury* (Oxford, 1952), 56–7. On their tardy recognition in the king's courts, W. Holdsworth, *A History of English Law*, i, 7th edn. (Oxford, 1956), 334, and J. G. Bellamy, *Criminal Law and Society in Late Medieval and Tudor England* (Gloucester/New York, 1984), 33–53.

[177] See Holdsworth, *History*, i. 334; cf. ibid., ix, 3rd edn. (Oxford, 1944), 182.

detinue and account.[178] Being, therefore, unfamiliar with witnesses as such, the royal courts were not well equipped to deal with malpractices among them. So, while false swearing was punishable in the case of juries formally attainted, perjury by witnesses was not a crime in common law.[179] The nature of the problem has been vividly described:

The origination and prosecution of suits that were based upon purely invented facts and supported by evidence that was wholly deliberate perjury seems . . . to have ranked almost as a recognized profession. Over and over again in the records we find instances of it. But to say so much is not to tell, nor even to hint at, half the full iniquity of these maintainers of false suits. When they had got a plaintiff well started on his action—a plaintiff who had based his action upon the advice these men had given him and upon the proofs of evidence which they had laid before him, and who had paid them for both advice and evidence, they then calmly went over to the other side, and got fresh fees for their advice and support on behalf of the defendant.[180]

This is the very situation of which the author of the *Memoriale* complains, though he has jurors in mind rather than witnesses.[181] Thomas Brinton, preaching *c*.1377, expresses his concern at the effects of false swearing in the courts, secular and ecclesiastical:

False jurors have to fear the hand of the Lord, who when they are produced so that they, being constituted in judgment, swear to tell the whole truth for either party, they conceal it, by reason of hatred or favour, bribe or fear, friendship or lordship; on pretext of their perjury, one man is deprived of his land, heredity, or right of patronage and another unjustly gains; one man gains a benefice before the

[178] Ibid., i. 306–7.

[179] See *The Eyre of Kent, 6 and 7 Edward II, AD 1313–1314*, ed. F. W. Maitland, L. W. V. Harcourt, and W. C. Bolland, Year Books of Edward II, v, Selden Society, 24 (1909), i. p. xxxiii.

[180] Ibid.

[181] MP, fos. 69ᵛ–70ʳ. For another reference to these 'ductores chorearum'—a feature, apparently, of the secular rather than of the ecclesiastical courts—see ibid., fo. 40ᵛ. The term 'ductores chorearum' appears to be coined; I have not found it used in this sense by other commentators. The author also uses it of (?)dancing, see ibid., fo. 51ʳ: 'Si puella fuerit sub potestate parentum constituta vel eciam sui iuris fuerit et forsan nimis la[s]civa fuerit discurrendo per vicos et plateas, de die choreas ducendo et de nocte ad vigilias et exequias mortuorum periculose accedendo, tu confessor graviter eam affligere debes ieiuniis et oracionibus ita quod metu penitencie a talibus de cetero abstineat se'; cf. ibid., fo. 10ʳᵇ. For 'choreae' in this sense, see e.g. John Bromyard, *Summa Predicantium* (Nuremberg, 1485), *sub voce* 'Choreizantium', art. 6. Cf. John de Burgo, *Pupilla Oculi* (London, 1510), fo. 132ᵛ. Prohibitions occur against allowing 'choreas duci' (vaguely disreputable revels) at academic inceptions: *Chartularium Universitatis Parisiensis*, ed. H. Denifle, i (Paris, 1889), 230 (AD 1252), 586 (AD 1280). I thank Professor C. H. Lawrence for suggesting this origin of the author's metaphor.

lawful age, since he swears that he is of lawful age; another obtains a benefice by a false title, so sworn, although in actual truth he has not title. Through such men's oaths, many are joined in marriage, in that when a lawful impediment is alleged against them, they proved by perjurors that there is no impediment, and so they stand at once in contravention of reason, canons, and God. Others are lawfully joined and sometimes unjustly divided, when by men's oaths they prove pre-contract or prior carnal union with someone related to the woman by consanguinity.[182]

William Doune's acerbic references to his half-brother, Aymer Fitzwarin, both provide an insight into corruption and reveal his own sensitivity on the subject.[183]

Purchase of office is a concern of the author of the *Memoriale*,[184] on grounds that officials who have bought their offices proceed to redeem the outlay from their subjects.[185] It is not quite clear that the author intends his comments on this matter to apply to ecclesiastical apparitors as well as to secular 'catchpoles', but this seems likely in the context.[186] The purchase of secular bailiwicks is well attested,[187] but no evidence has been found of it in the ecclesiastical sphere. The charge of deliberate harassment, on the other hand, is familiar from Chaucer's portrait of the summoner: [188]

> Brother, quod he, heere woneth an old rebekke,
> That hadde almoost as lief to lese hire nekke
> As for to yeve a peny of hir good.
> I wole han twelf pens, though that she be wood,
> Or I wole sompne hire unto our office;
> And yet, God woot, of hire I knowe no vice.[189]

A number of English diocesan statutes in the thirteenth century followed the terms of those promulgated for the diocese of Bath and Wells (*c.*1258), in attempting to curtail malicious citations. Noting complaints that apparitors called clerics and laymen before chapters 'over

---

[182] Brinton, *Sermons*, i. 62.   [183] See above, pp. 13–14.

[184] Cf. below, p. 130.   [185] MP, fos. 67vb–68^{r}.

[186] Initially it seems that the apparitor is included, ibid., fo. 67vb, but later in the passage, the emphasis is on 'catchpoles and bailiffs', ibid, fo. 68^{r}.

[187] See below, p. 132.

[188] Harassment by secular officials is considered below, pp. 132–5. For a severe judgement on the rural chapter see Scammell, 'The Rural Chapter', 17.

[189] *Canterbury Tales*, ed. Robinson, III D, 1573–8. For earlier evidence of hostility to apparitors, see 'A Satyre on the Consistory Courts', from the reign of Edward I, in *Political Songs*, ed. Wright, 157. The vein of satire continued into the seventeenth century; see 'The New Ballad of the Parator and the Devil', in C. H. Firth, 'The Reign of Charles I', *TRHS*, 3rd Ser., 6 (1912), 39–40.

crimes concerning which they are not previously defamed among good
and serious men, sometimes upon the suggestion of one man, and often
of none, but of their own volition', these enacted that no official, dean,
or apparitor should thenceforth cause anyone to be summoned before
a chapter who had not previously been defamed 'apud bonos et graves',
'on pain of removal from office, with the possibility of a further
penalty'.[190] From this it is clear that even at this date the apparitor is
exercising a police function, as well as being the bearer of citations,
though commissions authorizing him to do so are not found until much
later.[191] His fee in instance cases would be met from the costs, as borne
by the plaintiff or, if the case were successful, by the defendant.[192] In
ex officio proceedings it probably derived from 'a kind of commission
or percentage arrangement based on the fines levied'.[193] At Lincoln
in the late fifteenth century the costs of his citation were borne by the
defendant and were divided between the registrar and the apparitor.[194]
There was thus a premium on the latter's zeal, which the requirement
that there be sufficient defamation was aimed at curbing. Noting how
the machinery of appeal provided a check on abuses in the archdeacon's
court at Ely, Dr Aston observes that in many appeals from the latter
to the consistory court, the defendants questioned the authority of the
fama publica on which their prosecution had been based.[195] It is not,
however, possible to say how often this was more than a formal legal
exception.[196]

On the subject of extortion by apparitors, the Council of Lambeth
(1261) laid down that bedells and apparitors of archdeacons and rural
deans should not exact procurations from rectors, vicars, and chaplains
or other priests, clerics, or religious during the performance of their
duties, but should be content with what was freely offered to them.[197]
The use of the term 'procuration' suggests that they were laying claim
to a charge which was reserved to visiting prelates.[198] A few years earlier,

---

[190]   *CS*, ii. 609, c. 42.
[191]   See Haselmayer, 'The Apparitor and Chaucer's Summoner'.
[192]   See Woodcock, *Medieval Courts*, 60–2.   [193]   Haselmayer, 'The Apparitor', 50.
[194]   See Bowker, *Secular Clergy*, 34.
[195]   Aston, *Thomas Arundel*, 90. For episcopal scrutiny of unwarrantable citation in
Dunstable deanery in 1297, see *The Rolls and Registers of Bishop Oliver Sutton 1280–1299*,
ed. R. M. Hill, vi (LRS, lxiv, 1970), 16.
[196]   Frivolous prosecution was one of the Commons' complaints against the Ordinaries,
see C. H. Williams (ed.), *English Historical Documents*, v (London, 1967), 733; for discussion, see Bowker, 'Some Archdeacons' Court Books', 307.
[197]   *CS*, ii. 683, c. 17.
[198]   For a statement that apparitors are not entitled to a procuration in their own name,
see Lyndwood, *Provinciale*, iii, tit. 22, p. 221(b), gloss *ad vocem* 'ratione procurationis'.

in synodal statutes of Salisbury (1257), it was complained that apparitors proceeded through the deaneries on horseback and with servants, demanding immoderate hospitality.[199] Archbishop Stratford, in his constitutions of 1342, tried to limit their demands by ruling that apparitors should not spend more than one day and one night per quarter at the expense of rectors and vicars, unless specially invited.[200] In effect, this seems to concede a procuration to them, and one may suspect that invitations might not always be spontaneous.[201] It must be admitted, however, that while by the end of the fourteenth century 'the apparitor had become in literature a standard example of corruption and exploitation',[202] little documentary evidence can be adduced to support the charges generally levelled against them.[203] In forming an impression of their activities, we are as dependent on *fama publica* as, theoretically, they were in proceeding against those over whom they had authority.

Complaints against officialdom occupy an important place in the literature of complaint of fourteenth-century England. The interest of the *Memoriale Presbiterorum* in the vices common to the legal and administrative classes has a secular counterpart in the concern of juries— evidenced by the recurring charges on, for instance, the Hundred Rolls[204]—with offences committed by bailiffs 'per potestatem officii', itself a term equivalent to the canonist concept of 'concussio'.[205] As a comment on abuse, these chapters of the *Memoriale* invite particular

[199] *CS*, ii. 554, c. 9.

[200] *Concilia*, ii. 700. This constitution also aimed at preventing a proliferation of apparitors. It enacted that each suffragan should have only one mounted apparitor for his diocese; archdeacons should have only one for each deanery, who should not be mounted; ibid. It is criticized by Lyndwood on several points of law. Certainly, as he noted, it was open to the construction that what was restricted in the bishop's case was simply the number of mounted apparitors that he might have (Lyndwood, *Provinciale*, iii, tit. 22, p. 225 (b), gloss *ad vocem* 'duntaxat'); thus, Adam Orleton at Winchester in 1348 settled for two apparitors, one mounted and one on foot, see Haines, 'Adam Orleton', 21.

[201] For charges that the apparitors of the London archdeaconry in the second decade of the fourteenth century were sheltered by the clergy so that they might be allowed to continue in their vices, see *VCH London*, i, ed. W. Page (London, 1909), 199.

[202] See Haselmayer, 'The Apparitor', 55.

[203] Cf. Woodcock, *Medieval Courts*, 49. Two episodes at York, under Archbishop Wickwane illustrate their unsavoury reputation as well as the jealousy of a bishop's subjects in their regard. See *The Register of William Wickwane*, ed. W. Brown (SS, cxiv, 1907), 211, no. 505, 214–15, no. 518. The latter objection, though it concerned an apparitor described as 'preparatus ad predam', seems to have been against the office rather than the holder of it.

[204] See below, pp. 132–3.

[205] John Acton defines 'concussio' as follows, glossing Luke 3: 11: 'Est autem concutere, aliquid ultra debitum petere ratione officii alicuius. Dicitur autem concutere qui per oppressionem et minas pecuniam extorquet.' Acton, 'Septuplum', fo. 54ᵛ. Cf. the view of Alvarus Pelagius, *De Planctu*, art. 31 (fourteenth sin).

comparison with the *Speculum Vitae*.[206] The allegations there against the legal classes are familiar enough, as in the case of officials and deans:

> Officials and deans baþe
> Some done litel gode bot scaþe
> Ofte pair chaipitres þai wille sette
> To geder alle þat þai may gette
> þai take boþe of grete and smale
> ȝif þai done wrong þai ȝif no tale
> For þai have more affeccoun
> To silvir þan to correccoun
> And ȝit þai do nouȝt so grete reddoure
> To riche men als þai done to poure
> For riche men for mede þai forbere
> And poure men wrongwisely þai dere . . .
> Wiþ suche maner of ordinaunce
> þai chace men unto penance
> Ever to þai make redempcioun
> þat may be calde extorsioun;[207]

or of the assessor:

> þat es þe domesman conseillour
> And als his felawe sittes him by
> ȝit heldes he to þe tone party
> For ȝift þat he takes among
> He consailes him to do wrong
> Perchance to gife a fals iugement
> Or tarye þe riȝt be his assent.[208]

However, if the vices are in themselves unremarkable, and if in addressing them the poem is prompted by its source, the *Somme le Roi*, its marked concern with and elaboration of them is hardly less noteworthy than is the corresponding feature of the *Memoriale Presbiterorum*. While the problems that exercised their authors were widely recognized, the interest of the common element between the two works is accentuated by the suggestion of its common genesis in the Exeter context.[209]

---

[206] See above, pp. 59–60.   [207] Oxford, Bodleian Library, MS. Bodley 446, fo. 91ʳ.
[208] Ibid., fo. 93ʳ.   [209] Cf. above, pp. 57–9.

6

Society Under Scrutiny II:
The Examination of Lords and Knights

Compared with other commentators, the *Memoriale Presbiterorum* has surprisingly little to say of lords. In condemning injustices on the manor, the author's attention is concentrated on the officials. Given the importance at this period of the members of the lord's council in the administration of a great estate,[1] the emphasis is probably not misplaced. The *Memoriale* appears, too, to ignore with regard to lords the twin classic excesses of bastard feudalism—livery and associated maintenance[2]—which exercise other critics and modern historians markedly.[3] Though some of the author's concerns with corruption in courts might reflect the effects of systematic patronage, his remarks are on the whole insufficiently specific for him to be classed as a witness to more than an age-

---

[1] See H. M. Cam, 'The Decline and Fall of English Feudalism', *History*, 25 (1941), 222–3; and A. E. Levett, *Studies in Manorial History*, ed. H. M. Cam (Oxford, 1938), ch. 3, *passim*. Cf. G. C. Homans, *English Villagers of the Thirteenth Century* (New York, 1941), 229, on direct relations between lord and man as a mere figure of language; and the analysis of M. Hicks, *Bastard Feudalism* (London and New York, 1995), 52–7.

[2] For the distinction of a specific from a more general incidence of maintenance, see the highly pertinent remarks of Hicks, *Bastard Feudalism*, 121, and on the endemic nature of corruption, those of N. Saul, *Knights and Esquires: The Gloucestershire Gentry in the Fourteenth Century* (Oxford, 1981), 104. On a general aspiration to partial treatment, see C. Rawcliffe, 'Baronial Councils in the Later Middle Ages', in C. Ross (ed.), *Patronage Pedigree and Power in Later Medieval England* (Gloucester, 1979), 94 and R. W. Kaeuper, 'Law and Order in Fourteenth Century England: The Evidence of Special Commissions of Oyer and Terminer', *Speculum*, 54 (1979), 760–1. P. Morgan, *War and Society in Medieval Cheshire 1227–1403* (Manchester, 1987), 86–7, notes the implications of 'the bonds of association' for forensic corruption within a region.

[3] Cf. the strictures on the abuses of lordship of John Bromyard, *Summa Praedicantium*, *sub voce* 'Falsitas' (F. i), art. ii. sections ix, xi; and, later, Bishop Brinton on the aggravation of petty disputes: Brinton, *Sermons*, i. 213. On the corrupt sense that came to attach to 'good lordship', see C. Carpenter, 'The Beauchamp Affinity: A Study of Bastard Feudalism at Work', *EHR* 95 (1980), 525. For recent reviews of the concept of 'bastard feudalism', see J. M. W. Bean, *From Lord to Patron: Lordship in Late Medieval England* (Manchester, 1989), 1–9; P. R. Coss, 'Bastard Feudalism Revised', *Past and Present*, 125 (1989), 27–64 and Hicks, *Bastard Feudalism*; and of its operation, J. G. Bellamy, *Bastard Feudalism and the Law* (London, 1989).

old problem.[4] There are two possible explanations of the silence. The Exeter context, argued for in this study, with its two great lordships of Devon and Cornwall,[5] may have more urgently raised for the author's circle questions rather of the abuse of seignorial jurisdiction. Dr Pantin penetratingly noted this preoccupation of the treatise as a point of interest.[6] Grandisson's documented concern with the topic offers a valuable clue. In a letter to the archbishop of Canterbury of 3 December 1335, he denounced the servants of the earl of Cornwall who not only in secular matters excluded the exercise of royal jurisdiction but forbade the exercise of ecclesiastical jurisdiction, compelling all, even those who were not tenants of the earl, into his court 'which they have newly founded and established at their whim, in all civil and almost all ecclesiastical causes', to the point where the bishop warned of insurrection. By the same token, the newly styled earl of Devon, whose 'insanity' did not even have the excuse of youth, 'says openly . . . that he is the king's equal and that he can make laws and judge concerning all: that—under pretext of commissions issued to him—he can do what he likes', with the effect that 'simple Devonians' saw no other king.[7] It is not difficult to suppose that views so trenchantly articulated here would have been recurrent within the bishop's household. A second possible reason for the author's bias is quite simply that the canonical literature, being unacquainted with the social problems of maintenance and retinues, provided no stimulus to reflection on them. In dealing with the sins of lords, the *Memoriale* concentrates on matters that had been thoroughly investigated by the canons and their interpreters—questions such as tallage, enactment of unjust statutes, seizure of wreck, and infringement of ecclesiastical liberty.[8]

The important question of the validity of the lord's right to tallage is raised in section b. xxxviii:

It happens on occasion that temporal lords violently exact and extort many goods, both from their serfs and from their free tenants, beyond what the tenants should and are used to pay, and they impose tallage on them against their will and without

---

[4] He depicts the 'choir leaders' of whom he complains (see above, p. 13) as being available for hire, simply.

[5] For the former, see M. Cherry, 'The Courtenay Earls of Devon: The Formation and Disintegration of a Late Medieval Aristocratic Affinity', *Southern History*, 1 (1979), 71–97.

[6] Pantin, *Church*, 210.   [7] *RG*, i. 294.

[8] Many other matters raised in the interrogation of knights (MP, a. xxxvi), such as their abandonment of their wives, their attempts to exercise jurisdiction over clerics and their extortion of pensions from them, appear to be excerpted from or suggested by the *Summa* of Hostiensis. See Haren, 'The Interrogatories'.

cause, according to their whim, sometimes once in the year, sometimes more often, as they see fit, now more, now less, extorting a large number of their goods by violence. The result is sometimes that these tenants are impoverished and scarcely have the means to provide a livelihood for themselves and their families.[9]

These lords delude themselves that they are committing no sin, by quoting the maxim of civil law that whatever the serf acquires, he acquires for his lord,[10] but 'no temporal lord according to natural or to canon law should exact anything from his tenant beyond what is owed him by custom or from a convention established between him and his tenant or from an imposition made from of old'.[11] Liability to tallage was always one of the tests of serfdom in cases of disputed status.[12] It should not have been levied on free men, but even in cases of villeins, though in theory it was an arbitrary sum, assessed and imposed at the will of the lord, its amount and frequency were commonly determined by custom,[13] in the same way as were rents or labour services, which, in theory, were no less arbitrary. As these services were commuted, so tallage was replaced on some manors by the fixed aid to the lord, which in practice it had undoubtedly become already in many cases.

Like the author of the *Memoriale*, Chaucer's Parson is severely critical of

thise harde lordshipes, thurgh whiche men been distreyned by taylages, custume and cariages, moore than hire duetee or resoun is. And eek taken they of hire bondemen amercimentz, whiche myghten moore resonably ben cleped extorcions than amercimentz, of which amercimentz and raunsonynge of boonde-men somme lordes stywardes seyn that it is rightful, for as much as a churl hath no temporeel thyng

[9] MP, fo. 62[r].

[10] For this principle in the *Mirror of Justices* and on the practical restraint of custom, see J. Hatcher, 'English Serfdom and Villeinage: Towards a Reassessment', in T. H. Aston, *Landlords, Peasants and Politics in Medieval England* (Cambridge, 1987), 252.

[11] 'Conti[n]git interdum quod domini temporales violenter exigunt et extorquent tam a rusticis suis quam libere tenentibus multa bona, ultra id quod tenentes ipsi solvere debent et consueverunt, et ipsos invitos et absque causa talliant pro voluntate sua quandoque semel in anno, quandoque pluries, vel quociens videtur, nunc plus, nunc minus, quamplura bona per violenciam extorquendo. Unde quandoque evenit quod tenentes huiusmodi depauperati vix habent unde possunt sibi et suis in victualibus providere. Nec credunt tales domini se peccare in hoc, quia de iure civili, quod hodie in omnibus casibus in quibus vertitur periculum anime et peccatum committitur, si observetur ad litteram, tollitur omnino, cavetur quod quicquid servus adquirit domino adquirit . . . Set male decipiuntur, quia nullus dominus temporalis debet de iure naturali seu canonico aliquid exigere a tenente suo, preter id quod sibi debetur ab eodem de consuetudine vel ex convencione, inter ipsum et tenentem suum inita, vel ex imposicione facta ab antiquo.' MP, fo. 62[r].

[12] H. Bennett, *Life on the English Manor* (Cambridge, 1937), 138–9.

[13] Homans, *English Villagers*, 236.

that it ne is his lordes, as they seyn. But certes, this lordshipes doon wrong that bireven hire bondefolk thynges that they nevere yave hem.[14]

Robert Mannyng too condemns such unreasonable exactions:

> And ȝyf a lorde of a tounne
> Robbe hys men oute of resoune,
> þogh hyt be yn bondage,
> Aȝens ryȝt he doþe outrage . . .
> þogh god have ȝeve hym pe senyorye,
> He ȝaf hym no leve to do robberye.[15]

At the same time, he acknowledges that the lord may take 'þurgh ryȝt or þurgh cunnaunte'.[16] The moralists were in a dilemma, for while they opposed the laying of crippling burdens upon the peasant, they had no wish to derogate the customary rights of lordship.

The ambivalence had a long pedigree. Robert of Flamborough discusses tallage as a tax on both freemen and serfs. As a levy on the former it is only legitimate, he says, when it is based on an agreement between the lord and his tenant and when the amount and frequency of the imposition are fixed. 'Otherwise, in my opinion, your tallage is rapine and you are bound to restitution.'[17] On serfs, however: 'I neither counsel you to impose tallage, nor say that you sin mortally if you do so; but if they are reduced to extreme necessity by you, you are bound to sustain them.'[18] Robert of Courson, perhaps with English custom in mind,[19] stipulated that freemen ought to be exempt but allowed impositions on neifs.[20]

Though the subject received attention from the theologians and lawyers of the second half of the thirteenth century, their conclusions too failed to solve the dilemma. Like Flamborough, Simon Hinton distinguishes between the servile taxpayer and the free. In the case of the former, the lord sins in oppressing him excessively but he is not obliged to make restitution, though piety requires it. In the case of a freeman, however, his consent must be obtained and the demand must be related to a necessary expense of the lord.[21] John of Freiburg's discussion of the problem in essence resembles that of Flamborough and Hinton,

[14] *Canterbury Tales*, X (I) 750 (ed. Robinson, p. 252). Cf. the remarks of a Wyclifite critic: *The English Works of Wyclif*, ed. F. D. Matthew, EETS, os, 74 (1880), 233–4.
[15] *Handlyng Synne*, ed. Furnivall, ll. 2201–10.
[16] Ibid., l. 2199.   [17] *Liber Penitentialis*, ed. Firth, 186–7.   [18] Ibid.
[19] See Baldwin, *Masters*, i. 237.   [20] Ibid., ii. 174, n. 90.
[21] See B. Smalley, 'The Quaestiones of Simon of Hinton', in R. W. Hunt *et al.*, (eds.), *Studies Presented to F. M. Powicke* (Oxford, 1948), 211.

but is fuller, depending on the work of Raymund of Peñafort, Hostiensis, and Thomas Aquinas. In theory, upon the grant of land by a lord to his tenant, certain services and dues were agreed upon and perhaps written down. Such as were agreed upon without coercion and are consonant with the law of God may be demanded and must be rendered. If the subject withholds these against the lord's will, he is bound to restitution as a thief. Where no amounts were specified, the lord's demands should be regulated by a consideration of the subject's capacities. If the lord takes beyond what is customary or what is freely offered, he is bound to restitution and this applies to exactions made by him in person or by his servants, directly or indirectly—for example, by refusing to do justice or to protect his subjects otherwise. For Thomas Aquinas, to whom John refers, the justification for the lord's having revenues lies in his duty to serve the common good thereby, and where his revenues are insufficient to this end he may, in certain lands, by ancient custom, impose a tallage on his subjects. (This, of course, is the theory behind the king's right to tallage in England.) Examples are given of cases where a lord may demand more than is customary, all of them arising from unusual necessities such as extraordinary military expenditure in a just cause. Frivolous expenditure on his part does not justify such exactions.[22] Even on the level of theory, however, the ambivalence persists. To the question whether everything which has been paid from of old has necessarily been levied for a just cause, John replies that the presumption is that it has.[23] Even tallage at will seems permissible if it is well founded on custom:

What of those who avail themselves of a custom whereby they take as much and whenever they want from the moveable goods of their men . . . can they be excused by the custom from making restitution? I reply . . . If it is certain that such a burden was imposed from the beginning, without malice or fraud . . . it seems possible to allow that he may make use of such a constitution in such a way as not to weigh unreasonably on them . . . But where it is not certain or where it is believed

---

[22] John of Freiburg, *Summa Confessorum*, ii, 5, qq. 34–37. John Acton expresses a similar view: kings greatly sin who afflict the people of God with undue tallage and exactions. For this they shall give an account to God. This applies if out of pure greed or because of inordinate or immoderate expenses they wish to exact beyond what is established as due to them. In unusual circumstances, e.g. in case of enemy invasion or where the state of the prince requires it and where their own revenues and the customary levies are insufficient, princes may exact from their subjects, beyond what is customary, for the common utility. Unjust exactions, not required by the common utility, are forbidden. 'Septuplum': fo. 54ʳ·ᵛ, gloss *ad voces* 'contra iusticiam', 'potestate publica vel privata'.

[23] John of Freiburg, *Summa Confessorum*, q. 38.

that it was not lawfully instituted from the beginning, my belief is that since such spoliations in themselves are wickedly done, they who do so sin and are bound to make restitution.[24]

The author of the *Memoriale Presbiterorum*, like Simon Hinton, a voice from the valley,[25] is much more specific than the *Summae* on the evils of arbitrary tallage and on the necessity for restitution. 'You should tell such lords, if they confess to you concerning this, that all who do such things are robbers and in bad faith, and that no custom can excuse them from sin in this case. The reason is that that custom of tallaging and extorting is uncertain, for now it is to tallage more, now less, and as often as it pleases the lords.'[26]

In addition to oppressing their tenants in this fashion, lords and their ministers are accused of enacting statutes to the prejudice of churches and of ecclesiastics.[27] The author illustrates, somewhat inconsequentially, by referring to conspiracies among peasants against making customary offerings to their parish priests,[28] but otherwise gives no indication of the type of local legislation that he has in mind. John Bromyard, author of the *Summa Predicantium* (*c.*1330–40),[29] is more specific in describing how lords offend against the church. By evil customs, he says they take the goods of intestates, and they refuse to pay tithes on woodland, alleging that their ancestors never did so.[30] Friction over testaments was among the matters that engaged Grandisson's attention in relation to seignorial jurisdiction within his diocese. In the letter of 3 December 1335 to the archbishop of Canterbury, he complained that the servants of the earl of Cornwall forbade the exercise of ecclesiastical rights as regards personal injuries done to clerks and in testamentary cases, while the newly styled earl of Devon did not permit his men to make wills or that these be proved before the ordinary.[31]

While by the end of the thirteenth century the claims of the church courts in the matter of intestacy had won general recognition, canon and secular law were at variance over aspects of testamentary right. The

[24] Ibid., q. 39.   [25] See Smalley, 'The Quaestiones', 209, 211.

[26] MP, fo. 62[rb].   [27] Ibid., b. lvii.   [28] See below, p. 147.

[29] See L. E. Boyle, 'The Date of the *Summa Praedicantium* of John Bromyard', *Speculum*, 48 (1973), 553–7.

[30] Bromyard, *Summa Predicantium*, *sub voce* Dominatio (D. xii), art. vi, section xvi. A petition of the Commons in 1343 makes such an assertion concerning tithes of wood, see *Rot. Parl.*, ii, 18 Edw. III, p. 149 (b). For a directive of Archbishop Simon Sudbury to his commissary general to compel payment of tithe on deadwood under pain of *ipso facto* excommunication, see *Concilia*, iii. 113.

[31] *RG*, i. 293–4.

ecclesiastical authorities were uncompromising in maintaining the right of the serf, as of the covered woman, to make a will. The Council of Westminster, which had ordered the excommunication of lords interfering in cases of intestacy, ordered similar action against the impeding of wills by those of servile condition, 'contrary to the custom of the English church, hitherto approved'.[32] Among the clerical complaints at the parliament at Westminster in November 1280 is a charge that the wills of both freemen and serfs are impeded by feudal lords, so that the local ordinaries cannot cause them to be observed, even when the lord's customary rights over the dead man's property are safeguarded. According to the York version of the royal response, the ordinaries might deal with the offenders when the wills of free laymen or of clerics were involved. But the serf may be hindered by his lord, 'who can if he wishes, without injustice, take away from him all his goods, while he is alive', though if the lord consents to his making a will, it is valid and may not be impeded after his death.[33] There is evidence from several estates of the operation of a rule requiring this element of consent on the lord's part. The serfs of the abbey of Vale Royal, Cheshire, in the fourteenth century were forbidden to make a will or dispose of any of their goods, except for a mass penny and a mortuary, without the abbot's licence.[34] On one manor of the abbot of Ramsey, a will, to be valid, must be made in the presence of the reeve or bailiff.[35] In a court roll of Wiston, Hunts. (22 Edw. I) there is a directive to the bailiffs to seize all goods bequeathed by villeins in wills to the making of which the bailiffs had not been summoned.[36]

The canon law governing the making of a will, and its administration, was explained in detail by Bishop Quinel in his synodal statutes for the diocese of Exeter (1287), and it was there laid down that no one should impede the making of a will by clerk or layman, free or unfree, of those things which he possessed at the time of death.[37] The matter was included among the petitions to the king at the provincial Council of Canterbury in July 1295.[38] Interference with the wills of serfs was prohibited under pain of excommunication by Simon Mepham in his

[32] *CS*, ii. 585.
[33] Ibid. 878. For comment on this and on a reply of Edward III in 1344, see P. R. Hyams, *Kings, Lords and Commons in Medieval England: The Common Law of Villeinage in the Twelfth and Thirteenth Centuries* (Oxford, 1980), 72.
[34] Bennett, *English Manor*, 250–1.   [35] Ibid., 251.
[36] Homans, *English Villagers*, 432, n. 4. For the practice on St Albans manors, see Levett, *Studies*, 208–34.
[37] *CS*, ii. 1045–6.   [38] Ibid. 1143, c. 32.

constitutions of 1329,[39] and, definitively, by a constitution of the Council of London under Archbishop Stratford, which included a recension of Archbishop Boniface's enactment, the penalty decreed being that of major excommunication, *sententia lata*.[40] It was presumably against this latest expression of the serf's testamentary capacity that the Commons complained in 1343, declaring it to be 'against reason' that bondmen and wives might make a will.[41] The king's reply was to deny their right to do so.[42] On the level of theory, therefore, no concession was made to the church's view, though in practice servile wills were frequently allowed.[43]

Another notable point on which contemporary English custom was at variance with the canons was that of ownership to property lost at sea. The *Memoriale Presbiterorum* complains of the 'English custom, or rather, corruption'[44] by which, if there are no survivors of a shipwreck, the lord of the port to which their goods come occupies them as if they were his own by right of lordship. If a survivor does chance to appear, he will only with difficulty be able to reclaim a part but will never recover all his property. Lords, it cautions, may occupy wreck, but only in order to restore it to its true owners or to their heirs, notwithstanding any custom or statute to the contrary.[45] These absolute rights of the owner were not upheld in English law, by which the king had an interest in goods found on the sea or wrecked on the shore, and in which a distinction was made between *adventurae maris*—flotsam, jetsam, and lagan—and wreck of the seashore.[46] In the case of the former, goods found upon the sea, neither the lord of the port at which they were landed nor the original owner had any claim. The property ought to be divided between the finders and the king.[47] In the case of

---

[39] *Concilia*, ii. 553 (a).

[40] Ibid. 705. Commenting on this constitution, Lyndwood distinguishes between slaves and serfs. The former cannot make a will, being legally dead. *Provinciale*, iii, tit. 13, p. 172 (b), gloss ad vocem 'servilis conditionis'.

[41] *Rot. Parl.*, ii, 18 Edw. III, p. 149 (b). See also Levett, *Studies*, p. 210.

[42] *Rot. Parl.*, ii, 18 Edw. III, p. 149 (b).

[43] See M. M. Sheehan, *The Will in Medieval England* (Toronto, 1963), 253. On the attitude of the secular courts to the testamentary capacity of married women and of villeins, see J. L. Barton, *Roman Law in England, Ius Romanum Medii Aevi*, Pars v, xiii (a) (Milan, 1971), 85, and on the church's failure to establish the latter's right, see ibid. 86–7.

[44] MP, fo. 60ʳ.

[45] Ibid., b. xxxiv. Cf. the comments of John Bromyard, much of whose discussion of 'Consuetudo' is taken up with a discussion of wreck, *Summa Predicantium*, C. viii., especially arts. 5 and 6.

[46] For the definition of these terms, see Holdsworth, *History English Law*, i. 560. On the subject in general, see R. G. Marsden, 'Admiralty Droits and Salvage—Gas Float Whitton, No. II', *Law Quarterly Review*, 15 (1899), 353–66.

[47] See ibid. 355, where a case of 1310 is cited, in which the finders retained two-thirds while the king got the remainder.

wreck, which is what the *Memoriale* is concerned with—'if the goods contained in it should be carried to port by the tide'[48]—the lord of the land to which the goods came might indeed have an interest, by virtue of a royal grant to him of this droit.[49] However, the right of the owner of the goods remained, if he appeared to claim them within a year and a day.[50] A proclamation of Henry I, whereby a sole survivor should obtain all the wreck, was later successfully contested by Battle abbey as being valid only for his reign.[51] But the goods to which the survivor could prove a title must be restored to him, though one may well appreciate the difficulty in practice, and it is probable that, as the *Memoriale* suggests, the finder, if he did not keep all, claimed his reward.

Given the reputation of the Cornish coast into modern times, it is surprising that, while concerned with wreck, the *Memoriale* does not deal with wrecking nor with its near relation, the plundering of a stranded ship, as vividly described by Gerald of Wales.[52]

Several of the excesses with which knights, and, by implication, other temporal lords, are accused in the *Memoriale* involve infringements of ecclesiastical liberty or organization. Some of these are traditional offences: 'Item, if he hauled clerics to his court against their will, compelling them to litigate there or respond in spiritual actions or causes belonging to the ecclesiastical forum, and aggrieved them by amercing or mulcting them.'[53] The hearing of a spiritual plea would in itself be an infringement of church liberties, and is distinct from the other point raised—the lord's attempt to try clerics and fine them in his court. Among the list of grievances transmitted by Grandisson on 18 January 1329 for consideration at the Council of London later that month was that secular judges usurped spiritual jurisdiction and drew clerks into their courts in matters pertaining to the ecclesiastical forum.[54] When he wrote to Hugh de Courtenay in 1341 carefully explaining to him the effect of excommunication, the first three points concerned infringement of ecclesiastical liberties and of property and attachment of the person of clerks.[55] That parish clergy should appear both as litigants and as defendants in manorial courts was inevitable, given their involvement in the economic life of the community. Even the author

---

[48] MP, fo. 60ʳ.
[49] That he would be required to substantiate his claim to possess wreck is evidenced by *The Black Book of the Admiralty*, ed. T. Twiss (Rolls Series, 1871), i. 80–1, 158–9, 228.
[50] See Marsden, 'Admiralty Droits', 355.
[51] See H. W. C. Davis, 'The Chronicle of Battle Abbey', *EHR* 29 (1914), 434.
[52] Giraldi Cambrensis, *De Principis Instructione*, ed. J. F. Dimock (Rolls Series, 1891), viii. 120.
[53] MP, fo. 22ᵛᵇ.   [54] *RG*, i. 448.   [55] Ibid. 943–4. Cf. above, p. 48.

of the *Memoriale* seems to countenance the type of seizure of which he complains, when the clerk is a tenant of the lord, for he adds, 'especially if the cleric does not hold temporalities from him'.[56] The knight is also to be examined as regards violent assault on a cleric or his forcible detention.[57] The point is unremarkable. Cases could be documented from any episcopal register, but sensitivity to violence against the persons of clerks was, as has been noted, a constant preoccupation of Bishop Grandisson.[58]

Another harassment of ecclesiastics complained of by the *Memoriale* is the extortion of 'pensions or procurations'.[59] It is unclear whether the former are corrodies. Monasteries and other religious houses frequently made provision for old servants in their retirement by granting them lodgings and amounts of food, clothing, and other necessities in lieu of pensions, and it was a system which had a wider appeal.[60] By the end of the thirteenth century the king was making use of monasteries—usually of royal patronage—as a means of providing for retired servants of his household, and by the reign of Edward III the practice had come to be regarded as a right. The fact that the house concerned frequently attempted to excuse itself, with varying success, is evidence that such impositions were resented.[61] Founders also claimed rights in this regard, and the *Articuli Cleri* of 1316 contain a petition that the king should, in addition to refraining himself, prevent excessive demands by magnates and others.[62] When the grant was made in return for a capital payment, the arrangement could, of course, be greatly to the monastery's advantage, as in the case, recorded from early in the fifteenth century, of a corrodian of Westminster Abbey, who having bought his corrody, £5. 6s. 8d. annually, for £150, died after only five years.[63] In

---

[56] MP, fo. 23[r].   [57] Ibid.   [58] See above, pp. 44–7.   [59] MP, fo. 22[vb].

[60] On corrodies in general, see R. H. Snape, *English Monastic Finances in the Later Middle Ages* (Cambridge, 1926), 139–45; A. H. Thompson, 'A Corrody from Leicester Abbey, AD 1393–4, With Some Notes on Corrodies', *Transactions of the Leicestershire Archaeological Society*, 14 (1926), 114–34; K. Wood-Legh, *Church Life in England under Edward III* (Cambridge, 1934), 28–9; D. Knowles, *The Religious Orders in England*, iii (Cambridge, 1959), 28–9; Swanson, *Church and Society*, 236–7.

[61] See S. Wood, *English Monasteries and Their Patrons in the Thirteenth Century* (Oxford, 1955), 144–5. Cf. J. H. Tillotson, 'Pensions, Corrodies and Religious Houses: An Aspect of the Relations of Crown and Church in Early Fourteenth-Century England', *Journal of Religious History*, 8 (1974), 127–43.

[62] See *Statutes of the Realm*, ed. A. Luders et al., i (London, 1810), 173, c. xi. Cf. Snape, *Monastic Finances*, 139–40.

[63] See G. H. Cook, *English Monasteries in the Middle Ages* (London, 1961), 21. Cf. Snape, *Monastic Finances*, 143–4. It could also mean, however, that the house had a crippling burden to sustain in later years. See J. R. H. Moorman, *Church Life in England in the Thirteenth Century* (Cambridge, 1955), 270–1. Cf. Snape, *Monastic Finances*, 144.

this way corrodies were used simply as a means of raising ready money. But the practice was clearly open to abuse, for it was in the beneficiary's interests to have the capital sum fixed as low as possible, and one may presume that he might not always be above applying pressure to this end. Bishop Brinton tells of a bailiff who violently extorted a certain rent ('certum redditum') from a monastery and was struck down because he delayed repentance.[64] Corrodies which were subsequently found to be prejudicial to the house were sometimes revoked by royal authority on the plea of misrule by the head, the implication being that they were irregular, but whether this was more than a pretext, and what the nature of the irregularity might be in such cases, it is difficult to ascertain.[65]

Among the offences against ecclesiastical organization with which the knight is charged are simony—to which he might be presumed to be prone as patron of a church; sacrilege, 'carrying off consecrated things or non-consecrated things from a consecrated place,'[66] though not specifically infringement of sanctuary;[67] and keeping a private chapel without licence. Maintenance of a private chapel was a complaint of considerable antiquity. In about 830 Jonas of Orleans remarked how great folk had their private chapels, which they used as an excuse for not attending their parish church,[68] and in a synod at Pavia in 855 complaint was made to the emperor concerning lack of preaching, of which one cause was that rich and powerful layfolk heard divine service in chapels beside their dwellings and did not come very often to the mother churches.[69] The topic was ruled on both in the *Decretals*[70] and at diocesan and provincial level, with the object of protecting the interests of the parish church against the risk of the chapel's developing an independent life.[71] A statute of Bishop Nicholas of Farnham (1241–9) for the

---

[64] Brinton, *Sermons*, 183.   [65] See Wood-Legh, *Church Life*, 28–9.

[66] MP, fo. 23ʳ.   [67] See below, pp. 135–8.

[68] *Jonae Aurelianensis Episcopi, De Institutione Laicali*, i, c. ii (*PL*, cvi. col. 144). Cf. G. G. Coulton, *Medieval Village, Manor and Monastery* (New York, 1960), 281.

[69] *Sacrosancta Concilia*, ed. P. Labbé, viii (Paris, 1671), col. 147; cf. Coulton, *Medieval Village*, 281. For Eigenkirchen in the early period, see F. Barlow, *The English Church 1000–1066: A Constitutional Study* (London, 1963), 183–208, and W. Page, 'Some Remarks on the Churches of the Domesday Survey', *Archaeologia*, 66 (1915), 61–102. For policy on the minsters' rights, see Barlow, *English Church*, 194–201 and M. J. Franklin, 'Bodies in Medieval Northampton: Legatine Intervention in the Twelfth Century', in M. J. Franklin and C. Harper-Bill, *Medieval Ecclesiastical Studies in Honour of D. M. Owen* (Woodbridge, 1995), 71–2.

[70] X. 3. 1. 15.

[71] See Moorman, *Church Life*, 12. On the economic dimension, see R. N. Swanson, *Church and Society in Late Medieval England* (Oxford, 1989), 219, and on the tension, id., 'Parochialism and Particularism: The Dispute over the Status of Ditchford Frary, Warwickshire, in the early Fifteenth Century', in Franklin and Harper-Bill, *Medieval Ecclesiastical Studies*, 243–4, and N. Orme, 'Church and Chapel in Medieval England', *TRHS*, 6th ser., 6 (1996), 92–3.

diocese of Durham forbade the celebration of mass in newly erected chapels except by special authority of the bishop. Chapels erected of old must also have episcopal sanction, and archdeacons on their visitations were instructed to suspend such a chapel until episcopal licence be given.[72] The Legatine Council at London in 1268 advocated that control be maintained over the erection of private chapels, if the rights and revenues of the parish church were not to be prejudiced,[73] and just under twenty years later Bishop Quinel's statutes for Exeter dealt with the matter in detail. As usual, no new church or chapel was to be constructed without episcopal licence, nor might divine services be ministered there. Even when the chapel had been licensed, the mother church must suffer no prejudice and the customary offerings must continue to be made to the rector. This had parish chapels in mind, but the same was to apply to oratories in private houses. The upkeep of oratories and also of chapels not belonging to a parish church devolved on their founders.[74] As argued above, Bishop Grandisson's jealousy in the matter of chapels was a part of his general outlook.[75] With other bishops, he attempted to maintain strict control over oratories too. A clause safeguarding the rights of the parish church is standard in his licences.[76] As regards the precise stricture of the *Memoriale Presbiterorum*, one of Stratford's provincial constitutions of 1342 forbade the saying of mass in unconsecrated oratories, without episcopal licence, and severely curtailed the rights of his suffragan bishops to grant such licences.[77] The near-contemporary canonist John Acton, glossing the legatine constitutions, points out that while any of the faithful may have an unconsecrated oratory in his house, on his own authority, he may not have masses celebrated there, except in cases of necessity, without licence and consent of the bishop.[78]

Another transgression against canon law, according to the *Memoriale*, on which the knight ought to be examined was the frequenting of

---

On the driving force of choice, see G. Rosser, 'Parochial Conformity and Voluntary Religion in Late-Medieval England', *TRHS*, 6th series, 1 (1991), 173–89.

[72] *CS*, ii. 429.   [73] Ibid. 766.

[74] Ibid. 1002–4.   [75] See above, pp. 55–6.

[76] See e.g. *RG*, i. 492, 537, 556; ii. 652, 666; and *passim*; *Reg. Hethe*, 414, 679, 684–5, 699–700 and *passim*. For the control maintained over chapels in the later period, see Thompson, *The English Clergy*, 123–8. On the distinction between a 'proper chapel' and a 'room in a house', see Swanson, *Church and Society*, 49.

[77] *Concilia*, ii. 696; cf. ibid. 677. The constitution is from the unpublished series, cf. above, p. 27.

[78] Acton, *Commentary*, p. 6 (a), gloss *ad vocem*, 'Necessitatis causa'.

tournaments. The tournament from 1150 to 1350 has been described as, 'for the most part not a matter of individual jousting, but a mass-meeting of side against side, resulting in a mêlée which differed little from real war'.[79] It was the real chance of death ensuing from these conflicts that determined the attitude of the canon lawyers. In the *Decretals* the title *De torneamentis* follows immediately from *De homicidio voluntario vel casuali*.[80] In 1274 Gregory X wrote to Edward I that if men were not killed at tournaments, one could call them childish games.[81] It is in this vein that Hostiensis answers the question, 'Why are they forbidden? On account of the deaths of men and the peril of souls which frequently proceed from them . . . For future perils ought to be guarded against and every discerning person ought to look to the future, since he ought to think of the possibility of this outcome.'[82] Innocent II, at the Council of Clermont in 1130, had condemned 'those detestable fairs or feasts which commonly they call tournaments',[83] and a prohibition of Alexander III in similar language was incorporated in the *Decretals*.[84] Anyone dying at a tournament was to be allowed confession but denied ecclesiastical burial. This penalty does not seem to have been generally exacted in England, however. When Gilbert, earl of Pembroke, was killed in a tournament at Hertford in 1241 he was given Christian burial,[85] as was Arnold de Muntinni, a knight of the royal household, killed at a gathering in 1252.[86] Celestine III in 1192 had ordered the bishops and Richard I to forbid tournaments because of the wretched state of the Holy Land.[87] When John XXII relaxed the general ban in 1316, he did so, ironically, out of a consideration that knighthood was adversely affected and the relief of the Holy Land impeded thereby.[88] The *Memoriale*, while referring to the canonical ban on tournaments,[89] does not mention this latter ruling.[90]

---

[79] N. Denholm-Young, 'The Tournament in the Thirteenth Century', in Hunt *et al.* (eds.), *Studies to Powicke*, p. 240.

[80] X. 5. 13.   [81] Denholm-Young, 'The Tournament', 243.

[82] *SA*, v, De torneamentis, c. 2, col. 1243.

[83] Denholm-Young, 'The Tournament', 243.   [84] X. 5. 13. 1.

[85] See Denholm-Young, 'The Tournament', 252.   [86] Ibid., 255–6.

[87] Ibid. 243. Cf. M. Keen, *Chivalry* (New Haven/London, 1984), 97–8, for the dubious reasoning.

[88] *Extravagantes Johannis XXII*, De torneamentis, q. 1.

[89] MP, fo. 23ᵛ: 'Item si frequentaverit torneamenta, que de iure canonico sunt interdicta.'

[90] The author of the *Cilium Oculi Sacerdotis* is a little better informed in this respect, though short of being certain: 'Item qui in torneamentis occiduntur licet in titulo de torneamentis c. i. infra sacra sepeliri prohibentur, tamen secundum quosdam et capitulo novi iuris extravagante, sepeliri debent', Oxford, Balliol College, MS. 86, 'Cilium Oculi', fo. 238ᵛᵃ.

An even more serious topic for the moralist was the crimes attendant on other martial activity. The confessor ought to inquire whether the knight 'on occasion urged his lord—the king perhaps, or an earl or baron—to an unjust war'.[91] The requirements for a just war are expounded by the *Memoriale* in chapter b. xli. It was a question which had been thoroughly elaborated by the canonists.[92] Raymund of Peñafort, whose theory of the just war was repeated by Hostiensis and John of Freiburg and is inherited by the *Memoriale*, laid down five prerequisites: the war should be just with regard to the persons engaged in it, for clerics must not take part—another application of the doctrine of circumstances; it must be just with regard to its object and to its cause; it must be just in its intention, namely, to achieve justice; and it must be waged on valid authority, that is, on the authority of the Roman church or of a sovereign prince.[93] Closely linked with the question of the justice of the *casus belli* were the issues of the spoils of war, and of depredations in wartime. These are dealt with in a succession of chapters: b. xl 'De predonibus et raptoribus qui in bellis bona aliorum rapiunt';[94] b. xlii, 'De hiis qui recipiunt predam dono predonis';[95] b. xliii, 'De uxore et familia predonis';[96] b. xliiii, 'De hiis qui res raptas seu depredatas emunt'.[97] Although the discussion draws heavily on Hostiensis, and directly as well as indirectly on Raymund of Peñafort,[98] the author's engagement is evident. As suggested above, this dimension of the treatise plausibly relates to Grandisson's known interest in the morality of warfare. For that reason, it is unsafe to suppose—as would in the abstract be attractive—that the author's interest reflects the early stages of the Hundred Years War.[99]

---

[91] MP, fo. 23ᵛ.

[92] See M. Keen, *The Laws of War in the Late Middle Ages* (London/Toronto, 1965), chap. 5, and, comprehensively, F. H. Russell, *The Just War in the Middle Ages* (Cambridge, 1975). Cf. from a philosophical perspective, J. Barnes, 'The Just War', *The Cambridge History of Later Medieval Philosophy*, ed. A. Kenny and J. Pinborg (Cambridge, 1982), 771–84.

[93] Raymund of Peñafort, *Summa*, ii. 5, 17.   [94] MP, fo. 62ᵛᵇ.   [95] MP, fo. 64ʳᵃ.
[96] MP, fo. 64ʳᵃ⁻ᵇ.   [97] MP, fos. 64ᵛ–65ʳ.

[98] See esp. Hostiensis, *SA*, cols. 1469 (bis), 1470, 1470 (bis), 1473–4; Raymund of Peñafort, *Summa*, ii, sect. 21, pp. 191–2.

[99] Cf. Pantin, *Church*, 210.

7

Society Under Scrutiny III: The Examination of Manorial and Seignorial Officials

The *Memoriale*'s approach to the officials responsible for the exercise of seignorial or manorial jurisdiction or for the economic administration of estates is that of a moralist rather than of a writer on estate management. T. F. Plucknett has described the classic hierarchy among the lord's agents thus: 'At its head is the steward, who becomes a lawyer-financier, surveying the lord's fortune as a whole. In the middle rank is the bailiff in charge of a manor or small group of neighbouring properties. At the bottom there is, in each manor or estate, the reeve.'[1] All these factors of the lord may be generally referred to as bailiffs.[2] Their functions, theoretically distinct, were often confused. So, while in the classic pattern it was the function of the steward to hold the courts, pressure of business might mean that the ordinary three-weekly sessions would fall to the bailiff, while the steward attended the manorial court two or three times yearly—serious cases being perhaps reserved for his hearing on these occasions—or to hold the view of frankpledge, where his lord possessed this liberty.[3] In the chapter devoted to the interrogation of these persons[4] the *Memoriale* treats them jointly as 'seneschals and bailiffs'. Sometimes the queries to be put are those appropriate to the activities of a manorial officer; at other times it seems that the bailiff concerned exercises a form of public jurisdiction, as in the empanelling of juries 'in assizes and inquisitions'.[5] Here too, contemporary practice—as opposed to theory—often made no rigid distinction: many private bailiffs of lords also served as bailiffs of the

---

[1] T. F. Plucknett, *The Mediaeval Bailiff* (London, 1954), 7.

[2] On the breadth of meaning implicit in the term, see N. Denholm-Young, *Seignorial Administration* (London, 1937), 32. For the term 'seneschal', see ibid. 67. On the general distinction by the fourteenth century between the personnel of the household and of estate administration, see C. Given-Wilson, *The English Nobility in the Later Middle Ages: The Fourteenth-Century Political Community* (London/New York, 1987), 87–103.

[3] See Denholm-Young, *Seignorial Administration*, 72.

[4] MP, a. xxxv.   [5] ibid., fos. 21ᵛ–22ʳ.

hundred.[6] Again, in the section on restitution, the treatise considers how this obligation may fall on 'bailiffs and servants [or sergeants—*servientibus*] of magnates'.[7] Here the author has an accounting official in mind, but as the reeve sometimes discharged this function[8] his comments might equally apply to him. In short, the *Memoriale* is, in all of this, concerned with officialdom in general, those who exercise stewardship.

This attention to the officials in seignorial and manorial administration is an unusual feature in a confessional manual. They do not appear among the interrogatories prescribed by Hostiensis. The author's remarks on their behaviour seem to be original. With other critics of contemporary society—notably Bromyard—he clearly feels that a large part of the blame for the lord's mismanagement and oppression falls on these servants.[9]

In examining seneschals and bailiffs, the confessor is warned to be particularly on his guard: 'If it falls to you to hear any such person you must strive manfully to extract the truth, for such people are very devious and altogether given over to avarice and falsehood, and led by blind greed . . . they do not care about God or holy church or its ministers, but only about securing profits and bribes.'[10]

The first point to be established in examining a seneschal or bailiff is the penitent's personal status—whether, that is, he is a clerk or a layman. If he is a beneficed clerk, having cure of souls, 'and consequently, a priest', he is forbidden by canon law to exercise this jurisdiction, under pain of excommunication. If he is a non-beneficed clerk, he should be reminded that he may not proceed to sacred orders while he holds his secular office.[11] Grandisson, it has been noted, in addressing non-residence complained particularly of activities incongruent with the benefice-holder's order.[12] A long history underlay this concern.[13]

---

[6] See Denholm-Young, *Seignorial Administration*, 40; H. M. Cam, *The Hundred and the Hundred Rolls* (London, 1930), 157; A. Musson, *Public Order and Law Enforcement: The Local Administration of Criminal Justice 1294–1350* (Woodbridge, 1996), 155–8.

[7] MP, b. lii.

[8] See H. S. Bennett, 'The Reeve and the Manor in the Fourteenth Century', *EHR* 41 (1926), 360.

[9] For analogous remarks on the rapacity of officials, in thirteenth-century France, see A. de Poorter, 'Le Traité *Eruditio Regum et Principum* de Guibert de Tournai OFM (Étude et Texte Inédit)', in M. de Wulf (ed.), *Les Philosophes Belges*, ix (Louvain, 1914), 50—'De malis quae faciunt officiales in curiis.'

[10] MP, fo. 21ᵛ.   [11] Ibid.   [12] *RG*, ii. 1174. See above, p. 50.

[13] R. E. Rodes, *Ecclesiastical Administration in Medieval England: The Anglo-Saxons to the Reformation* (Notre Dame/London, 1977), 39–40, 43–4, sets it in context of the Gregorian reform.

Canon 12 of the Third Lateran Council forbade clerics in major orders to act as advocates in secular matters before a secular judge, except in certain specified circumstances, and added, 'nor shall they become proctors of vills nor [exercise] secular jurisdictions under any princes or secular men, nor become their justiciars'.[14] The only reason adduced by the canons for the prohibition is the text of the apostle, 'Nemo militans Deo implicet se secularibus negociis',[15] and the consideration that by immersing himself in secular affairs the cleric will neglect his clerical office. The injunction was repeated frequently in English diocesan legislation,[16] and this is usually more specific as to the dangers of such entanglements. Some of the early-thirteenth-century constitutions, indeed, link the holding of secular office with the extraneous question of involvement in judgments of blood.[17] It was expressly in order to enable him to proceed against this aspect of clerical association in secular administration that Grosseteste obtained a papal mandate in July 1236.[18] That was an element in a wider attempt on his part to define the relations between ecclesiastical and secular jurisdictions.

Concern for the pastoral interests of the benefice is not a wholly satisfactory explanation of the church's theoretically absolute ban on combining secular and ecclesiastical responsibilities, for the ecclesiastical bureaucrat who was also beneficed would have as little time for pastoral activities as the royal or seignorial official. The main objection, in fact, seems to have been to the idea of a cleric's holding a position in which he was answerable to a layman, an objection clearly enunciated by Grosseteste in his long survey of contemporary incursions on church liberties directed to Archbishop Edmund in 1236.[19] That particular consideration is a recurring feature of local legislation throughout the thirteenth century,[20] where the principal concern is with

[14] X. 1.37. 1; cf. ibid. 3. 50. 4.   [15] 2. Tim. 2. 4.
[16] The earliest instance seems to be in the statutes of Archbishop Stephen Langton for the diocese of Canterbury, 1213 × 1214, see *CS*, ii. 26–7.
[17] See Statutes of Exeter (1225 × 1237), *CS*, ii. 230; Council of Oxford (1222), canons 12 and 13, ibid. 110.
[18] *CPL*, i. 155; cf. ibid. 230. On the difficulties and uncertainties attaching, see R. W. Southern, *Robert Grosseteste, the Growth of an English Mind in Medieval Europe*, 2nd edn. (Oxford, 1992), 265–71.
[19] Robert Grosseteste, *Epistolae*, ed. H. R. Luard (Rolls Series, 1861), no. lxxii, p. 213.
[20] See e.g. Langton's statutes for Canterbury diocese, 1213 × 1214 (*CS*, ii. 26–7); Poore's for Salisbury (1217 × 1219), which forbid such a cleric's admission to ecclesiastical benefices before he has accounted for his administration (ibid. 187–8); canon 12 of the Council of Oxford (1222) (ibid. 110); the Lincoln statutes of 1239 (ibid. 270–1) and those of Worcester (1240) (ibid. 310–11). For a fourteenth-century restatement see Langham's Ely statutes (1364),

beneficed clerics or those in major orders. Ottobuono's prohibition on the exercise of secular jurisdiction by clerics was aimed at 'all rectors of churches and perpetual vicars, and further, all of the order of priest'.[21] This seems to represent in practice a concession in favour of sub-deacons, though the decree of the Third Lateran Council remained as part of the common law of the church. Acton, indeed, in his commentary on the legate's constitution, contends that the ruling applies to clerics in minor orders as well, priests being specified because the danger is greater in their case,[22] but this seems to be an unduly rigorous inter-pretation. The *Memoriale* certainly has priests in mind, though the inter-rogatory on this point does not make it clear whether the difficulty arises on account of their order or because they have the cure of souls.[23] Even Grosseteste thought that Hugh de Pateshull might lawfully continue in his secular involvements if he resigned his pastoral cure.[24]

That the prohibition was difficult to enforce in practice is evidenced by the frequency with which it was restated. After almost a century of recurring legislation, the topic is included under two heads among the articles of inquiry proposed by the papal nuncios at the Council of Westminster in January 1273.[25] In the first place, a concession was made, both explicitly and in practice, in favour of the king's interest in this respect,[26] and it was in this area that ecclesiastical interests were most likely to suffer from the cleric's liability to render an account of his stewardship, as the cases both of Stratford and Wykeham illustrate.[27]

Concilia, iii. 60. Cf. MP, fo. 22[vb]: 'Ordinari non potest nec debet de iure quamdiu fuerit astrictus tali officio seculari, et potissime si fuerit obligatus ad reddendum compotum de administracione sua.'

[21] *CS*, ii. 755.   [22] Acton, *Commentary*, p. 90(a), *sub voce* 'in sacerdotio'.
[23] MP, fo. 21[v].   [24] See Grosseteste, *Epistolae*, ed. Luard, no. xxv, p. 99.
[25] 'De clericis beneficiatis secularibus negotiis se immiscentibus', 'De clericis iustitiariis et advocatis curie secularis beneficiatis', *CS*, ii. 806.
[26] For the king's claim (1280) to a general papal privilege that his clerks should not be compelled to reside while in his service, see ibid. 879–80 and 879, n. 2. Cf. *CCR, 1302–7*, 193 and *Reg. Winchelsey*, i, xxii. Canon 6 of the Legatine Council (1268), dealt expressly with the tenure of secular jurisdiction, ibid. 755. Acton comments on this clause in a way which suggests that the royal privileges were not well defined even by the mid-fourteenth century. *Commentary*, 91 (a), *sub voce* 'privilegiis'. Reference too to his definition elsewhere of the 'commensal clerks' of a bishop as those who are with him continuously, if occasion-ally absent, implies that 'king's clerk' should also be interpreted restrictively: ibid. 38 (a), *sub voce* 'Commensalibus'.
[27] For an example of the analogous danger in the case of seignorial administration, see the outlawry of William, parson of Thoresby (*c*.1344), for failure to answer a plea of account in respect of his receivership, *CPR, 1343–5*, 208.

The extent to which the royal bureaucracy relied on ecclesiastical benefices is well known, and this feature, like so many others of government, was paralleled in the administration of the magnates. Service in a seignorial household was an important avenue of promotion in the church.[28] A good example is the career of Ralph Ergham, bishop of Salisbury (1375–88) and later of Bath and Wells (1388–1400).[29] He served as chancellor to the duke of Lancaster from April 1372 until 11 December 1375.[30] He had been a priest since 1362 and rector of Winstead, Yorks., from 1361 to November 1374, when he secured Preston, Lancs., at Gaunt's presentation.[31] His provision to Salisbury was also at Gaunt's instance.[32] It is to be noted, moreover, that he did not vacate the chancellorship until two days after his consecration as bishop, though before the temporalities of the see were restored to him.[33] An example of interest in context of the later career of William Doune is John Gynwell, bishop of Lincoln (1347–62). Besides holding a plurality of canonries and prebends, he was rector of Llanelly, Carmaths., in 1343–4, during which time he was also chaplain and steward of Henry, earl of Derby, the only cleric to act in this latter capacity.[34] Many other cases could be cited of beneficed clerks who served at one level or another in the administrations of great lords and whose masters took pains to advance their ecclesiastical careers. Cases can also be found in the fourteenth century of the association of religious with the worldly affairs of magnates. John de Stepulton, abbot of Wigmore, acted as receiver-general to Roger Mortimer, earl of March (1346–60).[35] The abbot of Walden was among the followers of Humphrey de Bohun, earl of Hereford, and on the latter's death in 1361 he was one of those to whom the earl's lands were farmed out.[36] Whether a monk—specifically an obedientiary or holder of claustral office—rendered himself *curialis*, a frequenter of the courts of princes or magnates, is included by the *Memoriale Presbiterorum* in the interrogatory for this class.[37]

If it is clear, therefore, that magnates too, like pope, bishops, and king, systematically relied on the separation of *beneficium* and *officium*

---

[28] See Highfield, 'The Hierarchy', 119–20, where it is observed that five members of the hierarchy in that period had been trained in lay households other than the king's. At a lower and particular level, see M. J. Bennett, *Community, Class and Careerism. Cheshire and Lancashire Society in the Age of Sir Gawain and the Green Knight* (Cambridge, 1983), 152–3.

[29] See *BRUO*, i. 644–5.   [30] See *Reg. John of Gaunt*, nos. 935, 1795.

[31] *BRUO*, i. 644–5; *Reg. John of Gaunt*, no. 199.   [32] *BRUO*, i. 644–5.

[33] Ibid.   [34] Ibid., ii. 842–3; *CPP*, i. 49. Cf. Fowler, *The King's Lieutenant*, 177.

[35] Holmes, *Estates*, 67.   [36] Ibid. 75.   [37] MP, fo. 14ʳ.

for the functioning of their administration,[38] at a purely casual and much humbler level, less capable of documentation, it may be supposed that the resident parson or vicar at least occasionally lent assistance in manorial management.[39] In *Piers Plowman*, Sloth appears in the guise of a parish priest, accomplished in this respect:

> Ich have be prest and person • passyng therty wintere,
> 3ut can ich nother solfye ne synge • ne a seyntes lyf rede.
> Ac ich can fynde in a feld • and in a forlang an hare,
> And holden a kny3tes court • and a-counte with the reyve.[40]

Having established the personal status of the steward, the confessor, according to the *Memoriale*, should inquire whether he obtained his office in return for payment or promise of payment, or by a bribe, 'for the law presumes that such a seneschal or bailiff, buying his bailiwick, will raise from the poor men of his bailiwick whatever he gave or paid to have it, by unjustly oppressing and burdening them'.[41] John Bromyard makes a similar point about the abuses attendant on the sale of offices. Sometimes, he says, lords sell an office to their servants, in the forest, on the land, in the castle, which is not sufficient to support them; the servants then proceed to extort the price from the people, without any qualms of conscience, since they think that they are entitled to do so. Bromyard claims to have seen one such who was put in charge of a prison in which there were many rich men, from whose wives and friends, wishing to visit them, he extorted large bribes. When taken to task over this, he replied that he had no conscience about the matter, for his lord had given him the office as a promotion and reward for his service and intended him to profit by it. 'But how could his lord give him what he could not in justice accept himself?'[42] Not only, he continues, do they afflict their wretched people financially; what is worse, they afflict them physically, for they place them in the deepest prisons, so that they must buy a freer one. From this traffic they live sumptuously and drink wine, and they who were poor and went on foot, so gnaw their wretched subjects that they become knights and rich men, as, Bromyard says, daily experience proves, and it is not without

---

[38] For the royal and papal bureaucracies, see Pantin, *Church*, 36. On the magnates, see the very specific Wycliffite criticism: *English Works of Wyclif*, ed. Matthew, 242.

[39] Cf. Bennett, *English Manor*, 187–8.

[40] *Piers Plowman*, C. Passus VIII, ll. 30–3. Cf. ibid., B. Passus V, ll. 427–8 and C. Passus I, ll. 93–4.

[41] MP, fo. 21^{ib}. On purchase of office cf. ibid., b. li, and above, p. 107.

[42] Bromyard, *Summa Predicantium, sub voce* 'Dominatio' (D. xii), art. iii, sec. viii.

hardship to their subjects that an office which used to maintain a man on foot now maintains a man on horse, with two or three scoundrels worse than their master, if that were possible. He concludes in the words of the prophet (Nahum 3: 17): 'Custodes tui quasi locuste et parvuli tui quasi locuste locustarum.'[43] Bailiwicks as a source of fortunes also attracted the notice of the author of a 'Song on the Venality of Judges' in the reign of Edward I:

> Clericos irrideo
> Suos, quos prius video
> Satis indigentes,
> Et quasi nil habentes,
> Quando ballivam capiunt;
> Qua capta mox superbiunt,
> Et crescunt sibi dentes,
> Collaque erigentes,
> Incipiunt perpropere
> Terras et domos emere
> Et redditus placentes
> Nummosque colligentes,
> Pauperes despiciunt,
> Et novas leges faciunt,
> Vicinos opprimentes.[44]

And a story found in both Bromyard and Brinton tells of the bailiff who resigned his office and then, finding that his wife and he were so much worse off, resumed it, only to be welcomed back by the devil in the form of an ape, which sat on his horse's neck and cried, 'Welcome to Wikke, welcome to Wikke'.[45]

---

[43] Ibid.

[44] *Political Songs*, ed. Wright, 230. The effect may be loosely captured:

> Their clerks arouse a smile
> Who just a little while
> Ago knew hunger pangs
> Until they got a bailiwick:
> Which gotten, double quick
> They start to grow their fangs.
> They buy up lands; they pile up dross;
> They smartly show the poor who's boss
> And grind men in the dust
> —With laws to make it just

[45] Bromyard, *Summa Predicantium, sub voce* 'Ministracio' (M.viii) art. v, sec. xv. Brinton, *Sermons*, 139.

Occasional extant seignorial appointments of bailiffs in private hundreds show the system of buying office in operation. So, in 1374 the bailiff of West Derby, Lancs., has a grant of the wapentake for three years, 'paying for the said office as much as any other will give for it'.[46] Similarly, the bailiwick of Salfordshire, Lancs., is farmed to two men for two years, at thirteen marks a year, on their giving security to govern well and loyally, and the wapentake of Staincliff, Yorks., is leased to Robert de Plesyngton, with all its issues and profits, for a term of twenty years, at an annual rent of £25.[47] 'The bailiff's profits', it has been observed, '. . . arose from those fees or tips or bribes which by custom or coercion he could claim from the people of the hundred as his commission.'[48] The complaint that the 'ferms' they took from the bailiffs were too high, and that the latter were thus forced to extortion, was commonly laid against sheriffs.[49]

Besides condemning this practice of buying offices, the *Memoriale* notes the various means by which the unjust steward might recoup his initial outlay. He might, for instance, take a bribe from someone who wished to initiate a false action against an adversary, or he might himself take the initiative and attach one of his subjects and cause him to lose his goods for failing to obey his will.[50] He is to be examined, too, on 'whether he imprisoned or ordered or procured the imprisonment of anyone unjustly, and so the imprisoned person lost his goods by conferring them on him or even on others to have his release and to redeem his harassment'.[51] These are the stuff of complaints at judicial inquiries of the period against bailiffs' activities in distraining: 'They are accused of taking beasts of the plough contrary to the statute, of distraining greatly in excess of the amount required, of distraining although payment was offered, of taking a bribe to allow manucaption, of wrongful seizure and imprisonment, of using undue violence in arresting persons, of treating them ill after arrest, of arresting them without warrant from the sheriff . . .'[52] Complaints concerning malicious

---

[46] *Reg. John of Gaunt*, xx. 667. Cf. J. F. Willard, W. A. Morris, and W. H. Dunham, *The English Government at Work*, iii, Medieval Academy of America (1950), 176.

[47] *Reg. John of Gaunt*, nos. 1392, 1445. Cf. Willard, Morris, and Dunham, *English Government*, 176.

[48] Willard, Morris, and Dunham, *English Government*, 176.

[49] See W. A. Morris, *The Medieval English Sheriff to 1300* (Manchester, 1927), 277. On the topic, cf. R. W. Kaeuper, *War, Justice and Public Order: England and France in the Later Middle Ages* (Oxford, 1988), 273–8.

[50] MP, fo. 21[vb].   [51] Ibid., fo. 22[r].

[52] Willard, Morris, and Dunham, *English Government*, 178–9.

imprisonment are various. They include allegations that sheriffs imprison persons 'per potestatem officii' until money is given them, as in a case at Black Torrington, Devon, where the sum involved was half a mark.[53] In Bedfordshire the sheriff, John de Chenee, exacted money from a man and his wife so that they should not be fettered until the gaol delivery.[54] Roger de Prideaus, sheriff of Devon, who had been involved in the abuse of power at Black Torrington referred to above, was accused of detaining one Richard FitzAmelot 'in the pit of the gaol' at Exeter castle for a day and a night, on the evidence of an approver, until he fined with him for four marks.[55] On occasion, we find that the *servientes* of the sheriff take six shillings of a man 'so that he should not go to prison'.[56]

The steward, according to the *Memoriale*, is to be questioned also on 'whether to extort money he placed any feeble and impotent or poor men or other simple persons on assizes and inquisitions, and thus they redeemed their harassment by giving him something'.[57] The jury of presentment for a hundred was empanelled by the bailiff, as were the assize juries summoned to the king's bench or common bench, the command to empanel the jury being transmitted through the sheriff.[58] Trickery in the summoning of juries was a common charge against bailiffs and sheriffs, as, for instance, in the 'Poem on the Evil Times of Edward II':

> And bailiffs and bedels under the shirreve,
> Everich fondeth hu he may pore men most greve.
> The pore men beth over al somoned on assise
> And the riche sholen sitte at hom and ther wole silver rise
> To shon.[59]

An attempt had in fact been made to combat such abuses by the Statute of Westminster (1285), clause 38 of which refers to the misdeeds of 'sheriffs, hundreders, and bailiffs of liberties' in 'putting in Assises and Juries men diseased and decrepit, and having continual or sudden disease, and men also that dwelled not in the Country at the time of the summons', alleging that they 'summon also an unreasonable multitude of Jurors, for to extort money from some of them for letting them go in peace, and so the assises and Juries pass many times

[53] *Rotuli Hundredorum*, i (Record Commissioners, 1812), 65(a).
[54] Ibid. 5(b).   [55] Ibid. 67 (b).   [56] Ibid. 436; cf. Morris, *English Sheriff*, 279.
[57] MP, fos. 21vb–22^r.   [58] Willard, Morris, and Dunham, *English Government*, 147.
[59] *Political Songs*, ed. Wright, p. 338, ll. 337–41.

by poor men, and the rich men abide at home by reason of their bribes'.
It ordained that no more than twenty-four persons should thenceforth
be summoned to an assize, excluded old men of over 70 years or the
sick or diseased from service on juries of petit assizes, and laid down
a property qualification for those required to serve in or out of their
shire, damages to be awarded to the parties aggrieved on any point
by the sheriff, his undersheriffs, or the bailiffs of liberties.[60] That
malpractices continued despite this is indicated both by contemporary
criticisms—the complaints of the 'Poem' are almost identical with those
listed in the statute—and by recorded examples. William Gazleek, a
bailiff of Suffolk, was amerced by the justices of assize in 1335 for maliciously empanelling a 16-year-old boy in an action in the court of common pleas.[61] One hundred bailiff was alleged to have made twenty-three
shillings a year for three years by letting men off jury service, while
another was accused of malicious harassment of a man by putting him
on juries and assizes at the bench at Westminster without giving him
due warning.[62] The consideration paid to the bailiff by those too weak
or ignorant to serve would presumably amount to something less than
the fine which the justices would impose if they failed to present themselves. This varied. Twenty-two delinquent jurors in Huntingdon in
1332 were fined between 3d and 13d.[63] This form of bribery features frequently on the Hundred Rolls. Thus in a Norfolk hundred, Richard,
the bailiff, took 12d for removing Alan de Aula from a jury. Philip,
the bedell, took 8d for removing another from an inquisition.[64] From
Stanford, Essex, there is a complaint that when the bailiffs place men
on assizes, some redeem themselves from serving.[65] Bromyard too
observes how men placed in great offices, such as justiciars and sheriffs, can excuse people from attending court and being included in assizes
and juries. Consequently, just and upright men, when they see that
those who judge thieves and give evidence against them suffer at their
hands because of the faults of those of higher rank, who because of
bribes, or kinship, or fear or favour support the criminals or at least
afford no protection from them, bribe the judges to be excused jury

---

[60] *Statutes of the Realm*, i. 89.

[61] Willard, Morris, and Dunham, *English Government*, 243–4.

[62] Ibid. 179. For a case in 1298 of a bailiff bribed by a villein not to place him on a jury, see Musson, *Public Order*, 193.

[63] Musson, *Public Order*, 244.   [64] *Rot. Hundred.*, i. 436 (b).

[65] Ibid., 137(b).

service. Dishonest men, on the other hand, when they see that on these juries there is much gain to be had, give bribes to be included in them.[66]

Several of the interrogatories prescribed by the *Memoriale* for the steward deal with infringements of ecclesiastical liberty.[67] Like the knight, he should be asked whether he laid violent hands on a cleric, whether he amerced any cleric in a personal action in his court, having no jurisdiction over him, whether he occupied the goods of a monastery or parish church of which his lord was the patron, during a vacancy in the same, or whether he simply despoiled churches or men of church of their goods. A constitution of Archbishop Boniface provided that those who invaded ecclesiastical goods or infringed ecclesiastical liberties should be pronounced excommunicate by the local ordinaries. Lyndwood argues that in general they are not excommunicate *ipso facto*, though those are who usurp the custody of a vacant church and occupy the goods on that pretext.[68] The *Memoriale*'s questionnaire is an interesting example of an attempt to restrain the misconduct through the medium of confession.

Under this heading of infringements come breaches of sanctuary: 'Item, whether he ever extracted anyone from a church or its cemetery or ordered the extraction of or consented to those who extracted anyone fleeing there to have its immunity and protection, or whether he prohibited the necessities of life from being ministered to him while he was in the church or prevented their being ministered to him.'[69] The privilege of sanctuary, enunciated in canon law, the subject of much local legislation, and with a recognized place in English law, by its nature was a source of frequent disputes. The right to sanctuary is found stated in several passages of the *Decretum Gratiani* and the *Decretals*. A section on ecclesiastical liberties in the *Decretum* pronounced that 'those who flee for refuge to a church ought not to be handed over but ought to be defended by the reverence and intercession of the place'.[70] Elsewhere, an attempt was made to delimit the extent of immunity. By area it was to be forty paces in the case of major churches and thirty in the case of chapels or lesser churches. Anyone infringing these limits or extracting thence a man or his goods, unless he were a public robber

[66] Bromyard, *Summa Predicantium*, *sub voce* 'Dominatio' (D.xii), art. iii, sec. ix.
[67] Cf. above, p. 116.
[68] Lyndwood, *Provinciale*, iii, tit. 28, p. 258, and gloss *ad vocem*, 'excommunicati'.
[69] MP, fo. 22[rb].   [70] *Decretum*, i. dist. 87, c. 6.

(*publicus latro*), should be excommunicate till he made amends.[71] A number of other fugitives are excepted from the privilege of sanctuary in the *Decretals*. Innocent III excludes the 'nocturnus depopulator agrorum' as well as the public robber. Other free men must be protected, but serfs shall be compelled to return to their lord after an oath has been obtained from the latter that they shall not be punished.[72] Gregory IX decrees that those who committed murders or mutilations in churches or their cemeteries ought not to be afforded protection of sanctuary,[73] and this had a parallel in English law, which prevented those who committed felonies in churches from enjoying the immunity.[74] John Acton queries whether the murderer should enjoy sanctuary, and distinguishes between murder by stealth ('per insidias') and unpremeditated murder. In the latter case, though not in the former, protection ought to be afforded. Where there is a doubt, the lenient interpretation is to be taken.[75] Eventually, Lyndwood summarized most comprehensively the understanding in English context of the canon law on this matter. Only the orthodox Christian is entitled to protection, and he is excluded if he commits the crime within a church. A serf may be protected if he is fleeing from the undue harshness of his lord, but if the latter guarantees not to molest him he is to be restored to him. If the serf fears punishment from someone other than his lord, however, he is to be treated as if he were a free man. If a free man flees to the church for non-payment of a tax he may be extracted from it; if on account of a crime, he is to enjoy immunity except in the cases specified in the canons. Lyndwood is of the opinion that debtors may be extracted where this is the local custom, an important concession in the English context.[76]

Medieval England had two classes of sanctuary.[77] Special sanctuary was the permanent immunity conferred by certain privileged abbeys and minsters, of which there were about thirty in various parts of the

---

[71] Ibid., ii, causa 1 7, q. 4, c. 6.; cf. Robert of Flamborough, *Liber Penitentialis*, ed. Firth, 252.

[72] X. 3. 49. 6.   [73] Ibid. 10.

[74] See Holdsworth, *History English Law*, iii, 5th edn. (London, 1942), 305.

[75] Acton, *Commentary*, 102 (a), *ad vocem* 'ut etiam reos sanguinis defendat'.

[76] Lyndwood, *Provinciale*, 257, gloss *ad vocem*, 'canones precipiunt'.

[77] See R. H. Forster, 'Notes on Durham and Other North-Country Sanctuaries', *JBAA*, NS, 11 (1905), 118–39, and R. F. Hunnisett, *The Medieval Coroner* (Cambridge, 1961), 37–54. G. Rosser, 'Sanctuary and Social Negotiation in Medieval England', in J. Blair and B. Golding (eds.), *The Cloister and the World: Essays in Medieval History in Honour of Barbara Harvey* (Oxford, 1996), 57–79, emphasizes the role of the community in the operation of the system.

country. These included Durham, Hexham, York, Ripon, and Beverley, in the north, and Westminster and St Martin's-le-Grand in London.[78] The special sanctuary of Durham extended over the palatinate.[79] Ordinary 'ecclesiastical' sanctuary, on the other hand, which was possessed by all consecrated places, in English common law conferred only temporary immunity, that is, for a period of forty days from the time of the criminal's taking refuge. Within this period he was required to acknowledge his guilt and abjure the realm before the coroner at his place of refuge. He ought then to be allowed to proceed in safety directly to the chosen point of exit from the realm. Abjuration, then, involving both exile and confiscation of property, replaced the more drastic penalty which would normally have attended the crime.[80]

No principle of canon law was violated by the English custom requiring abjuration of the realm, for it was not part of the church's claim that the criminal should escape all penalties but only that he should retain life and limb.[81] The difficulty arose in practice, in cases where the criminal refused either to submit himself to the law, when required by the coroner, or to confess and abjure. 'Bracton' will not countenance even the obdurate criminal's forcible extraction from sanctuary, but attempts to solve the difficulty by recommending that he be starved out.[82] This point the church would not concede. The Council of Merton in 1258 decreed that those who prevented food being provided to persons in sanctuary were liable to excommunication at the discretion of the ordinary, and those who maintained watch in the church or cemetery ought also to be excommunicated.[83] A similar provision was made by the Council of Lambeth, three years later.[84] The Legatine Council at London in 1268 went further, laying down that violent seizure of a person or property under safe-keeping in a church, as well as the direct or indirect denial of food to the fugitive—which was declared to be tantamount to murder—was to carry *ipso facto* excommunication,[85] and this enactment was duly recalled in the lists

---

[78] See Forster, 'Notes', 118; I. D. Thornley, 'Sanctuary in Medieval London', *JBAA*, NS, 38 (1932), 293–315.

[79] Forster, 'Notes', 125.

[80] See A. Réville, ' "L'Abjuratio Regni" , histoire d'une institution anglaise', *Revue Historique*, 1 (1892), 12.

[81] See X. 3. 49. 6. Lyndwood condemns exaggerated notions of the immunity of sanctuary. *Provinciale*, 256 (b).

[82] Bracton, *De Legibus et Consuetudinibus Angliae*, ed. S. E. Thorne and G. E. Woodbine (Cambridge, Mass., 1968), ii. 383.

[83] *CS*, ii. 581.   [84] Ibid. 679–80.   [85] Ibid. 763.

of excommunications issued by the Councils of Reading (1279) and Lambeth (1281).[86]

Besides being the subject of legislation, infringements of sanctuary were included among the abuses for which the clergy sought remedy of the king. The Council of London in 1257 complained that when someone fled to the immunity of the church, the cemetery or steps ('scalarium') of the church were sealed off by lay guards, so that the fugitive could hardly be maintained with victuals, that sometimes the fugitive was taken out by force, and sometimes, after having abjured the realm, he was ambushed on the public road and hanged.[87] These last two offences were also, of course, breaches of the secular law, though despite the attaching penalties, cases are recorded of abjurors' being pursued and decapitated on the highway.[88] The strict watch was required because of the very real dangers of escape, particularly in view of the fact that the criminal, having confessed before the coroner, might continue in sanctuary for a further period not exceeding forty days from his arrival before formally abjuring, and many chose this course, presumably with escape in mind.[89] The practical difficulties involved dictated an ambivalence in the royal responses to these complaints. A reply by Edward I in 1280 recognized that food should be allowed to the fugitive, though it made no reference to the mounting of a guard in the churchyard, a matter which had been included in the remonstrance.[90] Edward II did give an answer on the point, but qualified in such a way as to render it meaningless, allowing that 'their keepers ought not to abide in the churchyard, except necessity or peril of escape do require so'.[91] Observance varied. In 1344 a sanctuary-seeker who confessed but refused to abjure before a Nottinghamshire coroner, being still obdurate at the end of forty days, was left in the church, where he died five days later.[92] Forcible violations of sanctuary, however, are recurrent. For example, Grandisson wrote to the sheriff of Devon in 1328 about abstraction from the church of Alphington, and later that year denounced as excommunicate those who had laid violent hands on Mr Eustace de Teignmouth, proctor-general of his court, and violently extracted him from the church of Teignmouth where he sought sanctuary.[93]

---

[86] Ibid. 850, 907.   [87] Ibid. 543.   [88] See Hunnisett, *Medieval Coroner*, 49.
[89] Ibid. 43.   [90] *CS*, ii. 884.
[91] 9 Edw. II, stat. 1, 'Articuli Cleri', c. x; *Statutes of the Realm*, i. 172–3. Cf. J. C. Cox, *The Sanctuaries and Sanctuary Seekers of Medieval England* (London, 1911), 18.
[92] See Hunnisett, *Medieval Coroner*, p. 44.
[93] *RG*, i. 383–4, 440–1, 514–15. For other instances of concern with the problem, see ibid., ii. 817, 823.

A less specific question to be put to the steward regarding ecclesiastical liberties is 'whether he ever ordered or enacted anything to be done or observed by his subjects to the prejudice of the church or to the damage of men of church?'[94] Such interference would be most likely where church rights affected the economy of the manor, as in the case complained of by Grosseteste, while archdeacon of Leicester (*c*.1232), when one of the bailiffs of the countess of Winchester allegedly forbade men in the parish of Grosseteste's prebend to buy any tithes situated there, presumably with the aim of reducing their value and, as the archdeacon put it, of bringing it about that the parishioners will not pay tithes at all.[95] A desire to prevent his men from being fined and thus losing his goods might induce a lord to impede the exercise of ecclesiastical jurisdiction. The royal reply to the complaints of the clergy in June 1300 defended the lord's right to send his officials to observe the proceedings in court Christian where his naif stood in danger of being mulcted, on the grounds that 'everything belongs to the lord and the lord may procure an inhibition by the sheriff as regards them'.[96] A similar consideration prompted some lords to insist that their serfs, when convicted, took a flogging rather than alienate their goods, failure to obey being fined.[97] The Council of London in 1342 passed sentence of major excommunication—to be published four times annually in parish churches throughout the province—on all who forbade their lay tenants to appear in answer to citations before their ordinaries in criminal as well as in testamentary cases, complaining that ecclesiastics were being harassed for imposing pecuniary penances. Also included were temporal lords and their bailiffs who claimed the goods of intestates.[98]

As is to be expected, the steward's judicial functions attract attention. It is on this count that Robert Mannyng includes stewards under the vice of covetousness:

> Among hem stywardes mow be tolde,
> þat lordynges courtys holde,
> For nyrhand every a styward
> þe dome þat þey ȝeve ys over harde,
> And namely to þe pore man,
> þey greve hym alle þat þey kan.[99]

---

[94] MP, a. xxxv.   [95] Grosseteste, *Epistolae*, ed. Luard, no. v, pp. 37–8.

[96] *CS*, ii. 1217. Cf. the analogous stipulation, made in reply to the 'Articuli Cleri' of 1316, that pecuniary penances—though not commutations—could be opposed by writs of prohibition; see *Statutes of the Realm*, 171, and Logan, *Excommunication and the Secular Arm*, 144.

[97] See Scammell, 'The Rural Chapter in England', 17.   [98] *Concilia*, ii. 707–8.

[99] *Handlyng Synne*, ed. Furnivall, ll. 5241–6.

They are suspected by the author of the *Memoriale* of accepting bribes to favour one party against another, or to defer execution of a sentence.[100] But the steward or bailiff in search of riches did not need to confine himself to accepting douceurs: 'Item, if he ever coveted the lands, homes or possessions or other goods, moveable or immoveable, of his neighbour, and because he did not wish to sell, hire or make a present of these to him, he harassed him or procured his harassment in his goods or person, or perhaps he lost these goods by oppression for this reason.'[101] A case which illustrates oppression of this type is that of William Roculf, a bailiff of the city of Worcester in 1324, who abused his position as president of the borough court. In order to extract a pension from one William of Throckmorton, a tanner of the city, he had him indicted for forestalling, with the result that his victim granted him 40d annually for life. When Throckmorton refused to give him a horse, the bailiff had the animal confiscated in the king's name. Finally, by representing that William was the villein of the earl of Warwick, he enabled the earl to seize his goods to the value of £40. Roculf is recorded as having taken bribes in the manner complained of by the *Memoriale*. In one case he promised his favour to the plaintiffs in an action against the prior of Worcester cathedral monastery in return for one mark, only to reverse this on receiving an annual pension from the prior of one pound for life.[102]

The *Memoriale* accuses bailiffs of fraud in the collection of revenues and fines.[103] Two broad types of deception are envisaged. One involves simply falsifying the accounts, by exaggerating the expenditure or by including unnecessary or frivolous expenditure. On the same point, the author of the *Husbandry* begins his treatise by recommending that 'he who will render the account ought to swear that he will render true account and that he will charge himself honestly with as many goods belonging to his lord as he has received; and that he will spend them honestly and will not enter anything on his account roll except what he spent, honestly, and to the lord's advantage',[104] but as Walter of Henley warns the reader of his handbook, 'it cometh often to passe that those which buy and selle doe in their accompt increase the things bought and dyminishe the things solde'.[105] It was for this class that

---

[100] MP, a. xxxv.
[101] Ibid. Cf. the methods by which Mannyng describes the rich man as oppressing his neighbour out of a desire for his land: *Handlyng Synne*, ed. Furnivall, ll. 5979–96.
[102] See R. Hilton, *The West Midlands* (London, 1966), 260.   [103] MP, b. lii.
[104] See *Walter of Henley and Other Treatises*, ed. D. Oschinsky (Oxford, 1971), 419.
[105] Ibid. 341.

Robert Carpenter of Haslett composed his treatise on accounting.[106] The
other practice condemned by the *Memoriale*—that of recording debts
for which the full payment had been received as having been only partially settled[107]—injured the bailiff's subjects rather than the lord. Walter
of Henley notes a variation of this practice: 'And if any arrerages happen upon the finall accompt let it be quickly levyed. And if the accompt-
ant name any parson which oweth that arrerage than take youe the name
of that man for often tymes it chaunceth that the servauntes and reeves
be the debtors theimselves and yet do make other men the debtors which
neyther can nor ought to paye it. And this they doe to cover their
unfaythfulnesse withall.'[108] The abuse is one of the several complained
of in the thirteenth-century 'Song of the Husbandman':

> ʒet cometh budeles, with ful muche bost,—
> 'Greythe me selver to the grene wax:
> Thou art writen y my writ that thou wel wost'
> Mo then ten sithen told y my tax.[109]

As has already been suggested, the attention devoted by the moralists
to the vices of officials may be taken to reflect the dominance of the
professional element in the councils of magnates and in the administration of great estates. Bromyard bewails the evil effects of this screen
of officialdom separating lord and tenant. So, if the lord is rendered
destitute through hunting, tournaments, and so on, he calls on his flatter-
ing counsellors,

who say, 'Your land is wealthy; your men—blessed be God—are rich; you can
levy so much on them without causing hardship.' And if the lord, not yet accustomed to cruelty, should wish to act more mildly in anything and to say, 'This
way is better', they oppose him . . . saying, 'Sir, you attend to your delights and
pastimes and allow those who are more experienced to concern themselves with
the management of your estate.' They brush aside plaints, and those who wish to
lodge them with the lord they disparage and prevent, in case their nakedness and
shame should appear. They also inform their lords that if such people come to
them they should send them back to their servants. As a result, the following style
of reply on the part of lords is on the increase, 'Go to my seneschal or to my bailiff',
and so they neither know nor want to know the miseries of their subjects.[110]

---

[106] See Denholm-Young, *Seignorial Administration*, 121.   [107] MP, fo. 68[rb].
[108] *Walter of Henley and Other Treatises*, ed. Oschinsky, 341.
[109] *Political Songs*, ed. Wright, 151.
[110] Bromyard, *Summa Predicantium*, *sub voce* 'Dominatio', (D. xii), art. vii, sec. xix. Henry
of Lancaster was alive to the concept of offences committed by proxy. *Le Livre de Seyntz
Medicines*, ed. E. J. Arnould (Oxford, 1940), 19. He was also aware of the advantage to the
subject of bypassing the agent and of applying directly to the lord: ibid. 123.

It was one of the acknowledged virtues of St Louis that he recognized the dangers as well as the advantages of an expanding officialdom—though even his inquiries were, of necessity, conducted by proxy.[111] The ideal lord of the *Seneschaucie* too is expected to have to guard his guards by deputy.[112]

---

[111] *La Vie de Saint Louis: le témoignage de Jehan, Seigneur de Joinville. Texte du XIV siècle*, ed. N. L. Corbett (Sherbrooke, Quebec, 1977), 229–32. The tradition of his interest and accessibility in this regard was alive in fourteenth-century England. See Bromyard, *Summa Predicantium, sub voce* 'Dominatio' (D. xii), art. iii, sec. iv.

[112] *Walter of Henley and Other Treatises*, ed. Oschinsky, 295, where the auditors are to hear complaints. For an instance of appeal—close to Bromyard's time—from tenants directly to their lord (the prior of Christ Church, Canterbury) against the 'petty tyrannies of an over-zealous steward', see J. F. Nichols, 'An Early Fourteenth-Century Petition from the Tenants of Bocking to their Manorial Lord', *EcHR*, 2 (1929–30), 300–7. For a proxy investigation by the Earl of Stafford in 1386, see K. B. Macfarlane, 'Landlord versus Minister and Tenant', in *The Nobility of Later Medieval England* (Oxford, 1973), 220.

8

Society Under Scrutiny IV:
The Examination of Peasants

Scathing though he is in his criticism of the manorial officials, the author of the *Memoriale Presbiterorum* shows no real sympathy for their subjects, the peasants: 'You ought to know . . . that these peasants, like brutish men, possessed of a purse-string mentality, can scarcely ever be persuaded to obey God and his commandments in those matters in which they are bound to him and to his church.'[1] The contempt is matched in Alvarus Pelagius's treatment of the class:

Such is the avarice of some of them that although they are rich, for the sake of increasing their wealth—it would be different if they did so from humility or to avoid idleness— . . . they . . . labour with their own hands and do not cease, though bowed down by old age, torturing their bodies and corrupting their souls. Psalm 16, 'They have set their eyes bowing down to the earth.' For as they plough and dig the earth all day, so, wholly of the earth, they lick the earth, they eat the earth, they speak of the earth; in the earth they have altogether placed their hope and they care nothing for the heavenly substance which remains.[2]

Inevitably, the main problem concerns tithe-paying:

Inquire therefore, confessor, whether the peasant paid his praedial tithes in full, for some deduct their expenses, incurred in the collection of the fruits, paying the wages of their hired hands before they pay their tithes. And others pay the fifteenth part, others the twentieth or thirtieth, of the fruits, in place of the tenth, committing theft. Others pay an actual tenth, but they pay as tithe that which is worth least and is in worst condition, of fruit and animals, on the model of Cain.[3]

Medieval canon law distinguished three types of tithe: praedial, on the annual increase of the ground; mixed, on animals and animal products nurtured by the ground; and personal, on the legitimate profit of trade,

---

[1] MP, fo. 25rb. Cf. ibid., fo. 25vb: 'Rusticus dives in maioribus peccare nititur et minus peccare formidat quam nobilis, sensu regulato ductus.'

[2] Alvarus Pelagius, *De Planctu*, ii, art. 43. Cf. Coulton, *Medieval Village, Manor and Monastery*, 243–5.

[3] MP, fo. 25rb.

industry, and wages.[4] The duty of tithe-paying was seen as stemming from the need to recognize the universal dominion of God,[5] and it is so expounded by Archbishop FitzRalph, with whose views on dominion in general it is in perfect accord. In his sermon *Dic ut lapides isti panes fiant* of 26 February 1357, in which in Grandissonian fashion he defended the parish church against the friars' oratories as the divinely appointed place for confession, he explored at length the obligation to tithe honestly. Though he had merchants specifically in mind, several aspects of his analysis elucidate a general theory of tithe-paying such as may have been current in Grandisson's circle. Of particular interest is that, while FitzRalph implicitly countenances the deduction of necessary expenses before tithing the profits of trade, he requires immediate payment thereafter on each profit.[6]

Canon law distinguished between the deduction of expenses in the case of praedial and mixed tithes, on the one hand, and personal tithes on the other. One of the 'English' decretals of Alexander III (to the bishop of Exeter) directed that the men of 'Hortona', who, before paying their tithes from the harvest, allegedly paid their servants and hired hands their wages for the year, paying tithe only on the remainder, should be ordered to pay their praedial and mixed tithes 'without fraud or diminution' and to make satisfaction for what had been withheld.[7] The important statute of Archbishop Boniface, which attempted to enforce a uniform custom on tithing, enacted that tithes of fruits should be paid 'in whole and without any diminution, no expenses having been deducted'.[8] Similarly, Archbishop Stratford condemned those who paid the eleventh part as tithe, 'contending that they can pay their hired hands their wages from the untithed fruits, especially for their labours in the autumn'.[9] The temptation to deduct expenses at harvest would be strong.[10] By contrast, expenses were deductible in the case

---

[4] See A. G. Little, 'Personal Tithes', *EHR* 60 (1945), 68.

[5] On the Christian theory of tithes, see G. Constable, *Monastic Tithes From Their Origins To the Twelfth Century* (Cambridge, 1964), chap. 1. On divine lordship as the basis of tithe-paying, see the statutes of Bishop Chaury for Carlisle, *CS*, ii. 628.

[6] 'Sermons', London, British Library, MS. Lansdowne 393, fo. 120ʳ⁻ᵛ.

[7] X. 3. 30. 7; cf. ibid. 22.   [8] *CS*, ii. 795.

[9] Lyndwood, *Provinciale*, 188–9. Cf. *Concilia*, iii. 704.

[10] See ibid. 188, gloss *ad vocem* 'autumnali labore': 'Major enim videretur ratio ut deducantur expensae talium quam aliorum laborantium circa agriculturam. Sed verum est quod nulle expense circa talia sunt deducendae.' For a mandate of Archbishop Simon Islip (1352) directed against this practice, see *Concilia*, iii. 25–6.

of personal tithes, and however rationalized,[11] the distinction must have been an invidious one. The nature of the deductions to be made in personal tithing was itself a sensitive issue, at least in the perspective common to FitzRalph and the *Memoriale Presbiterorum*. FitzRalph condemns the merchants of Drogheda who, instead of paying tithe immediately at the time of profit, wait until the end of the year and then declare that they have no profit to show on the year's trading.[12] Possibly Drogheda had some convention, such as can be seen *c*.1345 in the borough customs of Torksey, Lincs., where profit was defined with 'allowance' for personal and domestic maintenance.[13] Or the practice was perhaps that described by the *Memoriale*, which inquires of the merchant 'whether he ever made compensation of profit against loss in this fashion, namely, today he buys wares and in selling them gains twenty, tomorrow he sells other wares and loses twenty, and so he does not wish to pay tithes from the twenty gained in the first case, because he loses another twenty on the other wares sold; but for certain, in this he sins mortally, defrauding the church of its right, for by law such compensation is wholly reproved'.[14] This interpretation was presumably based on the principle that tithes should be paid immediately, as was required in the case of praedial tithes.[15] Though there is no other evidence on the point, the articulation of concern by FitzRalph and the author of the *Memoriale* may perhaps be taken to indicate that the integrity of personal tithing, to be maintained by insistence on immediate payment, was a topic of discussion within Grandisson's circle.

Where not evaded, tithes might be resisted. 'Item, others, moved against their rector or vicar, to vindicate themselves or injure him, fling the tithed sheaves far from them, shaking off the ears from the blades, and set them before their animals to be devoured, and they care not what evil they do in this respect, provided that the rector or vicar can be injured.'[16] It has been argued that resistance to tithes in the middle ages has been greatly exaggerated, and that it was in fact comparatively rare, at least before the thirteenth century, though increasing in the

---

[11] X. 3. 30. 28. The gloss explains that expenses in business may be deducted, while those in connection with 'fruits and returns' may not, because in the former the hand of man is involved, in the latter, the hand of God. *Corpus Iuris Canonici cum Glossis*, ii (Lyons 1624), 1230.

[12] See A. Gwynn, 'Archbishop FitzRalph and George of Hungary', *Studies*, 24 (1935), 564. Cf. Walsh, *Scholar and Primate*, 314.

[13] M. Bateson, *Borough Customs*, Selden Society, 18, 21 (London, 1904–6), ii. 213.

[14] MP, fo. 23vb.   [15] X. 3. 30. 8.   [16] MP, fo. 25^r-v.

fourteenth and fifteenth centuries.[17] Certainly, diocesan and provincial legislation from the mid-thirteenth century in England witnesses to the concern of the ecclesiastical authorities over disturbances and even assaults in this connection. The statutes of Bishop Robert de Chaury for Carlisle diocese (1258 × 1259) complain that some people 'impede the parsons of churches to whom these tithes belong, and those deputed by them, from carrying them through the same places as the nine parts are carried and other convenient places, and from selling them and freely disposing of them, and maliciously harass them, and . . . some scatter the tithes in ditches or cast them before their beasts to be consumed'.[18] The case of a bailiff who tried to prevent the sale of tithes has already been noted.[19] A statute of Bishop Quinel deals with other restrictive practices. 'Some magnates too,' he complains, 'in an attempt to defraud the rectors, not only in the collection of tithes, but also when they have been collected, frequently by threats and terrors, now secret, now open, prevent their tenants from daring to purchase their tithes from the rectors, so that the latter, finding no buyers, shall be compelled for a slight price only, to sell their tithes to the same magnates.'[20] He refers to tithes being fed to animals, and to malicious damage.[21] Lyndwood, commenting on a constitution of Simon Mepham (1328/9), mentions the damage caused by scattering tithes, exposing them to the rain, and feeding them to beasts.[22] Mepham's constitution excommunicated those who impeded tithe-collection, complaining that ecclesiastics and their servants were denied free access to and egress from the meadows, to collect, guard, or remove the tithes. Some, allegedly, demanded a present in return for leaving the tithes undisturbed.[23] The Council of London in 1342 paid close attention to obstruction of tithe collection. Some, it is said, treat the servants of ecclesiastics, sent to remove tithes, as thieves and raise the hue and cry against them. Some implead ecclesiastics in secular courts for transporting the tithes across their land. Others force the collectors to use circuitous routes to and from the meadows, where a vehicle can hardly pass. Yet others will not permit the tithes to be removed from their land so long as one of the stalks remains, but allow them to be eaten by their animals.[24] At Exeter, the tithe-payers of Silverton were condemned in 1333 for banding together to diminish and withhold

[17] Constable, 'Resistance to Tithes in the Middle Ages', *JEH* 13 (1962), 185.

[18] *CS*, ii. 628.   [19] See above, p. 139.   [20] *CS*, ii. 1055–6.   [21] Ibid.

[22] Lyndwood, *Provinciale*, 186 (b), *ad vocem* 'damnum'. Cf. *Concilia*, iii. 553–4.

[23] Lyndwood, *Provinciale*, 186–7.   [24] *Concilia*, ii. 704.

tithes,[25] while a mandate issued by Grandisson in 1339 against viol-
ators of ecclesiastical liberty who have removed sheaves and other goods
from houses, manors, and granges looks as though it concerned a problem of disputed tithes.[26]

In London, on the question of tithes, 'it is possible to see the per-
sistence of organized opposition to the clergy, supported by the full
weight of the civic government'.[27] Praedial tithes there had been
commuted to an annual rate, payable in instalments, on the value of
buildings, though the assessment of this, made in the episcopacy of Roger
Niger (1229–41) and overtaken by inflation, was an object of dispute
in the fourteenth and fifteenth centuries. There was trouble also over
personal tithes—as evidenced by the teaching of Friar William Russell
—so that at one point, in 1457, their payment came to be left to the
devotion of the parishioners.[28]

The other 'ecclesiastical' offences on which the *Memoriale* examines
the peasant include working on saints' feast days[29] and conspiracies
against ecclesiastical liberties.[30] The latter point is not elaborated. Elsewhere, the author refers to parishioners who, incensed against their
rector or vicar, compact not to make an offering, or to make a diminished
offering, on such occasions as purifications, deaths, and anniversaries.[31]
An instance of exactly this type of action occurs in London in 1382,
where an ordinance of John of Northampton restricted offerings at
vigils of the dead or similar services to not more than one farthing a
mass—the priests having refused to accept farthings. If the person offering could not obtain change of the halfpenny, he was to leave the church
without offering. Payments at baptisms and weddings were also limited.[32]
Restriction of funerary offerings was among the condemned sanctions
taken by the parishioners at Paignton in support of their chapel.[33] A
restriction of unspecified offerings at Droitwich during William
Doune's tenure of the officiality of Worcester will be noticed later.[34]

---

[25] *RG*, ii. 689.   [26] Ibid. 914–16.
[27] J. F. Thompson, 'Tithe Disputes in Later Medieval London', *EHR* 78 (1963), 1.
[28] Ibid. 10–12.
[29] On this topic see B. Harvey, 'Work and Festa Ferianda in Medieval England', *JEH* 23 (1972), 289–308.
[30] MP, fos. 25[va], 25[vb].
[31] MP, fo. 71[r]. The author does not refer to offerings made on reception of the sacraments. On this custom and on conspiracy to withhold them, see C. R. Cheney, 'Some Aspects
of Diocesan Legislation in England During the Thirteenth Century', in *Medieval Texts*, 197–8.
[32] Thompson, 'Tithe Disputes' 3. On anticlericalism and resistance to offerings, see
D. M. Owen, *Church and Society in Medieval Lincolnshire* (Lincoln, 1971), 140–1.
[33] See above, p. 55.   [34] See below, p. 207.

As might be expected, part of the interrogatory for the peasants deals with 'social' sins. They are accused of malice towards each other. In an obscure reference to the *Institutes* of Justinian, the author reproves them for opposing manumissions.[35] He accuses them too of conspiring against their poorer neighbours who have not the means to bribe them, by disinheriting them and otherwise oppressing them by false presentments in the lord's court.[36] While inheritance of villein land was in theory at the will of the lord, in practice it passed according to manorial custom, and this, as well as the right of rival candidates for succession, was determined by an inquest in the manorial court.[37] The men of the court were liable to a fine for false presentation as well as for concealment,[38] but conspiracy by its nature was not likely to find its way frequently on to the court records.[39] A more commonly evidenced charge against peasants is that of filching land: 'Item, each peasant tries to tear up the limits placed to distinguish lands, stealing the land of his neighbour contiguous to his own.'[40] Removal of boundary marks was an offence known to Roman law, which prescribed the death penalty for the slave who did so without his master's knowledge, though the master had the option of paying a fine instead of losing his slave.[41] On this analogy, the author of the *Memoriale* thinks that excommunication would be an appropriate penalty, though no such sanction in fact appears in the canon law.[42] In champion country, boundaries between one holding and another were difficult to maintain.[43] The imposition of fines for the removal of boundary marks is relatively frequent in court records.[44] The removal of boundary marks is one of the vices ascribed

[35] 'Preterea rustici, lege fusiacanina, licet ab olim abrogata, more canino utentes, aliis nocere satagunt in quantum possunt; set sibi ipsis in nullo prosunt.' MP, fo. 25^{va-b}. For the *Lex Fufia Caninia*, which restricted manumission, see *Institut.*, 1. 7, ed. Moyle, p. 121.

[36] MP, fo. 25vb.

[37] See Homans, *English Villagers*, 119–21, and J. A. Raftis, *Tenure and Mobility* (Toronto, 1964), 55.

[38] Homans, *English Villagers*, 237.

[39] For malicious presentments, see e.g. *Wakefield Court Rolls*, ed. W. P. Baildon, Yorkshire Archaeological Society, 29 (1900), 99; *Wakefield Court Rolls*, ed. J. Lister, Yorkshire Archaeological Society 78 (1930), 78, 87.

[40] MP, fo. 26^r.   [41] *Digest*, 47. 21. 3 (iv. 792).

[42] 'Quanto magis de iure canonico debet excommunicari et certe multo magis, quia in hoc peccat mortaliter.' MP, fo. 26^r.

[43] See Homans, *English Villagers*, 72. Cf. Bennett, *English Manor*, 47.

[44] See e.g. *Select Pleas*, ed. Maitland, 93; *Halmota Prioratus Dunelmensis, 1296–1384*, ed. W. H. D. Longstaffe and J. Booth, SS, 82 (1889), 26; Raftis, *Tenure and Mobility*, 97. For other examples of ploughing away the balk between holdings, see Bennett, *Life on the English Manor*, 48.

to peasants by Alvarus Pelagius,[45] and Acton refers to it in his commentary on the legatine constitutions.[46] Avarice confesses in *Piers Plowman*:

> And yf ich ʒede to the plouh • ich pynchede on hus half-acre,
> That a fot-londe other a forwe • fecchen Ich wolde,
> Of my neyhʒboris next • nymen of hus erthe.
> And yf y repe, over-reche • other ʒaf hem red that repen,
> To sese to me with here sykel • that ich sew nevere.[47]

It was to limit the opportunities for stealing crops that special by-laws were enacted by the village community to regulate the method of harvesting.[48]

Peasants are presumed to be ill-disposed towards their lords, withdrawing customary services from them, stealing their goods, or conniving at malicious damage inflicted by others.[49] The withdrawal of services was an offence involving restitution according to the canonists, and is dealt with by Hostiensis, from whom the *Memoriale* borrows the interrogatory on this point, though the idea that they steal his goods or fail to warn him of the malice of others does not come from the source.[50]

Finally in the interrogatory for this class appears 'the all too superstitious rustic'.[51] 'Item, peasants trust in auguries and the chattering of birds, and follow them. Item, they trust in certain other evil casting of lots and superstitions, which many old women hold and practise, and so deviate from right and true faith and are ill believing.'[52] Robert Mannyng warns on the first point:.

> Beleve nouʒt yn þe pyys cheteryng,
> Hyt ys no trouþe but fals belevyng;
> Many belevyn yn þe pye:
> Whan she comyþ lowe or hye
> Cheteryng and haþ no reste
> þan sey þey we shal have geste.
> Manyon trowyn on here wylys
> And many tymes þe pye hem gylys.[53]

---

[45] Alvarus Pelagius, *De Planctu*, ii, art. 43; cf. Coulton, *Medieval Village, Manor and Monastery*, 243–5.

[46] Acton, *Commentary*, 78 (b).

[47] *Piers Plowman*, ed. Skeat, C. Passus VII, ll. 268–72.

[48] See W. O. Ault, 'Some Early Village By-laws', *EHR* 45 (1930), 208–31.

[49] MP, fo. 25ᵛ.   [50] Hostiensis, *SA*, art. 42, col. 1425 'tertio'.

[51] Owst, *Literature and Pulpit*, 147.   [52] MP, fo. 26ʳ.

[53] *Handling Synne*, ll. 355–63.

Condemnations of various other credulities recur in episcopal statutes. Those of Worcester (1229) instruct priests to preach to their parishioners against observing 'the times and moments', contrary to the apostle (Galatians 4: 10), adding that they are reluctant to contract marriage or enter a new home unless the moon is waxing.[54] Another set of Worcester statutes (1240) condemns the veneration of wells.[55] The veneration of stones, wood, trees, or springs 'on account of any dream', is condemned in Winchester statutes of c.1265.[56] Both the disposition to seek after religious novelties and episcopal vigilance as regards it are evidenced by an incident which occurred at Exeter cathedral on a morning in February 1341, when the bells were rung without authorization to announce a supposed miracle, resulting in a mandate from Grandisson for the citation of those responsible.[57] The bishop's opposition to the chapel at Frithelstock drew from him an allegation of sorcery.[58] The suspicion extended to individuals, as in his excommunication of Margery Rvyel for practising divinations at Modbury and Dartmouth.[59] The silence on witchcraft is noteworthy, however. Fourteenth-century England has no equivalent of Dame Alice Kytteler of Kilkenny.

[54] *CS*, ii. 179.   [55] Ibid. 303.   [56] Ibid. 722.
[57] *RG*, ii. 941; cf. ibid. 1231.   [58] See above, p. 56.   [59] *RG*, ii. 1044–5.

9

Society Under Scrutiny V: The Examination of Clerics, Regular and Secular

Regular Clergy

The interrogatories for the clerical order in the *Memoriale Presbiterorum* begin in the traditional manner with religious. Unlike Hostiensis, to whose treatment of this class he otherwise owes much,[1] the author devotes separate sections to simple religious, and to 'claustrales'—religious holding cloistral office—and obedientiaries.[2] The distinction between religious as a whole and religious as office-holders is in keeping with the author's general concern with the conduct of administration. Two other chapters deal with regulars: b. lxviii, 'De regularibus facientibus elemosinam', considers them as a 'legal class', whose capacity to give alms is restricted by prior obligations; b. lxi, 'De religiosis thesaurum et bona alia penes se deposita occupantibus et illicite consumentibus', apparently an original contribution by the author, considers the obligation of restitution that religious incur by stealing valuables deposited with them for safekeeping.

There is nothing in his relatively brief survey of religious to suggest that the author had any special interest in them. On this point he may be contrasted with William of Pagula, whose *Speculum Religiosorum* 'set out in an ordered fashion in its central or legal chapters all the monastic legislation of the Church and of legatine and provincial synods'.[3] In the context of the 'literature of complaint', one may compare the author's scanty treatment with the detailed survey of the vices of regulars in the *De Planctu Ecclesiae* of Alvarus Pelagius, article 24 of which notes forty-two sins to which monks are prone, including several suggested by the constitution 'Ne in agro dominico' of the Council

---

[1] Hostiensis, *SA*, V, tit. 'De penitentiis et remissionibus', art. 50, col. 1441.
[2] MP, a. xxviii, xxix.
[3] L. E. Boyle, 'The Summa Summarum and Some Other English Works of Canon Law', *Proceedings of the Second International Congress of Medieval Canon Law* (Vatican City, 1965), 437.

of Vienne, governing Benedictine monks.[4] The *Memoriale* makes no reference to this constitution, even though it is relevant to several points raised; for example, it laid down severe penalties for organized hunting by Benedictines:[5] an abbot or prior guilty on this count was to be suspended for two years from collation of benefices, while others were to be suspended for the same period from any administrations held by them. Similar suspension for a year was the penalty for less serious breaches of the constitution. Sentence of excommunication was decreed in the case of monks (or regular canons) who, not being the holders of administrations, removed 'ad curias principum', without licence of their prelates, or on monks who held arms within the confines of the monastery.[6] Aside from the technical deficiency, the paucity of treatment accords with the scope of the work. The ordinary parish priest will not be expected to have to deal with religious.[7] The principle governing the confession of religious was that which applied to all classes; each confessed to his superior.[8] A secular priest would not normally hear their confessions unless he were also an episcopal penitentiary. The fact, indeed, that religious confess to each other is the main point underlying chapter b. lxi: they are suspected of deferring to each other in the retention of goods deposited with them.[9] The most notorious theft was of the royal treasure at Westminster in 1303.[10] William Doune's anxiety upon the score has been noted above, as part of the argument for his authorship of the treatise.

Secular Clergy

The instruction provided by the *Memoriale* on the shortcomings of secular clerics, like that provided in respect of religious, covers a number of traditional disciplinary problems and may be classified under the following headings: abuses in the obtaining of benefices—such as illicit occupation, simoniacal acquisition (b. lxxi), and retention in plurality; irregular ordination; negligence, and other irregularities in the saying of mass or the performance of other divine services (a. xxxi); participation in activities prohibited to clerics, absolutely or with qualification

---

[4] Alvarus Pelagius, *De Planctu*, ii, art. 24, fo. 130ʳ⁻ᵛ.   [5] *Clementinarum*, 3. 10. 1.

[6] Ibid. For a question in the *Memoriale Presbiterorum* on worldly religious, see above, p. 129.

[7] MP, fo. 13ʳᵇ: 'Nullus presbiter parochialis poterit vel debebit audire confessionem religiosi nisi in casu necessitatis, vel hoc sibi fuerit commissum.'

[8] See e.g. Lyndwood, *Provinciale*, v., tit. 16, p. 341 (a).

[9] MP, fo. 71ᵛᵇ. Cf. above, pp. 12–13.   [10] See Cook, *English Monasteries*, 24.

—such as hunting, dicing, frequenting taverns, trading, or advocacy; and, related to this, extravagances in dress. There are also chapters of a specifically legal nature, explaining the restrictions on a prelate's use of church property, particularly as regards alienations to suspect persons (b. xxix, xxx). It may be observed that the author's concern with pluralism is of this technically legal character. The objection is to unlicensed pluralism.[11] On this count, the author is not a reformer of a system towards which he probably took the same view as William Doune's friend and associate Roger Otery. Otery's robust defence of pluralism— and incidental self-reference as an ecclesiastical administrator—carries the more conviction for what we know of Doune's character.[12]

As a preliminary, the confessor must know the limits of his jurisdiction over this class: 'If any secular cleric, especially a rector or vicar, shall come to you, O parish priest, and shall wish to confess to you, you ought not to hear him indiscriminately but remit him to his bishop, for no rector or vicar can or ought to by law choose as his confessor anyone, whether regular or secular, without licence of his own bishop. You should not, therefore, hear any such, except in the cases permitted to you.'[13] Conversely, the priest himself is warned to confess to 'your bishop or his penitentiary or another superior of yours to whom you are known to be subject temporally and spiritually, or to another by licence of your prelate'.[14] This advice derives from an accumulation of thirteenth-century legislation. Stephen Langton's diocesan statutes for Canterbury decreed that in every chapter there should be two confessors appointed by the archbishop to hear the confessions of priests, although every priest might have his own confessor by consent of the archbishop.[15] These diocesan measures were paralleled at provincial level in the Council of Oxford. According to canon 24, bishops were to constitute confessors in each archdeaconry to hear the confessions of rural deans, priests, and parsons. Secular canons of cathedral churches were to confess to the bishop or dean, or persons constituted by the bishop or dean and chapter.[16] The directive was approved in slightly differing terms by the Legatine Council of London, which prescribed constitution throughout the deaneries of confessors for use by 'parsons and minor

---

[11] MP, fo. 78[ra].

[12] See Thompson, *English Clergy*, 246–7; id., 'Will', 240. Cf. below, p. 203.

[13] MP, fo. 14[vb].   [14] Ibid., fo. 16[r].

[15] *CS*, ii. 27, c.13; cf. ibid. 75, c.46 (Salisbury), with respect to 'persone, vicarii, et sacerdotes annuales'; ibid. 235, c.27 (Exeter, 1225 × 1237).

[16] Ibid. 113.

clerics who are ashamed to confess to the deans'.[17] The effect of the two rulings can be seen in several bodies of mid-thirteenth-century diocesan legislation,[18] though the Council of Lambeth (1281), in re-affirming it, claimed that it was 'revoking this ordinance from desue-tude'.[19] As Lyndwood noted, this last was more specific in determining the status of the confessors thus to be deputed. The confessors envis-aged by the Council of Oxford were to be 'prudent and discreet', those of London were to be 'prudent and faithful', while Lambeth required a rector or vicar.[20] Lyndwood also drew attention to a difficulty in inter-preting the terms of reference of the legislation. Certainly, the status of the clerics bound to have recourse to these confessors is variously designated in the episcopal statutes consequent on the Oxford and London directives. Several of them mention simply priests;[21] elsewhere one finds rural deans, parsons, and parish priests,[22] or rectors, vicars, and annual priests,[23] or as specified by the Council of Oxford.[24] The anonymous synodal statutes issued shortly after Oxford condemned the view of some 'rectors . . . priests and those in sacred orders', 'that as regards the penitential forum they are subject to no one'.[25] Inter-pretation seems to have been fluid. When Lyndwood came to consider the word 'priests' in the Oxford canon, he suggested that it might bear two meanings:

One way is that this word, 'priests', stands for every priest, even one without cure (*simplici*), to the effect that such should confess to his bishop or to the latter's deputy, to be assigned, as is stated here. But I do not think this true, unless the priests in question are curates and immediately subject to the bishop; for otherwise, if they are stipendiaries or holders of chantries in parish churches, they ought to confess to the rector or vicar of that church where they celebrate divine services, extra. eodem c. Omnis,[26] and extra. de officio archipresbyteri, c. finale[27] is especially apt. It can be understood in another way, so that this word, 'priests', refers to his earlier, 'rural deans', to the effect that such, if they are priests, confess to the bishop or his deputy, as is stated here. This exposition is more to my liking, particularly

---

[17] Ibid. 247, c.5.

[18] See ibid. 173, Worcester (1229), c.15; 213, Coventry (1224 × 1237), c.17; 370, Salisbury (1238 × 1244), c.10; 455, Chichester (1245 × 1252), c.20; 595, Wells (1258?), c.7; 639, London (1245 × 1259), c.31.

[19] Ibid. 900, c.8.

[20] Lyndwood, *Provinciale*, v, tit. 16, 340 (b), gloss *ad vocem*, 'rector aut vicarius'.

[21] See e.g. *CS*, ii. 173, 213, 455.   [22] Ibid. 370.   [23] Ibid. 639.

[24] Ibid. 595.   [25] Ibid. 145, c.34.

[26] i.e. X. 5. 38. 12, 'Omnis utriusque sexus', requiring confession 'proprio sacerdoti'.

[27] i.e. X. 1. 24. 4, which states that rural archpriests (i.e. rural deans) have cure of priests and people in their custody.

in the case of such a dean, who holds cure of souls under the bishop or otherwise holds perpetual office under him, the office being such that he does not have in his deanery anyone to whom he is subject in the spiritual forum.[28]

This is an eccentric interpretation of the word in its context, but there is a presumption that Lyndwood's remarks correspond to the practice of his own time on the part of 'simple' priests. As intimated by his 'especially', the author of the *Memoriale*'s own instructions to the confessor in his admission of clerics to confession are finally unclear whether he considers that it is rectors, vicars, and parish priests who constitute a special case.[29]

Most of the matters raised in the course of the actual interrogations and in the chapters detailing the duty of restitution as incurred by clerics deal with breaches of canon law (b. lxxi, 'De hiis qui beneficia ecclesiastica illicite adquirunt seu retinent et fructus et proventus ipsorum percipiunt', for instance, is a good technical statement of the variety of ways in which clerics may err in this matter). The author's obvious special interest in particular malpractices, however, may be noted. One point to which he gives emphasis is indecorum in dress. In an age when there was no specific clerical uniform, there are frequent complaints that secular clerics render themselves indistinguishable from laymen.[30] The *Memoriale Presbiterorum* complains particularly of the failure to preserve a sufficient tonsure and of wearing coifs ('tenae').[31] These and other aspects of clerical costume were regulated in canon 5 of the legatine Council of London (1268). Clerics must wear clothes neither too long nor too short, and reaching at least halfway down their calves; their hair was not to cover their ears and their tonsure was to be sufficiently wide; 'and—unless they are journeying, and at no time when they are in churches or in the presence of their prelates or in the public,

---

[28] Lyndwood, *Provinciale*, v, tit. 16, p. 327, gloss *ad vocem* 'presbyterorum'.

[29] See also MP, fo. 14[vb]: 'Nullus rector vel vicarius potest vel de iure debebit eligere sibi confessorem quemcunque, sive religiosum sive secularem, sine licencia proprii episcopi'; ibid., fo. 16[rb]: 'Si aliquis capellanus secularis tibi velit confiteri et plenam forsan de eodem non habueris noticiam si sit parochianus tuus vel alius quem de iure audire potes . . .' Cf. more restrictive remarks at ibid.: 'Nulla consuetudo potest excusare eciam quoscumque presbiteros sive beneficiatos sive alios in hoc casu.'

[30] See P. Heath, *English Parish Clergy on the Eve of the Reformation* (London/Toronto, 1969), 108–9.

[31] 'Coyphae', 'Tenae', and 'Infulae' were used synonymously. See Acton, *Commentary*, p. 88 (a), *ad vocem* 'coyphas'. Lyndwood defines 'tena' as 'vittarum extremitas dependens diversorum colorum'; 'vittae' he defines as 'quae crinibus innectuntur, quibus fluentes religantur capilli'. However, he makes it clear that the prohibition on these contained in Pecham's statute of 1281 extends to all superfluity in headdress. *Provinciale*, iii, tit. 1, p. 120 (b), *ad vocem* 'Infulas'.

common sight of men—let them not dare or presume to wear the head attire [*infulas*] which they commonly call "coifs" [*coyfias*]'. The penalty for a priest or anyone in a dignity or having cure of souls, or for canons of cathedral churches, who offended against the statute in the matter of these coifs or of the tonsure or of dress, was *ipso facto* suspension from office if he did not heed a warning; if he persisted for three months under this suspension, he was to be suspended forthwith from benefice, and he was not to be absolved from these sentences by his diocesan until he had paid the latter a sixth part of his revenues for distribution to the poor. Other categories were to be dealt with by their prelates.[32] The statute was re-enacted by Archbishop Pecham at the Lambeth Council (1281), though in a severer form. Now there was to be no admonition, as, it was claimed, the statute had not been efficacious, 'in as much as minor prelates do not dare to admonish these monstrous clerics'. It also suspended any cleric in sacred orders wearing knightly attire from entry to a church until he reformed.[33] This must be the ruling to which the author of the *Memoriale* refers when he observes that 'priests and rectors of the province of Canterbury wearing these coifs in public are today suspended from office and benefice *ipso iure*'.[34] The matter received new attention from the Council of London (1342), but this restored the warning; any who persisted in breach of the statute—which included a detailed rehearsal of such abuses—for a period of six months after being warned, were to be suspended for three months and were then to be deprived of their benefice, or if unbeneficed, were to be rendered incapable of taking one for four months. Beneficed clergy were not to be absolved except by their bishop and not before they had distributed one-fifth of their annual revenue to the poor of the diocese. Exceptions were made for dress worn on journeys.[35] A mandate of Bishop Grandisson to his archdeacons just some four months before the council's legislation demonstrates his own marked concern with the problem.[36] This must be thought a further area in which he may have made a significant contribution to the council's deliberations.

Another point emphasized in the examination of priests is careless saying of divine office, which the author treats as a species of fraud.[37]

---

[32] *CS*, ii. 753–4.   [33] Ibid. 914–15.   [34] *MP*, fo. 15ʳ.

[35] *Concilia*, ii. 703. Archbishop Simon Islip issued a mandate in 1353 requiring the observance of Stratford's constitution; ibid., iii. 29–30.

[36] *RG*, ii. 959–60. The mandate, dated 18 June 1342, rails against the 'monstrous transformation' of clerks into laymen.

[37] *MP*, fo. 17ᵗʰ.

The perception was current. John Bromyard, who supplies a macaronic verse to sum up the range of malpractices ('Ecclesie tres sunt qui servitium male solvunt, | Forchipers, momelers, verlepers, non bene psallunt'), compares the office of such offenders to that of a thief in a kitchen. The thief, when he wishes to steal part of a fish, generally steals a piece from the middle and not the head or tail, which he joins to cover up the theft: 'so they join together the beginning of the verse and the end and leap over the middle, in their haste, so that I know not whether God or man understands it.'[38] The topic is no doubt perennial. In putative context, however, it is tempting to link the concern evinced in the *Memoriale Presbiterorum* with Grandisson's as evidenced in a mandate of 1330 graphically describing malpractices among the vicars choral of Exeter cathedral. Some deliberately let candle-grease drip on the heads of those below as a joke; mistakes are made in chanting and reading, while some, who know better, crack witticisms at the errors; some, 'in as much as their heart is in market or town or bed, though their body be in choir, managing to perform the *opus Dei* negligently and fraudulently themselves and to draw their accomplices to follow suit, order the conductor of the service, at the top of their voices, in English, to hurry matters up'.[39] Grandisson's Ordinal issued for the cathedral in 1337 specifically enjoined abstinence from 'quarrelling, gossiping, and merriment' in choir.[40]

The *Memoriale* mentions several irregularities in ordination on which the subject should be examined. One of these is the question of title: the source whereby the cleric intended to maintain himself, pending his obtaining a benefice, and in default of which the bishop who incautiously ordained him became liable to support him.[41] Religious houses were an increasingly important source of these, at least as an administrative device into which patrimonial or pensionary sources of

---

[38] Bromyard, *Summa Predicantium*, *sub voce* 'Ordo Clericalis' (O. vi), art. ii, section xxvi. On the history of Tutivillus, see Owst, *Literature and Pulpit*, 512–14. On negligence in divine office and in particular, with reference to the *Memoriale*'s condemnation of 'putting the cart before the horse' (MP, fo. 17ʳ), see Bishop Quinel's statutes for Exeter: *CS*, ii. 1018–19. Cf. *Piers Plowman*, ed. Skeat, B. Prologue, 97–98: 'Here masse and here matynes • and many of here oures | Are don undevoutlych.' Cf. ibid., C. XIV, 117–26, and C. XVIII, 117–19: 'Lord leyve that these preestes • leely seyn here masses, | That thei overhuppe nat for hast! • as ich hope thei do nat, | Though hit suffise for oure sauacion • sothfast by-leyve.'

[39] *RG*, i. 586–7.   [40] J. N. Dalton (ed.), *Ordinale Exon* (London, 1909), i. 12.

[41] X. 1. 14. 13. See Moorman, *Church Life*, 56. Cf. *Piers Plowman*, ed. Skeat, C. XIV, 104–7: 'The title that ȝe taketh ȝoure ordres by • telleth ȝe beth auaunced, | And needeth nat to nyme selver • for masses that ȝe syngen; | For he that tok ȝow title • sholde take ȝow wages, | Other the bishop that blessed ȝow • and embaumede ȝowre fyngeres.'

income may have been subsumed.[42] It has been shown that in the later period, at least, there was 'little relationship between the number of vacancies which a monastic house could be expected to have, whether in curacies or actual benefices, and the number of titles for ordination which it bestowed'.[43] Under pressure of candidates, fictitious title remained a problem till the Reformation. Thomas More urged that no one should be ordained 'but he that were, without collusion, sure of a living already'.[44] The collusion which he had in mind was probably something of the sort noted in the *Memoriale*: 'Item, whether, before he was thus presented to orders, he swore to his presenter that he would never disturb him over promotion or the making provision to him of an ecclesiastical benefice.'[45] Mid-thirteenth-century statutes for London deal with this very practice, enjoining under penalty of excommunication 'that no one being presented to sacred orders shall make a pact with his presenter that he will not trouble him over any provision or sustenance to be made to him', and inhibiting 'those who present . . . from receiving a pact or promise of this kind from any ordinand'.[46] Other statutes take pains to warn officials to admit no one to sacred orders who has not 'a certain and true title' without the bishop's being made aware of it, otherwise they should be deemed to have been promoted furtively.[47] Early in his pontificate, on 28 August 1328, Grandisson wrote to the archdeacons complaining of past abuses on the part of candidates for orders who relied on the support of the gentry, and directing that no one should impetrate prayers or letters addressed to the bishop or his clerks but should come with sufficient title, at the canonical times, and be prepared to submit to examination.[48] The *Memoriale* questions whether the penitent was ordained through 'inordinate prayers of any

[42] See R. N. Swanson, 'Titles to Orders in Medieval English Episcopal Registers', in H. Mayr-Harting and R. I. Moore (eds.), *Studies in Medieval History Presented to R. H. C. Davis* (London/Ronceverte, 1985), 239–40.

[43] Bowker, *Secular Clergy*, 62. Cf. Heath, *Parish Clergy*, 17. Cf. *Piers Plowman*, B. XIV, 110–14:

> For hit is a carful knight • and of a caitif kynges makynge
> That hath no londe ne lynage riche • ne good loos of hus handes.
> The same iche seye for sothe • by such that ben prestes,
> That han nother konnynge ne kyn • bote a corone one,
> And a title, a tale of nouht • to hus liflode, as hit were.

[44] See Bowker, *Secular Clergy*, 64.   [45] MP, fo. 16ᵛ.   [46] *CS*, ii. 644, c.50.

[47] See ibid. 373, c.19 (Salisbury, 1238 × 1244); ibid. 1001, c.8 (Exeter, 1287). 'Titulus certus et verus' was listed by the legate Otto (1237) as one of the prerequisites for orders, ibid. 243, c.6.

[48] *RG*, i. 384.

intercessors'.[49] It defines as furtive ordination any infringement of the ordaining bishop's specifications,[50] and notes two schools of thought on the matter. One view was that the offender might only be absolved by the pope, unless he entered religion, the other being, in essence, that recourse to the apostolic see was necessary only when the sentence was *ab homine*.[51] This is, in fact, the consensus of the decretals on the point.[52]

Two other items raised under this head which require comment are ordination 'per saltum' and ordination by the bishop of another diocese, without the candidate's having letters dimissory.[53] A decretal of Innocent III laid down that in the case of a cleric who had himself promoted in ignorance from subdeacon to priest, that is, 'per saltum', the recipient should, after a penance, be ordained deacon and then dispensed in his priesthood.[54] In the case of deliberate fraud, the penalty seems to have been that the culprit was suspended from office and benefice until satisfaction had been made for the offence and until he had been properly ordained.[55] Letters dimissory, as understood in this context, were a licence from the ordinand's bishop for his ordination outside his native diocese. From Quinel's statutes it appears that, even in the case of his own subject, a bishop might require formal testimony of fitness from the archdeacon of his locality before admitting to orders.[56] The term was also used of the testimonial which episcopal statutes generally demand from strange clerics, in proof of the orders claimed by them, before their admission to minister in a diocese.[57] There seems to be no firm distinction between the two uses of 'letters dimissory'. In Lyndwood's explanation, the letters differed in that, with the exception of an exempt prelate in the case of his own subject, only a bishop might issue letters dimissory for ordination, while testimonials to orders already received could be issued, in effect, by any prelate.[58] The legal requirement for both types of letter is stated in a number of rulings in

---

[49] MP, fo. 16ᵛ. On a later complaint in this vein, see Heath, *Parish Clergy*, 16.

[50] MP, fo. 16ᵛᵇ.   [51] Ibid.

[52] X. 5. 30. 1, 2, 3. See, however, *Registrum Johannis de Trillek*, ed. J. H. Parry, Canterbury and York Society, 8 (1912), 26–7, for papal letters to the bishop, instructing him to dispense a named priest to exercise his office, after a time of suspension and penance, despite his having obtained his orders by falsely swearing that his title was a sufficient one; the papal penitentiary has absolved him; it remains to the bishop to dispense him.

[53] MP, fo. 16ᵛ.   [54] X. 5. 29. 1. Cf. *CS*, ii. 651, c.82.

[55] X. 5. 30. 1. Cf. *CS*, ii. 374.   [56] *CS*, ii. 1001, c.8.   [57] See Ibid. 1032, c.37.

[58] See Lyndwood, *Provinciale*, i, tit. 9, 47 (a–b), gloss *ad voces* 'commendatitiis', 'vel dimissoriis'.

the *Decretum Gratiani*.[59] According to Lyndwood, clerics ordained by another bishop, without licence from their own, are suspended and may be dispensed only by their own bishop or by the pope or a papal legate.[60]

The clerical penitent is also to be examined on a number of activities prohibited to his order, absolutely or with qualification, such as trading[61] and the exercise of secular offices,[62] or professional advocacy, whether in a secular or an ecclesiastical court.[63] This and other aspects of clerical conduct, such as dicing, the frequenting of taverns, and patronage of actors and jesters—all of which occur in the *Memoriale*'s interrogatories for clerics[64]—were regulated by a canon of the Fourth Lateran Council,[65] which was the basis of much English legislation on the subject. He is to be examined too on associations with women,[66] though questions concerning clerical chastity do not bulk large in the interrogations.

Among the personal offences on which clerics are to be questioned are swearing—particularly by the limbs of Christ[67]—and loss of time. The latter is specifically associated with drunkenness: 'Item, he ought to confess and do penance over loss of his time, which he wasted over illicit gossiping, feasting, and drinking . . . and in which he ought to have done good work, for of such it is said, "Alas, nothing is more precious than time", but nothing is reputed more cheaply among clerics and especially among priests today.'[68] The remarks are probably suggested by similar observations of Hostiensis,[69] but the subject was an obvious topic of moralizing. The *Cloud of Unknowing* warns the mystical disciple: 'þerfore take good keep into tyme, how þat þou dispendist it. For noþing is more precious þan tyme. In oo litel tyme, as litel as it is, may hevene be wonne & lost . . . Man schal have none excusacion aзens

---

[59] *Decretum*, Ia pars, d. 71, 72.

[60] Lyndwood, *Provinciale*, gloss *ad voces* 'executionem', 'auctoritati sufficienti'.

[61] MP, fo. 15rb.   [62] Ibid., fo. 18vb.

[63] Ibid., fo. 15[v]. On clerics trading, see below, p. 164; on clerical advocacy, see above, p. 103. On their exercise of secular office, see above, p. 126.

[64] See e.g. MP, fos. 17[va-b], 18[vb], 15[va-b].

[65] X. 3. 1. 15. See *CS*, ii. 63, 151, 271, 348, 407, 431, 440, 565, 632; cf. ibid. 1013.

[66] MP, fo. 18[v].   [67] See below, p. 170.

[68] 'Item debet confiteri et penitere de amissione temporis sui quo vacavit circa confabulaciones, commessaciones et ebrietates huiusmodi illicitas, in quo debebat bonum operari, quia de talibus dicitur, "Heu nil carius tempore"; set nil vilius inter clericos et maxime presbiteros hodie reputatur.' MP, fo. 17vb.

[69] Cf. Hostiensis, *SA*, V, tit. 'De penitentiis et remissionibus', art. 50, 'a principibus secularibus', col. 1441.

God in þe dome & at þe ȝeuynge of acompte of dispendyng of tyme.'[70]
For Langland, too, time is a precious commodity:

> Lesyng of tyme • treuthe wote the sothe!
> Is moste yhated up erthe • of hem that beth in hevene,
> And sitthe to spille speche • that spyre is of grace,
> And goddes gleman • and a game of hevene;
> Wolde never the faithful fader • his fithel were intempred,
> Ne his gleman a gedelynge • a goer to tavernes.[71]

The topics which form the basis of the *Memoriale*'s interrogation of clerics are unidiosyncratic, deriving as they do from ecclesiastical law —common and local—and having many parallels in the literature of complaint. The general observations with which the author concludes his chapter on secular clerics, do, however, reveal a bias which is fundamental to his approach to the pastoral cure. He is aware that inadequacies on the part of secular clerics are regarded by 'religious'—that is, mendicants, in this context—as being a justification for their interference in parish life.

> Take note that modern clerics—almost universally, with a few exceptions— prodigal of their reputation, having in detestable fashion abandoned clerical honour, do not fear to lead an exceedingly dissolute life. Some too, on account of a defect of learning, are found little suited for the cure of souls committed to them. Considering all of which and making shift to be kings in the kingdom of the blind, these regulars scurry about through every parish and, collecting everywhere the grain which they find there, they scarcely leave the straw to those who minister in the parish churches, cordially embracing, for their own advancement mainly, the leonine society condemned by the law.[72]

Roman law did not admit of a partnership in which one partner was excluded from a share in the profits—the 'societas leonina'.[73] Richard

---

[70] *The Cloud of Unknowing*, ed. P. Hodgson, EETS, os, 218 (1944), 20.

[71] *Piers Plowman*, B. IX, 98–103; cf. C. VI, 92–3; C. XI, 185–7.

[72] MP, fos. 15vb–16^r: 'Ecce enim quod quasi communiter clerici moderni, paucis exceptis, fame sue prodigi, honestate clericali detestabiliter exulata, vitam non verentur ducere plurimum dissolutam. Nonnulli eciam propter defectum litterature quoad curam animarum sibi commissam minus ydonei reperiuntur. Que omnia religiosi huiusmodi [*sc.* mendicantes] considerantes et in regione cecorum regnare satagentes, per parochias singulas discurrunt et colligendo passim grana que ibi invenerint vix paleas in ecclesiis parochialibus ministrantibus relinquunt, societatem leoninam a iure reprobatam, pro sui recommendacione maxima, corditer amplexendo.'

[73] See W. W. Buckland, *A Text-Book of Roman Law from Augustus to Justinian*, 3rd edn., ed. P. Stein (Cambridge, 1963), 508.

FitzRalph makes a similar point, when, in the *Defensorium Curatorum*, he suggests that the friars only interest themselves in those aspects of the pastoral cure to which a profit attaches.[74] The canonist John Acton, in his own pastoral treatise, puts into the mouths of the secular clergy the text of Job 16: 2: ' "All of you are burdensome consolers": in these words, the rectors of churches, lamenting, inveigh against the mendicant friars; although the latter ought to be fellow workers with the rectors and partakers of their toils—rather as in the case of Eve, who was given as a helpmate—the rectors complain that they are defrauded of tithes and other church revenues, by the pestilential blandishments . . . with which, generally, they cozen laymen.'[75] The *Memoriale*'s criticism is, indeed, on this occasion qualified by a concession not made elsewhere in the work—that the mendicants are 'good clerks'.[76] The realization that the training of the secular clergy lags behind that of the friars is, for the author of a pastoral treatise for parish priests, an appropriate and significant sentiment.

---

[74] Richard FitzRalph, *Defensorium Curatorum*, 478.

[75] Acton, 'Septuplum', fo. 53ʳ, *ad vocem* 'consolatoris onerosi': ' "Consolatores onerosi omnes vos estis": que verba rectores ecclesiarum lamentantes invehunt contra fratres mendicantes, qui cum cooperatores ipsis rectoribus esse deberent et laborum participes . . . tamen velud Eva, data in adiutorium . . . persuasionibus pestiferis . . . quibus laicos plerumque dimulcent, rectores ipsi se defraudari decimis et aliis obveccionibus ecclesie conqueruntur.' For other criticisms of the friars in the 'Septuplum', see ibid., fos. 102ᵛ–103ʳ, and in his gloss on the legatine constitutions, see Acton, *Commentary*, p. 12, *ad vocem* 'ex penitentia proventus recipiunt', p. 14, *ad vocem* 'minores clerici'.

[76] MP, fo. 16ʳ. Cf. below, p. 185.

10

Society Under Scrutiny VI: Economic Activity: The Examination of Merchants; Usury, Trading, and the Duties of Almsgiving

The attempt by the medieval canon lawyers to impose controls on the use of wealth, and specifically to define the methods by which trade might be conducted, is an important example of the interest of the church in areas which in modern times are regarded as the responsibility of the state. The suspicion neatly expressed in the canonical warning that 'in buying and selling it is difficult not to incur sin',[1] coupled with a prohibition of usury, brought a whole range of commercial transactions within the purview of the ecclesiastical authorities. Even in cases where the public forum had no jurisdiction[2]—in many cases of usury, the proof of the crime rested on the intention of the lender—such dealings could be subjected to minute examination by the confessor. If the rising power of money in the twelfth and thirteenth centuries lent a special relevance to this manner of administering penance,[3] the interest of the canonists in the development of confessional practice may be seen from one aspect as a corollary of their preoccupation with business ethics.[4] Nor was it only to the process of acquiring wealth that social and moral considerations applied. The duty of almsgiving imposed particular demands upon its use. The *Memoriale Presbiterorum* evinces a pronounced interest in several aspects arising.

---

[1] *Decretum Gratiani*, 'De penitentia', D. 5, c.2.

[2] As in non-manifest usury, for remarks on which see B. N. Nelson, 'The Usurer and the Merchant Prince: Italian Businessman and the Ecclesiastical Law of Restitution 1100–1500', *JEcH*, Supplement 7 (1947), 109.

[3] Cf. A. Walz, 'Sancti Raymundi de Penyafort Auctoritas in Re Penitentiali', *Angelicum*, 12 (1935), 349.

[4] See J. W. Baldwin, 'The Medieval Theories of the Just Price', *Transactions of the American Philosophical Society*, NS, 49 (1959), part iv, p. 36. A major contribution to understanding the theological development of related themes is O. Langholm, *Economics in the Medieval Schools: Wealth, Exchange, Value, Money and Usury According to the Paris Theological Tradition* (Leiden/New York/Cologne, 1992).

Usury and Trading

In considering the attitude of the canonists to business transactions, a distinction must be made between the law relating to usury and that relating to 'dishonest gain' (*turpe lucrum*). The prohibition on usury as such was simple and absolute.[5] It was in connection with contracts where the usury was disguised that the confessor encountered difficulties.

'Dishonest gain' was the term applied by the canonists to the process of buying at a lower and selling at a higher price.[6] This increase was only justified where it was considered that an improvement had been effected in the goods in the meantime. One method was generally conceded to clerics and laymen alike. Both could receive profit from improvements involving skill—*ex artificio*—as in writing a book or in rearing animals. Even the latter activity had been considered illicit for clerics by Huguccio, *c.*1188–90, but his view was rejected by later canonists.[7] The only other justification for clerics' profiting by sale was from reason of 'utility' or 'necessity', in a case where an individual had bought goods for his own use and then had found that he had a surplus. Merchandising proper (*negotiatio*) was reserved for laymen; in their case, a profit could be made in recognition of the labour expended, for instance, in the transport of goods.[8] The practice of buying goods and storing them until the price should rise was prohibited even to laymen.[9]

Of usury, the *Memoriale Presbiterorum* says:

Here you should know that usury is exercised by many, both clerics and laymen, every single day, sometimes secretly, sometimes openly. In receiving something beyond the principal, they do not believe that they are sinning and in the penitencial forum they do not confess regarding this sin, nor do confessors of today make any inquiry regarding this sin. As for the judicial forum, justice is not done against usurers for this reason, that judges of today, in the execution of justice concerning this sin, are lukewarm and remiss and in no way wish to punish it.[10]

---

[5] The theories are fully discussed by T. P. McLaughlin, 'The Teaching of the Canonists on Usury', *MS* 1 (1939), 81–147; 2 (1940), 1–22.

[6] See ibid., i. 124. Baldwin, 'Theories', 45.   [7] See Baldwin, 'Theories', 45.

[8] Thomas de Chobham recognized the worth of this contribution: *Summa Conferorum* ed. Broomfield, 31.

[9] Baldwin, 'Theories', 45.

[10] 'Hic scire debes quod usura singulis diebus, aliquando occulte, aliquando manifeste, exercetur a plerisque, tam clericis quam laicis, qui, recipiendo aliquid ultra sortem in hoc non credunt se peccare nec in foro penitenciali de hoc peccato confitentur nec confessores moderni aliquid inquirunt de hoc peccato. In foro vero iudiciali, iusticia contra usurarios non redditur, eo quod omnes iudices moderni in exequenda iusticia circa hoc peccatum tepidi sunt et remissi nec aliqualiter volunt punire hoc peccatum.' MP, fo. 72ʳᵇ.

The confessor is therefore warned to consider the condition of each penitent, whether he was a merchant—cleric or lay—and whether he lent freely, receiving nothing beyond the principal. If by convention he received or hoped to receive anything in this way, he is a usurer.[11] In this context, it must be remembered that usury could be committed without an actual agreement when it was the intention of the lender that gain should arise from the contract and when this hope was the main cause of his giving the loan. The canonists' ruling on this was that 'Hope makes the usurer'.[12] If this hope was secondary, the guilt was less.[13]

The author then depicts what he considers a typical scene of the usurer at work:

Behold a poor man out of his necessity[14] comes to a rich parish priest or to a burgess or another neighbour and asks him for ten pounds, or the same number of measures of corn, or wine or other liquid, or other goods which are weighed, counted, or measured, to be given him on loan for a certain period, say for a year or six months, and the creditor says, 'If you like to pledge your lands or such and such revenues for a specified period as a bond, I will certainly give you a loan'; and the debtor pledges these lands and revenues for an agreed period. And when this loan has been taken, the creditor has the lands which have been pledged to him cultivated . . . and meantime receives the fruits which accrue and turns them to his own use. When the time comes to repay, the debtor repays him whatever he received from him as a loan, but the creditor does not deduct or allow the debtor on whatever he received in the meantime . . . freely appropriating to himself everything that he has gained in this way and so he commits usury by thus receiving beyond the principal.[15]

The loan on security—without allowance for the fruits—was known as mortgage and was one of the oldest and commonest types of

---

[11] Ibid., fo. 72rb.   [12] X. 5. 19. 10.   [13] McLaughlin, 'Teaching', 106.

[14] It was generally conceded that if the borrower resorted to a usurer out of necessity and as having no alternative, he did not participate in the usurer's sin. See Baldwin, *Masters*, i. 272.

[15] 'Ecce pauper homo pro sua necessitate venit ad presbiterum divitem, aut burgensem seu alium vicinum suum, et petit ab eo decem libras vel totidem mensuras bladi, vini vel alterius liquoris seu alias merces que consistunt in pondere, numero vel mensura, sibi dari mutuo usque ad tempus, puta ad annum vel dimidium, et creditor dicit sic: "Si vis obligare michi terras tuas vel redditus tales usque ad predictum tempus loco pingnoris, bene tibi mutuabo." Et debitor obligat sibi huiusmodi terras et redditus ad tempus conventum. Et tali mutuo sic recepto, creditor facit coli terras sibi impingnoratas . . . et fructus inde medio tempore provenientes percipit et in usus suos convertit. Adveniente vero termino solucionis faciende, debitor solvit sibi quicquid ab eo mutuo recepit, set creditor non deducit vel allocat debitori ea que de rebus sibi impignoratis seu earum fructibus, exitibus vel proficuis medio tempore recepit, omnia taliter percepta sibi libere appropriando, et sic usuram committit, sic ultra sortem recipiendo.' MP, fo. 72^{r-v}.

contract 'in fraudem usurarum', as the canonists described disguised usury.[16] It was condemned in two decretals of Alexander III.[17] The transaction in which the principal was reduced by the fruits accruing from the pledge—less the creditor's expenses—was known as 'vifgage', and was permitted.[18] Moreover, if in using the gage the gagee substantially improved it, he was, in Peter Cantor's view, entitled to remuneration for his effort.[19]

It is interesting that the parish priest should be specified as one of those likely to engage in concealed usury. Clerical usury had been condemned as early as the Council of Nicea in the fourth century.[20] A specific instance of usury involving the parish priest is raised elsewhere in the interrogatories.

The second example of disguised usury cited by the *Memoriale* is that of sale on credit:

Merchants commonly sell their goods to buyers in winter or at another time of year when they are worth such a price—say one hundred—but the buyers, not having in hand to pay the price, ask them to give such merchandise on credit. The merchants, however, say, 'If you paid me the money for these things now, I could gain many goods in the meantime from the same sum. Therefore, if you want to have this merchandise now, pay me one hundred in cash and I will be well satisfied, but if you wish to have a longer delay, you will pay one hundred and fifty.'[21]

This affair ranks as usury because of the merchant's willingness to accept less for immediate payment, and the author implicitly rejects the plea of *lucrum cessans* advanced by the creditor. Normally a certain amount of latitude was allowed by the moralists in sales on credit. A merchant might, in fact, sell now at higher than the current price for later payment, if he had not intended otherwise to sell the goods at this stage for cash.[22] In practice, it has been shown, credit generally played an important part in medieval trade, and was a feature particularly when

---

[16] It was also called 'interior usury'. See Baldwin, *Masters*, i. 273. For an example of the mortgage, see G. Mifsud, 'John Sheppey, Bishop of Rochester, as Preacher and Collector of Sermons', Oxford University B.Litt. thesis (1953), 85.

[17] X. 1. 19. 1; X. 5. 19. 2.　　[18] Baldwin, *Masters*, i. 275.　　[19] Ibid. 276.

[20] See *Decretum Gratiani*, D. 47. *c*.2. Cf. Baldwin, *Masters*, i. 296, 299–300.

[21] 'Item mercatores communiter vendunt emptoribus merces suas in yeme vel alio tempore anni, que tunc valet iusto precio, pone centum, set emptores non habentes in manibus precium quod solvant, petunt ut mutuo sibi concedant tales merces. Set mercatores dicunt sic: "Si nunc solveres michi peccuniam pro rebus istis, multa bona possem de dicta peccunia medio tempore lucrari. Unde si merces istas nunc habere volueris, solve centum in continenti et bene placet. Set si dilacionem habere volueris longiorem, solves centum quinquaginta."' MP, fo. 72ᵛ.

[22] See McLaughlin 'Teaching', 118.

goods were being handled in bulk and sold to intermediaries rather than to the final consumer.[23] Its importance can be deduced, for example, from the surviving ledger of the London merchant Gilbert Maghfeld, over 75 per cent of whose merchandise was sold on terms of deferred payment, though there is no indication of the rate of interest charged. It was also a factor in facilitating his own purchases on the home market.[24]

Another instance of disguised usury cited by the *Memoriale* concerns an advance tendered by the buyer for goods to be delivered later.

Many, and especially parish priests, given over to avarice, on occasion buy for a low price in advance, namely in the summer, on the feast of St John or of St Margaret, or at another time of year, certain measures of corn then growing on the stalk, to be delivered to them on the feast of St Michael next following, or at another time assigned for delivery, and the buyers have a fair presumption and think it probable, in accordance with the normal course and common custom, that the corn thus sold will be worth more at the time of delivery than it was when it was bought.[25]

Here too the intention of the trader is of prime importance in determining whether usury is involved. Gregory IX allowed payment in advance provided that a probable doubt existed as to the value of the goods at the future date,[26] but in the example cited no doubt exists, and again it seems that the local priest is to be included in the condemnation which Langland pronounces on the richer members of the clergy:

> On fat londe and ful of donge • foulest wedes groweth;
> Right for sothe • suche that ben byshopes,
> Erles and archdeknes • and other ryche clerkes,
> That chaffaren as chapmen • and chiden bote thei wynne.[27]

---

[23] See M. M. Postan, 'Credit in Medieval Trade', *EcHR* 1 (1927–8), 234–61. Cf. E. Lipson, *The Economic History of England*, i, 12th edn. (London, 1959), 616–17.

[24] See M. K. James, 'A London Merchant of the Fourteenth Century', *EcHR* 8 (1955–6), 364–76. On sale debts among Exeter merchants, see Kowalewski, 'Commercial Dominance', 376–7, and id., *Local Markets*, 203–5.

[25] 'Item multi et maxime presbiteri avaricie dediti quandoque pro modico precio emunt pre manibus, videlicet in estate, in festo sancti Johannis, sancte Margarete vel alio tempore anni, certas mensuras bladi in herba tunc crescentis, solvendas sibi in festo sancti Michaelis proximo sequente vel alio termino pro solucione facienda assignato et emptores bene presumunt et veraciter intelligunt iuxta cursum et communem consuetudinem patrie quod bladum sic venditum multo plus valebit tempore solucionis faciende, quam valuit tempore empcionis. Certe, omnes tales emptores sunt usurarii.' MP, fo. 72vb.

[26] See McLaughlin, 'Teaching', 117.

[27] *Piers Plowman*, C. xiii, 224–8. Analysis of Exeter litigation (1378–88), however, shows clerics (undifferentiated) marginally more likely to appear as debtors than as creditors. Kowalewski, 'Commercial Dominance', 369.

There are, says the author of the *Memoriale*, many other kinds of usury which he omits to mention for the sake of brevity. The *Myrour to Lewde Men and Wymmen*, prompted by its parent, the *Speculum Vitae*,[28] offers a concise and coherent account of twelve 'maneres'.[29] Besides those already dealt with, it lists three of some interest. If a man lends on the surety of a pledge and the debtor fails to repay the loan on the agreed day, despite the terms of the contract the creditor may not retain the whole pledge if it is worth more than the loan but must restore the surplus; otherwise he commits usury. So does the man who lends money to a merchant on the understanding that he is to have the entire sum repaid without risk or allowance for expenses, plus half the profits of the enterprise. Here, it is the refusal by the creditor to accept any loss which vitiates the contract, though some canonists held that even this might be lawful.[30] (A genuine partnership, with both parties sharing the risks as well as the profits, was allowed, as is implicitly recognized by the *Memoriale Presbiterorum*, which requires that a merchant should be asked whether he was involved in such a partnership (*societas*) and whether he committed any kind of fraud.[31]) Finally there is the case of the debtor who undertakes to labour for the creditor in return for a loan and who, if unable to refund on the appointed day, is compelled to continue his services in excess of the value of the debt.[32]

The emphasis on the evils of lending must not obscure the fact that the critics recognized that the borrower too had responsibilities. In *Piers Plowman*, Peace makes this complaint against Wrong:

> Ʒut he is bolde for to borwe • and baddeliche he payeth;
> He borwede of me bayarde • and brouʒte hym hom nevere,
> Ne no ferthyng ther-fore • for nouht ich couthe plede.[33]

John Bromyard has heard usurers excuse themselves by claiming that debtors are so deceitful that but for interest they would not pay back the loan at the appointed time. If this is true, he remarks, all that can be said is that on the one hand there are greedy usurers, and on the

---

[28] Cf. Oxford, Bodleian Library, MS. Bodley 446, fo. 85ᵛ.

[29] *Myrour*, ed. Nelson, 132–3.   [30] See McLaughlin, 'Teaching', 104–5.

[31] MP, fo. 24ʳ. This query is from Hostiensis, *SA*, col. 1424, 'sexto'. On the concept see M. M. Postan, 'Partnership in English Medieval Commerce', in *Studi in Onore di Armando Sapori* (Milan, 1957), 521–49. Peter Cantor and his circle allowed partnerships where risks were shared. See Baldwin, *Masters*, i. 288–90. On Exeter partnerships, see Kowalewski, 'Commercial Dominance', 375; cf. id., *Local Markets*, 202–12.

[32] For a discussion of this last form of disguised usury, see Baldwin, *Masters*, i. 278–9.

[33] *Piers Plowman*, C. v, 59–61.

other false and deceitful debtors. The usurer's trade cannot be justified by such an argument.[34] The *Memoriale Presbiterorum* treats any abuse
of the object lent as a form of theft: 'If anyone receives as a loan or a
favour, a horse or clothes or other things which deteriorate in use, from
his neighbour or from anyone else, and lends these things to another
without the knowledge of their true owner . . . or himself used the goods
lent to him in a way other than that permitted him, he commits theft.'[35]
Yet, when all is said, the author is more concerned, even in this matter,
with the creditor. The caution regarding the borrower is immediately
followed by a passage on the abuse of pledges by the lender.[36]

Besides usury, which lent itself to thorough investigation by the
canonists, merchants were suspected of a large number of fraudulent
practices.[37] Fundamentally, the price which the merchant was entitled
to charge was regulated in canon law. The *Memoriale Presbiterorum* questions the trader on 'whether he made a sale, knowingly deceiving the
buyer beyond one half of the just price, in which case, if anyone receives
more than the just price, he is considered by law to receive dishonest
gain'.[38] This stipulation was an extension by the canonists of the Roman
principle of 'extraordinary damage' (*laesio enormis*), which had originally protected the seller of land in cases where he had received less than
one-half of the just price. By the thirteenth century, following the decretals issued by Alexander III and Innocent III, the concept had become
a permanent feature of canon law in a form which protected the buyer
also, in cases where he had been overcharged by that amount—the just
price being, by this date, the current market value.[39] A whole range of
other misconduct would require inclusion in any rounded account of the
moralists' preoccupation with commercial malpractices. Late-medieval
vernacular literature—notably *Piers Plowman*—and pulpit literature,
both in the vernacular and in Latin,[40] is a rich source of satire and
denunciation on the themes of false weights and measures, hiding of
defects, artful display, attenuation of quality, shoddy workmanship, and

[34] Bromyard, *Summa Predicantium, sub voce* 'Usura', (U. xii), art. vi, sec. xix.
[35] 'Si quis recipit ex comodato vel precario a vicino suo vel aliquo alio equum seu aliud
animal vel vestes seu res alias que usu consumuntur, ad certum usum, et ipse res ipsas alii,
ignorante vero domino, accomodaverit vel tradiderit utendum vel eciam ipse per se rebus sibi
comodatis alio modo usus fuerit quam sibi fuit concessum, furtum committit.' MP, fo. 71ᵛ.
[36] Ibid., b. lx.
[37] For the idea that merchandising is now turned to treachery see especially 'Poem on the
Evil Times of Edward II', in *Political Songs*, ed. Wright, pp. 339–40, ll. 335–66, and John
Sheppey's sermon on the theme 'chevysaunce is mischief', Mifsud, 'John Sheppey', 85.
[38] MP, fo. 24ʳᵃ.   [39] See Baldwin, 'Theories', 43 ff.; cf. id., *Masters*, i. 268–9.
[40] For a summary review, see Owst, *Literature and Pulpit*, 352–61.

disparagement of competitors. These are the merchant's other sins, 'almost infinite in number',[41] to which the *Memoriale Presbiterorum* alludes without specification. Having elaborated the legal technicalities governing the conduct of business, especially in the matter of usury and the just price, the author clearly felt that the confessor might be left to his own devices in the investigation of the more commonplace deceits.[42]

One aspect of bargaining universally condemned by the moralists was the indiscriminate swearing that was deemed to accompany it.[43] The author of the *Memoriale* shares the concern. 'Item if he committed perjury or lying in selling, for example, the merchant says, "Look, this thing cost me so much and a better will not be found, and you will have it for such a price and not for less," and this he affirms, swearing by all Christ's limbs, and he lies expressly.'[44] Fra Bernardino, on the same subject, describes a man's going to the cobbler to buy a pair of shoes, neither of them even in such a simple transaction being able to open his mouth without perjuring himself.[45] The idea, portrayed in wall paintings,[46] that swearing disfigures Christ, has a long tradition and occurs frequently in contemporary and later literature. The author's aversion on the point, though it is evidenced again in the examination of sailors,[47] is unidiosyncratic.

In conclusion under this head may be noted the fact that Sunday trading, which was equally the subject of a long tradition of moralizing and regulation,[48] is not one of the author's concerns.

Almsgiving

The subject of almsgiving arises in the *Memoriale Presbiterorum* under the topic of restitution. The principal consideration is that in the matter of almsgiving the claims of justice are prior to the claims of charity. Examined are three classes of people whose ability to give alms is

---

[41] MP, fo. 24ʳᵇ.   [42] Ibid.   [43] See Owst, *Literature and Pulpit*, 414–25.

[44] MP, fo. 24ʳᵃ. The query about swearing is taken from Hostiensis, *SA*, col. 1424, 'sexto', but the reference to Christ's limbs is the author's.

[45] See I. Origo, *The World of San Bernardino* (London, 1963), 83.

[46] See C. Woodforde, 'A Medieval Campaign Against Blasphemy', *Downside Review*, 55 (1937), 357–62.

[47] MP, fo. 24ᵛᵇ.

[48] For prohibitions of Sunday trading, see *CS*, ii. 35, c.8; 194, c.83; 410, c.46; 461, c.51; 647, c.64; 1021, c.22. *Reg. Mortival*, ii. 12. *Reg. Hethe*, 117, 464.

restricted by higher responsibilities.[49] In the first place, the author condemns an outlook which, he claims, is prevalent in the society of his day:

A large number of people sin gravely by erring and deviating from right faith, the vision of their mind being darkened by the poison of avarice; for they believe that it is no sin, more than that, that it is a virtue and that it ought to win merit with God, if they unjustly and illicitly despoil the property of others and then give alms from the spoils. So it happens that many in our time illegally acquire an infinite number of goods, not distinguishing nor caring by what title. Some acquire them from an unjust war, some from hunting where it is forbidden . . . some from theft and rapine, some from simony . . . some from usury, some from unjust toll, some by unjust harassment . . . some from dicing . . . some from unjust tallage . . . some from unjust advocacy, some from unjust sentences, as do many judges, ecclesiastical and secular, and especially seneschals, who will not give definitive sentences in cases aired before them, except they receive Lady Meed or her equivalent, some by unjust extortions, as do judges and bailiffs; others acquire much from harlotry, others from the proceeds of prostitution, others from acting . . . And all such believe that they can be freed from this sin and be saved if they give alms frequently from goods wickedly acquired in this manner. But for certain in this they err and their belief is wrong. You will hold therefore, in brief, that in all the cases mentioned above, with the exception of prostitution and acting, since the recipient is held to restitution of his evil gains . . . alms cannot be given from goods received in this way.[50]

Hostiensis, who equates the capacity to give alms with the capacity to pay tithes, makes a similar concession, in the latter case, in favour of

---

[49] MP, b. lxvii, b. lxviii, b. lxix.

[50] 'In materia ista et circa istam plerique, errando et deviando a fide recta, sue mentis acie avaricie veneno tenebrata, graviter peccant, quia credunt non esse peccatum, immo magis se posse et debere apud Deum mereri, si aliena iniuriose et illicite rapuerint, et inde elemosinas fecerint. Unde contingit quod multi moderni bona infinita sibi adquirunt illicite, non distinguendo vel curando quo titulo. Aliqui enim adquirunt ex iniusto bello, alii ex venacione prohibita . . . alii ex furto et rapina, alii ex symonia . . . alii ex usura, alii ex iniusto pedagio, alii ex iniusta vexacione . . . alii ex ludo taxillorum . . . alii ex iniusta tallia . . . alii ex iniusta advocacione, alii ex iniustis sentenciis, secundum quod faciunt multi iudices, tam ecclesiastici quam seculares, et maxime senescalli, qui nolunt sentencias diffinitivas ferre in causis coram se ventilatis, nisi recepta domina pecunia vel aliquo equipol[l]ente, alii ex iniustis extorsionibus quas faciunt tam iudices quam ballivi, pauperes suos subditos exquisitis coloribus multipliciter gravando; alii adquirunt multa ex meretricio, alii ex mercede prostibuli, alii ex istronatu . . . Et omnes tales credunt se ab hoc peccato liberari et salvari posse si frequenter elemosinas dederint de huiusmodi male adquisitis, set certe errando in hoc male credunt. Tenebis igitur pro summa quod in omnibus casibus supradictis, exceptis meretricio et istronatu, ex quo recipiens tenetur ad restitucionem male adquisitorum . . . non potest de sic receptis fieri elemosina.' Ibid., fo. 75ʳ.

the prostitute and the actor, who were not bound to make restitution of their gains.[51]

The second case is that of a monk, who, since he has no property, is not allowed to give alms without his superior's permission. If he does so, except in a case of extreme necessity, he commits a grave sin. If, however, he holds an administrative position, he may give alms from whatever is superfluous, and indeed is bound to do so. Again, if he has been allocated a certain sum for study or pilgrimage, he may give alms from his expenses.[52] The question is discussed by Hostiensis, from whom the *Memoriale*'s account is taken.[53]

The third class of persons whose capacity to give alms is restricted are members of a family—wife, son, and servants. A wife may not give alms without her husband's consent from the goods they hold in common. If she has separate property, as breweresses or the wives of burgesses generally have, she may do so. She may also give 'moderately' from household stores entrusted to her administration, and wives would be well advised to do so, for there are few husbands who wish to give alms for the souls of their wives when they are dead.[54] A son may only do so, without his father's consent, if he has a personal allowance. Servants may only do so with their lord's consent. All these people who give alms from the goods of others commit theft and are held to restitution, despite the advice of the mendicant friars, who say that gifts made to them involve no sin. This is only true if the consent of the lord to the gifts can be presumed.[55]

These are the restrictions which the higher claims of justice impose on the right and duty of almsgiving. However, even when alms are given licitly, the donor has a responsibility to select a worthy object of his charity. The canonists and theologians did not consider that all poverty was a source of virtue. Nor did they regard all poverty as

---

[51] Hostiensis, *SA*, v, 'De penitenciis et remissionibus', sect. 61, q. 'Quid de facientibus eleemosynam de alieno sive de illicitis acquisitis?', col. 1479; iii, 'De decimis et primitiis', sec. 12, cols. 867–8. Cf. Thomas de Chobham, *Summa Confessorum*, ed. Broomfield, 296.

[52] MP, fos. 75ᵛ–76ʳ.

[53] Hostiensis, *SA*, v, 'De penitenciis et remissionibus', sec. 61, q. 'Quid de facientibus eleemosynam de alieno sive de illicitis acquisitis?', col. 1479.

[54] See the case (*c.*1480) of the London Franciscan, Eryk de Vedica, who, having tended and cured Alice, wife of William Stede, vintner, received from her 20 shillings, only to be sued by her husband for its return; A. G. Little, *Studies in English Franciscan History* (Manchester, 1917), 79–80. Cf. *Handlyng Synne*, ed. Furnivall, ll. 10792–10796: 'Truste ȝe nat moche on ȝoure wyves | Ne on ȝoure chyldryn, for noþyng, | But make þeself ȝoure offryng'.

[55] MP, fos. 76ᵛ–77ʳ.

deserving support.[56] Although the *Memoriale Presbiterorum* allows a wife to give alms to a poor man in extremity—even when her husband's consent is not forthcoming—it specifically excludes sturdy beggars as objects.[57] The distinction was to be forcefully propounded by Archbishop FitzRalph in his London sermon *Nemo vos seducat inanibus verbis*, which contains a pointed exegesis of the text 'When you hold a banquet, call the poor, the weak, the lame, and the blind and you shall be blessed, since they do not have wherewith to repay you' (Luke 14). The text, he argues, is to be read as a whole. There are weak who are rich and poor who are physically robust. These are not invited. Voluntary beggars injure those who must beg.[58] The immediate context is an attack upon the friars' cult of mendicancy, and there was an obvious moral to be drawn, but basically it is a statement of a more general doctrine, shared with the *Memoriale Presbiterorum*, of the need for prudence in the matter of almsgiving.

[56] See Tierney, *Medieval Poor Law* (Berkeley/Los Angeles, 1959), 11.
[57] MP, fo. 76ᵛᵇ.
[58] London, British Library, MS. Lansdowne, 393, fos. 127ᵛ–128ʳ.

Society Under Scrutiny VII: Miscellaneous Penitents: Pardoners, Collectors, Doctors, Hosts, Actors, Servants, Sailors, Women, and Children

The penultimate chapter in the section on restitution is an account of pardoners. They are a class neglected by the *Summae Confessorum*, and the discussion of them in the *Memoriale Presbiterorum* seems to be original to the author. No interrogatory is provided for them: there is no explicit indication that the parish priest is likely to have to hear their confessions. The author's account serves two purposes. He makes clear—presumably with their confessions in mind—how fraudulent pardoners must discharge their obligation to make restitution, to their principals, that is, if they have been duly constituted, and to the bishop of the diocese if they have acted on their own authority, and he advises the parish priest on the precautions necessary in admitting pardoners.[1]

The admission and conduct of pardoners was governed principally by a number of rulings in the official collections of canon law, and, in English context, by supplementary episcopal statutes. There seems to be no surviving provincial legislation in England dealing with them. A canon of the Fourth Lateran Council, besides exemplifying the form in which papal letters on this subject should be cast and which bishops were recommended to follow when issuing similar credentials, laid down that pardoners might not be admitted without such letters either from the pope or from the ordinary, and required them while on their mission to behave discreetly, avoiding taverns and places of ill repute, and refraining from incurring excessive expenses and from fraudulently adopting a religious habit.[2] A canon of the Council of Vienne reinforced that of the Lateran Council and ordered bishops to examine strictly

---

[1] MP, b. lxx.

[2] X. 5. 38. 14. Chaucer's pardoner makes a point of stopping off at the 'ale-stake' before beginning his tale. See *Canterbury Tales*, ed. Robinson, VI (C), 321–2.

the credentials of such persons before admitting them. It also recited a number of abuses said to be common among pardoners and revoked any authority they might have for practising them.[3]

The *Memoriale*'s instruction is addressed to the 'parish chaplain'. He should admit no pardoner without a mandate from his bishop testifying to the authenticity of the indulgence and letters carried by him. In particular, the pardoner is not to be allowed to preach, under penalty of excommunication.[4] It is an object of satire in *Piers Plowman* that a pardoner should preach, 'as he a prest were'.[5] The bishop's responsibility in this is emphasized,[6] but the parish priest is not always the pardoner's 'ape',[7] for Langland satirizes a collusion denounced in the *Memoriale* as widespread, whereby false pardoners are sometimes admitted by parish priests in return for a share of the profits:[8]

> Ac it is noȝt by the bysshop • that the boye prechith,
> The parsheprest and the pardoner • parten the selver.[9]

In a mandate to his archdeacons, Robert Grosseteste complained that parish clergy admitted pardoners to preach 'who preach only such things as extract money the more readily', this although he did not license any pardoner to preach, but only to have his business explained in a simple fashion by the parish priest.[10]

A good example of the exercise of episcopal control over this type of preaching, as also of the attempt to ensure the diplomatic integrity of the pardoner's documents, is Bishop William Bitton's statutes for Bath and Wells (*c*.1258). He forbade the admission of questors unless they were authorized by the bishop's letters; even then, they should not be allowed to preach unless the bishop had specially licensed them to do so. Instead, the 'parish chaplains' should publish the questor's business and indulgences, as evidently contained in the body of a genuine letter of the pope or bishop, and not in codicils, which, it was claimed, were often forged. They were also to see that the money collected was committed to two trustworthy people in each parish, for safekeeping, until it was assigned to a 'faithful messenger' (who would convey it to the pardoner's principals), in the presence of the 'local ordinary' in full chapter.[11] At Exeter similar instructions were issued by Bishop

---

[3] *Clementin.*, 5. 9. 2.   [4] MP, fo. 77ᵛ.
[5] *Piers Plowman*, ed. Skeat, C. Passus I, 66.   [6] Ibid. 76.
[7] Cf. *Canterbury Tales*, ed. Robinson, I (A), 706.   [8] MP, fo. 77ᵛ.
[9] *Piers Plowman*, ed. Skeat, C. Passus I, 78–9. Cf. MP, fo. 77ᵛᵇ.
[10] *CS*, ii. 480.   [11] Ibid. 623.

Quinel, who complained that pardoners, having collected alms, afterwards openly spent them in drunkenness and lecheries.[12] This local legislation may have been the stimulus for the author's special attention to the class, though pardoners would have been suspect within the Grandissonian ecclesiology, hostile as it was to all intrusions into the parish context.

The publication of pardoners' letters in a chapter was a practical method of reducing the opportunities for fraud. It also served from the pardoners' point of view as a means of advertisement, and their privileges sometimes required that this facility should be extended to them. This, and the general procedure surrounding the admission of pardoners, is exemplified in the case of the agents of the hospital of St James of Altopascio, who in the early years of the fourteenth century vindicated their rights within the province of Canterbury against opposition. The house—which was on the route of the northern pilgrims to Rome and to the Holy Face at Lucca—was concerned with the provision of hospitality to travellers and with the construction of roads and bridges,[13] as noted in the *Memoriale*.[14] Two letters issued in favour of the hospital by Clement IV, in 1265 and 1266, were rehearsed by Archbishop Winchelsey in a mandate, dated 19 August 1303, to the bishops and other prelates of the province. He ordered them to admit the brothers of the hospital and their agents, bearing letters whose contents were certified under the seal of the archbishop or his official, to protect their collections from seizure and to summon convocations of rectors—in accordance with Clement's second letter—who should be instructed to publish the necessities of the hospital and the indulgences granted to it, on the three or four Sundays following and whenever expedient, as an aid to the agents.[15] The 'seizure' against which the agents were thus protected may well have been custodial action of the sort provided for by Bishop Bitton.

Clement's first letter had been addressed to the archbishop of Canterbury and his official, and Winchelsey is styled in his mandate 'judge conservator or executor of the privileges' of the hospital.[16] Winchelsey's mandate nullified an ordinance of his predecessor and of the latter's suffragans, to the effect that the proctors of the hospital should not be permitted to hold convocations or collections in the

---

[12] Ibid. 1043.
[13] See *Dictionnaire d'histoire et de géographie ecclésiastiques*, A. Baudrillart *et al.*, ii (Paris, 1914), cols. 831–4.
[14] MP, fo. 77[r].   [15] See *Reg. Winchelsey*, ii. 783–7.   [16] Ibid. 783.

province, as they had been accustomed to do, until investigation had been made of the hospital's privileges, 'on account of certain grievances which were said to have been inflicted on the subjects of the province by runners of the hospital or of the brothers or their ambassadors, on many occasions, against the tenor of the above-mentioned privileges and perhaps without the knowledge of the brothers themselves'.[17] There does not appear to be any primary record of such an ordinance,[18] but it seems to have been obsolete by 1291. On 27 July of that year Bishop Oliver Sutton of Lincoln informed his dean and chapter and archdeacons that the hospital had been exempted by Pope Nicholas IV from his revocation of apostolic privileges granted to pardoners,[19] and ordered them, at the instance of a letter of Archbishop Pecham, to allow genuine brothers of the house to have their business expounded.[20]

There is only slight evidence from Grandisson's register of his dealing as regards pardoners. It seems safe to assume, though, that his policy was one of vigilance rather than of complete exclusion. At the beginning of his pontificate he sequestrated all monies collected by pardoners between his election and 26 July 1328, and moved specifically against pardoners on behalf of Thomas of Lancaster and of the Holy Sepulchre.[21] In 1356 he issued a mandate that pardoners were not to be admitted to preach and complained that archdeacons' officials and the commissaries and registrars of the latter had been admitting pardoners and transmitting their privileges to curates in return for a levy on the receipts.[22] The restriction on preaching can hardly be interpreted as a new departure, but must be rather a measure evoked by the abuse that occasioned the intervention.

Another type of collecting official occurs, like pardoners, in the *Memoriale*'s section on restitution, and not among the interrogatories. There is no precedent in the penitential genre for chapter b. xlvii, 'On the collectors of the procurations of a legate or other nuncio of the apostolic see'.[23] Several points call for comment in relation to them. In

---

[17] Ibid. 787. Winchelsey's action was probably the result of a suit initiated by the hospital, at the curia, to have its privileges implemented. See *Registrum Simonis de Gandavo*, ed. Flower and Dawes, i. 97–8; cf. ibid. 134.

[18] It is not found in the printed edition of Pecham's register: *Registrum Epistolarum Fratris Johannis de Pecham*, ed. Martin; *Registrum Johannis Pecham*, ed. C. Jenkins, Canterbury and York Society (1908–19).

[19] See *Les Régistres de Nicholas IV*, ed. E. Langlois, Bibliothèque des Écoles Françaises d'Athènes et de Rome (1887–93), 410 (b), for the exception referred to.

[20] *The Rolls and Register of Bishop Oliver Sutton*, ed. R. M. Hill, LRS (1948–75), iii. 133–4.

[21] *RG*, i. 344–5, 351, 426–7.   [22] Ibid., ii. 1178–9.   [23] MP, b. xlvii.

the first place, it should be noted that the author does not echo the complaint, frequently voiced by chroniclers,[24] against the financial burden which such procurations imposed. He is concerned only with fraud on the part of the agents. Secondly, the method of collection which he describes, in combination with the sum nominated as a procuration, poses a difficulty. 'It sometimes happens', he says,

> that collectors, such as officials and deans, deputed to collect the procurations, imposed on churches, of legates or of other nuncios of the apostolic see, aggrieve those churches fraudulently, as for instance, the legate or other nuncio . . . shall have in a day sixty shillings for a procuration and it is ordered that procuration be raised from six churches; and so the collector ought to receive only ten from each church; but from each church he receives twelve or more and pays only sixty, keeping the surplus for himself.[25]

The canonical principles regarding procurations were that all churches were liable for them,[26] and that when a nuncio stayed long in one place, neighbouring places should contribute to his upkeep.[27] In England, however, the practice was, until the late thirteenth century, that only prelates and conventual or capitular communities paid this tax,[28] which since Ottobuono's mission was fixed at six marks per day in the case of cardinals, and which, in the case of legates and nuncios of inferior hierarchical status, was determined by their letters of commission.[29] The mission of Bernard, cardinal bishop of Albano, and Simon, cardinal bishop of Palestrina, in 1295–7, established what was probably a new method of collection.[30] In their second year they ordered their procurations to be exacted according to the valuation used for the collection of the tenth, at a rate of four pence in each mark of assessed value, rectors being liable as well as prelates, chapters, and convents. They proceeded similarly in their third year, fixing the rate on this occasion at three pence in the mark.[31] The new method produced a larger

---

[24] See W. E. Lunt, *Financial Relations of the Papacy with England to 1327* (Cambridge, Mass., 1939), and id., *Financial Relations of the Papacy with England, 1327–1534* (Cambridge, Mass., 1962), *passim*.

[25] 'Conti[n]git interdum quod collectores, utputa officiales et decani, deputati ad colligendum procuraciones legatorum vel aliorum nunciorum sedis apostolice ecclesiis impositas, gravant ipsas ecclesias fraudulenter, ut ecce legatus vel alius nuncius sedis apostolice habebit in die sexaginta solidos pro procuracione et precipitur quod ista procuracio levetur a sex ecclesiis et sic debet collector recipere a qualibet ecclesia tantum decem; set de qualibet recipit duodecim vel plus et tantum sexaginta solvit, quod ultra recipit sibi retinendo.' MP, fo. 66^{r-v}.

[26] X. 3. 39. 17.   [27] X. 3. 39. 23.

[28] See Lunt, *Financial Relations to 1327*, 569.   [29] Ibid. 550–1.

[30] A tradition that Ottobuono was the first to levy procurations as an income tax was probably not well founded; see ibid. 555.

[31] See ibid. 553–5.

sum than the old and, despite protests by the convocations of Canterbury and York in 1297, continued to be used by later envoys.[32] Papal envoys in 1309, 1313, 1318, 1324, 1326–7, and 1335 raised their procurations as an income tax.[33] Those sent in 1335 to make peace between England and Scotland, Hugh, bishop of St Paul-de-Trois-Châteaux, and Roland d'Aste, papal chaplain and auditor, were to receive six pounds of small Tours and fifty shillings, respectively, per day. The rate of income tax in Canterbury province to meet this was a halfpenny in the pound.[34] By this time the 'maior summa' which was customarily granted to a cardinal had come to be a tax of four pence in the mark of clerical incomes as assessed for the tenth, with the exception that payers having an exceptionally large income were allowed to compound.[35]

'Officials and deans' might be agents under either method of collection. Under the new method the diocesans were burdened with the collection, which they entrusted to deputies. In 1337 we find appointed as deputy collectors, in Ely diocese, the archdeacon's official, in Exeter and Salisbury, the archdeacons.[36] The archdeacons would no doubt act through their officials and possibly through rural deans. The *Memoriale* is therefore correct on this point. Otherwise, however, the author's understanding of the method of raising these procurations is out of keeping with the development whereby the sum was levied as a smaller tax, fixed for the occasion, on a large number of subscribers.[37] The mention of sixty shillings as a procuration denotes envoys rather than papal collectors, whose expenses continued to fall on a restricted number of traditional payers, but who were entitled to receive only seven shillings per day.[38] The new system appears in retrospect to have been well established by the third decade of the fourteenth century, though, since it was not accompanied by a formal statement, contemporaries may have been less sure that the administrative change was permanent.[39] The easiest explanation of the discrepancy would be to assume that the author confused the procurations of envoys with those of collectors.

[32] Ibid. 556.
[33] Ibid. 560–1, 563, 565, 568–9; id., *Financial Relations 1327–1534*, 621.
[34] Ibid.   [35] Ibid.
[36] In several other dioceses, various religious houses were deputed. See Lunt, *Financial Relations 1327–1534*, 627, n. 32.
[37] See Lunt, *Financial Relations to 1327*, 569; id., *Financial Relations 1327–1534*, 693.
[38] See W. E. Lunt, *Papal Revenues in the Middle Ages*, i (New York, 1934), 45; cf. *RG*, i. 302–4.
[39] William de Lauduno, OP, during his short mission of 1320–1, was authorized to take three florins a day of all the clergy, of England and Wales. He did not formally raise it as an income tax but demanded a specified quota from each bishop, who might levy it as he thought fit. See Lunt, *Financial Relations to 1327*, 568.

The intermediate agents may well have profited from raising these, as they certainly did from Peter's Pence, and there may even have been some mixing of the systems of collection.[40] One way or another, the author's understanding was defective. His sensitivity to abuse over procurations may have been indirectly founded. They were, in fact, a topic of controversy at Exeter. Grandisson distinguished himself in 1337–8 by a fierce onslaught on the papal collector Bernard de Sistre and his deputy Master Durantus. Among his complaints was that Bernard was collecting arrears for his own benefit, and that excommunication and interdict were being deployed against alleged delinquents who had paid in full.[41] That was the external confrontation of the problem. The *Memoriale*'s chapter might represent a corresponding awareness of abuses practised by the agents within the diocese.

Doctors too occur in the section on restitution, an obligation which they incur through inexpertise or malpractice.[42] The prescription that a divine gift should not be sold[43] was not held to forbid the physician's receiving payment, since the entitlement to the fee arose from the labour expended by him and not out of consideration for a restoration of health.[44] The 'turpe lucrum' stigmatized by the *Memoriale*[45] arises, therefore, from the negligence or fraud rather than from the practice of medicine for remuneration. Similarly, the physician was held responsible for the death of his patient[46] only if he had been negligent.[47]

The other aspects of medical ethics discussed by the author concern the personal status of the physician (specifically as regards the

---

[40] For Peter's Pence, see Lunt, *Papal Revenues*, 68–9. Cf. *RG*, i. 217–18, 299. Grandisson accused Bernard de Sistre of collecting his procuration by the wider method: ibid. 302–4; cf. Lunt, *Accounts*, p. xxxi. Ibid., n. 318, confuses the two procurations. There may have been confusion in practice.

[41] *RG*, i. 217–18, 298–300, 302–4. Cf. Lunt, *Accounts*, pp. xxx–xxxi.

[42] MP, b. liii. The Lincoln archidiaconal court in 1520 imposed a heavy penance on a doctor who confessed to being illiterate and to having no knowledge of medicine. See Bowker, 'Some Archdeacons' Court Books and the Commons' Supplication', 306–7. On the public image of the profession, see R. S. Gottfried, *Doctors and Medicine in Medieval England 1340–1530* (Princeton, 1986), 58–65.

[43] See *Decretum*, IIa pars, causa 1, q. 1, c. xi.

[44] See the gloss of Joannes Andreae on X. 1. 14. 7; *Corpus Juris Canonici* (Lyons, 1671), ii. 495, ll. 79–84. Cf. the case of teachers.

[45] MP, fo. 68ᵛ.   [46] Ibid.

[47] Cf. X. 1. 14.7, where the question of responsibility in this case is left to the conscience of the practitioner. For the contractual relationship between doctor and patient, see M. R. McVaugh, *Medicine Before the Plague: Practitioners and their Patients in the Crown of Aragon 1285–1345* (Cambridge, 1993), 174–81, and on the patient's expectation of competence, ibid. 185–7. For general remarks on culpability, see C. Rawcliffe, *Medicine and Society in Later Medieval England* (Stroud, 1995), 71–2.

prohibition on study of medicine by religious and priests, and on practice of surgery which he presents as forbidden to religious in general
as well as to priests),[48] and incautious, experimental use of medicine.[49]

The *Memoriale*'s summary of the subject omits several points which
one might have expected to find raised. A good global account of the
doctor's responsibilities is provided by the *Summa* of St Antoninus of
Florence.[50] This deals with a number of perennial problems, such as
whether a doctor summoned by the relatives may treat a patient against
the latter's will,[51] or whether the doctor, believing death to be immin-
ent, should tell the patient,[52] as well as some arising from the archbishop's own social milieu[53] or the contemporary legal context.[54] The
review of the sins of physicians includes other immoralities or technical faults not mentioned in the *Memoriale*. So, the doctor is deemed
guilty if he 'gives medicines and remedies contrary to the salvation of
souls, such as by procuring an abortion or by counselling any other
evil';[55] if he does not induce the patient to call a priest;[56] if he refuses
to visit the poor, who cannot pay;[57] if he prolongs the patient's infirmity 'so that he may have greater gain from frequent attendance', when
he could as easily heal him;[58] if he induces his patients to infringe church

[48] MP, fo. 68ᵛ; the legal basis of the remarks is X. 3. 50. 9, 10. The history of the question is examined in D. W. Amundsen, *Medicine, Society and Faith in the Ancient and Medieval
Worlds* (Baltimore and London, 1996), 222–47.

[49] MP, fo. 69ʳ. Cf. Amundsen, *Medicine, Society and Faith*, 256–7.

[50] *Summa* (Lyons, 1542), iii, tit. 7, 'De statu medicorum'.

[51] Ibid., sec. 3: the answer is that he may do so on the presumption that the patient is
mad.

[52] Ibid., sec. 4: he sins mortally by not doing so, if he knows or is in doubt that the patient
is in mortal sin or has made proper disposition of his property. If he considers that the patient
is in a good state on these counts, he may decide not to tell him—though he should bear in
mind that there is always room for the patient to effect an improvement in his state or arrangements. In no circumstance may he lie 'as they are accustomed to do'.

[53] Such as whether a physician salaried by the commune might make an extra charge, ibid.,
sec. 3.

[54] Such as whether canon law required that the doctor should refuse to treat a patient
unless he agreed to confess. Antoninus rejected Hostiensis's opinion that he should, 'cum
in periculo constitutis quantumcunqe obstinatis sit subveniendum secundum ordinem
charitatis': ibid., sec. 4.

[55] Ibid., sec. 7, 3rd sin.

[56] Ibid., 4th sin; this obligation was imposed on the doctor by X. 5. 38. 13; for an example
of English synodal legislation on this point, see *CS*, ii. 993.

[57] St Antoninus, *Summa*, iii, tit. 7, sect. 7.

[58] 'cum eque bene citius possent [sc. medici] liberare', ibid., 8th sin. This might be a temptation for the physician who, as a psychological measure, exaggerated the time required for
a cure—in accordance, for instance, with John Arderne's advice; see John Arderne, *Treatises
De Fistula in Ano*, ed. D'Arcy Power, EETS (1910), 6.

fasts, without good cause;[59] or if he boasts about his own expertise and depreciates his colleagues.[60] However, although the *Memoriale*'s consideration of this topic is thus incomplete by the sophisticated standard of the fifteenth-century Florentine analysis, it represents an important innovation on the author's part in the schema of Joannes de Deo and Hostiensis, neither of whom includes physicians in his review of the professions.

The host of an inn is accorded a brief chapter in the section on restitution as being responsible for the safe custody of mislaid property.[61]

Also included in the section on restitution is a discussion of the actor's remuneration. The actor, whose profession was traditionally an object of the moralists' suspicion,[62] is not considered elsewhere in the treatise. He is included at this point, with the prostitute, in so far as the obligation of restitution may fall on him as the recipient of ecclesiastical property, donated to him by a prelate—whose title to the goods is not an absolute one.[63]

Several persons have a place in the section on interrogation only.[64] The interrogation of servants seems to be original to the author and has no equivalent in the *Summa Hostiensis*, though it may have been suggested in part by the latter's queries for 'mechanici', who are to be questioned 'on mendacity, on perjury, on theft, on work fictitiously done'.[65] The *Memoriale*'s examination, too, concerns general conduct and is non-technical.

The inclusion of sailors in the schema is original and highly appropriate given the provenance argued for the treatise. 'So great is their wickedness', says the author 'that it exceeds the sins of all other men.'[66] Several questions concern their hostility to ecclesiastics or their spiritual shortcomings, notably failure to confess.[67] Sailors, as wandering entities, would have found it easier than most classes to avoid the obligation imposed by *Omnis utriusque*. The case is noted in a later period of a sailor from Wainfleet who found himself under suspicion of Lollardy because every year at Lent he went to Norfolk and did not return until

---

[59] St Antoninus, *Summa*, iii, tit. 7, sect. 7, 9th sin.

[60] Ibid., 10th sin. Omitted from this account of Antoninus's review of physicians' sins are the several abuses which occur in the *Memoriale* and those noted above from other sections of the *Summa Antonini*, which are repeated under this head.

[61] MP, b. xxxvi, a section perhaps suggested by a remark in Hostiensis, *SA*, v. tit. 'De penitentiis et remissionibus', art. 61, 'De naufragiis', col. 1470.

[62] See E. Faral, *Les Jongleurs en France au moyen âge*, 2nd edn. (Paris, 1964), chaps. 2, 3.

[63] MP, b. xxxii, a canonical problem simply.   [64] Ibid., a. xxxviii.

[65] Hostiensis, *SA*, v. tit. 'De penitenciis et remissionibus', art. 50, col. 1441.

[66] MP, fo. 24ᵛ.   [67] Ibid., fo. 24ᵛᵇ.

a fortnight after Easter, so that it was not known whether he had confessed and communicated. When he eventually appeared to answer, he
produced a witness who swore that he had seen him communicate.[68]
Matrimonial discipline too might be expected to be less capable of
enforcement among sailors. The author suspects them of having a wife
in every port.[69]

As for 'social' sins, sailors are accused of practising 'fenus nauticum',[70]
the sea-loan, condemned in the decretal *Naviganti*.[71] In this, the sailor
would be more sinned against than sinning, for the main objection to
this form of disguised usury was that the lender, although he assumed
the sea-risk, was safe from the misfortunes of the business enterprise
as a whole, the loan being repayable even though no profit was forthcoming.[72] Sailors commit fraud in merchandising.[73] They practise
piracy, for which they are excommunicated by canon law,[74] and commit murder.[75] Finally, they infringe the law on jettison: 'And for a
certainty, they sin frequently against the intention of the Rhodian law
on jettison. That is, when they stand in peril of the sea, they fling merchandise from the ship to lighten it, sparing the goods of one merchant,
corrupted by a bribe, and inflicting damage on another merchant in
his goods.'[76] Roman civil law—as quoted by the author—required that
the loss should be shared in this event.[77] The Laws of Oléron laid down
in greater detail the procedure to be observed. The master could order
the jettison without the consent of the owners, but it was prescribed
that on arrival at shore he should take an oath with three of his com-
panions that he did so only in order to save lives and the ship. The
goods lost should be appraised at the market price of those which had
been saved and the cost borne equally by the merchants, the master
and crew contributing if they had cargo on board. Originally the ship
was also liable to contribute, but Edward I enacted to the contrary in

---

[68] See J. A. F. Thomson, *The Later Lollards* (Oxford, 1965), 103.   [69] MP, fo. 25^r.
[70] Ibid.   [71] X. 5. 19. 19.
[72] See R. de Roover, 'The Organization of Trade', in *The Cambridge Economic History*, iii
(Cambridge, 1965), 53–5.
[73] MP, fo. 25^r.
[74] Ibid., fo. 24vb. Cf. X. 5. 17. 2. On piracy in the Channel, see C. L. Kingsford, 'West
Country Piracy: The School of English Seamen', in id., *Prejudice and Promise in Fifteenth
Century England* (London, repr.1962), 78–106. See also C. Ewen, 'Organised Piracy Round
England in the Sixteenth Century', *The Mariner's Mirror*, 35 (1949), 29–42, which has some
observations on the earlier period, and R. F. Wright, 'The High Seas and the Church in the
Middle Ages', *The Mariner's Mirror*, 53 (1967), 118–19.
[75] MP, fo. 24vb.   [76] Ibid., fo. 25^r.
[77] *Digest*, 14. 2 (i. 419–22). Cf. L. A. Senigallia, 'Medieval Sources of English Maritime
Law', *The Mariner's Mirror*, 26 (1940), 7–14.

1285.[78] Conversely, the merchants were required to contribute to jettison of the ship's mast or cables.[79] The Laws of Oléron were more equitable with regard to jettison than Roman law, according to which goods lost were appraised at the price of purchase and goods saved, at their market price.[80] The author does not, however, refer to them.

Women penitents are dealt with under a number of headings in the treatise. In the first place, there is a traditional warning to the confessor that he should be especially on his guard in receiving them to confession.[81] Then there is a detailed and original interrogatory for use with them.[82] This consists for the most part of non-technical matters such as their addiction to fashion or to the use of cosmetics—both well tried objects of criticism[83]—irreverence towards their husbands, harlotry, overlying of children,[84] exposure of children, procuring of abortion, sorcery, hypocrisy in religious practice, adultery or fornication, bigamy, scandal-mongering, and so on. One of the points raised in the interrogatory—the substitution of a putative child for the true heir[85]—is the subject of a separate chapter, in the section on restitution,[86] as posing a particularly thorny problem for the confessor. Women are also given special attention in the imposition of penance, as wives[87]—for whom the performance of a penance for non-public sin may be difficult—and as widows, whose special place in ecclesiology renders them more culpable if they err.[88]

Children too are considered as a separate class of penitent, whose responsibility is diminished by their age.[89] In regard to them, the *Memoriale* follows, with amplification, the tradition of Joannes de Deo and Hostiensis.[90]

---

[78] See *The Oak Book of Southampton*, ed. P. Studer, ii, Southampton Record Society (1911), 66–9; 69, n. 21. The Oak Book preserves a good mid-fourteenth-century text of the laws. *The Black Book of the Admiralty*, ed.Twiss, i. 89–131, contains a fifteenth-century text.

[79] *Oak Book*, ed. Studer, ii. 68–71.

[80] Ibid., 69, n. 20.   [81] MP, fo. 2ʳ.   [82] Ibid., a. xli.

[83] See Owst, *Literature and Pulpit*, 391–2, 396, 404, 520.

[84] See Pantin, *Church*, 199.   [85] MP, fo. 26ᵛ.

[86] Ibid., b. xxxiii.   [87] Ibid., b. xvii.

[88] Ibid., b. xviii. On the status, see especially A. Rosambert, *La Veuve en droit canonique jusq'au XIVᵉ siècle* (Paris, 1923), 55–92.

[89] MP, a. xlii. Cf. ibid., b. xix. H. C. Lea, *A History of Auricular Confession*, i (London 1896), 400–4, describes mainly later doctrine on this subject. R. Meens, 'Children and Confession in the Early Middle Ages', in D. Wood (ed.), *The Church and Childhood* (Oxford, 1994), 53–65, surveys the early penitentials, and N. Orme, 'Children and the Church in Medieval England', *JEH* 45 (1994), 573–4, the views of William of Pagula and John de Burgh.

[90] See Hostiensis, *SA*, v. tit. 'De penitentiis et remissionibus', art. 43, col. 1425.

12

Friars as Confessors—The Author's Criticisms

The attitude of the author to friars as confessors is conveyed internally in some dozen asides, where he interrupts his main theme to castigate their laxity or rapacity. One such has been noted already—his condemnation of the friars' aggressive competition in exploiting the deficiencies of the secular clergy.[1] The underlying point there is ecclesiological. 'For this they [sc. the regulars] do not deserve in a just judgment to be commended and let them take care, since, although they are good clerks, they ought not however to criticize with biting tooth, secretly or openly, prelates or simple priests, detracting them in any respect, who on account of the prerogative of their office are to be venerated as though the vicegerents of God.'[2] Office has an intrinsic integrity that commands respect. The conviction finds its counterpart in Richard FitzRalph's bold assertion at the height of the controversies over the friars' pastoral privileges that God will give greater assistance in execution to the man elected or deputed by his church to an office than he will to an outsider perhaps with four times the learning.[3] In the context argued for the *Memoriale Presbiterorum*, the perspective is part of a world-view. 'Vicegerents of God' might be from the mouth of Grandisson himself.[4]

Specifically as regards confessional practice, there is a list of complaints. The friars impose unsatisfactory penances and absolve in reserved cases:

Who dies impenitent dies as though excommunicated by the canon, and therefore the church ought not at all to pray for such a one, impenitent and dying in mortal

---

[1] See above, p. 161.

[2] MP, fos. 15ᵛ–16ʳ: 'Ex hoc tamen non merentur iusto iudicio commendari et caveant quia, licet sint boni clerici, non tamen debent reprehendere dente mordaci, clam vel palam, prelatos sive sacerdotes simplices, sibi aliqualiter detrahendo, qui propter prerogativam officii sui tamquam vices Dei gerentes sunt merito venerandi.' For complaints that the friars slandered the secular clergy, see C. Erickson, 'The Fourteenth-Century Franciscans and their Critics. II: Poverty, Jurisdiction and Internal Change', *Franciscan Studies*, 36 (1976), 130.

[3] In the sermon 'Nemo vos seducat inanibus verbis' (12 March 1357): London, British Library, MS. Lansdowne 393, fo. 133ʳ.

[4] Cf. above, p. 46.

sin. But it is truly a cause for lament in this case, in that almost all rich people, and ordinary people too, shy from having penances imposed on them and even want to evade them easily, and especially women, and therefore, rejecting their proper judges, having the cure of their souls, they confess their sins in these times to confessors of the orders of mendicants who of their own head and without lawful authority absolve, *de facto*, without distinction all and sundry confessing to them, remitting no one to the bishop in cases specially reserved to the bishop, as the law requires.[5]

While 'almost all' modern confessors err in the matter of canonical penances, the criticism is particularly directed to regular confessors 'who serve and dwell in the courts of princes and magnates'.[6] After long discussion of the question whether goods seized in war must be restored, the author concludes:

But whatever may be written here or elsewhere of this matter, there is hardly to be found anyone who may confess concerning this sin, and if from time to time perhaps this should happen, then many confessors and especially of the orders of mendicants, blind and leaders of the blind, having no power at all of absolving a sinner in this case [he means that this is episcopally reserved], some part of the booty or some other thing having been given them, *de facto* absolve the plunderer and others adhering to him, caring not at all about the restitution which, as the law demands, should be made. But woe to all such confessors.[7]

A similar deficiency is noted as regards appropriation of wreck, though here also the criticism includes secular confessors.[8] Evasion of

---

[5] MP, fos. 85vb–86ra: 'Si talis impenitens moriatur, tamquam excommunicatus a canone decedit, et ideo non debet ecclesia pro tali impenitente et in mortali peccato constituto decedente aliqualiter orare. Set valde dolendum est in hoc casu, quia quasi omnes divites et eciam plebei affectant quoad penitencias sibi iniungendas et eciam volunt de facili evadere et potissime mulieres, et ideo, spretis propriis iudicibus animarum suarum curam habentibus, confitentur hiis temporibus peccata sua confessoribus de ordinibus mendicancium, qui proprio capite et absque auctoritate legitima absolvunt indistincte de facto totaliter sibi confitentes ab omnibus peccatis sibi confessatis, neminem in casibus episcopo specialiter reservatis ad episcopum, prout ius exigit, remittendo.'

[6] MP, fo. 55rb.

[7] Ibid., fos. 63^v–64^r: 'Set quicquid hic vel alibi scribatur de materia ista, vix reperitur aliquis qui de hoc peccato confiteatur, et si aliquociens forsan hoc contingat, plerique tunc confessores moderni, et maxime de ordinibus mendicancium, ceci et duces cecorum, nullam penitus talem peccatorem in hoc casu absolvendi potestatem habentes, data sibi aliqua parte huiusmodi prede vel re alia, predonem et alios sibi adherentes absolvunt de facto, de restitucione prout ius exigit facienda penitus non curantes. Set ve omnibus talibus confessoribus.'

[8] Ibid., fo. 61^r: 'Set timendum est quod confessores tam religiosi quam seculares moderni multociens sunt in causa perdicionis et dampacionis animarum taliter peccancium, eo quod non exponunt sibi confitentibus pericula sua in hoc casu; et si exposuerint, tamen pro modico de suo sibi dato ipsos absolvunt de facto, nulla facta restitucione illis quibus de iure fieri debet; et male, quia ad hoc de iure nullam habent potestatem nisi in casu necessitatis, vel de licencia episcopi loci, seu auctoritate domini pape speciali; quo casu debet quilibet confessor iniungere restitucionem integre fore faciendam ut supra scribitur.'

restitution, too, is the reason why 'catchpoles and bailiffs' allegedly hie to mendicant confessors to whom they tell what they wish to tell.[9] The implication here would seem to be that the friars, as reliant only on what is confessed, will be less searching in interrogation than a parish confessor who, knowing the avocation of his penitent, will establish the obligation of restitution and remit to a competent penitentiary. This suspicion of the friars as a point of 'exit' from a system[10] that should otherwise be closed seems, in context, characteristically Grandissonian.

In regard to the obligations arising from the relationship between confessor and penitent, the author says of the penitent:

He is obliged to relieve the indigence of his confessor if the latter is a poor man and in great need and if the penitent is someone of substance, and even if the penitent is poor he has the same obligation in so far as he can conveniently do so. But many confessors of our time and especially those of the orders of mendicants consider well that obligation and hold it as affects them, who from such a practice acquire to themselves many unlawful goods, enjoining light penances in cases where a fixed penance is laid down by the canon, and especially in cases in which it is not permitted them by law to loose or bind.[11]

It is precisely this last danger that FitzRalph much later (1357) adduced in the *Defensorium Curatorum* against the penitent's entrusting himself to a friar rather than to the 'tutior persona' of his parish priest, whose livelihood does not depend on confessions and who can therefore be trusted to impose a fitting penance.[12]

While there are similarities between the criticisms of friars to be found in the *Memoriale* and those later broadcast by FitzRalph, there are important divergences between them, or at least between the *Memoriale* and

---

[9] Ibid., fo. 68ra–b: 'Tales cacherelli et ballivi nolunt confiteri proprio suo episcopo vel eius penitenciario qui solus et non alius eo inferior regulariter de iure potest vel debet absolvere tales, set vadunt ad confessores de ordinibus mendicancium et sibi dicunt quod volunt. Constat tamen quod non possunt tales confessores privilegio suo quo se dicunt munitos aliquem talem in casu isto absolvere et nullo modo liberantur pena legis qua ligantur.'

[10] I echo a thought-provoking observation of Mr Alexander Murray on structures for confession. Cf. M. J. Haren, 'Confession, Social Ethics and Social Discipline in the *Memoriale Presbiterorum*', in P. Biller and A. Minnis (ed.), *Handling Sin: Confession in the Middle Ages*, York Studies in Medieval Theology, 2 (1998), 118.

[11] MP, fo. 82^r: 'Tenetur ipsius confessoris relevare inopiam si pauper fuerit et multum indiguerit et confitens habundans fuerit, et licet confitens pauper fuerit ad id tamen obligatur in quantum com[m]ode facere poterit. Istam autem obligacionem bene considerant et tenent quoad se plerique confessores moderni et maxime illi de ordinibus mendicancium, qui ex tali questu bona plurima illicita sibi adquirunt, penitencias leves iniungendo in casibus in quibus certa penitencia a canone est statuta et maxime in casibus in quibus de iure sibi non permittitur absolvere vel ligare.'

[12] Richard FitzRalph, 'Defensorium Curatorum', in E. Brown, *Fasciculus Rerum Expetendarum et Fugiendarum* (London, 1690), 469.

FitzRalph in full flow. The *Memoriale* shows no concern whatever with the dogmatic question of poverty. On one occasion the author repeats 'the common report' that the mendicants build churches and other edifices on the proceeds of corruption, whereas the confessor ought to keep his hands clean of any bribe, though he should be humble enough not to refuse an alms if offered it.[13] Here was an obvious opportunity to attack. Again, in a passage where he is at pains to remind proud prelates that the whole church is sustained by alms, and that, according to Augustine, 'Our Lord Jesus lived by alms', he makes no reference to the poverty controversy.[14] It is worth noting here that in FitzRalph's case the preoccupation with poverty was a relatively late development, canvassed in the *De Pauperie Salvatoris* but not in the *Propositio* of 1350.[15] As regards the mendicant orders, the sole interest of the author of the *Memoriale Presbiterorum* is in the abuse of privileges. Neither is he an apologist for the removal, or indeed the redefinition of the privileges. Only on one occasion does he observe that dissension exists between seculars and mendicants over their interpretation. In listing the cases in which confessions must be repeated, he states that where a parishioner has confessed to another confessor—secular or regular, of whatever order—without his own priest's consent, except it be to the bishop's penitentiary, he must confess the same sins, 'specie et numero', to his own priest, 'in accordance with the tenor of the constitution of the general council'. He notes, however, without comment that the mendicant confessors do not approve this case. His conclusion seems to be that as a general rule it is safer to confess to one's own priest than to external confessors.[16] It must be remembered, as a final distinction between the author and FitzRalph, that the author is a lawyer and the lawyers' tradition was extremely circumspect on the points which FitzRalph, a theologian, came tendentiously to challenge in the 1350s.[17]

Within the context which has been argued for it, the *Memoriale Presbiterorum* represents on the question of friars as confessors the first evidence of a hostility that subsequently becomes an overt feature of Grandisson's regime.[18] That the hostility was deeply laid within

---

[13] MP, fo. 84ᵛ: 'Premissa tamen non observant per omnia confessores moderni ordinum mendicancium, qui de tali turpi questu fabricant sibi ecclesias et alia edificia, prout eis vulgariter imponitur.'

[14] Ibid.   [15] Cf. Walsh, *Scholar and Primate*, 350.   [16] MP, fo. 31ʳ.

[17] M. J. Haren, 'Friars as Confessors: The Canonist Background to the Fourteenth-Century Controversy', *Peritia*, 3 (1984), 503–16.

[18] Cf. Haren, 'Bishop Gynwell', 277.

Grandisson's own outlook may be deduced from the fact that when he first declares himself, at the height of the FitzRalph campaign in 1359, he is revealed as nothing short of apocalyptic in his language.[19] Quite apart from any specific influence, such as may have been contributed by his studies in the Paris of Jean de Pouilli,[20] antipathy to the pastoral role of the friars—except where, as notably in Cornwall, their participation was specially invited[21]—is readily seen as of a piece with a general policy. That policy centred on the rights of the parish church and on responsibility for souls discharged within the parochial and diocesan structure. Evidently, the issue here is ecclesiological. Aside from gleanings in the proems of episcopal mandates, however, and inferences from praxis, the ecclesiological dimension is not explicit on Grandisson's part. The explicit evidence comes from the polemics of his protégé FitzRalph, who in the heat of battle may have carried the standard further than was strategic (though hardly further than envisaged if Jean de Pouilli was indeed the model). As no doubt befitted the work, putatively, of a young lawyer, written well before controversy erupted, the *Memoriale Presbiterorum* is notably silent on such a larger agenda. Its tenor is strictly legalistic. Strictly, but not narrowly so: the insights that the treatise offers are consistent with an underlying programme— the direction of society in accordance with the demands of abstract justice. To judge by the *Memoriale Presbiterorum*, a central component of the programme was the raising of moral sensitivities to social abuse through confessional practice, or at least the maintenance of a confessional practice, that, through rigorous interrogation, emphasized social responsibilities and posited the demands of justice, expressed in the obligation of restitution, as an effective pre-requirement for absolution.

---

[19] Ibid. and cf. Haren, 'Confession, Social Ethics and Social Discipline', 119–20.
[20] Cf. A. Gwynn, *The English Austin Friars in the Time of Wyclif* (Oxford, 1940), 81.
[21] See Haren, 'Bishop Gynwell', 280.

13

The Career of an Ecclesiastical
Administrator II: Lincoln and Worcester

William Doune's later career is of potential interest to the present study on two counts. First, it might be expected to provide a basis from which to hypothesize towards his early outlook, contemporary with the *Memoriale Presbiterorum*. In fact, only his will (and, on one cardinal point, the will of his own official and successor) offers substantial and unmistakable documentation of his views. The humdrum record of administrative activity, as so often,[1] disappoints when looked to for the personal dimension, though it is tempting to see in reforms enacted in 1361 for the Lincoln consistory an expression of the same preoccupation that has been noted at Exeter and a pulse of the indignation at forensic abuse that so heavily characterizes the *Memoriale Presbiterorum*. By the same token, the clear evidence of support at Lincoln for Archbishop FitzRalph's campaign against the friars accords with the outlook of the treatise as considered in Chapter 12. Secondly, Doune's later career constitutes the parameters within which would have to be assessed any long-term and wider, contextual, effect of the doctrine of the *Memoriale* and of the disciplinary programme with which Doune has been associated in Chapter 3. In this respect the evidence is highly suggestive.

It will be procedurally convenient, if inevitably somewhat artificial, to separate for the purposes of documentation the two dimensions of Doune's later administrative career, in the dioceses of Lincoln and Worcester.

Doune's Career in Lincoln Diocese

Apart from his studies at Oxford, William Doune's earliest documented association with Lincoln diocese is through benefice. On 1 September 1349 he was admitted, at Aymer Fitzwarin's presentation, to the

---

[1] On this defect of administrative records, see Haren, 'Will', 121.

church of Quainton, Bucks., vacant by the death of its rector.[2] At this point there is no indication that he was contemplating an administrative career in the diocese. Indeed, the evidence is to the contrary. Among a list of supplications to the pope granted in favour of Reginald Brian, as elect of St Davids, on 18 October 1349 is one for a canonry of Exeter with expectation of a prebend to William Doune, described as licentiate in laws and the bishop-elect's clerk.[3] At this point he had evidently entered on the connection which was eventually to bring him to the officiality of Worcester.

Bishop Gynwell was provided to the see of Lincoln on 23 March 1347 and consecrated on 23 September following.[4] Although he had been a king's clerk,[5] the most likely factor to which he owed his promotion was that he had served (*c*.1343–5) as chaplain and steward to Henry, earl of Derby and later duke of Lancaster.[6] He had been in the civil law faculty at Oxford *c*.1337.[7] He would probably have encountered Doune in that context. The first evidence of Doune's attachment to his service is a commission to him and John de Carleton, both described as professors of civil law, dated 27 October 1351, to visit Chacombe priory.[8] By the date of the next reference to him in Gynwell's register, he had proceeded doctor of laws and had already been appointed official of Lincoln: on 12 October 1352, described as such, he was present with John de Belvoir, William de Spaldewick, John de Denton, and Richard de Asschule, notary public, at the new bishop's visitation of his cathedral.[9] The description 'clerks of Exeter diocese' in the witness clause to this document must, minimally, apply to John de Denton and Richard de Asschule, who may therefore be thought to have been recruited by Doune from his old context. As will be seen, John de Belvoir, who was a native of Lincoln diocese, was to become official in the archdeaconry of Leicester, of which Doune had collation on 12 May 1354,[10] and, eventually, Doune's successor as official of the diocese.

The specific references to Doune as official in Gynwell's register need not be thought to provide a comprehensive view of his contribution to

[2] LAO, Reg. IX, fo. 240ʳ (roman numeration).
[3] ASV, *RS* 21, fo. 52ʳ. *CPP*, i. 182. Cf. *CPL*, iii. 345.
[4] *BRUO*, ii. 842–3.   [5] Ibid.
[6] Ibid. See further Highfield, 'The Hierarchy', 119, and Fowler, *The King's Lieutenant*, 177, 179–180.
[7] *BRUO*, ii. 842, notes his depositing Justinian's *Institutiones* as surety.
[8] LAO, Reg. VIII, fo. 5ʳ.   [9] Ibid., fo. 167ᵛ.
[10] LAO, Reg. IX, fo. 319ᵛ (roman numeration).

the administration of the diocese. (Of his judicial functions they certainly do not.)[11] Nor do the specific references, mainly consisting of episcopal mandates, always guarantee his personal discharge of the business committed. They do, however, provide the securest guidance on the extent, and occasionally on the location, of his activity and are therefore worth detailing. For the remainder of 1352 there is a short series of commissions to him: on 14 October 1352 to visit the archdeaconry of Lincoln with John de Belvoir, now rector of Faldingworth, and William de Spaldewick;[12] on 25 October to preside over an exchange;[13] on 12 December to receive in St Michael's the Great, Stamford, the purgation of a clerk defamed of theft.[14]

During the spring of 1353 there are three commissions to the official: on 5 January to act in a divorce case;[15] three days later to act in the church of St Michael the Great, Stamford, regarding papal dispensation of a married couple for affinity;[16] and on 1 March 1353 to act over the estate of the late Richard Tonk, merchant and citizen of Lincoln.[17] On 6 April Doune was present with Thomas de Wikham, 'literatus', and John de Kelleseye, notary public, when the bishop admonished John de Stowe, rector of St Mary's, Mablethorpe, Lincs., to take up personal and continuous residence within a month.[18] After this there is a silence until, on 3 August, the official was commissioned to admit John de Lyberd to the vicarage of Luton, Beds., at the presentation of the abbot of St Albans. The institution took place at Stowe Park next day.[19] The vacancy arose by the deprivation of William of St Neots for non-residence, or rather for desertion of his cure following adultery with the wife of a parishioner.[20] The commission for his removal is registered underneath the new admission. The reason for the deprivation may explain the very particular note made of the form by which Doune instituted Lyberd, 'cum onere personaliter ministrandi et continue residendi sub debito iuramenti a se ad sancta evangelia in forma constitucionis domini Octoboni quondam sedis apostolice in Anglia legati in hoc casu edite prestiti'.[21] However, the proviso that an oath be taken to personal residence, in accordance with the legatine constitution, was also included in the commission issued on 15 October

---

[11] The case determined by him on 31 July 1359 (see below, p. 198), is known only from Northants. Record Office, Box X643, no. 1, fos. 42ʳ–43ᵛ.

[12] LAO, Reg. VIII, fo. 24ʳ.   [13] Ibid., fo. 23ᵛ.

[14] Ibid., fo. 29ʳ. For the circumstances, see ibid., fo. 32ʳ⁻ᵛ.   [15] Ibid., fo. 33ʳ.

[16] Ibid., fo. 34ʳ.   [17] Ibid., fo. 41ʳ.   [18] Ibid., fo. 43ʳ.   [19] Ibid., fo. 50ʳ.

[20] Cf. ibid., fos. 119ᵛ–120ʳ.   [21] Ibid., fo. 50ʳ.

to Doune, as official, to admit John de Herthull' to the vicarage which the abbot and convent of St Mary de Pratis, Leicester, claimed to exist in the church of Hungarton, Leics., and to which they had presented.[22] This last concludes the business specifically directed to Doune in that year.

For 1354 there are no references to Doune's activity as official. On 12 May he had episcopal collation of the archdeaconry of Leicester, vacant by death of Mr Henry Chaddesden.[23] In making the collation, Gynwell ignored or acted in ignorance of a papal reservation of the archdeaconry, for which a rival claim had been entered on the part of Arnold de Gavarreto, of the diocese of Bazas.[24] Although Doune also secured papal provision to the archdeaconry, on 12 October following,[25] and was evidently in firm possession of it,[26] the resulting dispute continued to rumble in the background for the rest of his career.[27] As late as 1 February 1361 a suit over the archdeaconry was pending in the papal palace.[28]

The next reference to Doune in the episcopal register is also to do with benefice. On 4 May 1355 the abbot of Osney, a house with which Doune had close associations, was commissioned to receive any resignation made by him of his rectory of Quainton. The manoeuvre of which this commission was the first stage was a response to a difficulty generated by the form of Innocent VI's provision to Doune of the archdeaconry of Leicester. No doubt because of the existence of the rival claim to the archdeaconry, Doune (or his proctor) had considered it more prudent in securing his provision to offer that he would resign the church of Quainton rather than that he should take advantage of the fact that he was already dispensed to hold additionally any dignity, parsonage, or office, even if—as in the case of the archdeaconry—it had cure of souls. On 11 December 1354 Doune supplicated again, stating that reference to his dispensation had on the earlier occasion been omitted through inadvertence, that, by virtue of the

[22] Ibid., fos. 50ᵛ–51ʳ.   [23] LAO, Reg. IX, fo. 319ᵛ (roman numeration).

[24] See *CPL*, iii. 566.

[25] Ibid. 517, and as rehearsed in a petition to Innocent VI, granted on 11 December 1354. ASV, *RS* 27, fo. 296ᵛ (modern foliation). Cf. *CPP*, i. 267–8.

[26] As attested by the recurring references to him by the title in Gynwell's register, by Doune's statement in his petition of 11 December 1354 to Innocent VI (see above, n. 25), by his payment of annates (Lunt, *Accounts*, 88), and, finally, by the evidence of his will.

[27] Hamilton Thompson is not quite correct in stating that the dispute was resolved in his favour by 10 December 1355: Thompson, 'Will', 240. In fact, a provision to him of the archdeaconry on that date was to hold good if his rival had ceded: *CPL*, iii. 566.

[28] *CPP*, i. 366–7.

dispensation, he had held Quainton together with the archdeaconry for several months before the pope's letter of provision—on the strength, in fact, of Gynwell's legally flawed collation—and that he still held it. He now sought a grant in the form 'Perinde valeat', emending the previous provision to the effect that it should hold good from its date of issue as if all these circumstances had been expressed in it but with omission of the requirement that he resign his church of Quainton. There was express cognizance of the fact that he held also a prebendal portion in the church of St Endellion. As a specific consideration in favour of his being allowed to retain Quainton, the supplication adduced the information—corroborated otherwise—that no prebend or dwelling attached to the archdeaconry.[29] In vain: the pope's reply granted only that Quainton might be retained until the feast of All Saints (1 November of the following year), and that it must meanwhile be exchanged for a benefice compatible with the archdeaconry or otherwise be wholly resigned. The request for backdating was also denied[30] —a point that further complicated Doune's legal position in the face of his rival's claim to the archdeaconry. Although there is no record of his actual resignation of Quainton, he evidently did resign, no doubt just before the term set by the pope. On 29 May 1357 the abbot of Osney was commissioned to supervise an exchange between Doune, described as canon of the collegiate church of St Mary *prope castrum*, Leicester, and prebendary of prebend 'D' in the same, and John Godman, rector of Quainton.[31] In all probability the exchange envisaged in the commission of May 1357 was a straight reversal of an earlier, nominal exchange between Godman and Doune, designed to provide for the latter's temporary difficulty. In breaking his tenure of Quainton by exchanging it for the prebend of the collegiate church, a compatible benefice, Doune complied with the terms of the pope's reply to his supplication. The technical arrangement by which he did so depended on his having a compliant partner in the exchange, willing to exchange again after an interval. Nothing more is known with certainty of John Godman. He may have been of Worcester provenance: a John Godman, more likely a relation than the same, occurs in Brian's register among an undated list of ordinands to first tonsure, that refers perhaps to the period 1354–5.[32] The possibility strengthens slightly the

---

[29] ASV, *RS*, 27, fo. 296ᵛ (modern foliation). For the confirmation that the archdeaconry had no dwelling-house, see the petition of the bishop, dean and chapter, and mayor and commonalty of Lincoln, at n. 43, below.

[30] Ibid.   [31] LAO, Reg. VIII, fo. 78ʳ.   [32] Brian's Register, 95.

presumption that the Godman of the exchange was a client of Doune, perhaps recruited by him for his administration within the archdeaconry of Leicester.

There are no references to Doune's activity as official of Lincoln or as archdeacon of Leicester in 1355. The silence on this point over two years is open to several interpretations. It may reflect his newly acquired responsibility in the diocese of Worcester, where, as will be seen, he was appointed official early in 1354. It may mean that during this time he was principally engaged at Oxford in exercises leading to the doctorate in canon law. A papal indult of 16 June 1351, dispensing him from residence in benefice for five years while studying at a university or residing at the Roman curia or elsewhere,[33] suggests that he had had this course in mind. It would have been particularly opportune that he should take advantage of the licence in the prelude to its expiry. However, as already noted, there is no firm evidence that he ever proceeded doctor of canon law.[34] Nor need residence at Oxford have excluded the issue to him of episcopal commissions. As regards the officiality, the silence on this point may, at least in part, be an effect of deficiency in the preservation of business in the register of memoranda, which is relatively thin at this juncture.

By contrast, the first half of 1356 is well documented as regards Doune's activity in the diocese. On 9 January, styled archdeacon of Leicester rather than official, he is named as one of the witnesses to the submission of the dean and chapter and treasurer of Lincoln cathedral regarding their responsibility for vestments and ornaments of the cathedral found to be defective during the bishop's visitation.[35] He is named again in the notarial instrument which follows, dated 6 February.[36] On 24 March he was present with William Cloune, abbot of St Mary of the Meadows, Leicester, the archdeacon of Richmond, William of Loughborough, LL D, John de Belvoir, and John de Kelleseye at the installation of Richard de Hanslope of Tanworth as dean of the New College of St Mary, Leicester.[37] Here again he is styled archdeacon of Leicester, and it would have been equally appropriate that he should be present in that capacity as in that of Gynwell's official. However, it is clear that the distinction of functions is not always preserved in references to him. In much of the subsequent business directed to him in the register he is addressed as archdeacon of Leicester even

---

[33] *CPL*, iii. 427. [34] See above, p. 18. [35] LAO, Reg. VIII, fos. 152ᵛ–153ʳ.
[36] Ibid., fo. 153ʳ⁻ᵛ. [37] LAO, Reg. IX, fo. 364ʳ⁻ᵛ (arabic numeration).

when the matter at issue did not pertain to him as archdeacon. It was, properly, as official that on 6 April he was commissioned with John de Belvoir, William de Spaldwick, and John de Longedon, 'iurisperitis', to proceed against a wife refusing conjugal debt. The case was fixed to commence before them in St Michael's the Great, Stamford, the next Thursday, continuing until determination.[38] On 28 May, with William de Askeby, canon of Lincoln, and Henry, perpetual vicar of Liddington, Rutland, he was commissioned to proceed in a case of detention of tithe of deadwood.[39] The alleged offence was within the parish of Woburn, Beds., so that the reference to Doune as archdeacon is evidently loose. In a return by him to an episcopal commission for confirmation of the election of Ralph Mareschall, canon of Missenden, Bucks., OSA, as abbot of same, he is more circumspectly styled archdeacon of Leicester and official of Lincoln. The episcopal commission, rehearsed in the return, is dated 3 June. The scrutiny and proceedings took place in the church of St Michael the Great, Stamford, on Friday, 10 June. The certificate of the proceedings is dated by Doune 11 June, and is noted and entered as received on same day.[40] Finally as regards 1356, he was present with William de Askeby, John de Kelleseye, Henry, vicar of Liddington, John de Denton, Robert de Navesby, 'and other Christian faithful in a copious multitude' when on 14 June, in the prebendal church of Liddington, the bishop passed sentence of excommunication and suspension directed against unseemly behaviour and even bloodshed such as occurred in the past on the third feria of the feast of Pentecost, 'circa delationes vexillorum Pentecostalium'.[41]

There is now a gap of almost two years, unexplained as in the case of the previous gap, in Doune's recorded activity. The only references to him in Lincoln context in 1357 have to do with benefice and are indirect. One has already been noted: the commission, on 29 May, to the abbot of Osney to preside over what I have interpreted as the reversal of the exchange of Quainton.[42] This reversal coincides suggestively with the presentation of a petition on Doune's behalf by an impressive coalition of the bishop, the dean and chapter, and the mayor and commonalty of Lincoln, dated by its grant five days before, that the pope deign to

---

[38] LAO, Reg. VIII, fo. 59ʳ⁻ᵛ.   [39] Ibid., fo. 63ʳ⁻ᵛ.

[40] LAO, Reg. IX, fos. 260ᵛ–261ʳ (roman numeration).

[41] LAO, Reg. VIII, fo. 84ᵛ. The name of another witness on the occasion, J. de Wa(?) is obscured in the binding.

[42] Ibid., fo. 78ʳ. Cf. above, p. 194.

provide 'to their beloved clerk and official of Lincoln' a canonry of the cathedral with expectation of a prebend, notwithstanding his holding the prebendal portion of St Endellion in Exeter diocese, 'especially since to his archdeaconry of Leicester which he holds there is not annexed prebend or manse or habitation where he may lay his head, neither can he without a prebend conveniently reside in the said church [sc. of Lincoln] nor take anything from the common goods of the same nor even participate in its dealings or affairs'.[43] As a consequence, Doune did get title, at a date that is not established, to the prebend of Empingham.[44] Though backdating of the supplication cannot be excluded, the most economical supposition is that news had just reached Lincoln of its success. Steps were then quickly taken to enter into titular possession of Quainton, which, had it been held at the date of the petition, would have had to be declared. Doune's second period as rector of Quainton lasted until his vacating it on securing corporal possession of nearby Swalcliffe, by 17 May 1360.[45]

On 14 March 1358 Doune was commissioned with John de Kelleseye to examine and confirm the election of the prioress of Hinchingbrook, Hunts, OSB.[46] On 29 March he was commissioned with William de Askeby, canon of Lincoln, Robert de Kynebelle, rector of Horwood Magna, and Thomas Pepir, notary public by apostolic authority and bishop's commissary, to conduct episcopal visitation in the archdeaconries of Buckingham, Oxford, and Northampton and to receive the procurations due accordingly, in accordance with an indult of Innocent VI granted to the bishop for visiting by proxy.[47] Doune was individually appointed for the archdeaconries of Oxford and Buckingham.[48] He probably undertook that part of the visitation at least. The visitation of even the two archdeaconries would certainly have absorbed some four to six weeks of that year.[49]

---

[43] ASV, *RS*, 29, fo. 135ᵛ (modern foliation). 'presertim cum archidiaconatui suo leycestrie quem obtinet in dicta ecclesia non sit annexa aliqua prebenda nec mansu[s] vel habitacio ubi caput suum valeat reclinare nec eciam possit sine prebenda in dicta ecclesia com[m]ode residere neque de bonis communibus dicte ecclesie quicquam percipere nec eciam in tractatibus seu certis ipsius ecclesie negociis interesse.' The date is 9 *Kalendas Junii* (24 May) not 11 *Kalendas* as in *CPP*, i. 297.

[44] *CPP*, i. 366–7. Cf. Le Neve, *Fasti*, i (Lincoln Diocese), 63.

[45] 17 May 1360 is the date of admission to Quainton of Doune's successor, John de Syngelton'. LAO, Reg. IX, fo. 270ᵛ (roman numeration).

[46] LAO, Reg. VIII, fo. 99ᵛ.   [47] Ibid., fo. 86ʳ⁻ᵛ.   [48] Ibid., fo. 86ᵛ.

[49] *Visitations in the Diocese of Lincoln 1517–1531*, ed. A. H. Thompson, i (LRS, xxxiii. 1940), 144, 146–7, estimates that the visitation of Buckingham archdeaconry in 1519 occupied from 9 May to 26 May, and that of Oxford archdeaconry in 1520 from 23 April until early–mid-May.

There are three testimonials to Doune's activity in 1359. On 29 April he had a commission that would have been wholly congenial to the author of the *Memoriale Presbiterorum* and that, with due deference paid to the difficulty of distinguishing between the part of principals and their agents in the construction of diocesan policy,[50] might readily be supposed to relate to the rigorous outlook maintained in the treatise. In his capacity as official principal, Doune was to investigate archidiaconal encroachments on the bishop's exclusive jurisdiction over matrimonial cases in the diocese.[51] The discharge of this brief may be inferred from the reforms instituted in 1361, as detailed later. On 14 June he is noted as a witness with John de Warsop, rector of Loughborough, to the notarial act of John de Northkelleseye, recording the bishop's admission of the resignation of the rector of Baldock, Herts. Finally as regards the record for 1359, on 31 July in the church of St Michael the Great, Stamford, he gave sentence in a case between the abbot and convent of Osney, plaintiffs, and Philip de Hamburth, rector of Ducklington, Oxon.[52] That the act is preserved at all is accidental.[53] It is a reminder of how incomplete must be our knowledge in particular of Doune's judicial activity during some eight working years as official.

On 27 June 1360 a glimpse of judicial business is provided by the bishop's revoking a case of breach of faith pending before the official principal in his consistory at Stamford between Christiana de Thorp of Grimsby, plaintiff, and John Barber, also of Grimsby. On account of the defendant's lack of means to attend for examination at Stamford, the bishop committed the case to the dean of Grimsby.[54] A routine measure in the abstract, the concession is compatible with the sensitivity displayed in the *Memoriale Presbiterorum* to the inconveniences suffered by litigants in being dragged beyond their places of abode.

Besides the instances of recorded activity in the years 1358–60, an inference arises from other matter in the register. Doune's hand is probably to be detected behind the scenes in manifestations of support at Lincoln for Archbishop FitzRalph's campaign against the confessional privileges of the mendicant orders. First to be noted is the suggestion of a diminution, from about 1356, in the issue by Gynwell of

---

[50] Cf. Haren, 'Will', 121.   [51] LAO, Reg. VIII, fo. 125ᵛ.
[52] Northants. Record Office, Box X643, no. 1, fos. 42ʳ–43ᵛ.
[53] See above, pp. 10–11.   [54] LAO, Reg. VIII, fo. 150ʳ.

penitentiary commissions to friars.[55] Next is the evidence for a hardening of policy in the diocese on the obligation of annual confession. This is explicit in a letter of 24 January 1358 publishing the names of fifteen penitentiaries with powers in episcopally reserved cases and revoking similar powers previously granted. The letter required that the text of the constitution *Omnis utriusque sexus* should be circulated to the clergy and expounded to the people 'so that none of our subjects may plausibly plead ignorance' of it.[56] Although, in the abstract, the publication of *Omnis utriusque* might merely be a reminder to the faithful of their duty to confess annually to their 'proper' priest, and although within the terms of canon law as authoritatively interpreted this duty would be discharged by confession to a friar licensed under the constitution *Super cathedram*,[57] exposition of the text at a time when the issues arising from it were the subject of litigation would readily invite restrictive interpretation. Moreover, there are unambiguous indications of sympathy on the part of the regime at Lincoln for the FitzRalph campaign against the friars' pastoral privileges. In the years 1359 and 1360 attempts were being made to collect from the clergy of the diocese in support of the archbishop's expenses as a litigant.[58] The fact that the response would appear to have been less than enthusiastic makes the endeavour more noteworthy. Most remarkably, Gynwell's register is, so far as is yet known, the only source for an interesting development at Avignon in the course of the FitzRalph suit. From a notarial instrument drawn up by the archbishop's party on 16 October 1359, recording the reissue on behalf of the pope as bishop of Avignon of synodal legislation formidably bolstering the authority of parish clergy, it appears that there was in course some attempt at a compromise between FitzRalph's demands and the established state of canon law.[59] The presence of this extraneous item in the Lincoln register, where it must plausibly have been entered at latest before FitzRalph's death reduced its topicality, indicates contact with the litigants—uniquely close

[55] For detailed exposition of what follows, see M. J. Haren, 'Bishop Gynwell of Lincoln, Two Avignonese Statutes and Archbishop FitzRalph of Armagh's Suit at the Roman Curia against the Friars', *Archivum Historiae Pontificiae*, 31 (1993), 275–92. As regards the diminution referred to, which is hazardous of interpretation, see ibid. 282 and n. 42.

[56] LAO, Bishops' Registers 8, fo. 97ʳ. Haren, 'Bishop Gynwell', 282–3.

[57] See Haren, 'Friars as Confessors', 503–16.

[58] See Haren, 'Bishop Gynwell', 283–5.

[59] The instrument is registered at LAO, Reg. VIII, fo. 53ʳ⁻ᵛ. For discussion and text, see Haren, 'Bishop Gynwell', 285–92.

contact in terms of what is so far known—and considerable interest in a strategic manoeuvre that they had relayed back. How much of this interest and of the other indications of sympathy with the FitzRalph campaign is due to Gynwell and how much to his administration is, so far as the content of the register goes, imponderable. However, the independent evidence for Doune's hostility to the friars[60] makes him a prime candidate to be thought an agent in these matters. To this consideration may be added some uncertain but suggestive evidence from Worcester, discussed in context of Doune's career as official of that diocese.[61]

By the early autumn of 1360 Doune was preparing to leave for Avignon on the journey to the curia from which he would not return. On 22 September Masters William de Spaldewick and John de Belvoir were appointed *locum tenentes* of the officiality. The reason for Doune's absence was given as 'lawful causes that must necessarily be pursued touching him'.[62] Since there are some grounds from which to hypothesize a close relationship between them, Doune's departure may have been prompted by news of FitzRalph's illness.[63] That, however, can be no more than surmise. Though a combination of interests is not excluded, there is a ready and exact explanation of 'lawful causes touching him', sufficient perhaps to warrant his presence in person. That is the continuing issue of title to the archdeaconry. The suit pending in the papal palace over it was noted in a petition granted on 1 February 1361 confirming to Doune the prebend of Empingham in Lincoln cathedral, nothwithstanding his church of Swalcliffe, portion of St Endellion, and archdeaconry.[64]

William Doune died by June 1361 at Barbentane,[65] a hill town south of Avignon where he had no doubt retreated to escape or recuperate from the plague then raging. It is a reasonable assumption a priori that he maintained contact with the administration at Lincoln in the interval between his departure and his death. There is, in fact, specific cause to consider that he might have done so. On 15 January 1361, by which time Doune must have been gone for some months, an episcopal mandate was issued to the commissary or *locum tenens* of the official principal or of the president of the consistory dealing extensively with

[60] See below, p. 209.   [61] See below, pp. 205–7.

[62] 'ex causis legitimis ipsum tangentibus necessario prosequendis se habet a nostra diocesi per tempus aliquod absentare'. LAO, Reg. VIII, fo. 146ᵛ.

[63] Cf. Walsh, *Scholar and Primate*, 448 for a similar speculation.

[64] *CPP*, i. 366–7.   [65] Ibid. 370, 381.

matrimonial jurisdiction. It related complaints that matrimonial cases and cases of divorce, which ought to be dealt with in the consistory, were in times past (*ante hec tempora*) committed to rural deans 'and other men not having knowledge of the sacred canons', with the result that, among other scandals, 'there were rather frequently separated without due process those lawfully joined' and the jurisdiction of the consistory was diminished. The bishop now forbade under penalty of excommunication delegating 'a matrimonial case or case of divorce or any other ecclesiastical case' to any person outside the place of the consistory, without previously consulting the bishop. He directed that all spiritual cases pertaining to the consistory be heard within it.[66] The measure was probably part of a general programme to reform the consistory. A mandate of 8 April 1361 required that advocates of the court must henceforth, as of old, wear long togas or tabards.[67] The intention was evidently to demarcate the personnel clearly. The real purpose is evident from a mandate of 17 April to the president of the consistory —in the absence of the official principal—insisting on strict enforcement of the statute that only advocates should be given audience, to the exclusion of proctors, who it was complained had been encroaching on the advocates' function, particularly since the last pestilence.[68] As so often, it is impossible to distinguish here between concerns that were particularly urgent for an individual administrator, that may have been shared within the administration as a whole, or that may have emanated spontaneously from the bishop. As regards the other members of the administration, John de Belvoir, one of the two *locum tenentes* of the official and Doune's own official in the archdeaconry of Leicester, is revealed in his will as enduringly loyal to Doune's memory and was himself putatively a tenacious reformer of official abuse.[69] However, when all reservations have been entered, curial reform is a subject with which Doune may plausibly be linked. He had had a model of it in general in Grandisson's reforms at Exeter, long before.[70] Particular sensitivity to jurisdiction over marital litigation is a feature of the *Memoriale Presbiterorum*. As already noted, Doune had been appointed specifically to investigate the issue in 1359. While this last evidence is ambivalent and might well argue for Gynwell's personal interest, the inference is possible from the reforms of 1361 that Doune, now no doubt at the curia and perhaps conscious that his return would be delayed, was

---

[66] LAO, Reg. VIII, fo. 132[r]. [67] Ibid., fo. 155[r]. [68] Ibid., fo. 156[r].
[69] See below, pp. 210–15. [70] See above, pp. 53–4.

anxious to order the matter for the future and to ensure the perman-
ence of a reform over whose genesis he had presided.

Doune's Career in Worcester Diocese

Even less than at Lincoln can William Doune's career at Worcester be
documented continuously. The fact must be thought attributable at least
in part to the imperfect survival of Bishop Brian's acts. It is certain
that these were once recorded more fully, in either a temporary or permanent form, as drawn on, probably *c.*1389–96, by the compiler of the
formulary erroneously known as 'Register Brian 2'. The latter contains
a series of documents that can be definitely assigned to Brian's episcopate, and others that may with plausibility be thought to date from
it, but that are not now extant in the register proper.[71]

As has been noted already, Doune's association with Reginald Brian
preceded the latter's translation from St Davids to Worcester. The translation is dated 22 October 1352 and the temporalities were restored on
31 March 1353.[72] Brian too was an Oxford civilian, who had proceeded
to the licentiate by May 1349.[73] Of particular relevance, however, to
Doune's recruitment by him are likely to have been their common links
with Exeter. Reginald Brian's father was Sir Guy de Brian, of Walwyns
Castle, Pembs., and Torbryan, Devon.[74] If Doune was indeed of Down
Thomas, the Brian family were near neighbours. Doune was one of
several natives of Exeter to be seen at various levels in Brian's administration at Worcester. At the first reference to him in that context, on
4 November 1353, where he witnesses the bishop's decree consequent
on a letter of the papal penitentiary in favour of a brother of the hospital of St John the Baptist, Wells, he is listed along with Sir Robert
Modicombe and Sir Richard Crede.[75] Crede is identified elsewhere as
a priest of Exeter diocese.[76] Although there is no further information
on Modicombe, his may be a Devon toponymic.[77] Another, certainly
identifiable, Exeter figure at Worcester was Roger Otery. He is the Roger
Boghemore of Ottery St Mary, clerk of Exeter diocese and papal notary

---

[71] See R. M. Haines, 'The Compilation of a late Fourteenth-Century Precedent Book—Register Brian 2', *SCH* II (1975), 173–85.

[72] *HBC* 279.   [73] *BRUO*, i. 290.

[74] See Highfield, 'The English Hierarchy', 121.

[75] Brian's Register, 9.   [76] Ibid., 18.

[77] 'cumb', though frequent also in Dorset and Somerset, is, except for 'tun', 'the commonest of all elements found in Devon': *Place-Names Devon*, ii. 676.

public, who witnessed an act on 5 March 1354.[78] In 1360 he is found
serving as Brian's sequestrator.[79] Much later, in 1366, when he had
passed into the service of Lewis Charlton, bishop of Hereford, he was
to return the well-known justification of himself as 'industrious in
temporal and spiritual matters, and above all concerning the correction
and reformation of the morals of bishops' subjects in accordance with
the custom of the English and Welsh church as experience teaches and
has taught these many years'.[80] The statement was made in the context of a defence of pluralism. Interest in it has chiefly focused on the
spirited terms in which the apologia for pluralism was conceived. The
self-regard of the professional administrator and lawyer is hardly less
noteworthy, and the evidence of the present study is in favour of its
being taken seriously. Had 'reformation of morals' through the established disciplinary framework required similarly spirited defence, there
need be little doubt that it might equally have been mounted.

On 10 February 1354 Brian appointed Doune his official.[81] From
this juncture, therefore, he was simultaneously official at Lincoln and
at Worcester. In thus combining the officiality of two dioceses, one of
them the largest territorially of the English church, and in his tenure
besides of the archdeaconry of Leicester, he must be counted one of
the most important ecclesiastics of his time below the level of bishop,
and certainly one of the most powerful of fourteenth-century ecclesiastical administrators.

Among the earliest pieces of business that Doune had to handle at
Worcester was the case against the cathedral sacrist John de Powick,
whose removal from office was being sought by the prior. The sacrist's
appointment by the bishop, in accordance with his long-standing
claim to this right,[82] was contentious in itself, but John de Powick,
a Worcester monk, was specifically accused of incontinence and

---

[78] Brian's Register, 17–18. The identification is certain since it was by the surname
'Boghemore' that Grandisson, on 9 October 1361, collated to him the eighth prebend in Ottery
St Mary, vacant by the death of its holder from 1338: *RG*, iii. 1463, 1320. (Emden's date of
14 July 1364 is erroneous. *BRUO*, ii. 1409.) For his tenure of the prebend, see Thompson,
English Clergy, 246–7, id., 'Notes on the Ecclesiastical History of the Parish of Henbury',
Transactions of the Bristol and Gloucestershire Archaeological Society, 37 (1914), 127, and
id., 'Will', 255–6, though Thompson wrongly says that Grandisson's register is silent as regards
the collation of it to him.
[79] Brian's Register, 200–1.   [80] See Thompson, *English Clergy*, 246.
[81] Brian's Register, 16.
[82] See R. Graham, 'The Metropolitical Visitation of the Diocese of Worcester by
Archbishop Winchelsey in 1301', *TRHS*, 4th ser., 2 (1919), 72–5.

malversion.[83] On 29 February 1354 Masters Richard de Cleangre, professor of sacred theology, and William de Doune, professor of civil law, the bishop's official, were present at a representation on the part of the prior of Worcester against him.[84] The case, which continued during this year, was heard at least in part before Doune, as is established by an inhibition of the Court of Canterbury directed to him on behalf of the prior on 20 July 1354,[85] and from an undated instrument of appeal to the apostolic see and for tuition of the Court of Canterbury against his proceedings.[86] In an evident attempt to take advantage of a possible confusion stemming from Doune's dual administrative personality, it was alleged by Nicholas Chastel, proctor of the prior, that he had executed certain of the acts as official of Lincoln.[87]

Doune is specifically noted as having been present[88] at the episcopal manor of Hartlebury, on 26 March 1354, when the bishop granted a licence to Robert de Utilicote, rector of Kinwarton, Warwicks, for a year's leave of absence while in the service of the duke of Lancaster.[89] It is not possible to say, though, whether Doune had a particular concern with the licence or whether his mention is purely incidental.

Doune presided at further judicial business in 1354. On 4 June he sat as commissary in the consistory over the purgation of John de Waddesworth, clerk, accused of rape.[90] The case was long drawn out. Doune sat also on 5 June[91] and on 24 July.[92] The remainder of the proceedings as preserved (eight hearings between 22 September and 18 February 1355) were before the prior of Worcester and Richard de Medmenham who, on 21 September 1354, were commissioned by the bishop to hear it.[93]

For almost three years after there is no reference to Doune's activity in Brian's service until, on 20 April 1357, he was constituted with Adam de Houton and Richard de Medmenham bishop's proctor for the convocation to be held in St Bride's, London, on 26 April.[94] There ensues a further silence of over a year before there is definite evidence

---

[83] *LAW*, fo. 239[r]. The circumstances and charges are contained in an instrument of Nicholas Castel, the prior's proctor, part of a quire (fos. 236[r]–245[v]) relating to the case. Cf. Joan Greatrex, *Biographical Register of the English Cathedral Priories of the Province of Canterbury c.1066 to 1540* (Oxford, 1997), 864.

[84] *LAW*, fo. 236[r].   [85] Ibid., fos. 239[v]–240[r].

[86] Ibid., fo. 245[r-v]. The instrument has to be read in context of the entries at ibid., fos. 239[v]–240[r], and in particular with the inhibition of the Court of Canterbury directed to Doune on 20 July 1354.

[87] Ibid., fo. 245[r-v].   [88] 'presentibus Magistro Willelmo de Donne et aliis'.

[89] Brian's Register, 126.   [90] 'Register Brian 2', 115.   [91] Ibid. 120.

[92] Ibid. 121.   [93] Ibid. 122.   [94] Brian's Register, 155.

of his presence in the diocese. On 21 September 1358, designated as official, he was present in Gloucester abbey with the chancellor of the diocese, Richard de Medmenham, William de Rothewell, notary public, and two evidently minor members of the bishop's household, Thomas Mount and John de Wych, described as donsels, when the bishop made an ordinance regarding the annual levying of Peter's Pence in the parish of Henbury, Worcs.[95] Just over a week later, on 29 September, described as doctor of laws and archdeacon of Leicester, he was commissioned with Masters Richard Cleangre, Adam de Houton, LL D, William Wroth, LL D, Giles de Staneford, canon of Hereford, Nicholas de Iford, canon of Wells, the abbots of Tewkesbury and Alcester, and the prior of Stanley, to visit Worcester cathedral and priory.[96]

In 1359 there are two references to Doune. On 22 January 1359, designated as official, with Richard de Medmenham, chancellor, and William de Rothwell, notary public, he witnessed the assignment of a penance to Alice de Zeldyngtre for adultery with Sir William Corbet, knight.[97] On 12 December he made a return as official of Worcester —but executed by him at Northampton—over an exchange between Bernard Rycherii, canon of Westbury on Trim and prebendary of the prebend of 'Holleye' alias of St Werburgh in the same, and William de Navesby, holder of a perpetual chaplaincy or chantry in the church of Louth, Lincs.[98]

On 27 January 1360, in the last reference to him in Worcester sources, Doune was constituted with Adam de Houton as Brian's proctor for the forthcoming council at London, held at St Paul's, 3–9 February.[99] On the same day the bishop made an interesting ordinance between the rector of St Andrew's, Droitwich, and his parishioners. Doune is not mentioned in connection with the ordinance, but it seems likely that he was an influence upon it. Among the responsibilities that the bishop defined was that the parishioners should attend personally at the parish church 'at least' on Sundays and feast days, 'as all catholic Christians are by precept obliged and ought to do', should devoutly pray there, 'duly venerating it', should there 'take care especially on those days, to hear and with due humility attend to masses and other divine offices and the monitions of salvation, zealously to pay their devotions and prayers to the Lord Jesus Christ our Saviour and with marked diligence to render parish rights, to the complete abandonment and utter

[95] Ibid. 5.   [96] Ibid. 173.   [97] Ibid. 5.
[98] Ibid. 61.   [99] Ibid. 198. For the dates of the council, see *HBC* 596.

exclusion of all intricate demurrals and shady or fictitious excuses'. The obligation was enforced by sentence of major excommunication.[100]

Under cover of the requirement that mass be heard on Sundays and feast days, this regulation specified that it be heard in the parish church. In context of the topography of Droitwich it is reasonably interpreted as aimed at diverting the parishioners of St Andrew's from the neighbouring priory of Austin friars.[101] As a measure jealously protective of the parish church, its pedigree could be readily traced to the policy of Bishop Grandisson. However, more specific prompting may be suggested. This provision of the ordinance resembles in general tone, and perhaps in some of its wording, the measure enacted a few months before in faraway Avignon and recorded, as already noted, in Gynwell's register.[102] At Avignon, the vicars-general and official of Innocent VI in the bishopric—at the time reserved to and governed by the pope—had republished a statute requiring, under penalty of excommunication, that parishioners of the churches of the city and diocese 'in the absence of lawful excuse . . . attend in person at their parish churches at least on all Sundays at the main mass, to hear the word of God, salutary monitions and divine offices, and to receive the sacraments, with effect that from every household one person at least shall remain and hear completely the whole mass'.[103] The proceeding had been carefully recorded by the party of Archbishop FitzRalph, eager to see in this a concession by the pope to their case against the friars. The Droitwich measure is in one respect more rigorous than that enacted at Avignon. Its obligation is not satisfied by the attendance of one member of every household but binds all individuals. In one respect its formulation is weaker. The qualification 'in the absence of lawful excuse' of the Avignonese text is in the Droitwich case 'in so far as they can conveniently': but this would not evidently facilitate alternative attendance

---

[100] 'Item volumus et ordinamus et sub excommunicacionis maioris sentencie pena iniungimus et mandamus quod omnes et singuli ipsius ecclesie parochiani eidem in qua etiam ex precepto tenentur et debent utpote universi catholici Christiani diebus dominicis et festivis personaliter interesse ipsam ecclesiam quantum comode possunt saltem huiusmodi diebus dominicis et festivis adeant ibidemque devotis oracionibus insistant eandem debite venerantes et in eadem presertim diebus huiusmodi missarum solempnia aliaque divina officia et monita salutis audire ac cum humilitate debita ascultare devocionesque et oraciones domino Ihesu Christo salvatori nostro impendere studiose et iura parochialia curant diligencius exhibere quibuscumque exquisitis coloribus et confucatis seu fabricatis occasionibus omnino postpositis et penitus pretermissis.' Brian's Register, 198–9. The ordinance was sufficiently noteworthy to be copied in 'Reg. Brian 2', 81–4. Cf. Haines, 'The Compilation', 185.

[101] See J. Willis-Bund (ed.), *VCH Worcestershire* (London, 1913), iii. 87.

[102] Cf. above, p. 199.   [103] See Haren, 'Bishop Gynwell', 286, 290.

at the Austin priory, and the forthright disparagement of feigning amply compensates for the attenuation of wording. With allowance made for variation, the coincidences of timing and of Doune's officiality strongly suggest that he had taken the opportunity to apply at Droitwich a measure of parish discipline that had shortly before been received by him at Lincoln as capable of claiming the personal support of the pope himself. Another provision of the Droitwich ordinance, insisting that oblations were not to be limited to one penny, may have been intended to counteract a by-law of the borough—the kind of restrictive convention which the *Memoriale Presbiterorum* decried among villeins.[104] This too would be a tempting point on which to discern Doune's influence, though the provision is not so idiosyncratic as to warrant that deduction.

Although there is no specific arrangement extant in Brian's register covering Doune's absence at Avignon, a letter to the archdeacon of Worcester dated 22 March, and evidently by context of the year 1361, communicating a demand of the papal nuncio Hugh Pelegrini for payment of his procurations, was written by Richard de Medmenham as *locum tenens* of the official.[105] The arrangement is consonant with the evidence of Doune's will, of which Medmenham was both executor and a beneficiary, for a close relationship between the two.

Doune's Relationship With his Colleagues and the Continuity of a Programme

Several of Doune's colleagues as episcopal administrators were beneficiaries of his will. The fact that William of Nassington predeceased him removes an occasion of testing the closeness of their relationship. Of his surviving colleagues at Exeter, Mr Benedict de Paston received forty shillings, in a clause that immediately preceded a bequest to Doune's kinsman, Ralph Halford, who had succeeded Paston as portioner of St Probus.[106] Of those at Worcester, Roger Otery was not a beneficiary, at least as the will is extant, though he is named as having lent a book to the testator.[107] Mr Richard de Cleangre, mentioned twice in association with him at Worcester, was bequeathed a 'silk belt decorated with silver on which birds are sculpted over the whole'.[108]

---

[104] See above, p. 147. For the suggestion that the borough had a by-law on the subject see *VCH Worcestershire*, iii. 87.

[105] *LAW*, fo. 223ᵛ.   [106] Thompson, 'Will', 275, 246–7.

[107] Ibid. 275.   [108] Ibid. 274.

Cleangre had been a fellow of Merton, a college with which Doune also seems to have been connected.[109] This, more than the Worcester context, may have been the basis of their friendship. Richard de Medmenham too was a Mertonian as well as putatively a close colleague of Doune at Worcester.[110] Doune bequeathed him 'use or usufruct at least in the manner that follows [sc. with reversion to the abbot of Osney after Medmenham ceased to have personal need] of my book of Joannes Andreae in the Novels upon the old decretals', and of a thick book relating to practice in the Roman curia,[111] also

a large quire, rather a book, which I used to carry with me, written in part on parchment and in part on paper, in which I signalled and referred to gobbets organized more or less alphabetically, where will be found sayings of Innocent [IV] and of the Archdeacon in the *Rosarium* and matters written in the said thick book [sc. of curial praxis], and I often refer to my own repetitions and my *lectura* written on paper, which I also leave to him and also usufruct of a certain book containing the text of the *Liber Sextus*. Item, the text of the *Clementines* written in my own hand and the provincial and legatine constitutions and the statutes of the court of the Arches and copies of bulls, judicial and of grace, of inhibitions, of articles, and many other things useful for the practitioner.

Medmenham was left, too, 'my second-best belt, decorated, and one of my table-cloths, namely third-best, with matching napkin, one of my mazers, namely a second-best, at his choice after Master John de Belvoir has exercised his, and ten pounds sterling beyond reasonable expenses which he shall incur in the completion of the present testament'. Medmenham had custody of some of Doune's goods—presumably at Worcester—because the will stipulated that the bequests were made 'under the condition that he shall have faithfully kept my goods deposited with him and shall have made answer concerning them and shall have restored them, saving and excepting accidents of fire, theft, and robbery'.[112]

Mr John de Belvoir, Doune's official in the archdeaconry of Leicester and his second executor, was left the

use or at least the usufruct as follows [sc. with reversion again to Osney] of my book of Hostiensis in the *Summa* and of my Mandegout which I have well

---

[109] For Cleangre's fellowship at Merton, in 1331 and still in 1346, see *BRUO*, i. 430–1. The basis for supposing Doune to have been a Mertonian is his bequest to the college. Thompson, 'Will', 271.

[110] For the extensive evidence of Medmenham's Mertonian status 1339–40/1353 see *BRUO*, ii. 1255.

[111] See above, p. 36, n. 166.　　　　[112] Thompson, 'Will', 282–3.

corrected and in which I have written many useful things, and a certain book of
sermons which I had by his gift and a certain knife with ivory handle which I had
by his gift and my best belt of black silk, decorated with gilded silver and hooped
in the middle and enamelled as it hangs, and my crystal goblet and my second-
best tablecloth with matching napkin, and ten marks sterling beyond all reasonable expenses which he shall incur in the completion of the present testament and
the administration of my goods.[113]

Only in the case of John de Belvoir can one go beyond the bare evidence of the record of association and the content of Doune's will to
reconstruct the quality of the relationship between them. In his own
will de Belvoir reveals his continuing loyalty to the memory of his
former principal, whom he had eventually succeeded in the officiality
of Lincoln. In his provision for obits he links Doune's name with his
own and with those of his relations and wards and of all others to whom
he is obliged 'by bond of equity' in an arrangement for two chaplains
to celebrate for seven years, and the conjunction is repeated with slight
variation in a provision for daily celebration over five years in the
priory of Belvoir.[114] A book of decrees bound, without boards, in leather,
that had belonged to Doune, was to be sold and the price distributed
for his soul,[115] and de Belvoir further left the large sum of 100 marks
to be distributed for Doune's soul specifically in his old archdeaconry.
As regards these distributions, he directed that the friars were not to
benefit.[116] Since he himself evinces no antipathy on this score, his reserve
here may be taken as deference to Doune's personal engagement, perhaps well known among contemporaries but uniquely certified by this
careful provision which complements what might be deduced from
Gynwell's register and is in keeping with the views of the *Memoriale
Presbiterorum*.[117] The fact that Doune makes bequests to the friars[118]
does not tell against the inference from de Belvoir's will. The largest
bequest, ten marks 'for the clothing of old, weak, and abject friars', is
made with a suggestive rider—'provided they be honest and devout'.[119]
Eirenicism, in so far as it is present, may be thought a proper testamentary sentiment. Cardinal Hugh of Evesham's dispositions included
ten marks for the Oxford Franciscans whom he had opposed in their
1269 poverty debate with the Dominicans.[120] Grandisson himself made

---

[113] Ibid.   [114] See Haren, 'Will', 135, 139, 141.   [115] See ibid. 135, 145.
[116] See ibid. 135, 146.   [117] Cf. above, pp. 198–200, and Chapter 12.
[118] See Thompson, 'Will', 267–8, 276; cf. Haren, 'Will', 136.
[119] Thompson, 'Will', 276.
[120] See R. Brentano, *Two Churches* (Princeton, 1968), 53–4, and references there.

bequests to Franciscans, Dominicans, and Carmelites—though only five marks to the Exeter Franciscans, as compared to 100 shillings to the Dominicans of that city (who were also to have the bishop's copy of the writings of Thomas Aquinas). He left forty shillings to the Franciscans of Bodmin.[121]

Hardly less significant of de Belvoir's regard for Doune, or of the latter's influence on him, would seem the provision which he made for a public proclamation in each deanery of the archdeaconry of Leicester, 'that if anyone can prove in good faith that I received anything from him unjustly it shall be restored to him'.[122] This may in context be plausibly thought an imitation of the more elaborate provision in Doune's will for a similar proclamation.[123] The specification of the archdeaconry suggests that his concern was with archidiaconal procurations, for which as Doune's official—and perhaps as official after Doune's death—he would have had responsibility.

To this dimension of John de Belvoir's will may be added the evidence from the register of Bishop Buckingham of an urgent preoccupation with the right conduct of archidiaconal office in the very matter of procurations and other exactions. John de Belvoir served Buckingham as bishop's official from 1369 until 1391, actively at least until October 1389.[124] The preoccupation with archidiaconal exactions is revealed by a series of measures, beginning with a vigorous attack, dated 22 September 1377, on the archdeacon of Stowe. In a mandate to his sequestrator in the archdeaconries of Lincoln and Stowe, the bishop complained that the archdeacon of Stowe was extorting unaccustomed and excessive procurations annually, 'without support of any privilege in this respect, even though he has not personally discharged the office of visitation'.[125] Despite the mention of 'unaccustomed' levies, the reference to absence of privilege shows that the objection was to any levy at all where there had not been personal visitation. The concerns evinced in the mandate were in fact complex and interwoven: objection to procurations and complaint that by defect of visitation discipline was

---

[121] *RG*, ii. 1553, 1555.   [122] Haren, 'Will', 136–7, 145.
[123] Thompson, 'Will', 280.   [124] See Haren, 'Will', 125–6.
[125] 'assidua tamen et frequenti querela ac rei notorietate cui populus testis adest tutus nostris auribus est delatum quod archidiaconus Stowe . . . nullo privilegio in ea parte fulsitus procuraciones insolitas et excessivas ab ecclesiarum rectoribus ceterisque personis ecclesiasticis extorquet et exigit annuatim eciam visitacionis officio per eum personaliter non impenso eorum ecclesiis seu beneficiis in forma iuris minime visitatis'. LAO, Reg. XII, fo. 156ʳ.

impaired.[126] The policy would seem to have been not only to restrain unaccustomed levies but to compel the discharge of duty by denying procurations otherwise. The mandate declared that anyone receiving procurations by reason of visitation where the visitation had not been discharged was suspended from office and benefice until he made double satisfaction in full, 'no remission by liberality or grace on the part of those who made the payment being of any avail'.[127]

If both the legal principle of double restitution and the insufficiency of any remission will be recognized as dear to the author of the *Memoriale Presbiterorum*, the next target of Buckingham's mandate is also familiar in those terms. The archdeacon, it is complained,

abusively piling error on error, scurries through multiple churches of his archdeaconry, encompassing four or five or more on a single day, at his pleasure, and, in respect of each church . . . heedless of the order of law, exacts and extorts individual procurations for one day's livelihood, although each church thus visited in whirlwind would of itself suffice for payment in full of the due procuration, . . . whence he seems rather to gape for monetary gain than to will to conserve the state of churches or to seek the gain of souls; rectors and vicars and other ecclesiastical persons objecting to him in this matter he improperly compels and binds by ecclesiastical censures to payment of the unwarranted procuration, whence his archidiaconal office, which was of old salubriously ordained to healing, tends to poisonous effect in these days, as desire and greed grow apace.[128]

---

[126] 'sic quod in defectu ipsius visitacionis annue non impense grave periculum im[m]inet animarum, status ecclesiasticus in dicto archidiaconatu non modicum denigratur dum, ipsius necligencia et cupiditate irrefrenata exigentibus, lupus rapax querens quem devoret gregem invadit dominicum et eundem dilaniat et dispergit . . . necnon excessus clericorum et laicorum, conniventibus ipsius archidiaconi oculis, eciam graves, quod dolendum est, transiunt impuniti, dum referenda per eundem suo episcopo et prelato non refert seu detegit ut tenetur set referenda . . . tacet et abscondit, tot et tantos excessus hor[r]ibiles, nunc precibus nunc muneribus, Dei timore postposito, palliando, unde dum ipse contra dictorum subditorum crimina et excessus notorios in emendacione eorundem se non opponens videtur eosdem tacite approbare (scribitur enim, *error cui non resistitur approbatur et sic animarum fit interitus plurimorum*): absurdum namque est simul et miserum et dissonum racioni ut qui non seminavit colligat quod non seminavit, cum ergo procuracio debetur racione visitacionis, visitacione cessante quicquid racione eiusdem quocumque colore quesito recipitur male et contra bonam fidem est exactum et indebite persolutum'. Ibid.

[127] 'nulla sibi dancium remissione liberalitate seu gracia valitura'. Ibid.

[128] 'predictusque archidiaconus hiis erratis non contentus set abusive errores erroribus cumulando, plures ecclesias sui archidiaconatus, quatuor vel quinque seu plures unico die prout sibi placuerit circu[m]eundo, discurrit et pro singulis ecclesiis sic per eum unico die decursis, iuris ordine non servato, singulas procuraciones pro victu unius diei exigit et extorquet, licet qu[e]libet ecclesia sic vento visitata per se sufficiat ad debitam procuracionem integre persolvendam, paternas tradiciones et legum doctrinam non servando, unde videtur magis lucris pecuniariis inhiare quam ecclesiarum statum velle conservare seu lucrum querere

The bishop went on to direct that the archdeacon be given solemn threefold warning under penalty of excommunication from receiving a procuration that perverted the name,[129] where the canonical form had not been observed. Any sentences that might be passed by reason of non-payment of an illicit procuration were decreed null. The bishop's mandate was to be published in the next synod held within the archdeaconry, in the presence of 'clergy and people, even if need be in the vernacular', and, as a final precaution, all rectors, vicars, and other ecclesiastics were strictly forbidden to make any unwarranted payment, 'on pretext of donation, liberality, [or] subsidy, or under cover of other contrivance of whatever kind', or to exceed the canonical limit in making payment even when the office of visitation had been discharged.[130]

In itself, this mandate constitutes the most ferocious condemnation of archidiaconal abuse and the most determined attack upon it noted in any fourteenth-century episcopal register—even Grandisson's. It turned out only to be the opening shot of a campaign. On 26 July 1381 Mr John Neuport, canon of Lincoln, was authorized to proceed against

animarum, rectores et vicarios ceterasque personas ecclesiasticas eidem in premissis obviantes ad solucionem procuracionis indebite per censuras ecclesiasticas compellit indebite et astringit, unde ipsius officium archidiaconale quod olim ad medelam extitit salubriter ordinatum, desidia et cupiditate succres[c]entibus, tendit ad noxia hiis diebus.' Ibid.

[129] 'nomen eiusdem procuracionis fugata veritate in legis fraudem pervertendo'. Ibid., fo. 156ᵛ.

[130] 'et si forsan dictus archidiaconus, forma premissa non servata, occasione non solucionis procuracionis indebite fronte impetuosa sentenciam interdicti in locis seu excommunicacionis sentenciam in personis sibi in solucione huiusmodi resistentibus presumpserit fulminare ipsas declaramus prout iura declarant et decernimus fore nullas ac omnibus viribus evacuatas et subditos dicti archidiaconatus casu quo idem archidiaconus huiusmodi sentencias presumpserit fulminare eisdem parere nullatenus obligari, et licet iuris ignorancia, paucis exceptis personis, neminem debeat excusare, volumus tamen ex habundanti, ne locus alicui pateat ignorancie, quatinus presens nostrum mandatum in proxima sinodo in prefato archidiaconatu celebranda, clero et populo congregatis, eciam, si oporteat, in vulgari publicetis seu faciatis de sensu in sensum publicari, execucione vero pene canonis contra eundem archidiaconum, si et quatenus eam inciderit racione huiusmodi forme per eum non servate per nos facienda pro tempore oportuno nobis specialiter reservata. Insuper ut omnis ambicionis improbitas et illicite exaccionis via solerciis precludantur, omnibus et singulis ecclesiarum rectoribus, vicariis ac personis ecclesiasticis quibuscumque qui dicto archidiacono procuraciones in pecunia numerata seu alias solvere de iure vel consuetudine sunt astricti inhibemus ne ipsi aut eorum aliquis eidem archidiacono exquisitis fraudibus contra dictarum constitucionum instituta et nostre inhibicionis formam antedictam pretextu donacionis, liberalitatis, subsidii seu sub alterius machinacionis cuiuscumque velamine quicquam racione visitacionis persolvant aut offerant persolvendum set secundum constituciones memoratas ac presertim Extravagantem B[enedictinam] que incipit *Vas eleccionis* dicto archidiacono, eis officium visitacionis debite impendenti, procuraciones huiusmodi exhibeant secundum taxacionem et limitacionem in dicta constitucione Benedictina contentam et non ultra.' Ibid.

abuses by the archdeacons of the diocese, especially those of Lincoln and Stowe, in terms virtually identical to those of the 1377 mandate—except for a circumspect exclusion of cardinals of the Roman church from the effect of the censures contained.[131] The archdeaconry of Leicester was at this time held by Poncellus de Orsini, cardinal priest of S. Clemente.[132] On 30 September following Neuport was given a new mandate, this time to issue a monition against the levying of excessive charges on presentees to churches by the archdeacons of Lincoln and Stowe for inquiries into the vacancy, and also against their letting the deaneries of their archdeaconries to farm.[133] On 24 October following Mr Stephen de Saresham, the bishop's sequestrator in the archdeaconry of Leicester, was ordered to inhibit and denounce the official of that archdeacon, who had failed to appear to show his authority for exercising the office of visitation but who was presuming to visit nonetheless, 'unwarrantedly extorting single procurations . . . for multiple churches *de facto* temerariously visited by him, scurrying about, on the one day'.[134] In the case of the archdeacon of Lincoln at least, Richard de Ravenser, the censures stood until 16 May of the following year, when Buckingham issued a relaxation of them. The relaxation, dated at the Old Temple, London, came at the request of Archbishop Courtenay on the very eve of the 'earthquake council'. Probably Buckingham had been prevailed on to accept that some concession was needed to safeguarding the image of ecclesiastical authority at a time of crisis. Even so, the relaxation was grudgingly couched, being made with the qualification 'in so far as we can by law do so'.[135]

The issue as regards the archdeaconry of Lincoln was revived just over four years later, when Ravenser had been succeeded by Mr Nicholas de Chaddesden. In a mandate of 28 September 1386, again issued to John Neuport, the bishop proceeded on two fronts. One was jurisdictional. Chaddesden, he protested, was claiming that a composition over archidiaconal jurisdiction that the bishop regarded as personal between him and Ravenser, arrived at reluctantly on his part 'at the pleas of

---

[131] Ibid., fos. 245ᵛ–246ᵛ.   [132] See Le Neve, *Fasti*, i. 12.

[133] 'iidem archidiaconi decanatus suorum archidiaconatuum contra constituciones canonicas ad firmam pro certis pecuniarum summis dimittunt'. LAO, Reg. XII, fo. 246ᵛ.

[134] 'subditos nostros dicti archidiaconatus locaque eiusdem de facto visitare presumit et presumpsit contra iuris prohibicionem procuraciones singulas ab eis pro ecclesiis pluribus per eum unico die discurrendo de facto temere visitatis indebite extorquendo et eos molestiis et vexacionibus plurimis pregravando'. Ibid., fo. 230ʳ.

[135] Ibid., fo. 246ᵛ.

the king and queen and other notables of the kingdom', was still valid.[136] The second part of the letter then addressed archidiaconal procurations in terms similar to those of the 1377 mandate, though with some recasting and emendations, the most substantial of which was an addition making explicit that the inhibition applied not only to the archdeacon personally but also to his official and servants.[137] That the bishop remained vigilant over Chaddesden's conduct in the matter of procurations is shown by a letter of 10 November 1389. This was directed against a specific instance of alleged abuse on his part. Although Chaddesden, it notes, has not personally visited the parish church of Bytham, Lincs., and has indeed been absent for a year and more, and although he has and has had no authority for otherwise levying procurations, nevertheless Mr Robert Swerston, who claims to be the archdeacon's official, attempts to extort them from the rector, in a quantity of money beyond the statutory sum, without the archdeacon's personal visitation, and on that pretext has imposed sentences of suspension and interdict. These, at the complaint of the rector and parishioners, the bishop hereby quashes and declares void. Bytham was of episcopal collation, which both gave the bishop particular interest and may have made the rector readier to resist. It is more likely that the ground was chosen for a stand than that the case was isolated.

The bitter contest over archidiaconal procurations is not the only dimension of Buckingham's regime from which parallels might be drawn with the sensitivities of the *Memoriale Presbiterorum*. There are in the register marked signs of vigilance, for instance, as regards the admission of pardoners[138] and the lax and supposedly corrupt constitution of penitentiaries.[139] However, in view of the prominence of this theme both in the treatise and in the outlook, as deduced from their wills, of William Doune and of John de Belvoir, archidiaconal exactions are the obvious point at which to test whether there is a real influence. Caution is necessary. Evidently, the question of abuse in practice had become enmeshed with a jurisdictional conflict that may well have been the principal engine driving the campaign for reform of the conduct of archidiaconal office under Buckingham, or that is at least the probable explanation for some part of its timing. On the other hand, although the most concentrated thrust of the campaign was against the

---

[136] On the terms of the Ravenser composition, see C. Morris, 'The Commissary of the Bishop in the Diocese of Lincoln', *JEH* 10 (1959), 60–1.

[137] LAO, Reg. XII, fo. 332ʳ⁻ᵛ.   [138] Ibid., fos. 297ᵛ (AD 1371), 387ʳ (AD 1391).

[139] Ibid., fo. 336ʳ (AD 1387).

archdeacon of Lincoln—the prime figure in the jurisdictional dispute—
the campaign had begun as an attack on the archdeacon of Stowe and,
in all, only four of the eight archdeacons were selected for specific
mention in its whole course. The genesis and selection suggest that
abuse was a real concern. Whether the campaign should be principally thought of as proceeding from Bishop Buckingham himself or
from the senior members of his administration is, as usual with this
attempted distinction, imponderable. No doubt the jurisdictional issue
would have ensured that the bishop's own attention was thoroughly
engaged. That, in turn, might have allowed the administration to indulge
a preoccupation. To the extent that there might be supposed to have
been a significant administrative contribution to the formulation and
pursuit of policy on this count, John de Belvoir, as official, is the
favourite candidate to whom to attribute it. His views on the point
cannot, however, be thought peculiar to him. By the date of the later
complaint about the behaviour of Nicholas de Chaddesden, John de
Belvoir was probably less active: a coadjutor, Mr John Keele, had been
joined with him in the officiality some weeks before.[140] If one cannot
demonstrate an empathy between official and coadjutor on the issue
of exactions, it is not unreasonable to suppose that the choice of assist-
ant was a broadly congenial one: and Keele was named by de Belvoir
as one of his executors. To endow policy and the administration of
policy with personality (rather than to label it by the mere addition of
names) is for this period a difficult task in all but the most exceptional
circumstances. A large dimension of the present study has been the
combination of evidence that promises to make the task fitfully possible, and the conclusions that derive in consequence. If continuity of
outlook in the matter of archdeacons' exactions has indeed here been
correctly diagnosed under Buckingham, it is part of a remarkable
programme, characterized by a wide-ranging preoccupation with
justice and right order, that spans some fifty years and affects two and
putatively three dioceses.[141] In principle, the programme could without
any prompting be discerned at its inception in the bare documentary
narrative of Grandisson's administration. It is discerned the more
readily both at inception and in its continued dynamism in so far as
the argument for authorship of the *Memoriale Presbiterorum* directs

---

[140] See Haren, 'Will', 125–6.
[141] The character of Brian's register forbids a study of policy at Worcester comparable to
what is possible at Lincoln.

attention first to the character of the regime at Exeter, and then to William Doune's career as a whole. On that argument, the *Memoriale Presbiterorum* adds to its intrinsic interest as a pastoral manual of unusual forcefulness its utility as a lens bringing into sharper focus insights latent in the administrative record.

APPENDIX A SUMMARY ACCOUNT OF
THE MANUSCRIPTS OF THE TREATISE

CORPUS CHRISTI COLLEGE, CAMBRIDGE, MS. 148 (= C)

This, the earliest manuscript, is in a hand characterized as of the first half of the fourteenth century.[1] The press-mark, P viii, in the top right-hand corner of fo. 1[r], may indicate that it was part of the library of Norwich Cathedral Priory.[2] If so, it would probably have been acquired by the library well before 1407, when Cardinal Adam Easton's large gift of books was classified under the letter 'X', and indeed its acquisition would be expected to have preceded or to have been contemporaneous with the cataloguing of the books of Simon Bozoun, prior from 1344 to 1352.[3] Although the late Dr Ker judged it to be one of the manuscripts having weakest claims to being accepted as a Norwich priory book,[4] and although such a location would in the abstract seem unlikely for a manual of the type, two considerations may be pleaded in favour of that interpretation of the press-mark. A note on fo. 1[r], in a fourteenth-century hand—'Pecunia nihil aliud servis Dei est quam coluber et serpens venenosus'—suggests monastic custody at that point. Moreover, the interest of the Norwich monks in such a book could be readily explained by the strictures which it contains against the friars. A bitter quarrel between the Benedictines and the mendicants was raging at Norwich just about the time when the FitzRalph campaign was at its height.[5] The book was one of the 433 manuscripts bequeathed to Corpus Christi College by Archbishop Matthew Parker in 1575,[6] and it is to its classification in his collection that the press-mark, D. 2, on the verso of the first original flyleaf, refers.

The manuscript is at present constituted as follows: binding twentieth century; one modern flyleaf, with a note of rebinding, September 1952; flyleaves i–iv, medieval: i is pasted on a modern backing sheet so that recto is covered but it appears to have been blank; verso has press-mark, D. 2, in left margin, and notes in several hands of the fifteenth century, including a satirical prophecy, beginning

---

[1] See N. R. Ker, *Medieval Libraries of Great Britain*, 2nd edn. (London, 1964), 137. It is described in M. R. James, *A Descriptive Catalogue of the Manuscripts in the Library of Corpus Christi College, Cambridge* (Cambridge, 1912), i. 336–7, where it is dated 'fourteenth century, early'.

[2] See Ker, *Medieval Libraries*, and id., 'Medieval Manuscripts From Norwich Cathedral Priory', *Transactions of the Cambridge Bibliographical Society*, 1 (1949–53), 1–28.

[3] Ker, 'Medieval Manuscripts', 137; cf. H. C. Beeching and M. R. James, 'The Library of the Cathedral Church of Norwich', *Norfolk Archaeology*, 19 (1917), 72. Ker, *Medieval Libraries*, 135–139, 284.

[4] Ker, 'Medieval Manuscripts', where it is no. 77 in the list.

[5] See Pantin, *Church*, 175–7.   [6] See James, *Catalogue*, i., pp. xxxiv, xii.

'Anno cephas mille, canis, catulus et cocadrille', and pieces of biblical exegesis; ii verso–iv verso contain a table of chapters to the *Memoriale Presbiterorum*, in a hand contemporaneous with that of the text, but in darker ink; fos. 1–96, *Memoriale Presbiterorum*, written in double columns, frame ruled, with chapters numbered a. i–lxlix, b. i–lxxxxviii (of which the designation b. vii occurs twice); collation: a–h^{12}, catchwords throughout; fo. 1^r has press-mark, P viii, in top right-hand corner and a large illuminated initial 'C' to chapter 1; at top of fo. 1^r is the note already referred to as suggesting monastic provenance; illuminated capitals throughout, with rubrics for most of the text; at end: flyleaves v–vi, medieval; v recto has a collection of epigrams in alphabetical arrangement, ending under letter 'b', with doodled sketch of human face; verso is blank except for an indecipherable scribble, possibly 'domini . . .', which recurs in a more contracted form on vi recto; vi verso is pasted on a modern backing sheet but appears to have been blank; two flyleaves, modern. Parchment, except for modern flyleaves. 31.5 cm × 21 cm; text: 21.6 cm × 12.7 cm; second folio, 'et tunc propter'.

Of the several hands which have annotated the text, the following are the most important:

Hand A: fourteenth-century; black ink. It supplies mainly internal cross-references, but on two occasions contributes phrases to the text. On fo. 5ra it adds 'quin fiat mortale'. On fo. 28va it adds 'virginem vel non'. On fo. 52vb, it adds 'debes iniungere mundiciam'. In the first instance—for which S is not a witness—the phrase is attested by H. In the second and third instances the phrases are attested by S and H—authoritative witnesses to them, according to the arrangement of the manuscripts in the stemma below. The author of these additions would therefore appear to have had access to the exemplar or to another copy of the text. Notes on fo. 49ra ('Nota quid sit faciendum si peccator dicat se non posse penitenciam facere'), on fo. 52vb ('Nota quod non attenditur ista mora quantum ad diuturnitatem temporis set quantum ad consensum racionis, quia quando racio perpendit cogitacionem esse illicitam et consentit, statim mortaliter peccat'), on fo. 59va ('Nota qui non potest in toto, in parte saltem satisfacere debet. Concor. infra in titulo ubi agitur de forma restitucionis faciende'), on fo. 70va ('Nota de restitucione fame alicuius per diffamatorem faciendi, quibus verbis fiet'), and on fo. 79va ('Nota quid iuris si male adquirens vel dampnum dans non possit restituere ablata propter paupertatem vel absque periculo sustentacionis proprie totum'), are in this same hand. The author of these comments is also interested in the criticisms of mendicant confessors, highlighting occurrences of these by noting 'Contra mendicantes' (fo. 19rb) or 'Contra fratres' (fos. 63vb, 68rb, 79rb, 82ra, 86ra) against them.

Hand B: fourteenth-century; brown ink. It makes two additions to the text, which are present in W but absent in H: on fo. 6ra it adds 'et eciam mitigant', and at fo. 32va, 'exequatur'. It is also responsible for the following marginal gloss on fo. 30rb, *ad vocem* 'benedictus': 'Nota, quidam dicunt quod papa Johannes vicesimus secundus dispensavit cum episcopis quod ipsi possent absolvere sacerdotes qui secundas nupcias benedixerint', a note which was incorporated into the text of W, in the form 'set quidam dicunt [etc.]'. This amplification had some currency in the pastoral genre. For example, in Oxford, Bodleian Library, MS. Bodley, 293 ('Summa Summarum'), against the statement in the text that the priest concerned must be sent for absolution to the apostolic see, is the note: 'Hoc tamen cor[r]igitur quia per constitutionem que incipit "Concertationi", diocesanus loci potest absolvere hodie.'[7] The constitution referred to is found published under the title 'Concertationi antiquae', attributed rather to Benedict XII, in a letter of Archbishop Whittlesey, dated 23 October 1370.[8] The form of reference in the note to C may indicate that it pre-dates Whittlesey's publication.

Hand C: fourteenth-century; black ink. It supplies the following comments: fo. 4vb, 'Nota bene', on the necessity of confessing mortal sins; fo. 16rb, 'Nota bene totum', on a passage concerning clerical confessions; fo. 32vb, partly lost in binding: 'Nota pro presbitero fornicante . . .'; fo. 59^v, at head, 'Nota qui non potest in toto, in parte saltem satisfacere debet. Require ad talem in folio xi^o sequente'; fo. 70^v, at head, 'Nota quibus verbis fiet restitucio fame alicuius per diffamatorem'; fo. 86va: 'Nota bene totum', on a passage concerning clerical avarice; fo. 87rb: 'Hic nota', on the parish priest's responsibility for souls committed to him.

The interest of these commentators was evidently pastoral. If the book has a connection with Norwich Cathedral Priory, rather than being copied specially it was evidently acquired after it had passed through several sets of hands as a working manual.

WESTMINSTER DIOCESAN ARCHIVES, MS. H. 38 (= W)

This is a composite book containing, fos. 1–78^v, a fifteenth-century text, entitled in the incipit, *Memoriale presbiterorum parochialium*, with chapters numbered in two series, a 1–119 and (b) 1–98, and with a table of contents, fos. 78^v–81. The second item in the book is a late-fourteenth/early-fifteenth-century collection of Carthusian provenance. The manuscript was first noticed in N. R. Ker, *Medieval Manuscripts in British Libraries*, I (Oxford, 1969), 419–21, and is there fully described.

BODLEIAN LIBRARY, MS. SELDEN SUPRA 39 (= S)

Parchment, in a late-fourteenth-century hand; provenance, Merton Priory, OSA, Surrey. Binding modern; the spine of a former binding is preserved with the press-mark '39'. One modern flyleaf; flyleaves ii–iii are part of a sixteenth-century lease, in English, to Thomas Alen, from the master and wardens of a company; on ii recto are three press-marks: D. 14; 39; (3427), of which the second is the Selden mark and the last the classification of the *Summary Catalogue*. Fos. 4–68: the penitential canons of the *Memoriale Presbiterorum*, without title or chapter numbering, beginning 'Pro quibus culpis et penitentiis sit penitens ad episcopum proprium

---

[7] Oxford, Bodleian Library, MS. Bodl. 293, fo. 166^v. Cf. John de Burgh, *Pupilla Oculi* (London, 1510), part viii, cap. 18, fo. 112^v.

[8] *Concilia*, iii. 88.

remittendus' (= C, fo. 28ʳ) and continuing to '. . . facienda et observanda' (= C, fo. 53ʳ), but omitting two chapters (= a. xlvi and a. xlvii in C). Collation, a–i⁸, with catchwords throughout. Miniatures on fo. 4ʳ and 68ʳ and illuminated capitals and rubrics throughout. Second folio, 'quo casu talis'. On fo. 68ᵛ, in a late-fifteenth-century hand, is the note: 'Joannes Ramsey canonicus Merton hunc librum possidet. Qui est ex deo verbum Dei audit; Joannes octavo. Pro cuius declaracione notandum quod per verbum possunt duo significari. Joannes Ramsey.' At end: one flyleaf, modern. 21 cm × 15 cm. The manuscript is described in *Summary Catalogue of Western Manuscripts in the Bodleian Library*, ed. F. Madan and H. H. E. Craster, II (Oxford, 1922), no. 3427, and is noticed in Ker, *Medieval Libraries*, 131.

Memoriale Sacerdotum [i.e. 'Presbiterorum'] (fos. 1–104) and other tracts and statutes of a pastoral nature (fos. 105–22).[9] Parchment. Rebound, 1968. Three modern flyleaves; one flyleaf, parchment, with press-marks: 111 A. 5.; 3120. At end, one modern flyleaf. Collation: a¹⁰b⁸c¹⁰d–l⁸m¹²n–o⁸p². Second folio, 'parochianum alienum'.

(1) Fos. 1–2, table of contents to *Memoriale Sacerdotum*, numbering chapters 1–198 (but with errors of numeration so that 196 chapters are actually listed). Fos. 3–104: text of *Memoriale Sacerdotum*, in double columns, with chapters numbering 1–176; in addition to minor deficiencies both of chapter headings and occasionally of their content as against C, the text is continuously defective from the middle of a sentence in chapter b. lxiv (as witnessed by C) to the middle of a sentence in chapter b. lxxvi (as witnessed by C). On fo. 104ᵛ is the following colophon: 'Explicit memoriale sacerdotum compositum a quodam doctore decretorum apud Avenon', Anno domini millesimo CCCᵒ quadragesimo quarto, ad informacionem iura non intelligencium, ita quod, ex frequente iteracione, iura penitencialia, que in canonibus reperiuntur, secundum diversa capitula, aliqualiter sciunt et eciam modum penitencie penitentibus sciunt inponere, secundum quod ordo iuris exigit.' The colophon is written by the scribe of the text, though in a *textura* hand, whereas the text is in a book hand of the early fifteenth century. The ink of the colophon is the same as that used for the text and the colophon has several capitals illuminated in the same blue illuminating ink as that used for initial capitals in the text. 20.4 cm × 14.5 cm; text: 15.1 cm × 10.7 cm.

This is a composite manuscript, containing:

(1) fos. 1–8ᵛ, Clement of Llanthony, *De alis Cherubim et Seraphim*, thirteenth century;

(2) fos. 9–39, *Oculus Sacerdotis, Pars Oculi*, mid-fourteenth century;

⁹ For a full description of the contents, see Haren 'A Study', i. 9–11.

(3) fos. 40ʳ–60ʳ, anonymous *Speculum lucidum*, with incipit, 'Quoniam circa Deum non est sciencia salubrior', late fourteenth or early fifteenth century;

(4) fos. 60ʳ–68ʳ, an extract from Pecham's *Ignorantia Sacerdotum*, followed by a hotchpotch of legislation: of Pecham, fo. 61; papal excommunications, fo. 63; of Pecham, fos. 63ᵛ–64; constitutions of Ottobuono, fos. 64ᵛ–66; constitutions of the Council of Vienne, fos. 66–68;

(5) fos. 68ʳ–69ᵛ, an unacknowledged version of the chapters of the *Memoriale Presbiterorum* on provincial legislation (corresponding approximately to C, fos. 92ᵛ–93ᵛᵃ = chapters b. lxxxxii–lxxxxv), followed, fos. 69ᵛ–70ᵛ, by Archbishop Boniface's statute on tithing (cf. *CS*, ii. 795, c. 2), by a list of the cases where ecclesiastical burial is refused, fos. 70ᵛ–71ᵛ, and, fos. 71ᵛ–73ʳ, by the chapter from the *Memoriale Presbiterorum*, without acknowledgement, on the burial of a pregnant woman (corresponding to C, fos. 95–6, chapter b. lxxxxviii);

(6) fos. 73–89ᵛ, a treatise on the virtues and vices, of which the first chapter is entitled, 'Quod superbia sit peccatum videtur Tobie quarto'.

The miscellany, (4) and (5), is in the same hand as (3).

CLASSIFICATION OF THE MANUSCRIPTS

In general, the best, as it is the earliest, text for the treatise as a whole is that of C. S witnesses to the central part only of the treatise. H, while preserving the major portion, contains many errors and unintelligibilities. There are few crucial readings, but the evidence is sufficient to allow the construction of a stemma.[10] Since U contains only a small part of the text, and that—except for the letter on burial—in an edited form, its positioning in the stemma is tentative. The final outline of the stemma depends on what hypothesis is advanced to explain the fact that only one witness, H, transmits a colophon. Figure 1 makes no assumption that the colophon is at core authorial.

Since S does not even preserve the title of the treatise, of which it constitutes only a middle portion, no significance can be attached to its lacking the colophon.

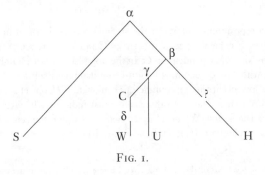

FIG. 1.

[10] The evidence, based on a complete collation, is recorded ibid. 13–21.

In Figure 1, α may represent either the treatise as originally written (without addendum on burial or colophon) or the edited treatise (with addendum on burial and, perhaps, the information of the colophon regarding date and place of 'composition'), argued for in Chapter 3.[11] β represents the agreement of CH against S and represents a point by which the addendum on burial had attached. As the colophon, if at core authorial, would most economically be supposed also to have been present at that point, it would in those terms be taken to have been lost in the transmission of the text to CU, and would have been absent at γ. The loss putatively of a quire or, more likely perhaps, of two quires in transmission of the text to H is the most likely explanation of the large, unsignalled defect in the latter. It is not, strictly, necessary to postulate an intervening exemplar as the loss could have occurred in β after copying of the ancestor of C.

While it cannot be excluded that a particular copy of the treatise, after the attachment of the addendum on burial, received a note of place and date of composition after β, that is not a point on which the surviving manuscripts can assist. To suppose that such an addition was authorial is uneconomical as requiring two editorial interventions. The hypothesis of addition rather than loss would generate a stemma as in Figure 2.

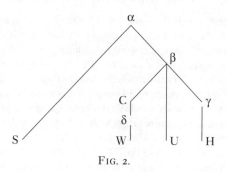

FIG. 2.

W'S POSITIONING IN THE STEMMA

The precise positioning of W on the stemma may be justified in summary.[12] Although there is general agreement between C and W, there are prima facie difficulties in making W dependent on C. In the first place, it has a number of errors in common with H—de dampnato coitu *C*: de dampnatu coitu *WH*; cervisia *C*: servicia *WH* (two occurrences); coniuncti *C*: coniuncte *WH*; ope et auxilio *C*: opere et auxilio *WH* (where there is other, contextual indication in favour of 'ope'). On a few occasions, too, W and H agree against C where the sense is neutral— inhibetur *C*: prohibetur *WH*; favebat *C*: fovebat *WH*; ligandi et solvendi *C*:

---

[11] Cf. below. pp. 37–8.
[12] For precise locations of the readings cited here, with reference to the edited text, see Haren, 'A Study', i. 15–21.

ligandi et absolvendi *WH*. In addition, W and H several times agree to omit, as against *C*: socio *om. WH* (with clearly defective sense); eciam *C*: *om. WHS*; suam *CS*: *om. WH*; quod *CS*: *om. WH*; in hoc *C*: *om. WH*. Discounted is the omission of a whole phrase by WH attributable to homoioteleuton.

In the second place, W has several strong readings not derived from C— perhibendo *WS*: prohibendo *CH*; *add.* sunt *WS*; *add.* pro *WS*; dignum *C* (with defective sense): indignum *WH*; infligunt *C* (with defective sense): infligit *WH*; efficaciter *C* (with defective sense): efficiatur *WH*. Here, if W is to be considered as a descendant of C, one must postulate emendation. (The readings noted are hardly such as require access to another exemplar, and it is otherwise clear that W's scribe, at least, did not have such access.) There is in fact suggestive evidence at a number of junctures that W or a mediator attempted to resolve difficulties.

Several instances of addition in the text of W as against other witnesses, where whole clauses are in question, are of the type that might be explained by the absorption of glosses into the text. As noted above, absorption of marginalia into the text as witnessed by W can in fact be demonstrated, and they constitute crucial evidence for W's descent. The marginal comment of Hand B at C, fo. 30rb, appears in the text of W (fo. 25^{r}) as follows: 'set quidam dicunt quod papa Johannes vicesimus secundus dispensavit [. . .] benedixerint'. The note of Hand A at C, fo. 52^{v}, is reproduced verbatim in the text of W, fo. 43^{r}. Neither passage is attested by the other witnesses, SH. The fact that these annotations in C are in different hands and inks is against the hypothesis that they might have derived from corresponding notes in C's exemplar and have reached W from there, and it is improbable that they are both independent additions to the latter, even though, as observed, the legal amplification contained in the first passage had some currency.

If W is thus made dependent on C, its dependence is indirect. Evidence of mediation is provided by four lacunae in W, with the omission in each case of a single word, where the text of C is whole and affords no problem of legibility (W, fos. 34^{v}, 36^{v}, 38^{v}, 50^{r}).

BIBLIOGRAPHY

MANUSCRIPT SOURCES

Cambridge, Corpus Christi College, MS. 148, 'Memoriale Presbiterorum'.
Cambridge, Gonville and Caius College, MS. 282/675, 'Septuplum'.
Cambridge University Library, MS. Mm. v. 33, ('Memoriale Presbiterorum'), extract.
Devon Record Office, Exeter Diocesan Records, Chanter Catalogue 3, 4, 5 (Register of John Grandisson).
Hereford and Worcester Record Office, b 716.093-BA. 2648/3 (iii) (Register of Reginald Brian); b 716.93-BA. 2648/3 (iv) ('Register Brian 2').
Lincolnshire Record Office, Episcopal Registers VIII–IX (Register of John Gynwell), XII (Register of John Buckingham).
London, British Library, MS. Cotton Cleopatra C. XI, 'Psalter of Bishop Grandisson'.
—— MS. Harley 3120, 'Memoriale Sacerdotum'.
—— MS. Lansdowne 393, 'Richard FitzRalph, Sermons'.
—— MS. Royal 6 E. vi, vii, 'Omne Bonum'.
—— MS. Royal 10 D. x, 'Summa Summarum'.
—— MS. Royal 19 C. ii, 'Somme le Roi'.
Northamptonshire Record Office, Delapré Abbey, Box X643, no. 1.
Oxford, Balliol College, MS. 86, fos. 231^r–246^r, 'Cilium Oculi Sacerdotis'.
Oxford, Bodleian Library, MS. Auct. F. infra 1. 2, 'Richard FitzRalph, Sermons'.
—— MS. Bodley 293, 'Summa Summarum'.
—— MS. Bodley 446, 'Speculum Vitae'.
—— MS. Bodley 490, fos. 118^r–132^r, 'Interrogations'.
—— MS. Bodley 643, 'Memoriale Iuniorum'.
—— MS. Laud Miscellaneous 112, fos. 325^r–338^v, 'Joannes de Deo, Liber Poenitentiarius'.
—— MS. Selden Supra 39, ('Memoriale Presbiterorum', extract).
Oxford, New College, MS. 292, 'Oculus Sacerdotis'.
Vatican City, Archivio Segreto Vaticano, *Registra Avenioniensia*; *Registra Supplicationum*.
Worcester Cathedral Muniments, A. 5, 'Liber Albus'.

PRINTED PRIMARY SOURCES

ALAN DE LILLE (Alanus de Insulis), *Summa de Arte Praedicatoria*, in J. P. Migne, *Patrologia Latina*, ccx (Paris, 1855), cols. 184–98.
—— *Penitenciale*, edited in J. P. Migne, *Patrologia Latina*, ccx (Paris, 1855), cols. 179–304.

ALVARUS PELAGIUS, *De Planctu Ecclesiae* (Lyons, 1517).

Annales Monastici, ed. H. Luard, 5 vols., Rolls Series (1864–9).

ANTONINUS OF FLORENCE, *Summa Summarum* (Lyons, 1542).

ASTESANUS DE ASTI, *Summa Confessorum* (Strasbourg, incunabule edition, sine anno).

Aȝenbite of Inwit, ed. R. Morris, EETS, os, 23 (1886).

BATESON, M., *Borough Customs*, 2 vols., Selden Society, 18, 21 (1904–6).

The Black Book of the Admiralty, ed. T. Twiss, i, Rolls Series (1871).

The Book of Vices and Virtues, ed. W. N. Francis, EETS, os, 217 (1942).

Bracton, De Legibus et Consuetudinibus Angliae, ed. S. E. Thorne and G. E. Woodbine, 4 vols. (Cambridge, Mass. and London, 1968–77).

BURCHARD OF WORMS, *Decretum*, in J. P. Migne, *Patrologia Latina*, cxl (Paris, 1853), cols. 943–1014.

Calendar of Close Rolls (London, 1892–1963).

Calendar of Entries in the Papal Registers relating to Great Britain and Ireland: Petitions to the Pope (1342–1419), ed. W. H. Bliss (London, 1896).

Calendar of Entries in the Papal Registers relating to Great Britain and Ireland: Papal Letters, i, ed. W. H. Bliss (London, 1893); ii, ed. W. H. Bliss (London, 1895); iii, ed. W. H. Bliss and C. Johnson (London, 1897).

Calendar of Inquisitions Post Mortem and Other Analogous Documents preserved in the Public Record Office, iv (London, 1913).

Calendar of Patent Rolls, Edward III (London, 1891–1916).

Chartularium Universitatis Parisiensis, ed. H. Denifle, i (Paris, 1889).

CLAY, T., *York Minster Fasti being Notes on the Dignitaries, Archdeacons and Prebendaries in the Church of York prior to the year 1307*, ii, Yorkshire Archaeological Society, Record Series, 124 (1959).

Clément VI (1342–1352): Lettres closes, patentes et curiales se rapportant à la France, ed. E. Déprez, J. Glenisson, and G. Mollat, 3 vols. (Paris 1910–61).

The Cloud of Unknowing, ed. P. Hodgson, EETS, os, 218 (1944).

Concilia Magnae Britanniae et Hiberniae, ed. D. Wilkins, 4 vols. (London, 1737).

Corpus Juris Canonici, ed. A. Friedberg, 2 vols. (Leipzig, 1879–81).

Corpus Iuris Canonici cum Glossis (Lyons, 1671).

Corpus Juris Civilis, ed. T. Mommsen and P. Krueger, 2 vols. (Berlin, 1899–1928).

Councils and Synods of the English Church in the Thirteenth Century, ed. F. M. Powicke and C. R. Cheney, 2 vols. (Oxford, 1964).

Devon Feet of Fines, ii, ed. O. J. Reichel, F. B. Prideaux, and H. Tapley-Soper (Exeter, 1939).

The Digest of Justinian, Latin text ed. T. Mommsen and P. Krueger and English translation ed. A. Watson, 4 vols. (Philadelphia, 1985).

Documents illustrating the Activities of the General and Provincial Chapters of the English Black Monks, 1215–1540, ed. W. A. Pantin, 3 vols., Camden Society, 45, 47, 54 (1931–7).

Dominorum de Rota Decisiones Novae, Antiquae et Antiquiores (Cologne, apud Iohannem Gymnicum, 1581).

The English Works of John Wyclif, Hitherto Unprinted, ed. F. D. Matthew, EETS, os, 74 (1880).

An Episcopal Court Book for the Diocese of Lincoln 1514–1520, ed. M. Bowker, Lincoln Record Society, 61 (1967).

The Exempla or Illustrative Stories from the Sermones Vulgares of Jacques de Vitry, ed. T. F. Crane, Folklore Society (1890).

GERALD OF WALES, *De Principis Instructione Liber*, in *Giraldi Cambrensis. Opera*, ed. J. F. Dimock, viii, Rolls Series (1891).

GUIDO DE MONTE ROCHERII, *Manipulus Curatorum* (Rouen, apud Jacques le Forestier, sine anno).

GULIELMUS DURANDUS ('Speculator'), *Speculum Juris* (Frankfort, 1592), containing, in a second series of pagination, his *Repertorium Aureum* and *Aureum Confessorium et Memoriale Sacerdotum*.

GUILELMUS LYNDWOOD *see* Lyndwood.

Halmota Prioratus Dunelmensis, 1296–1384, ed. W. H. D. Longstaffe and J. Booth, Surtees Society, 82 (1889).

HAREN, M. J., 'The Will of Master John de Belvoir, Official of Lincoln (d. 1391)', *Mediaeval Studies*, 58 (1996), 119–47.

—— 'The Interrogatories for Officials, Lawyers and Secular Estates of the *Memoriale Presbiterorum*', in P. Biller and A. Minnis (eds.), *Handling Sin: Confession in the Middle Ages*, York Studies in Medieval Theology, 2 (1998).

HENRY DE SUSA (Hostiensis), *Lectura in Quinque Decretalium Libros* (Paris, 1512).

—— *Summa Aurea* (Basle, 1573).

HENRY OF LANCASTER, *Le Livre de Seyntz Medicines*, ed. E. J. Arnould (Oxford, 1940).

HONORIUS AUGUSTODUNENSIS, *Speculum Ecclesiae*, edited in P. Migne, *Patrologia Latina*, 172 (Paris, 1854), cols. 861–70.

Imperatoris Iustiniani Institutiones, ed. J. B. Moyle, 5th edn. (Oxford, 1912).

Inquisitions and Assessments relating to Feudal Aids with Other Analogous Documents Preserved in the Public Record Office AD 1284–1431, i (London, 1899).

JOANNES ANDREAE, Gloss on the *Liber Clementinarum*, ed. Baptista de Tortis (Venice, 1491).

—— Gloss on the *Liber Sextus* and *Liber Clementinarum*, in *Corpus Iuris Canonici cum Glossis*, 3 vols. (Lyons, 1671).

—— *Novella in Sextum* (Venice, 1571).

JOANNES DE DEO, *Liber Poenitentiarius*, partially edited in P. Migne, *Patrologia Latina*, xcix (Paris, 1851), cols. 1085–108.

JOHN ACTON, 'Commentary on the Legatine Constitutions', printed with separate pagination following G. Lyndwood, *Provinciale* (Oxford, 1679).

JOHN BROMYARD, *Summa Predicantium* (Nuremberg, 1485).

JOHN DE BURGH, *Pupilla Oculi* (London, 1510).

John Lydford's Book, ed. D. M. Owen (London, 1974).

JOHN OF FREIBURG, *Summa Confessorum* (Paris, 1519).

The Liber Albus of the Priory of Worcester Parts I and II, ed. J. M. Wilson, Worcestershire Historical Society (1919).

Liber Ecclesiae Wigorniensis: A Letter Book of the Priors of Worcester Preserved in the Public Record Office Among the Miscellaneous Books of the Exchequer, ed. J. Harvey Bloom, Worcestershire Historical Society (1912).

LUNT, W. E. (ed.), *Accounts Rendered by Papal Collectors in England 1317–1378*, ed. E. B. Graves (Philadelphia, 1968).

LYNDWOOD, G., *Provinciale* (Oxford, 1671).

MAITLAND, F. W., *Select Pleas in Manorial and Other Seignorial Courts*, i, Selden Society (London, 1889).

—— *The Court Baron*, Selden Society (London, 1891).

MARCHESINO DI REGGIO D'EMILIA, *Confessionale*, in *Sancti Bonaventurae Opera*, vi (Lyon, 1688), 45–66.

Minor Latin Poets, ed. J. W. and A. M. Duff (London, 1934).

A Myrour to Lewde Men and Wymmen: A Prose Version of the Speculum Vitae edited from B. L. Ms.Harley 45, ed. V. Nelson (Heidelberg, 1981).

The Oak Book of Southampton, ed. P. Studer, Southampton Record Society (1911).

Ordinale Exon., ed. J. Dalton, 2 vols. (London, 1909).

Peter Abelard's Ethics, ed. D. Luscombe (Oxford, 1971).

PETER CANTOR, *Summa de Sacramentis et Animae Consiliis*, ed. J.-A. Dugauquier, 3 vols., Analecta Mediaevalia Namurcensia (Louvain/Lille, 1954–67).

—— *Verbum Abbreviatum*, in P. Migne, *Patrologia Latina*, 205 (Paris, 1855), cols. 21–554.

POORTER, A. DE, 'Le Traité Eruditio Regum et Principum de Guibert de Tournai OFM (Etude et Texte Inédit)', in *Les Philosophes Belges*, ed. M. de Wulf, ix (Louvain, 1914), 1–92.

RAYMUND DE PEÑAFORT, *Summa de Casibus Conscientiae* (Rome, 1603).

The Register of John of Gaunt, ed. S. A. Smyth, 2 vols., Camden Society, 3rd Series, 56–7 (1937).

The Register of John de Grandisson, Bishop of Exeter (AD 1327–1369), ed. F. C. Hingeston-Randolph, 3 vols. (London/Exeter, 1894–9).

The Register of Ralph of Shrewsbury, Bishop of Bath and Wells 1329–1363, ed. T. S. Holmes, ii, Somerset Record Society, 10 (1896).

The Register of William Greenfield, 1306–1315, ed. W. Brown and A. H. Thompson, 5 vols., Surtees Society, 145, 149, 151–3 (1931–40).

The Register of Walter de Stapeldon Bishop of Exeter (1307–1326), ed. F. C. Hingeston-Randolph (London, 1892).

The Registers of Roger Mortival, Bishop of Salisbury, 1315–1330, ed. K. Edwards, C. R. Elrington, S. Reynolds, and D. M. Owen, 4 vols., Canterbury and York Society, 55, 58–9, 68 (1959–75).

Les Régistres de Nicholas IV, ed. E. Langlois, Bibliothèque des Écoles Françaises d'Athènes et de Rome (1887–93).

Registrum Epistolarum Johannis Pecham, ed. C. T. Martin, 3 vols., Rolls Series (1882–5).

Registrum Hamonis Hethe, ed. C. Johnson, 2 vols., Canterbury and York Society, 48–9 (1948).

Registrum Johannis de Trillek, ed. J. H. Parry, Canterbury and York Society, 8 (1912).

Registrum Ludovici de Charltone, ed. J. H. Parry, Canterbury and York Society, 14 (1914).

Registrum Palatinum Dunelmense, ed. T. D. Hardy, Rolls Series (1873).

Registrum Radulphi Baldock, Gilberti Segrave, Ricardi Newport et Stephani Gravesend, 1304–1338, ed. R. C. Flower, Canterbury and York Society, 7 (1911).

Registrum Roberti Winchelsey, ed. R. Graham, 2 vols., Canterbury and York Society, 51–2 (1952–6).

Registrum Simonis de Gandavo, ed. C. T. Flower and M. C. B. Dawes, Canterbury and York Society, 40–1 (1934).

Regulae Cancellariae Apostolicae: die päpstlichen Kanzleiregeln von Johannes XXII. bis Nikolaus V., ed. E von Ottenthal (Innsbruck, 1888).

RICHARD DE BURY, *Philobiblon*, ed. M. Maclagan (Oxford, 1960).

RICHARD FITZRALPH, *Defensorium Curatorum*, in E. Brown, *Fasciculus Rerum Expetendarum et Fugiendarum* (London, 1690), 466–86.

ROBERT GROSSETESTE, *Epistolae*, ed. H. Luard, Rolls Series (1861).

Robert of Brunne's 'Handlyng Synne', ed. F. J. Furnivall, 2 vols., EETS, os, 119, 123 (1901–3).

ROBERT OF FLAMBOROUGH, *Liber Penitentialis*, ed. J. Firth, Pontifical Institute of Mediaeval Studies, Studies and Texts, 18 (Toronto 1971).

The Rolls and Registers of Bishop Oliver Sutton 1280–1299, ed. R. M. Hill, 6 vols., Lincoln Record Society, 39, 43, 48, 52, 60, 64 (1948–69).

Rotuli Hundredorum, i, Record Commissioners (1812).

Rotuli Parliamentorum, ii (London, 1767).

RYMER, T., *Foedera, Conventiones, Literae et cujuscunque generis Acta Publica inter Reges Angliae et alios quosvis Imperatores, Reges, Pontifices, Principes vel Communitates habita aut tractata*, ii–iii (London, 1821–5).

Sacrosancta Concilia, ed. P. Labbé, viii (Paris, 1671).

The Sermons of Thomas Brinton, Bishop of Rochester, 1373–1389, ed. M. A. Devlin, Camden Society, 3rd Series, 85–6 (1954).

SIMON HINTON, *Summa Iuniorum*, printed in Joannes Gerson, *Opera Omnia*, i (Antwerp, 1706).

Statuta Antiqua Universitatis Oxoniensis, ed. S. Gibson (Oxford, 1931).

Statutes of the Realm, i (London, 1810).

THOMAS DE CHABHAM (Chobham), *Summa Confessorum*, ed. F. Broomfield, Analecta Medievalia Namurcensia, 25 (Louvain/Paris, 1968).

Thomas Gascoigne, Loci e Libro Veritatum, ed. J. E. T. Rogers (Oxford, 1881).

THOMPSON, A. H., 'The Will of Master William Doune, Archdeacon of Leicester', *Archaeological Journal*, 72 (1915), 233–84.

La Vie de Saint Louis: Témoignage de Jehan, Seigneur de Joinville. Texte du XIV Siècle, ed. N. L. Corbett (Sherbrooke, Quebec, 1977).

The Vision of William Concerning Piers the Plowman, ed. W. W. Skeat, 2 vols. (Oxford, 1886; reprinted with bibliographical additions, 1968).

Visitations in the Diocese of Lincoln 1517–1531, ed. A. H. Thompson, i, Lincoln Record Society, 33 (1940).

Wakefield Court Rolls, ed. W. P. Baildon and J. Lister, Yorkshire Archaeological Society, 29 (1900); 78 (1930).

Walter of Henley and Other Treatises, ed. D. Oschinsky (Oxford, 1971).

WILLIAM DE MONTE LAUDUNO, 'Apparatus on the Clementines', printed in *Repetitiones Juris Canonici*, vi (Cologne, 1618).

The Works of Geoffrey Chaucer, ed. F. N. Robinson (London, 1966).

The Works of John Gower, ed. G. C. Macaulay, 4 vols. (Oxford, 1899–1902).

WRIGHT, T., *The Political Songs of England from the Reign of John to that of Edward II*, Camden Society, 1st Series, 6 (1839).

ZUTSHI, P. N. R., *Original Papal Letters in England 1305–1415* (Vatican City, 1990).

SECONDARY SOURCES

ABERTH, J., *Criminal Churchmen in the Age of Edward III: The Case of Bishop Thomas de Lisle* (University Park, Pa., 1996).

ALLEN, H. E., 'The Speculum Vitae—Addendum', *Publications of the Modern Language Association of America*, 32 (NS, 25) (1917), 133–62.

ALLMAND, C. T., 'The Civil Lawyers', in C. H. Clough (ed.), *Profession, Vocation and Culture in Later Medieval England* (Liverpool, 1982), 155–80.

AMUNDSEN, D. W., *Medicine, Society and Faith in the Ancient and Medieval Worlds* (Baltimore/London, 1996).

ANCIAUX, P., *La Théologie du sacrement de pénitence au XIIᵉ siècle*, Universitas Catholica Lovaniensis: Dissertationes ad gradum magistri in Facultate Theologica . . . conscriptae, Series II, xli (Louvain/Gembloux, 1949).

ASTON, M., *Thomas Arundel: A Study of Church Life in the Reign of Richard II* (Oxford, 1967).

AULT, W. O., 'Some Early Village By-laws', *English Historical Review*, 45 (1930), 208–31.

BALDWIN, J. W., 'The Medieval Theories of the Just Price', *Transactions of the American Philosophical Society*, NS, 49 (1959), part iv, pp. 1–92.

—— 'Critics of the Legal Profession: Peter the Chanter and his Circle', in *Proceedings of the Second International Congress of Medieval Canon Law* (Vatican City, 1965), 249–59.

—— *Masters, Princes and Merchants: the Social Views of Peter the Chanter and his Circle*, 2 vols. (Princeton, 1970).

BALE, J., *Scriptorum Illustrium Maioris Britanniae Catalogus*, 2nd edn. (Basle, 1557–9).

BARLOW, F., *The English Church 1000–1066: A Constitutional Study* (London, 1963).

BARNES, J., 'The Just War', in A. Kenny and J. Pinborg (eds.), *The Cambridge History of Later Medieval Philosophy* (Cambridge, 1982), 771–84.

BARTON, J. L., *Roman Law in England, Ius Romanum Medii Aevi*, Pars v, xiii (a) (Milan, 1971).

BEAN, J. M. W., *From Lord to Patron: Lordship in Late Medieval England* (Manchester, 1989).

BEECHING, H. C., and JAMES, M. R., 'The Library of the Cathedral Church of Norwich', *Norfolk Archaeology*, 19 (1917), 67–116.

BELLAMY, J., 'The Coterel Gang: An Anatomy of a Band of Fourteenth Century Criminals', *English Historical Review*, 79 (1964), 698–717.

—— *Crime and Public Order in Medieval England* (London/Toronto, 1973).

—— *Criminal Law and Society in Late Medieval and Tudor England* (Gloucester/New York, 1984).

—— *Bastard Feudalism and the Law* (London, 1989).

BENNETT, H. S., 'The Reeve and the Manor in the Fourteenth Century', *English Historical Review*, 41 (1926), 358–65.

—— *Life on the English Manor* (Cambridge, 1937).

BENNETT, M. J., *Community, Class and Careerism: Cheshire and Lancashire Society in the Age of Sir Gawain and the Green Knight* (Cambridge, 1983).

BERGES, W., *Die Fürstenspiegel des hohen und späten Mittelalters* (Leipzig, 1938).

R. BLOMME, *La Doctrine du péché dans les écoles théologiques de la première moitié du XII siècle* (Louvain, 1958).

BLOMEFIELD, F., *An Essay towards a Topographical History of the County of Norfolk*, 11 vols. (London 1805–10).

BOLTON, B., 'The Council of London of 1342', in *Studies in Church History*, vii (Cambridge, 1971), 147–160.

BOWKER, M., *The Secular Clergy of the Diocese of Lincoln 1495–1520*, Cambridge Studies in Medieval Life and Thought, NS, 13 (Cambridge 1968).

—— 'Some Archdeacons' Court Books and the Commons' Supplication against the Ordinaries of 1532', in D. A. Bullough and R. L. Storey (eds.), *The Study of Medieval Records: Essays in Honour of Kathleen Major* (Oxford, 1971), 282–316.

BOYLE, L. E., 'The Oculus Sacerdotis and Some Other Works of William of Pagula', *Transactions of the Royal Historical Society*, 5th Series, 5 (1955), 81–110.

—— 'A Study of the Works Attributed to William of Pagula, With Special Reference to the Oculus Sacerdotis and Summa Summarum', Oxford University, D.Phil. thesis, 1956.

—— 'The Curriculum of the Faculty of Canon Law at Oxford', in *Oxford Studies presented to Daniel Callus*, Oxford Historical Society, NS, 16 (Oxford, 1964).

—— 'The "Summa Summarum" and Some Other English Works of Canon Law', *Proceedings of the Second International Congress of Medieval Canon Law* (Vatican City, 1965), 416–56.

—— 'The Date of the Summa Praedicantium of John Bromyard', *Speculum*, 48 (1973), 533–7.

—— 'The Summa Confessorum of John of Freiburg and the Popularization of the Moral Teaching of St Thomas and Some of his Contemporaries', in *St Thomas Aquinas Commemorative Studies* (Toronto 1974), 245–68.

—— *Pastoral Care, Clerical Education and Canon Law 1200–1400* (London, 1981).

—— 'The Inter-Conciliar Period 1179–1215 and the Beginnings of Pastoral Manuals', in F. Liotta (ed.), *Miscellanea Rolando Bandinelli Papa Alessandro III* (Siena, 1986), 45–56.

BRENTANO, R., *Two Churches: England and Italy in the Thirteenth Century* (Princeton, 1968).

BREWER, D., 'Class Distinction in Chaucer', *Speculum*, 43 (1968), 290–305.

BRIQUET, C. M., *Les Filigranes: Dictionnaire historique des marques du papier dès leur apparition vers 1282 jusqu'en 1600*, 2nd edn. (Paris, 1923).

BROWN, C., and ROBBINS, R. H., *The Index of Middle English Verse* (New York, 1943).

BUCKLAND, W. W., *A Text-Book of Roman Law from Augustus to Justinian*, 3rd edn., ed. P. Stein (Cambridge, 1963).

CAM, H. M., *The Hundred and the Hundred Rolls* (London, 1930).

—— 'The Decline and Fall of English Feudalism', *History*, 25 (1941), 216–33.

CAMPBELL, B. M. S. (ed.), *Before the Black Death: Studies in the 'Crisis' of the Early Fourteenth Century* (Manchester, 1991).

CAPES, W. W., *The English Church in the Fourteenth and Fifteenth Centuries* (London, 1900).

CARPENTER, C., 'The Beauchamp Affinity: A Study of Bastard Feudalism at Work', *English Historical Review*, 95 (1980), 514–32.

CAWTHRON, D. J., 'The Episcopal Administration of the Diocese of Exeter in the Fourteenth Century, With Special Reference to the Registers of Stapeldon, Grandisson and Brantingham', London University MA thesis, 1951.

CHENEY, C. R., 'Legislation of the Medieval English Church', *English Historical Review*, 1 (1935), 193–224, 385–417.

—— 'Textual Problems of the English Provincial Canons', in *Medieval Texts and Studies* (Oxford, 1973), 111–37.

—— 'William Lyndwood's Provinciale', in *Medieval Texts and Studies* (Oxford, 1973), 158–184.

—— 'Some Aspects of Diocesan Legislation in England During the Thirteenth Century', in *Medieval Texts and Studies* (Oxford, 1973), 185–202.

CHENEY, M., 'The Compromise of Avranches and the Spread of Canon Law in England', *English Historical Review*, 56 (1941), 177–97.

CHENU, M. D., 'Les Quaestiones de Thomas Buckingham', in *Studia Medievalia in Honorem R. J. Martin* (Bruges, 1949), 229–41.

CHERRY, M., 'The Courtenay Earls of Devon: The Formation and Disintegration of a Late Medieval Aristocratic Affinity', *Southern History*, 1 (1979), 71–97.

COKAYNE, G. E., *The Complete Peerage*, vi (London, 1926).

COLEMAN, J., *English Literature in History 1350–1400: Medieval Readers and Writers* (London, 1981).

CONGAR, Y., 'Aspects ecclésiologiques de la querelle entre mendiants et séculiers dans la seconde moitié du XIIIe et le début du XIVe siècle', *Archives d'Histoire Doctrinale et Littéraire du Moyen Age*, 28 (1961), 33–161.

CONSTABLE, G., 'Resistance to Tithes in the Middle Ages', *Journal of Ecclesiastical History*, 13 (1962), 172–85.

—— *Monastic Tithes from their Origins to the Twelfth Century* (Cambridge, 1964).

COOK, G. H., *English Monasteries in the Middle Ages* (London, 1961).

COPELAND, J., 'The Relations Between the Secular Clergy and the Mendicant Friars in England During the Century After the Issue of the Bull *Super Cathedram*', London University MA thesis, 1937.

COSS, P. R., 'Bastard Feudalism Revised', *Past and Present*, 125 (1989), 27–64.

COULTON, G. G., 'A Visitation of the Archdeaconry of Totnes in 1342', *English Historical Review*, 26 (1911), 108–24.

—— *Medieval Village, Manor and Monastery* (New York, 1960).

COURTENAY, W. J., *Schools and Scholars in Fourteenth-Century England* (Princeton, 1987).

COX, J. C., *The Sanctuaries and Sanctuary Seekers of Medieval England* (London, 1911).

CUTTS, E. L., *Parish Priests and their People in the Middle Ages in England* (London, 1898).

DAHMUS, J., *William Courtenay Archbishop of Canterbury, 1381–1396* (Philadelphia/London, 1966).

DAVIS, H. W. C., 'The Chronicle of Battle Abbey', *English Historical Review*, 29 (1914), 426–34.

DENHOLM-YOUNG, N., *Seignorial Administration* (London, 1937).

—— 'The Tournament in the Thirteenth Century', in R. W. Hunt, W. A. Pantin, and R. W. Southern (eds.), *Studies Presented to F. M. Powicke* (Oxford, 1948), 240–68.

—— 'Richard de Bury (1287–1345) and the Liber Epistolaris', in *Collected Papers of N. Denholm-Young* (Cardiff, 1969), 1–41.

Dictionary of National Biography, ed. L. Stephen and S. Lee, 21 vols. (London 1908–9).

Dictionnaire de droit canonique, directed by R. Naz, 7 vols. (Paris 1935–65), various articles.

Dictionnaire d'histoire et de géographie ecclésiastiques, A. Baudrillart *et al.*, ii (Paris, 1914) (article 'Altopascio').

Dictionnaire de théologie catholique, ed. A. Vacant, E. Mangenot, *et al.*, 15 vols. (Paris 1903–50).

DOHAR, W. J., 'Medieval Ordination Lists: The Origins of a Record', *Archives*, 20: 87 (1992), 17–35.

—— *The Black Death and Pastoral Leadership: The Diocese of Hereford in the Fourteenth Century* (Philadelphia, 1995).

EMDEN, A. B., *A Biographical Register of the University of Oxford to A.D. 1500*, 3 vols. (Oxford, 1957).

—— *A Biographical Register of the University of Cambridge to A.D. 1500* (Cambridge, 1963).

ENGEN, J. VAN, ' "God is no Respecter of Persons": Sacred Texts and Social Realities', in L. Smith and B. Ward (eds.), *Intellectual Life in the Middle Ages* (London/Rio Grande, 1992), 243–64.

ERICKSON, C., 'The Fourteenth-Century Franciscans and their Critics', *Franciscan Studies*, 35 (1975), 107–35; 36 (1976), 108–47.

EWEN, C., 'Organised Piracy Round England in the Sixteenth Century', *The Mariner's Mirror*, 35 (1949), 29–42.

FARAL, É., *Les Jongleurs en France au moyen âge*, 2nd edn. (Paris, 1964).

FIRTH, C. H., 'The Reign of Charles I', *Transactions of the Royal Historical Society*, 3rd Series, 6 (1912), 39–40, for 'The New Ballad of the Parator and the Devil'.

FIRTH, J. J., 'The Penitentiale of Robert of Flamborough: An Early Handbook For the Confessor in its Manuscript Tradition', *Traditio*, 16 (1960), 541–56.

FORSTER, R. H., 'Notes on Durham and Other North Country Sanctuaries', *Journal of the British Archaeological Association*, NS, 11 (1905), 118–39.

FOSTER, J., 'The Activities of Rural Deans in England in the Twelfth and Thirteenth Centuries', Manchester University, MA thesis, 1955.

FOURNIER, P., *Les Officialités au moyen âge* (Paris, 1880).

FOWLER, K., *The King's Lieutenant: Henry of Grosmont, First Duke of Lancaster 1310–1361* (London, 1969).

FRANKLIN, M. J., 'Bodies in Medieval Northampton: Legatine Intervention in the Twelfth Century', in M. J. Franklin and C. Harper-Bill, *Medieval Ecclesiastical Studies in Honour of D. M. Owen* (Woodbridge, 1995), 57–81.

DE GHELLINCK, J., 'Un bibliophile au XIV siècle: Richard d'Aungerville', *Revue d'Histoire Ecclésiastique*, (1920), 271–312, 482–502; 19 (1923), 157–200.

GILLESPIE, V., 'The Literary Form of the Middle English Pastoral Manual, With Particular Reference to the *Speculum Christiani* and Some Related Texts', Oxford University, D.Phil. thesis, 1981.

GIVEN-WILSON, C., *The English Nobility in the Later Middle Ages: The Fourteenth-Century Political Community* (London/New York, 1987).

GLORIEUX, P., 'Prélats francais contre religieux mendiants (1281–1290)', *Revue d'Histoire de l'Église de France*, 11 (1925), 309–31, 471–95.

GOERING, J., *William de Montibus (c.1140–1213): The Schools and the Literature of Pastoral Care* (Toronto, 1992).

—— and TAYLOR, D. S., 'The Summulae of Bishops Walter de Cantilupe (1240) and Peter Quinel (1287)', *Speculum*, 67 (1992), 576–94.

GONZÁLEZ, J. L., *Faith and Wealth: A History of Early Christian Ideas on the Origin, Significance and Use of Money* (San Francisco, 1990).

GOTTFRIED, R. S., *Doctors and Medicine in Medieval England 1340–1530* (Princeton, 1986).

GOVER, J. E. B., MAWER, A., and STENTON, F. (eds.), *The Place-Names of Devon*, 2 vols. (Cambridge, 1931–2).

GRAHAM, R., 'The Metropolitical Visitation of the Diocese of Worcester by Archbishop Winchelsey in 1301', *Transactions of the Royal Historical Society*, 4th series, 2 (1919), 59–93.

GRANSDEN, A., 'Some Late Thirteenth-Century Records of an Ecclesiastical Court in the Archdeaconry of Sudbury', *Bulletin of the Institute of Historical Research*, 32 (1959), 62–9.

234 *Bibliography*

GREATREX, J., *Biographical Register of the English Cathedral Priories of the Province of Canterbury c.1066 to 1540* (Oxford, 1997).

GRÜNDEL, J., *Die Lehre von dem Umständen der menschlichen Handlung im Mittelalter*, Beiträge zur Geschichte der Philosophie und Theologie des Mittelalters, Band xxxix, Heft 5 (Münster, 1963).

GUILLEMAIN, B., *La Cour pontificale d'Avignon (1309–1376)*. *Étude d'une société* (Paris, 1962).

GWYNN, A., 'The Black Death in Ireland', *Studies*, 24 (1935), 25–42.

—— 'Archbishop FitzRalph and George of Hungary', *Studies*, 24 (1935), 558–72.

—— 'Richard FitzRalph, Archbishop of Armagh', *Studies*, 25 (1936), 81–96.

—— 'Archbishop FitzRalph and the Friars', *Studies*, 26 (1937), 50–67.

—— 'The Sermon Diary of Richard FitzRalph', *Proceedings of the Royal Irish Academy*, 44 (1937), Section C, No. 1, pp. 1–57.

HAINES, R. M., *The Administration of the Diocese of Worcester in the First Half of the Fourteenth Century* (London, 1965).

—— 'Adam Orleton and the Diocese of Winchester', *Journal of Ecclesiastical History*, 23 (1972), 1–30.

—— 'The Compilation of a Late Fourteenth-Century Precedent Book—Register Brian 2', in D. Baker (ed.), *Studies in Church History*, xi (Oxford, 1975), 173–85.

—— *The Church and Politics in Fourteenth-Century England: The Career of Adam Orleton* (Cambridge, 1978).

HAMMERICH, L. L., *The Beginning of the Strife between Richard FitzRalph and the Mendicants* (Copenhagen, 1938).

HARDING, A., *A Social History of English Law* (Harmondsworth, 1966).

HAREN, M. J., 'Friars as Confessors: The Canonist Background to the Fourteenth-Century Controversy', *Peritia*, 3 (1984), 503–16.

—— 'Social Ideas in the Pastoral Literature of Fourteenth-Century England', in C. Harper-Bill (ed.), *Religious Belief and Ecclesiastical Careers in Late Medieval England*, Studies in the History of Medieval Religion, 3 (Woodbridge, 1991), 45–59.

—— 'Bishop Gynwell of Lincoln, Two Avignonese Statutes and Archbishop FitzRalph of Armagh's Suit at the Roman Curia against the Friars', *Archivum Historiae Pontificiae*, 31 (1993), 275–92.

—— 'Confession, Social Ethics and Social Discipline in the *Memoriale Presbiterorum*', in P. Biller and A. Minnis (eds.), *Handling Sin: Confession in the Middle Ages*, York Studies in Medieval Theology, 2 (1998), 109–22.

—— 'Richard FitzRalph and the Friars: The Intellectual Itinerary of a Curial Controversialist', in J. Hamesse (ed.), *Roma Magistra Mundi. Itineraria Culturae Medievalis* (Louvain-la-Neuve, 1998), i. 349–67.

HARVEY, B., 'Work and Festa Ferianda in Medieval England', *Journal of Ecclesiastical History*, 23 (1972), 289–308.

HASELMAYER, L. A., 'The Apparitor and Chaucer's Summoner', *Speculum*, 12 (1937), 43–57.

HATCHER, J., 'English Serfdom and Villeinage: Towards a Reassessment', in T. H. Aston, *Landlords, Peasants and Politics in Medieval England* (Cambridge, 1987), 247–83.

HAY, D., 'The Division of the Spoils of War in Fourteenth-Century England', *Transactions of the Royal Historical Society*, 5th Series, 4 (1954), 91–109.

HEATH, P., *English Parish Clergy on the Eve of the Reformation* (London/Toronto, 1969).

HELMHOLZ, R. H., *Marriage Litigation in Medieval England* (Cambridge, 1974).

—— 'Ethical Standards for Advocates in Theory and Practice', in S. Kuttner (ed.), *Proceedings of the Fourth International Congress of Medieval Canon Law* (Vatican City, 1975), 283–99.

HICKS, M., *Bastard Feudalism* (London/New York, 1995).

HIGHFIELD, J. R. L., 'The English Hierarchy in the Reign of Edward III', *Transactions of the Royal Historical Society*, 5th Series, 6 (1956), 115–38.

—— 'The Early Colleges', in J. I. Catto (ed.), *The Early Oxford Schools = History of Oxford University*, i (Oxford, 1984), 225–63.

HILL, R., 'Public Penance: Some Problems of a Thirteenth Century Bishop', *History*, 36 (1951), 213–26.

HILTON, R. H., *A Medieval Society: The West Midlands at the End of the Thirteenth Century* (London, 1966).

—— *The English Peasantry in the Later Middle Ages* (Oxford, 1975).

HOLDSWORTH, W., *A History of English Law*, 17 vols. (London, 1923–66).

HOLMES, G., *The Estates of the Higher Nobility* (Cambridge, 1957).

HOMANS, G. C., *English Villagers of the Thirteenth Century* (New York, 1941).

HUGHES, J., *Pastors and Visionaries: Religion and Secular Life in Late Medieval Yorkshire* (Woodbridge, 1988).

HUNNISETT, R. F., *The Medieval Coroner* (Cambridge, 1961).

HUNT, R. W., 'Oxford Grammar Masters in the Middle Ages', in *Oxford Studies Presented to Daniel Callus*, Oxford Historical Society, NS, 16 (1964), 163–93.

HYAMS, P. R., *Kings, Lords and Peasants in Medieval England: The Common Law of Villeinage in the Twelfth and Thirteenth Centuries* (Oxford, 1980).

JAMES, M. K., 'A London Merchant of the Fourteenth Century', *Economic History Review*, 8 (1955–6), 364–376.

JAMES, M. R., *A Descriptive Catalogue of the Manuscripts in the Library of Corpus Christi College, Cambridge* (Cambridge, 1912).

JARRETT, B., *Medieval Socialism* (London, 1913).

—— *S. Antonino and Medieval Economics* (London, 1914).

KAEUPER, R. W., 'Law and Order in Fourteenth Century England: The Evidence of the Special Commissions of Oyer et Terminer', *Speculum*, 54 (1979), 734–84.

—— *War, Justice and Public Order: England and France in the Later Middle Ages* (Oxford, 1988).

KANE, G., 'Some Fourteenth-Century "Political" Poems', in G. Kratzmann and J. Simpson (eds.), *Medieval English Religious and Ethical Literature: Essays in Honour of G. H. Russell* (Cambridge, 1986), 82–91.

KEEN, M., *The Laws of War in the Late Middle Ages* (London/Toronto, 1965).
—— *Chivalry* (New Haven/London, 1984).
KELLOGG, A., and L. A. HASELMAYER, 'Chaucer's Satire of the Pardoner', *Publications of the Modern Language Association of America*, 66 (1951), 251–77.
KEMP, E., 'The Origins of the Canterbury Convocation', *Journal of Ecclesiastical History*, 3 (1952), 132–43.
KER, N. R., 'Mediaeval Manuscripts from Norwich Cathedral Priory', *Transactions of the Cambridge Bibliographical Society*, 1 (1949–53), 1–28.
—— *Medieval Libraries of Great Britain*, 2nd edn. (London, 1964).
—— *Medieval Manuscripts in British Libraries*, i (Oxford, 1969).
KINGSFORD, C. L., 'West Country Piracy: The School of English Seamen', in *Prejudice and Promise in Fifteenth Century England* (Oxford, 1925, reprinted 1962), 78–106.
KNOWLES, D., *The Religious Orders in England*, ii (Cambridge, 1955); iii (Cambridge, 1959).
KOCH, J., 'Der Prozess gegen den Magister Johannes de Polliaco und seine Vorgeschichte 1312–1321', *Recherches de Théologie Ancienne et Médiévale*, 5 (1933), 391–422.
KOWALEWSKI, M., 'The Commercial Dominance of a Medieval Provincial Oligarchy: Exeter in the late Fourteenth Century', *Mediaeval Studies*, 46 (1984), 355–84.
—— *Local Markets and Regional Trade in Medieval Exeter* (Cambridge, 1995).
KUTTNER, S., 'Pierre de Roissy and Robert of Flamborough', *Traditio*, 2 (1944), 492–9.
—— and SMALLEY, B., 'The "Glossa Ordinaria" to the Gregorian Decretals', *English Historical Review*, 60 (1945), 97–105.
LANGHOLM, O., *Economics in the Medieval Schools: Wealth, Exchange, Value, Money and Usury According to the Paris Tradition* (Leiden/New York/Cologne, 1992).
LEA, H. C., *A History of Auricular Confession and Indulgences in the Latin Church*, 3 vols. (London, 1896).
LEFF, G., *Bradwardine and the Pelagians* (Cambridge, 1957).
LE GOFF, J., 'Métier et profession d'après les manuels de confesseurs au moyen âge', in P. Wilpert (ed.), *Beiträge zum Berufsbewusstsein des mittelalterlichen Menschen, Miscellanea Mediaevalia*, 3 (Berlin, 1964), 44–60.
LE NEVE, J., *Fasti Ecclesiae Anglicanae 1300–1541*, 12 vols., revised edn. (London, 1962–7).
LEPINE, D. N., 'The Origin and Careers of the Canons of Exeter Cathedral, 1300–1455', in C. Harper-Bill (ed.), *Religious Belief and Ecclesiastical Careers in Late Medieval England*, Studies in the History of Medieval Religion, 3 (Woodbridge, 1991), 87–120.
LEVETT, A. E., *Studies in Manorial History*, ed. H. M. Cam (Oxford, 1938).
LEWIS, N. B., 'The Organization of Indentured Retinues in Fourteenth-Century England', *Transactions of the Royal Historical Society*, 4th Series, 27 (1945), 29–39.
LIPPENS, H., 'Le Droit nouveau des mendiants en conflit avec le droit coutumier du clergé séculier du Concile de Vienne a celui de Trente', *Archivum Franciscanum Historicum*, 47 (1954), 241–92.

LIPSON, E., *The Economic History of England*, 1, 12th edn. (London, 1959).

List of Escheators for England and Wales, Public Record Office List and Indexes, 72 (London, 1932).

List of Sheriffs for England and Wales, Public Record Office List and Indexes, 9 (London, 1898).

LITTLE, A. G., *Studies in English Franciscan History* (Manchester, 1917).

—— 'A Royal Inquiry into Property Held by the Mendicant Friars in England in 1349 and 1350', in J. G. Edwards, V. H. Galbraith, and E. F. Jacob (eds.), *Historical Essays in Honour of James Tait* (Manchester, 1933), 179–88.

—— 'Personal Tithes', *English Historical Review*, 60 (1945), 67–88.

—— and EASTERLING, R. C., *The Franciscans and Dominicans of Exeter* (Exeter, 1927).

LOGAN, F. D., *Excommunication and the Secular Arm in Medieval England*, Pontifical Institute of Mediaeval Studies, Studies and Texts, 15 (Toronto, 1968).

LOTTIN, O., *Psychologie et morale aux XIIe et XIIIe siècles*, 1 (Louvain/Gembloux, 1942).

LUNT, W. E., *Financial Relations of the Papacy with England to 1327* (Cambridge, Mass., 1939).

—— *Financial Relations of the Papacy with England, 1327–1534* (Cambridge, Mass., 1962).

LUSCOMBE, D., *The School of Peter Abelard* (Cambridge, 1969).

McFARLANE, K. B., *The Nobility of Later Medieval England* (Oxford, 1973).

McLAUGHLIN, T. P., 'The Teaching of the Canonists on Usury', *Mediaeval Studies*, 1 (1939), 81–147; 2 (1940), 1–22.

McVAUGH, M. R., *Medicine Before the Plague: Practitioners and their Patients in the Crown of Aragon 1285–1345* (Cambridge, 1993).

MADAN, F., and CRASTER, H. H. E. (eds.), *A Summary Catalogue of Western Manuscripts in the Bodleian Library*, 2 (Oxford, 1922).

MADDICOTT, J. R., 'Poems of Social Protest in Early Fourteenth-Century England', in W. M. Ormrod (ed.), *England in the Fourteenth Century*, Proceedings of the 1985 Harlaxton Symposium (Woodbridge, 1986), 130–44.

MAITLAND, F. W., *Roman Canon Law in the Church of England* (Cambridge, 1898).

—— HARCOURT, L. W. V., and BOLLAND, W. C. (eds.), *The Eyre of Kent, 6 and 7 Edward II, AD 1313–1314*, Year Books of Edward II, 5; Selden Society, 24 (1909).

MANN, J., *Chaucer and Medieval Estates Satire: The Literature of Classes and the General Prologue to the Canterbury Tales* (Cambridge, 1973).

MARSDEN, R. G., 'Admiralty Droits and Salvage—Gas Float Whitton No. II', *Law Quarterly Review*, 15 (1899), 353–66.

MAUGENOT, E., 'Astesanus de Asti', in *Dictionnaire de théologie catholique*, i (Paris, 1903), col. 2142.

MEENS, R., 'Children and Confession in the Early Middle Ages', in D. Wood (ed.), *The Church and Childhood* (Oxford, 1994), 53–65.

MICHAUD-QUANTIN, P., *Sommes de casuistique et manuels de confession* (Louvain/Lille, 1962).

MIFSUD, G., 'John Sheppey, Bishop of Rochester, as Preacher and Collector of Sermons', Oxford University, B.Litt. thesis, 1953.

MOORMAN, J. R. H., *Church Life in England in the Thirteenth Century* (Cambridge, 1955).

MORENZONI, F., *Des écoles aux paroisses: Thomas de Chobham et la promotion de la prédication au début du XIIIᵉ siècle*, Collection des études Augustiniennes (Turnhout/Paris, 1995).

MOREY, A., *Bartholomew of Exeter, Bishop and Canonist* (Cambridge, 1937).

MORGAN, P., *War and Society in Medieval Cheshire 1227–1403* (Manchester, 1987).

MORRIS, C., 'The Commissary of the Bishop in the Diocese of Lincoln', *Journal of Ecclesiastical History*, 10 (1959), 50–65.

—— 'A Consistory Court in the Middle Ages', *Journal of Ecclesiastical History*, 14 (1963), 150–9.

—— 'The Ravenser Composition—A Fourteenth Century Dispute between the Bishop and Archdeacons of Lincoln', *Lincolnshire Architectural and Archaeological Society, Reports and Papers*, NS, 10, Part 1 (1963), 24–39.

—— 'From Synod to Consistory: The Bishops' Courts in England, 1150–1250', *Journal of Ecclesiastical History*, 22 (1975), 115–23.

MORRIS, W. A., *The Medieval English Sheriff to 1300* (Manchester 1927).

MUSSON, A., *Public Order and Law Enforcement: The Local Administration of Criminal Justice 1294–1350* (Woodbridge, 1996).

NELSON, B. N., 'The Usurer and the Merchant Prince: Italian Businessmen and the Ecclesiastical Law of Restitution 1100–1500', *Journal of Economic History*, Supplement 7 (1947), 104–22.

—— *The Idea of Usury: From Tribal Brotherhood to Universal Otherhood*, 2nd edn. (Chicago, 1969).

NELSON, V., 'Problems of Transcription in the *Speculum Vitae* MSS', *Scriptorium*, 31 (1977), 254–9.

The New Catholic Encyclopaedia, 15 vol. (San Francisco/London/Toronto/Sydney, 1967).

NICHOLS, J. F., 'An Early Fourteenth-Century Petition from the Tenants of Bocking to their Manorial Lord', *Economic History Review*, 2 (1929–30), 300–7.

OAKLEY, T. P., *English Penitential Discipline and Anglo-Saxon Law in their Joint Influence*, Columbia University Studies in History etc., 107 (New York, 1923).

OLIVER, G., *Monasticon Diocesis Exoniensis* (Exeter, 1846).

—— *Lives of the Bishops of Exeter and a History of the Cathedral* (Exeter, 1861).

ORIGO, I., *The World of San Bernardino* (London, 1963).

ORME, N., *Education in the West of England 1066–1548: Cornwall, Devon, Dorset, Gloucestershire, Somerset, Wiltshire* (University of Exeter, 1976).

—— 'Bishop Grandisson and Popular Religion', *Reports and Transactions of the Devonshire Association for the Advancement of Science, Literature and Art*, 134 (1992), 107–18.

—— 'Children and the Church in Medieval England', *Journal of Ecclesiastical History*, 45 (1994), 563–87.

—— 'Church and Chapel in Medieval England', *Transactions of the Royal Historical Society*, 6th Series, 6 (1996), 75–102.

OWEN, D., 'The Records of the Bishop's Official at Ely: Specialization in the English Episcopal Chancery of the Later Middle Ages', in D. A. Bullough and R. L. Storey (eds.), *The Study of Medieval Records, Essays in Honour of Kathleen Major* (Oxford, 1971), 189–205.

—— *Church and Society in Medieval Lincolnshire* = *History of Medieval Lincolnshire*, v (Lincoln, 1971).

—— *The Medieval Canon Law: Teaching Literature and Transmission* (Cambridge, 1990).

OWST, G. R., *Preaching in Medieval England* (Cambridge, 1926).

—— *Literature and Pulpit in Medieval England*, 2nd edn. (Oxford, 1961).

PAGE, W. (ed.), *The Victoria County History of London*, i (London, 1909).

—— 'Some Remarks on the Churches of the Domesday Survey', *Archaeologia*, 66 (1915), 61–102.

PANTIN, W. A., 'Grosseteste's Relations With the Papacy and the Crown', in D. Callus (ed.), *Robert Grosseteste Scholar and Bishop* (Oxford, 1955), 178–215.

—— *The English Church in the Fourteenth Century* (Cambridge, 1955; reprinted Notre Dame, 1962).

—— 'John of Wales and Medieval Humanism', in J. A. Watt, J. B. Morrall, and F. X. Martin (eds.), *Medieval Studies Presented to Aubrey Gwynn* (Dublin, 1961), 279–319.

PARSONS, H. R., 'Anglo-Norman Books of Courtesy and Nurture', *Publications of the Modern Language Association of America*, 38 (1923), 383–485.

PAYER, P. J., 'The Humanism of the Penitentials and the Continuity of the Penitential Tradition', *Mediaeval Studies*, 46 (1984), 340–54.

PEARCE, E. H., *Walter de Wenlok, Abbot of Westminster* (London, 1920).

PETERSEN, I. J., *William of Nassington, Canon, Mystic and Poet of the Speculum Vitae* (New York/Berne/Frankfurt am Main, 1986).

PHILLIPS, J. R. S., *Aymer de Valence, Earl of Pembroke 1307–1324* (Oxford, 1972).

PLUCKNETT, T. F., *The Mediaeval Bailiff* (London, 1954).

POLLOCK, F., and MAITLAND, F. W., *A History of English Law*, 2nd edn. (Cambridge, 1898).

POOLE, R. L., 'Thomas de Hanneya', in *Dictionary of National Biography* (London, 1908–9), viii. 1190.

POSTAN, M. M., 'Credit in Medieval Trade', *Economic History Review*, 1 (1927–8), 234–61.

—— 'Some Social Consequences of the Hundred Years War', *Economic History Review*, 12 (1942), 1–12.

—— 'Partnership in English Medieval Commerce', in *Studi in Onore di Armando Sapori* (Milan, 1957), 521–49.

PUTNAM, B. H., 'Shire Officials: Keepers of the Peace and Justices of the Peace', in J. W. Willard, W. A. Morris, and W. Dunham Jr. (eds.), *The English Government at Work*, iii (Cambridge, Mass., 1950), 185–217.

QUANTIN, P. M., 'A propos des premières *Summae Confessorum*', *Recherches de Théologie Ancienne et Médiévale*, 26 (1959), 264–306.

QUERA, M., 'De Contritionismo et Attritionismo in Scholis usque ad Tempus S. Thomae Traditio', *Analecta Sacra Tarraconensia*, 4 (1928), 183–202.

RAFTIS, J. A., *Tenure and Mobility: Studies in the Social History of the English Village*, Pontifical Institute of Mediaeval Studies, Studies and Texts, 8 (1964).

RAWCLIFFE, C., 'Baronial Councils in the Later Middle Ages', in C. Ross (ed.), *Patronage Pedigree and Power in Later Medieval England* (Gloucester, 1979), 87–108.

—— *Medicine and Society in Later Medieval England* (Stroud, 1995).

RÉVILLE, A., ' "L'Abjuratio Regni", Histoire d'une institution anglaise', *Revue Historique*, 1 (1892), 1–42.

RIGBY, S. H., *English Society in the Later Middle Ages: Class, Status and Gender* (London, 1995).

ROBERTSON, C. A., 'The Tithe Heresy of Friar William Russell', *Albion*, 8 (1976), 1–16.

ROBERTSON, D. W., Jr, 'A Note on the Classical Origin of Circumstances in the Medieval Confessional', *Studies in Philology*, 43 (1946), 6–14.

ROBINSON, J. A., 'Convocation of Canterbury: Its Early History', *Church Quarterly Review*, 81 (1915), 81–137.

DE ROOVER, R., 'The Organization of Trade', in M. M. Postan *et al.* (eds.), *The Cambridge Economic History*, iii (Cambridge, 1965), 42–118.

RODES, R. E., *Ecclesiastical Administration in Medieval England: The Anglo-Saxons to the Reformation* (Notre Dame/London, 1977).

ROSAMBERT, A., *La Veuve en droit canonique jusq'au XIVe siècle* (Paris, 1923).

ROSE-TROUP, F., *Bishop Grandisson, Student and Art Lover* (Plymouth, 1929).

ROSSER, G., 'Parochial Conformity and Voluntary Religion in Late-Medieval England', *Transactions of the Royal Historical Society*, 6th Series, 1 (1991), 173–89.

—— 'Sanctuary and Social Negotiation in Medieval England', in J. Blair and B. Golding (eds.), *The Cloister and the World: Essays in Medieval History in Honour of Barbara Harvey* (Oxford, 1996), 57–79.

ROTH, F., *The English Austin Friars*, 2 vols.: i, *History* (New York, 1966); ii, *Sources* (New York, 1961).

SANDLER, L. F., 'Face to Face with God: A Pictorial Image of the Beatific Vision', in W. M. Ormrod (ed.), *England in the Fourteenth Century*, Proceedings of the 1985 Harlaxton Symposium (Woodbridge, 1986), 224–35.

SAUL, N., *Knights and Esquires: The Gloucestershire Gentry in the Fourteenth Century* (Oxford, 1981).

SAVINE, A., 'English Monasteries on the Eve of the Dissolution', in P. Vinogradoff (ed.), *Oxford Studies in Social and Legal History*, i (Oxford, 1909), Part i, pp. 240–5.

SAYERS, J., *Papal Judges Delegate in the Province of Canterbury 1198–1254* (Oxford, 1971).

SCAMMELL, J., 'The Rural Chapter in England from the Eleventh to the Fourteenth Century', *English Historical Review*, 86 (1971), 1–21.

SCHIMMELPFENNIG, B., 'Zisterzienserideal und Kirchenreform: Benedikt XII. (1334–42) als Reformpapst', *Zisterzienser-Studien*, iii, Studien zur europäischen Geschichte, Bd. 13, (Berlin, 1976), 11–43.

SENIGALLIA, L. A., 'Medieval Sources of English Maritime Law', *The Mariner's Mirror*, 26 (1940), 7–14.

SHEEHAN, M. M., *The Will in Medieval England*, Pontifical Institute of Mediaeval Studies, Studies and Texts, 6 (1963).

—— 'The Formation and Stability of Marriage in Fourteenth Century England: Evidence of an Ely Register', *Mediaeval Studies*, 33 (1971), 228–63.

SIKES, J. G., 'John de Pouilli and Peter de la Palu', *English Historical Review*, 49 (1934), 219–40.

SMALLEY, B., 'The Quaestiones of Simon of Hinton', in R. W. Hunt, W. A. Pantin, and R. W. Southern (eds.), *Studies Presented to F. M. Powicke* (Oxford, 1948), 209–22.

SNAPE, R. H., *English Monastic Finances in the Later Middle Ages* (Cambridge, 1926).

SOUTHERN, R. W., *Robert Grosseteste, the Growth of an English Mind in Medieval Europe*, 2nd edn. (Oxford, 1992).

SPENCER, H. LEITH, *English Preaching in the Late Middle Ages* (Oxford, 1993).

STEELE, M. W., 'A Study of the Books Owned or Used by John Grandisson, Bishop of Exeter (1327–1369)', Oxford University, D.Phil. thesis, 1994.

STONES, E. L. G., 'The Folvilles of Ashby-Folville, Leicestershire and their Associates in Crime, 1326–47', *Transactions of the Royal Historical Society*, 7 (1957), 117–36.

SWANSON, R., 'Titles to Orders in Medieval English Episcopal Registers', in H. Mayr-Harting and R. I. Moore (eds.), *Studies in Medieval History Presented to R. H. C. Davis* (London/Ronceverte, 1985), 233–45.

—— *Church and Society in Late Medieval England* (Oxford, 1989).

—— 'Parochialism and Particularism: The Dispute over the Status of Ditchford Frary, Warwickshire, in the Early Fifteenth Century', in M. J. Franklin and C. Harper-Bill (eds.), *Medieval Ecclesiastical Studies in Honour of D. M. Owen* (Woodbridge, 1995), 241–57.

SZITTYA, P. R., *The Antifraternal Tradition in Medieval Literature* (Princeton, 1986).

TANNER, T., *Bibliotheca Britannico-Hibernica* (London, 1748).

TAYLOR, J., *English Historical Literature in the Fourteenth Century* (Oxford, 1987).

TEETAERT, A., 'La Doctrine pénitentielle de St Raymond de Penyafort', *Analecta Sacra Tarraconensia*, 4 (1928), 121–82.

—— 'Marchesino di Reggio d'Emilia', in *Dictionnaire de Théologie Catholique*, tom. xiii (Paris, 1936), cols. 2102–4.

THOMPSON, A. H., 'Notes on the Ecclesiastical History of the Parish of Henbury', *Transactions of the Bristol and Gloucestershire Archaeological Society*, 37 (1914), 125–9.

THOMPSON, A. H., 'The Will of Master William Doune, Archdeacon of Leicester', *Archaeological Journal*, 72 (1915), 233–84.

—— 'The Registers of the Archdeaconry of Richmond, 1361–1442', *Yorkshire Archaeological Journal*, 25 (1920), 129–268.

—— 'A Corrody from Leicester Abbey, AD 1393–4, With Some Notes on Corrodies', *Transactions of the Leicestershire Archaeological Society*, 14 (1928), 114–34.

—— 'William Bateman, Bishop of Norwich, 1344–1355', *Norfolk Archaeology*, 25 (1935), 102–37.

—— 'Diocesan Organization in the Middle Ages, Archdeacons and Rural Deans', *Proceedings of the British Academy*, 29 (1943), 153–94.

—— *The English Clergy and Their Organization in the Later Middle Ages* (Oxford 1947).

THOMPSON, J. A. F., 'Tithe Disputes in Later Medieval London', *English Historical Review*, 78 (1963), 1–17.

—— *The Later Lollards* (Oxford, 1965).

THOMSON, S. H., *The Writings of Robert Grosseteste* (Cambridge, 1940).

THORNLEY, I. D., 'Sanctuary in Medieval London', *Journal of the British Archaeological Association*, NS, 38 (1932), 293–315.

TIERNEY, B., *Medieval Poor Law* (Berkeley/Los Angeles, 1959).

TILLOTSON, J. H., 'Pensions, Corrodies and Religious Houses: An Aspect of the Relations of Crown and Church in Early Fourteenth-Century England', *Journal of Religious History*, 8 (1974), 127–43.

DE LA TORRE, B. R., *Thomas Buckingham and the Contingency of Futures: The Possibility of Human Freedom* (Notre Dame, 1987).

WALSH, K., *A Fourteenth-Century Scholar and Primate: Richard FitzRalph in Oxford, Avignon and Armagh* (Oxford, 1981).

WALZ, A., 'Sancti Raymundi de Penyafort, Auctoritas in Re Penitentiali', *Angelicum*, 12 (1935), 346–96.

WILLIAMS, A., 'Relations Between the Mendicant Friars and the Secular Clergy in England in the later Fourteenth Century', *Duquesne Studies, Annuale Médiévale*, 1 (1960), 22–95.

WILLIAMS, G., *The Welsh Church from Conquest to Reformation* (Cardiff, 1962).

WILLIS-BUND, J. (ed.), *The Victoria County History of Worcestershire*, iii (London, 1913).

WOOD, S., *English Monasteries and their Patrons in the Thirteenth Century* (Oxford, 1955).

WOODCOCK, B., *Medieval Ecclesiastical Courts in the Diocese of Canterbury* (Oxford, 1952).

WOODFORDE, C., 'A Medieval Campaign against Blasphemy', *Downside Review*, 55 (1937), 357–62.

WOOD-LEGH, K., *Church Life in England Under Edward III* (Cambridge, 1934).

WRIGHT, R. F., 'The High Seas and the Church in the Middle Ages', *The Mariner's Mirror*, 53 (1967), 3–32.

YUNCK, J. A., *The Lineage of Lady Meed: The Development of Medieval Venality Satire* (Notre Dame, 1963).

INDEX